Higher Education and the Law

SRHE and Open University Press Imprint
General Editor: Heather Eggins

Higher Education and the Law

A Guide for Managers

Edited by
David Palfreyman
and David Warner

The Society for Research into Higher Education
& Open University Press

Dedicated to Julia, Tessa and Laurie

David Palfreyman

Published by SRHE and
Open University Press
Celtic Court
22 Ballmoor
Buckingham
MK18 1XW

and 1900 Frost Road, Suite 101
Bristol, PA 19007, USA

First published 1998

A catalogue record of this book is available from the British Library

ISBN 0 335 19876 7 (hb)

A catalog record for this book is available from the Library of Congress

Typeset by Graphicraft Typesetters Limited, Hong Kong
Printed in Great Britain by St Edmundsbury Press Ltd, Bury St Edmunds, Suffolk

Coventry University

Contents

Abbreviations

ACT	advanced corporation tax
AGM	annual general meeting
CCTV	closed-circuit television
CUC	Committee of University Chairmen
CVCP	Committee of Vice-Chancellors and Principals
DDA 1995	Disability Discrimination Act 1995
DfE, DfEE	Department for Education (previously DES, Department of Education and Science) and subsequently Department for Education and Employment
DoE	Department of the Environment
DPA 1984	Data Protection Act 1984
DTI	Department of Trade and Industry
EA 1994	Education Act 1994
ECJ	European Court of Justice
EEA	European economic area
ERA 1988	Education Reform Act 1988
EU	European Union
FE	further education
FEI	further education institution
GPA 1994	Government Procurement Agreement 1994
HE	higher education
HEC	higher education corporation
HEFCE	Higher Education Funding Council for England
HEFCW	Higher Education Funding Council for Wales
HEI	higher education institution
HEQC	Higher Education Quality Council
HMO	house in multiple occupation
ICTA 1988	Income and Corporation Taxes Act 1988
IP	intellectual property
JR	judicial review

LEA	local education authority
NUS	National Union of Students
QAA	Quality Assurance Agency
SU	Students' Union
UCAS	Universities and Colleges Admissions Service
UCL	University College London
UTCCR 1994	Unfair Terms in Consumer Contracts Regulations 1994
WTO	World Trade Organization

Part 1

Contexts

1

Setting the Scene

David Palfreyman and David Warner

Rationale for this book

The business we are in

Higher education (HE) in the UK is big business in every sense of the term, and it is growing. At the time of writing in 1997, the three national funding councils for England, Scotland and Wales directly fund 147, 21 and 15 HE institutions (HEIs) respectively, plus, in the case of the first named, a large number of Further Education (FE) institutions for their HE work. In addition, the Department for Education in Northern Ireland funds several HEIs and there are a number of private institutions, such as the University of Buckingham, the Royal Agricultural College and the Royal Academy of Dramatic Art. The sector employs approximately 225,000 staff and teaches more than one-and-a-half million students on award-bearing courses alone. It is not surprising, therefore, that turnover is also massive. On 18 June 1996, Professor G. Roberts, the then Chairman of the Committee of Vice-Chancellors and Principals (CVCP), commented:

> The annual turnover of the higher education sector has now passed the £10 billion mark. The massive increase in participation that has led to this figure, and the need to prepare for further increases, now demands that we make revolutionary advances, in the way we structure, manage and fund higher education.
>
> (CVCP, 1996)

We entirely agree with these sentiments and, for similar reasons to those enunciated by Professor Roberts, jointly edited *Higher Education Management: The Key Elements* (Warner and Palfreyman, 1996). That volume ended with a section entitled 'Notes on the Legal Framework within which HEIs Operate'. This companion volume takes those Notes as a starting-point and inevitably expands them into a full-length work. This book is not, however, a law textbook: we give many references to them in the Further reading section at the end of each chapter and in the extensive Bibliography. It is a *guide* for busy HEI managers who need to familiarize themselves with the legal content in which HE operates and who, from time to time, need to purchase legal services on behalf of the HEI.

The growth of consumerism

There is no doubt that we live in an era of increasing consumerism and, indeed, 'charterism', if that is the correct description of the last Government's policy. Each year, full-time students pay either directly or through their families a larger percentage of the costs of their time in HE and it seems quite probable that in the near future (post-Dearing) they will not only contribute even more towards their living costs, but also their tuition fees. The majority of part-time students, who are increasing rapidly in numbers, already pay for their own tuition fees and the remaining fees are not paid for by the State but usually by employers. As paying customers, students will readily resort to law if they feel that their HEI has not provided value-for-money. The *Times Higher* of 12 July 1996, carried an Editorial, 'The natives are restless', referring to the student community 'getting stroppy', to 'a growth in litigiousness', to 'slow, anachronistic, secretive or apparently excessively cosy' complaints procedures and to the risk of UK HE 'getting mired in expensive and unsatisfactory litigation which can only undermine public confidence'. A few weeks later Laurie Taylor addressed the issue in his inimitable style:

> *More and more students are suing their universities over marks and grades –*
> *Leading article in* The Independent, *August 22.*
> Lapping speaking.
> **Ah, good morning, Professor Lapping. It's Gerald Stiggins, of Stiggins, Lipton and Harcourt.**
> Good morning, Gerald. How's tricks?
> **Not bad at all. We've a sexual harassment in philosophy, an unfair dismissal in earth sciences, and the usual crop of student business. In fact, we are currently representing a Miss Rebecca Tomkins who has recently completed her first year in your department.**
> Tall with fair hair and a tattoo?
> **My client is small and dark haired with no tattoos.**
> That Rebecca Tomkins. Small, dark, un-tattoed Rebecca Tomkins. How is she?
> **Not at all well, Professor Lapping. She feels strongly that her C brackets plus mark on her** Coronation Street **essay may jeopardise her chances of obtaining a good degree and pursuing her chosen career in facilities management. She alleges that the marking system in your department**

**is arbitrary and unreasonable and that in any case her low essay mark
was a direct result of inadequate supervision by her senior tutor, a
certain Professor Lapping. She intends to pursue these matters through
the High Court.**

And, purely as a matter of curiosity, what mark does Rebecca feel she
might have obtained if her essay had been appropriately marked and
supervised?

An A plus.

A plus!

**Imagine the scene in the High Court, Professor Lapping. Your marking
system held up to judicial scrutiny.**

How about a B double minus?

**Imagine the usher's voice: 'Call Professor Lapping. Call Professor
Lapping'.**

B-minus. And I'll throw in a year's subscription to *Media Studies* and a
three-drawer filing cabinet.

And two dozen A4 lined pads.

Agreed.

**A Daniel come to judgement. And now if I might have Doctor
Piercemuller's extension number.**

With great pleasure.

(Times Higher, 30 August 1996)

Already the 'grapevine' suggests that some international students from
outside of the European Union, and especially those from the USA, have
threatened legal action, reflecting the more litigious culture back home
and also the heightened sense of grievance at having paid increasingly large
sums of money for their allegedly inadequate British university courses. For
example, the Birmingham *Evening Mail* carried this news item, indicating
that the virus of litigation may already have spread to the UK:

SUE THREAT TO COLLEGES

MIDLAND colleges and universities are facing a threat of legal action
from students who claim their education is inadequate.

About a dozen mature or postgraduate students across the country
are already claiming a breach of contract or educational negligence
and others may follow.

Birmingham solicitor, Nicola Hart, a partner at Martineau Johnson,
said allegations ranged from failure to provide enough teaching sessions to claims that marking was biased on the grounds of gender.

(Evening Mail, 1 March 1996)

The Birmingham Post (11 March 1996), reporting the same story, noted
that 'students have been encouraged to make complaints since the introduction of the Higher Education Charter by the Government' and that 'a
few of the claims have resulted in the students asking for large amounts of
money, as much as £200,000 as compensation'.

At almost the same time, the Senior Proctor of the University of Oxford, on demitting office at the end of his year, made the following comments in a speech to Congregation:

> Traditionally the Senior Proctor has been concerned with graduate examinations, predominantly the DPhil. Complaints have, very approximately, tripled over the last decade (or doubled, proportionately to student numbers).
>
> Echoing the words of my predecessor of last year, I have to report that nearly 70 per cent of all graduate examination complaints have come from overseas students. I have no single explanation for this, since not everything can be explained by cultural differences.
>
> (*Gazette*, 21 March 1996: Vol. 126, No. 4396)

In a somewhat different publication from the Oxford University *Gazette*, Brendan O'Neill (*Living Marxism*, April 1997, Should failed students sue?) wrote: 'More students are turning to the courts to challenge their university's failure to provide the education they require, claiming that they failed their degrees because of inadequate teaching and a lack of resources. Educational lawyers predict that growing numbers of dissatisfied students will demand compensation through the courts'. A solicitor, Jaswinder Gill, specializing in student complaints, is quoted: 'there are those who are aggrieved at the mark awarded for their degree, so they go through the normal appeals mechanism at their university. But they feel that the appeals mechanism has also let them down so legal action becomes necessary. These cases can usually be resolved by way of a judicial review. The second, more serious grievance is where students feel they have not received the service for which they paid . . . I am arguing that a student is a consumer, no different to a consumer purchasing any other kind of product or service. Like other consumers I think that students should have recourse if a university fails in its obligation to provide a satisfactory course or full programme of study'.

Another solicitor, Ivan Walker (Lawfords & Co) is cited in the same article, establishing the HEI perspective, '. . . sometimes the reason they have failed is simply that it is part of a university's function in life to pass some students and to fail others, that is what higher education is all about'. Dennis Farrington is also reported as commenting, 'the relationship between university and student is not as straightforward as that between provider and consumer. I see the contract as a bi-lateral one. There are obligations on the institution to provide certain things, but there are also obligations on the student to participate fully: to attend lectures, to participate in seminars, to hand essays in on time. It is a partnership approach, rather than a commercial consumer approach'.

In fact, the author of the article concludes, 'The fact is that students are much more than consumers and university is not the same as school . . . Higher education should demand that students work hard and contribute fully to their own learning . . . Establishing a legal precedent that students are consumers can only degrade higher education and the role of the student within it even further. And who will benefit from that?'.

On 9 February, 1997, *The Sunday Times* carried a front-page article 'Students Sue Over Course Failures', in which it was reported that three ex-students, with legal aid, are suing their former HEI 'in legal test cases that could pave the way for a flood of costly compensation claims'. They are seeking damages for loss of future earnings arising from allegedly unsatisfactory courses which have reduced their job prospects. Their solicitor is quoted: 'Universities have a duty to provide a proper programme of study. . . . People are increasingly having to pay for their own tuition and they have every right to expect what they are promised.' The same article also reports on a separate case where a student who failed the first year of an HND course at another HEI, allegedly because of inadequate teaching, is claiming 'more than £120,000'. Further afield, a *Times Higher* article on 21 February 1997, reported that four graduates were suing a New Zealand university over an allegedly substandard masters course. Their legal costs are being met by the New Zealand equivalent of the NUS. One of the claimants is quoted as declaring: 'This is the 90s, and quality is what it is all about. It was a huge cost for us to do this course, and we haven't got time to muck around.' (If the concept of the student as a customer causes difficulty for any 1998 British reader, it should be noted that the earliest reference the Editors have come across to the student-customer is, unsurprisingly, from the USA, although even for the norms of US HE, the year (1888) is perhaps surprisingly early, especially given the then tendency for US colleges to adopt the Oxbridge Christian/Liberal Arts 'young gentlemen' model (Duke, 1996): 'College administration is a business in which trustees are partners, professors the salesmen and students the customers', the inaugural address of the new President of Princeton University.)

Meanwhile, following problems of management at a number of HEIs and FE institutions in recent years, Lord Nolan is currently scrutinizing 'governance' and engendering a general debate about the legal liabilities of governors/members of council. The result seems to have been a fairly clean bill of health, that is that 'mismanagement, maladministration, and misconduct seem to be isolated occurrences'. There is, however, a recommendation for 'publicly available registers of interests' in relation to members of council/governing body. In addition, the Nolan Committee (1996) has recommended that a system be established to allow senior managers complaining about (or even 'whistle-blowing' over) issues of governance and students challenging procedures and decisions to take their disputes to an independent review panel/appeals body. However, it is not entirely clear whether such independent, external mechanisms will *de facto* supplement or replace the traditional role of the Visitor in the chartered HEIs and whether the mechanism for the statutory HEIs will be based on the Visitor (or an enhanced version of same) in the chartered HEIs. Inevitably, this chapter will be out of date by the time of publication since Nolan-related events in UK HE may well move fairly fast in 1998. Indeed, a National Audit

Office Report (January 1997) on 'a breakdown in both governance and management' at Swansea Institute of Higher Education floats the concept of an Ombudsman for HE.

Other recent works

All of the points raised so far make the legal status of the (changing?) student–university relationship (contract?) topical and emphasize the need for the fiduciary duties of governors/members of council to be clarified and stressed. In 1990 *Universities and the Law*, edited by Farrington and Mattison, was published by the Conference of University Administrators (CUA, now AUA). This was followed by the useful work by Farrington, *The Law of Higher Education* (Farrington, 1994). Also in 1994, the report of Sir Michael Davies as the Visitor examining a dispute at University College, Swansea, was published in book form – the first time a Visitor report has been made so widely available (Davies, 1994). Attention is also drawn to the journal *Education and the Law*, edited by Geoffrey Bennett and Paul Meredith, published by Carfax; and to the *Education Law Monitor*, edited by Richard Clutterbrook and Charlotte Skeet, Monitor Press Ltd. (In addition, a book by Oliver Hyams is due in 1998 on education law, to be published by Sweet & Maxwell.)

More recently Farrington has established UCELNET (the Universities and Colleges Education Law Network), the first annual conference for which was held in June 1996, with a focus on the student–HEI relationship. (See the Note on UCELNET on page 361.) In addition, Lancaster University's School for Independent Studies has run a course entitled 'Academic judgement: academics, managers and the judges' *twice* in 1996, at £495 per participant. The 'flyer' for the 'briefing workshop' refers to a growing 'culture of complaint' and notes that 'a case which involves the University Visitor or judicial review can cost many thousands of pounds in legal fees'.

Prior to these books there had been virtually nothing on the Law of HE until one reaches back as far as 1910 when Butterworths published *The Law of the Universities* by Williams, who noted that there were 'very few works dealing directly with the law of a university or universities' and that coverage of the topic 'has hardly been done before in England', or indeed (until the 1990s), since!

In the USA, by contrast, extensive modern coverage of the interaction between the law and the academic world was to be found as early as 1979 in the first edition of Kaplin, *The Law of Higher Education*, which noted: 'The law has arrived on the campus . . . The challenge is to make law more a beacon and less a fog.' The second edition (1985) ran to over 600 pages, and the third (Kaplin and Lee, 1995a) comes to 1023 pages! The third edition notes:

> In the decade since publication of the second edition, many new and newly complex legal concerns have arisen on the campuses . . . it is difficult to think of any other entities . . . that are subject to as great an array of legal requirements as colleges and universities are . . . Litigation

has extended into every corner of campus activity . . . It is said that the law reaches too far and speaks too loudly . . . Traditionally, the law's relationship to postsecondary (or higher) education was much different from what it is now . . . The higher education world, moreover, tended to think of itself as removed from and perhaps above the world of law and lawyers.

(Kaplin and Lee, 1995a: 9)

Some 1500 cases are cited. There is an entirely new chapter on relationships between HEIs and 'the business/industrial community' in the third edition of Kaplin and Lee. We will refer to US law and Kaplin and Lee (1995a) where appropriate in our 'Editors' introduction' at the start of each chapter.

There appears to be no equivalent of Farrington or Kaplin for Australia, Canada or New Zealand, whose case law, as Commonwealth countries broadly sharing the English Common Law system, would be of relevance to cases in English Courts. A 1975 publication from the Legal Research Institute at the University of Manitoba, *Universities and the Law* (ed. Thomas), noted, even then, that in the context of Canadian universities, 'Life becomes more legalistic by the day . . . Administrators, in response, are also turning to legal advisors with increased frequency.' Certainly, over the last three decades, Canadian Courts do seem to have considered a number of cases generated over the university–student contractual relationship – Farrington, for instance, cites an article by Lewis, 'The legal nature of a university and the student–university relationship' (1983, *Ottawa Law Review*, XV) which discusses the relevant Canadian cases.

The objectives of this book

We have set ourselves three objectives in preparing this book. First, this is not an encyclopaedia which covers every aspect of the law applicable to HE. There are numerous texts covering those legal issues which apply to all employers, whether they relate to individual employees, premises or whatever. We mention, however, as potentially interesting areas of development within employment law, the issues of employee claims for work-related/-induced stress and of employee actions and/or claims in relation to the Criminal Justice and Public Order Act 1994, which created a new criminal offence of intentional harassment (largely aimed at the 'stalker' problem – not unknown in HE circles – but possibly also applicable to bullying in the workplace). Otherwise, we have concentrated on those topics which are peculiar to HE (and in many cases other sectors of education), such as the discipline and dismissal of academic staff, legislation on houses in multiple occupation and its relationship to halls of residence, the contract(s) of employment of academic staff, intellectual property and the status of student unions in relation to contract and tort. In particular, we have also attempted to cover some of the topics not covered in the excellent work by Farrington.

Second, whenever possible, we have asked the contributors to attempt to solve problems rather than just to identify them. This is not, of course, always practicable because many of the points at issue have not yet been tested in the Courts. However, the aim is for each chapter to be a clear, comprehensive and concise explanation of the relevant law, with concrete examples of how it affects day-to-day management within institutions, including identification of the legal pitfalls and the provision of possible avoidance mechanisms (for example, draft clauses for use in relevant documentation and examples of good practice). The book is intended to be 'hands on' and accessible to the non-lawyer.

Finally, we have eschewed the single-author approach and have brought together a team of solicitors who as individuals are all experts in the particular topics which they are dealing with and whose firms have a significant number of HE clients. However, the 'insider' experience of the HE manager has not been lost because we have added an 'Editors' introduction' at the head of each chapter when appropriate. Inconsistencies have been removed, but we have not attempted to homogenize individual styles, nor to eliminate repetition which is necessary to understand a chapter read in isolation.

There is one objective, however, which we have not set ourselves, namely to make the book relevant to the whole of the UK. The law used throughout is the law of England and Wales, and hence we regret that the book is of less value to those managing institutions in Scotland and in Northern Ireland. Nevertheless, we trust that it will still be of some value to them.

A note on terminology

In the first chapter of Warner and Palfreyman (1996), we argued that the debate over the use of the terms 'administrator' or 'manager', 'administration' or 'management' is a sterile one and adds little to understanding. Nevertheless, the 'm' word has emotively good connotations (similar to 'marketing' which is always used in educational circles rather than 'selling') and, therefore, that is the term which will be used throughout this book (except in quotations and in historical context). It will also be used to describe both academic and other managers.

The language of HE is in need of significant overhaul because, as yet, there is no generally accepted terminology to distinguish between those institutions which gained the title of 'university' as a result of the Further and Higher Education Act 1992 and those which already had it. Many commentators use 'old' and 'new', but how could we accept these terms as one of us is a Fellow of New College, Oxford (Founded 1379) and the other has worked at both of the 1960s Universities of East Anglia and Warwick which were previously called 'new universities'? 'Modern' is slightly better, but perhaps a little jaded. Suffice it to say that we have decided on 'chartered' and 'statutory', even though we know that some pre-1992 institutions were founded by Act of Parliament (see Chapter 2) and that a small

Table 1.1   Response rates

	No. sent out	No. returned	Percentage return
Chartered university	62	38	61
Statutory university	41	24	59
College of HE	59	29	49
Overall	162	91	56

number do not have charters. In any case, this debate completely omits the colleges and HEIs which are legally, and, in most cases, managerially in the same category as statutory universities. Wherever possible, therefore, we have used 'higher education institution' (HEI).

Legal problems in HE

Whilst organizing the conference which provided part of the stimulus for the writing of this book, we realized that there was little or no information available about the nature and frequency of legal problems which HEIs face or about the way in which they are handled. Consequently, we prepared a questionnaire survey which was sent to the registrars/heads of administration of all HEIs in the UK.

Putting on one side the definitional problem of deciding exactly how many HEIs there are in the UK, 162 questionnaires were sent out: 62 to chartered universities, 41 to statutory universities and 59 to colleges/HEIs. The response to a single questionnaire, which was not followed up by a prompt, was very good as Table 1.1 indicates. Within these categories there are, of course, wide variations in size. By almost every criterion, the University of Birmingham is at least 15 times larger than St David's University College, Lampeter, and Southampton HEI has 30 times more students than Rose Bruford College. However, the categories reflect historical differences which still have management implications and, therefore, they have been used for the analysis of the survey results.

The questions asked were as follows.

1. *What types of legal problem arise in your institution and approximately how often in an average year?*

In order to keep the questionnaire brief and, thereby, increase the likelihood of it being answered, explanations of terminology were kept to a minimum. As a result, the majority of respondents interpreted 'legal' in the narrow sense of requiring the expertise of a lawyer, whereas others used a broader definition along the lines of 'contravening the institution's rules, regulations, etc., and requiring significant action or judgement'.

The 13 areas in Table 1.2 were prompted with the average and median results as set out for an individual HEI.

Table 1.2 Type and annual frequency of legal problems

	Chartered		Statutory		HE colleges		All	
	Average	Median	Average	Median	Average	Median	Average	Median
Employment issues	16	5	16.1	10	5.4	5	12.2	5
Staff discipline	4.8	2	7.5	3	3.5	2	5.4	2
Student admission issues	2	2.5	2.7	2	2.7	2	2.7	2
Student matriculation issues (including examinations)	2.1	2	12.2	5	2.6	2	6.1	2
Student discipline	3.7	2.5	7	5	3	2	4.6	2
Students' union issues	3.4	2	3	3	1.5	1	2.7	2
Health and safety	2.3	2	12	5	3	2	5.3	2
Residential accommodation	3	3	6.2	5	2.8	3	4.1	2
Property-related issues	9	10	8.9	10	5.3	4	7.8	6
Charitable status issues	4.5	1	3.9	3	2.1	2	3.7	2
Trading company issues	3.9	3	9.7	9	3.2	2	5.4	3
Intellectual property and similar	38.1	3	7.3	3	1.8	1	16.7	2
Security issues	1.5	1	5.3	5	2.7	2	3.3	2

There are several interesting conclusions which can be drawn from these responses. First, the statutory universities have, on average, more legal problems than the chartered universities. This is entirely to be expected because, on average, the statutory universities:

• are larger than the chartered universities
• have just undergone significant constitutional and human resource management changes (see Chapters 2, 3 and 12 in Warner and Crosthwaite, 1995)
• have many more part-time and mature students.

Second, a number of chartered universities are experiencing considerable difficulties with intellectual property and related issues. Again, this is not especially surprising given the recent stimulus the Research Assessment Exercise (RAE) has given to this area. We would predict a similar growth in those statutory universities and colleges of HE which are giving an increasing emphasis to research. Third, there arises, on average, one substantial legal issue in every HEI in the UK every working week of the year!

Respondents were also asked to indicate which other types of legal problem had occurred in their institution. Some 29 separate topics were mentioned, but about half of these could be subsumed in the categories just given. Of the new issues, the most common were of a constitutional nature (e.g., concerning the charter or the function of the Visitor) or involved finance (at the corporate level, VAT, raising of loans and, especially, debt collection). Other interesting references were to defamation, medical negligence and licensing.

2. Are legal problems increasing or decreasing in your institution?

The results, expressed as a percentage, unequivocally point to an increase in legal activity. (See Table 1.3)

Indeed, the overall increase would probably have been slightly higher had there not been a recent decrease in activity in the statutory universities and colleges of HE resulting from the completion of incorporation and the consequent difficult asset transfer issues.

Table 1.3 Frequency of legal problems: increasing or decreasing?

	Increasing	*Decreasing*	*Constant*
Chartered university	86.8	0	13.2
Statutory university	87.0	0	13.0
College of HE	76.7	3.3	20.0
All institutions	83.8	1.2	15.0

3.   *Does your principal and/or head of administration have any legal qualifications?*

The results set out in table 1.4 are self-explanatory. It would perhaps have been of even more interest to have found out the actual subject discipline of each of the principals. Would engineering or physics have been more common than sociology or management? However, that is another story. It is of significance to note that several universities (e.g. the Universities of Birmingham, Leeds and Salford) have appointed an internal legal officer/ adviser. This is a trend which is almost certain to continue, at least amongst the larger institutions. (Note the existence of the National Association of College and University Attorneys (NACUA) in the USA and its many excellent publications.)

Table 1.4   Whether senior management legally qualified?

	Chartered universities %	*Statutory universities* %	*HE colleges* %	*Overall* %
Principal	10.5	4.1	7.2	7.5
Head of administration or similar	15.8	33.3	10.7	18

4.   *Do you deal with legal problems internally or externally?*

This question foundered a little on the difficulty in defining a 'legal problem' as mentioned earlier. Suffice it to say that virtually all HEIs employ a mixed economy. When asked to specify what internal processes are used, the following responses were all given:

1. *refer to individuals*:
   - chair of the board of governors
   - clerk to the board of governors
   - deputy director/vice principal
   - head of human resources
   - legal officer/part-time solicitor
   - head of finance
   - office of academic affairs
   - head of personnel
2. *use procedures*:
   - informal approach
   - disciplinary committee
   - internal tribunal
   - NATFHE/UNISON
   - reference to agreed procedures
   - use *Croner's Law Line* for reference and advice.

Clearly, HEIs would benefit from the identification and publication of some good practice case studies. Perhaps the establishment of UCELNET by Farrington will help.

5. If externally, please state:
   (a) How many firms of solicitors you use.

Table 1.5 gives these results.

   (b) If you use a tender procedure to select your main firm of solicitors.

These results (in Table 1.6) are particularly interesting because they indicate that many HEIs may be breaking their own financial rules. We did not ask how much each institution spends each year on legal advice, but anecdotal information leads us to believe that the figure is in excess of £100,000 for many large institutions. Not only would this financial level normally entail a tendering procedure, but, of course, the arrangement is effectively perpetual. To be fair, however, several HEIs did indicate that they were about to introduce or were considering a change in their practice towards tendering.

   (c) The criteria you use for selection.

All of the following are used and, in most cases, in combination (e.g. cost was only mentioned on its own by one institution!):

- competence
- expertise
- quality of individual solicitor involved
- specialisms (e.g. corporate law)
- suitability
- familiarity with institution and knowledge of procedures

Table 1.5 Number of legal firms used

Chartered universities	Statutory universities	HE colleges	Overall
2.4	1.9	1.7	2.1

Table 1.6 Whether legal firm(s) selected and appointed on the basis of tendering

Chartered universities %	Statutory universities %	HE colleges %	Overall %
31.4	52.4	28.5	34.5

- efficiency
- good working relationship with client
- track record
- response time
- speed
- by recommendation
- by references
- insurer's solicitor
- price
- competitive tender
- value for money
- proximity to institution.

Survey conclusions

In order to secure a good response from busy people, many of whom are suffering from 'survey overload', we deliberately produced a brief questionnaire. The results, as given earlier, are tantalising – at best, they provide some important new insights, and at worst they raise far more questions than they answer. Indeed, this whole area seems to us to be ripe for further in-depth research. Who will take up the challenge? Certainly, the survey results show that HE and the Law is an expanding territory in the UK, just as Kaplin and Lee (1995a) trace the already greatly increased impact of the law on US HEIs. They introduce the concept of 'legal audits' to check whether an 'office or function is in compliance with the full range of legal constraints to which it is subject'. The contrast between firefighting, defending and reacting in legal terms, and a 'preventive law' approach is drawn: the latter 'focuses on initiatives that an institution can take before actual legal disputes arise . . . this approach becoming increasingly valuable as the presence of law on the campus increased [since the 1980s]'. Reference is made to *The Formbook* produced by the US National Association of College and University Attorneys (NACUA, 1994) as including 'nearly one hundred legal forms and checklists covering a wide range of institutional functions and transactions . . . A practical resource'. How long before we need something similar for UK HEIs? It would be much cheaper than each HEI independently employing law firms to reinvent the wheel.

Final thoughts

It hardly needs pointing out to anyone who works in HE how rapidly the system changes – particularly, those aspects of the system which are determined by external agencies. Legislation which impinges on HE (and almost all legislation seems to do so) changes equally rapidly. New laws are introduced, existing laws are amended and, above all, new interpretations and rulings are made. This last point is especially important to HE because many issues of relevance have simply not yet been tested in the English courts, let alone those of Europe. It is stressed, therefore, that, although we and the contributors have made all reasonable efforts to ensure that this book is comprehensive and useful, none of us can accept any responsibility or liability if a reader and his or her institution rely on the material within this book. It is advised that up-to-date legal advice should always be taken in relation to each particular set of circumstances.

Acknowledgements

We would like to thank the following for commenting on the scope of the book in relation to the perceived needs of HEI managers: John Lauwerys, Registrar, University of Southampton; David Neave, Secretary-General, Brunel University; and Harold Thomas, HE Consultant. Thanks are also due to Kate Hunter and Anita Rowlands at New College for their skill in coping with the handwriting of one of the Editors, and also to Maureen Duggan from UCE. This book arises from a seminar held in March 1996, at New College, Oxford, on 'Key issues in the Law of HE', at which the following provided valuable commentaries on papers given by solicitors: Peter Cane, (1996), Harvey McGregor, QC (1997), Hubert Picarda, QC (1995), and Michael Shattock OBE (1994); and at which Sir Michael Davies, QC (1994), spoke on the role of the Visitor. We also thank Richard Ramsey, Law Lecturer, Oxford Brookes University, for his valuable comments on the Bibliographical Essay on the Visitor. We gratefully acknowledge the kind permission of Laurie Taylor for the reproduction of one of his *Times Higher* columns earlier in this chapter.

2

What is a Higher Education Institution as a Legal Entity?

Nicola Hart (Martineau Johnson)

Editors' introduction

The observations in this chapter are intended to provide an introductory platform for diving into any other chapter in this book, by generally and briefly setting out some fundamental concepts one needs to be aware of in applying the law to an HEI (higher education institution).

The corporation

An HEI is a peculiar kind of legal entity, probably best generally described as a corporation. A corporation is a body of persons recognized by the law as having a personality distinct from the separate personalities of its members. It is, thus, a distinct legal entity, which continues in existence as its members change from time to time. HEIs fall into various subcategories of corporation. The basic distinction is between those created by statute (for example, the provisions of the Education Reform Act (ERA) 1988 allowed the incorporation of what we now call the 'new' universities), and those created by charter. Only the Crown can create a corporation by grant of a charter.

The distinction is important because statutory and non-statutory corporations have quite different powers. A chartered university has power, generally speaking, to do anything in law which could be done by an individual. So express powers need not be spelled out in its charter or statutes. Although academic lawyers have maintained the argument that a chartered university, as a corporation with all the powers of an individual, will not be susceptible to claims that it has acted *ultra vires*, in practice there are restrictions on its freedom to act. If such a university acted in direct contravention of its charter, at least in theory the charter might be revoked by the Crown. More realistically, an individual member could sue the university or petition its Visitor to enforce the charter's provisions.

The notion of an Alsatia in England (where the King's writ does not run and where, presumably, no act is *ultra vires*) is becoming increasingly attenuated for chartered universities in the present day. There have been a number of warning signs in recent years. The role of the Visitor has been severely curtailed by Parliament's enactment of Section 206 of the ERA 1988, removing the Visitor's jurisdiction in employment disputes and introducing the role of the university commissioners. The issues raised by the handling of the rape allegations against Mr. Donnellan at King's College, London – the criminal case, the judicial enquiry and the CVCP (Committee of Vice-Chancellors and Principals) investigation and report (CVCP, 1994) – are so significant in practical terms, in relation to what a chartered university generally used to consider to be its freedom to act, as to make that case effectively a watershed. The *vires* issue which the Donnellan case raised was a practical and immediate one concerning the extent to which the HEI really could rely on its own internal regulatory framework and its entitlements within that framework to investigate, to discipline and to penalize. Post-Donnellan, a tendency has become visible for chartered universities to see themselves as more circumscribed by external considerations (including public relations and media, as well as the criminal and civil courts) than ever used to be the case, and, accordingly, to be less self-confident in terms of their perceived freedom to act.

Erosion of powers

Whereas the previous paragraph may tend to suggest that as between 'old' and 'new' universities the distinction as to their powers is starting to be eroded, a statutory university (as opposed to a chartered university) is clearly a creature of its originating statute and it can be said quite definitively that its only rights and powers to act are only those expressly or impliedly conferred by that statute.

However, from this side of the fence as well, it is possible to blur the distinction. The ERA 1988, Section 124(2), provides for a subjective test: that which *appears to it to be necessary or expedient* in the exercise of its principal powers, the corporation has power to do. The exercise of this judgement is still distinct from the exercise of the powers of a chartered university: while the subjective test provides some comfort to governors, the power in question, as an express statutory one, is clearly subject to the usual public law requirements that it should be exercised reasonably and for its proper purpose. The courts can be expected in future to take a narrow view of the powers of all statutory corporations, following the Court of Appeal's decisions in the *Allerdale* and *Waltham Forest* cases (about local authorities' powers to participate in companies and to give guarantees).

Generally, under the terms of the enacting statute, the statutory university will have power to delegate its duties and functions, subject to any restriction as to those which may be carried out only by the statutory university's governing body itself. Acting beyond its express powers may be *ultra vires* and lead to transactions being set aside as of no effect in law. The impact of this may be felt in areas where a statutory university tests the boundaries of its freedom to operate commercially (e.g. in terms of borrowing, lending or giving guarantees in relation to the operations of subsidiary or joint venture companies). The statutory university may be required to demonstrate to a commercial lender that it has power to enter into a particular commercial arrangement. Although in theory the risk might rest with the lender, in practice the statutory university first needs the funds and, second, does not want the scheme called in as a nullity, no doubt with the implication that new and unfavourable terms will be substituted. *Ultra vires* actions may also give students grounds for challenge by way of judicial review, for example in relation to suspension (pursuant to powers under the statutory university's articles of government).

Charitable status

An HEI will usually be a charity. Although exempt from the jurisdiction of the Charity Commissioners, it will be subject to the control of the High Court. The principal advantages of the HEI's charitable status are:

1. that any charity, as a charity, is assured in society at large of a special status, which will assist it in areas such as fundraising
2. that particularly favourable tax treatment is available to charitable bodies
3. the generally helpful fact that the parameters of the charity's operations and essential nature are clarified by a body of statute and case law.

These advantages are balanced by the impact charitable status has on the HEI's ability to engage in commercial operations. Generally, the following questions need to be asked.

1. Is trading permissible?
2. May the HEI properly establish subsidiary non-charitable trading companies?
3. To what extent and in what way might the HEI fund, guarantee or otherwise facilitate the operations of such companies?

Charity law may also have an impact on the HEI in the form of duties equivalent to those of charity trustees being imputed to those in charge of its governance.

Public body

The HEI will be treated as a public body for certain purposes in law. This classification is liable to introduce further complications and to bring the HEI within the jurisdiction of various external regimes. If an HEI were to

be classified as an emanation of the State for the purposes of European law
– a question still tantalisingly undecided – the consequences would include
the possibility of claims by individuals under the Treaty of Rome (for example, on equal-pay issues) being made directly against the institution. Other
obligations which do not depend upon being an emanation of the State
also arise in connection with European law, such as the requirement to
advertise in the *Official Journal* for tenders for public works contracts over
a certain value.

External control and regulation may be exerted on the HEI from a number
of different quarters. The State has power, through Parliament or the Privy
Council, to make constitutional changes. Ministers make regulations with
statutory force. Quangos (e.g. the funding councils) impose their requirements and criteria unilaterally in effect. The High Court provides third
parties with the opportunity of judicial review of a statutory HEI's decisions.
The Visitor in chartered universities has wide powers to intervene and
to right wrongs. Nolan (1996) may lead ultimately to the creation of an
approximately comparable independent appeal or review function for universities which are statutory corporations and have no Visitor. Statutory
inspectorates (for example, in health and safety, pollution, radiation and
food hygiene) inspect and prosecute in the criminal courts.

As a community

The HEI finally is a community, originally of academics but ultimately
encompassing a wide range of individuals and groups with correspondingly
diverse interests: academic and non-academic staff, undergraduates, postgraduates, honorary postholders, administrators and managers. These are
examples of interest groups or stakeholders within the university – perhaps
they could be grouped under the name of the 'home community'. In relation to any of these, the HEI may be one or more out of, for example,
employer, supplier of educational services and qualifications, landlord or
even partner in a joint venture company.

In addition to these various internal groupings, the HEI will also have
'foreign relations' at a variety of diplomatic or other levels with, for example,
other HEIs, the media, legislators, Parliament and civil servants, the courts,
commercial partners, external validating agencies and people, institutions
and governments outside the UK jurisdictions. The way in which the members of its home community interact with these outsiders is also a subject
likely to be of interest from the legal point of view.

The HEI arguably has an obligation to regulate its home community and
activities, to ensure that good order is maintained for the benefit of all
participants. This obligation (in the context of both the home and foreign
communities) has to be seen as the basis for the HEI's ability to make,
change and, effectively, impose disciplinary regulations on its students in a
way which would not ordinarily be effective within the accepted boundaries

of contract law. The principle is also invoked from time to time in dealing with issues such as the immediate removal of a student from the campus in a situation where allowing that person to remain on the premises would endanger the good order and effective operations of the home community, again taking into account the background of foreign relations. In other words, heretical as this assertion may seem against a prevailing individualistic culture, in practice it is likely that there will be times when the responsibility for a universal community may outweigh, even temporarily, the interests of an individual and the requirements of natural justice.

Part 2

Governance

3

Governance in an Era of Accountability and Potential Personal Liability

John Hall and Oliver Hyams (Eversheds)

Editors' introduction

'Governance' is a rather pompous term for the total management of an HEI (higher education institution). It is, however, useful in a wider sense than simply 'the management of an HEI' in circumstances where 'the management' within an HEI has become distorted or confused about its power and duties. Sometimes 'the management' in any organization can assume too readily that *its* best interests as a constituency and as an interest group are automatically the same as those of the organization *as a whole.*

Hence, we have seen problems at University College, Cardiff, in the late 1980s, and more recently at Portsmouth, Brighton, Glasgow Caledonian and Huddersfield (plus, in the FE (further education) sector, at Coventry Technical College, at Hereward College, Coventry, at Derby Wilmorton College and at St Philips Roman Catholic Sixth Form College). Such problems prompted the extension of the original Nolan Inquiry (1995) into an investigation of HE (higher education) and FE governance in the UK. The result seems to be a fairly clean bill of health from Nolan (1996): 'On the evidence we received, the rare cases of mismanagement, maladministration and misconduct, seem to be isolated occurrences. We have been impressed by the remedial action which has been taken by regulators, funding bodies, and representative associations.' The inquiry notes: 'Many of the institutions have evolved systems of governance over many years and it would require evidence of substantial misconduct to justify sweeping changes. We received no such evidence.' It does, however, call for 'publicly available registers of interests'. Yet the fourth Nolan Report (1997b), whilst noting that there has been a willingness to take up the Nolan (1996) anti-sleaze and whistleblowing recommendations in principle, implementation in practice has been slow and there is complacency.

At Portsmouth University the governing body has recently established a Chancellor's Court to consider complaints presented by a minimum of four governors. This kind of move, with variations on the theme at other statutory HEIs, reflects a search for the equivalent of the Visitor to be found in the chartered universities (see Chapters 8 and 9, and the bibliographical essay on the Visitor at the end of this volume.) At the Swansea Institute a governor resigned over the conduct of a governors' meeting, the alleged use of 'a gagging order', and the alleged lack of independence of the governing body (*Times Higher*, 5 July 1996). Certainly the Government White Paper response (*The Governance of Public Bodies: A Progress Report*, January 1997) calls for HEI governing bodies to receive guidance on codes of practice.

The concept of governance is about checks and balances within the HEI to ensure that it is well managed, about the allocation of responsibility and appropriate power to fulfil that responsibility, and about duties. It links with the concept of trusteeship explored in Chapter 4, and to the conduct of meetings examined in Chapter 5. It also rapidly blends into other areas beyond the law – the concept of the culture of an organization, of its management style and of managerial lines of reporting. These aspects are all explored in Warner and Palfreyman (1996: Chapters 1 and 2). This chapter examines governance from the legal perspective, which is essentially

- what functions exist to do what
- how the functions are distributed within an HEI's management structure (officers, governing body, committees)
- the duties, responsibilities and potential liability of members of governing bodies, individually and collectively as committees.

Editors' note: See also the relevant sections and recommendations in Dearing (1997) on HEI governance (paragraphs 15.32 to 15.68 of the main report, pp. 236–47; Recommendations 54–60). Dearing proposes a code of practice for institutional governance, and a review of the effectiveness of the governing body and of the HEI to be undertaken at least once every five years. It is also proposed that governors should have effective arrangements to address complaints by students (see Chapters 6–9, and the section on 'The Visitor post-Nolan' in the bibliographical essay on the Visitor, plus CVCP, 1997), and to deal with 'whistleblowing' (including the outlawing of confidentiality or 'gagging' clauses). In essence, Dearing follows Nolan (1995, 1996) and endorses the steps already taken by way of the 'good practice' guides referred to above (in addition to which the CUC has speedily produced 'Advice on Whistleblowing', CUC, 1997). Nolan (1997) seems to feel, however, that HEIs have been a bit slow in establishing appropriate practice in 'whistleblowing' even if the principle on how to handle it is accepted. Note the 1997 furore at Glasgow Caledonian University surrounding the 'whistleblowing' of a former member of academic staff concerning the alleged undermining of academic standards by putting financial interests first. In a separate incident, the Principal of the University departed in September 1997 following allegations of misconduct and mismanagement.

'Whistleblowing' is discussed in Evans (1996), Cripps (1994) and Miceh (1992); see also Davies (1994) on the use of a 'gagging clause' in the University College, Swansea saga (pp. 78–80). One organization, Abbey National Bank plc, not only provided a whistleblower exposing major fraud at senior level with a new job but also with a £25,000 cash reward!

The collegiality–managerialism spectrum in styles of governance is discussed in Palfreyman and Turner's forthcoming article.

Governance under scrutiny

For the past decade, the spotlight of public scrutiny has turned with increasing intensity on the governance and management of HEIs. The Jarratt Report (1985) contained seminal recommendations to the Committee of Vice-Chancellors and Principals (CVCP) and the University Grants Committee (UGC) which embraced the important acknowledgement that universities are, first and foremost, corporate enterprises to which the academic community is accountable. The granting of corporate independence to the former polytechnics and HE colleges from LEA (local education authority) control in 1989 gave impetus to the move to a more corporate model of governance in HE, the enhancement of the principal's role as chief executive, and the growth in the power of the governing body (council or board) in relation to the supreme academic authority (the senate or academic board).

These developments coincided with the harsh economic climate of the late 1980s, which placed the work of the Cadbury Committee (1992) in the eye of the storm following BCCI, Maxwell and public disquiet about executive pay and pay-offs. The quest for effective governance thus became an imperative in the private sector:

> The country's economy depends on the drive and efficiency of its companies. Thus the effectiveness with which their boards discharge their responsibilities determines Britain's competitive position. They must be free to drive their companies forward, but exercise that freedom within a framework of effective accountability. This is the essence of any system of good corporate governance.
>
> (Cadbury, 1994: 18)

Close on the footsteps of Cadbury came a flurry of reports which emphasized the importance of independent remuneration committees to curb the worst excesses of executive pay, culminating in the Greenbury Report and Code (1995). This was, in large measure, prompted by fierce media criticism of the chief executives of privatized utility companies and the accusation that too many 'fat cats' were being rewarded for failure. There emerged from the gloom, in gleaming armour, 'the new philosophy of full transparency' (proclaimed with a transatlantic accent), which required company shareholders to have access to all information which they might reasonably require to enable them to assess a board's policy on issues such as executive pay and packages. (See also the Report of the Hempel Committee on corporate governance due at the end of 1997.)

Wider still was cast a net for governance structures which would command public confidence. Studies were undertaken into comparative models in other countries, but these only emphasized the diverse range of corporate governance systems worldwide. Perhaps inevitably the quest for good governance moved to that most indefinable and controversial area of human conduct – ethics. A fall in public confidence in the financial probity of Members of Parliament and other holders of public office (exemplified by the public furore concerning 'cash for questions'), and the development of a 'culture of sleaze' led to the then Prime Minister setting up the Committee on Standards in Public Life under the chairmanship of Lord Nolan in 1994. The terms of reference of the Nolan Committee were drawn in the widest possible terms:

> To examine current concerns about standards of conduct of all holders of public office, including arrangements relating to financial and commercial activities, and make recommendations as to any changes in present arrangements which might be required to ensure the highest standards of propriety in public life.
>
> (Nolan, 1995)

The challenge was taken up with alacrity. The Committee's First Report (Nolan, 1995) concentrated on Members of Parliament, ministers and civil servants, executive quangos, and National Health Service bodies. Certain weaknesses in the procedures for maintaining and enforcing appropriate standards of behaviour in public life were identified, and the Committee recommended 'urgent remedial action'. In particular, it identified seven principles of public life to serve as a yardstick against which the personal qualities and conduct of those charged with public responsibilities could be measured and to which they should aspire:

1. selflessness
2. integrity
3. objectivity
4. accountability
5. openness
6. honesty
7. leadership.

The Nolan Committee then announced (June, 1995) a second inquiry which would review local public spending bodies, that is to say 'not-for-profit' bodies which are neither fully elected nor appointed by ministers, but which provide public services, often delivered at local level, and which are wholly or largely publicly funded. Thus, in response to this remit, the Nolan Committee turned its sights on HEIs together with their FE counterparts and grant-maintained schools. As a catalyst for the submission of evidence it produced an 'Issues and Questions' paper, which identified three 'common threads' as mechanisms for maintaining standards of conduct and attaining the seven principles of public life, namely:

1. the use of codes of conduct
2. the encouragement of independent scrutiny
3. the availability of guidance and training for governing bodies and managers.

The Committee also made plain in the Issues and Questions paper that it intended to focus its attention on the following three broad themes:

1. the appointment and accountability of board members
2. the role of boards in relation to the officers and staff
3. safeguards in respect of conflicts of interest.

The Nolan Committee published its Second Report in May 1996 (Nolan, 1996). Whilst acknowledging the existence of high standards of conduct in the governance of HEIs, the Committee made several recommendations directed at FE and HE which are considered later in this chapter. In the main, such recommendations were aimed at HEIs achieving greater consistency in standards of openness and responsiveness, rather than any radical overhaul. The recommendations made in the Second Report are not binding on the Prime Minister or government of the day, but carry considerable moral authority.

The Second Nolan Report was received with particular interest since HE and FE have been no strangers to allegations of 'mismanagement and maladministration' in recent years. It is beyond the scope of this chapter to chronicle the well-publicized governance problems in 1994 at two statutory universities (Huddersfield and Portsmouth), and in 1994 and 1995 at two FE colleges (Derby Tertiary College Wilmorton and St Phillip's Roman Catholic Sixth Form College). These have been fully analysed elsewhere (NAO, 1995; Lever, 1995; FEFC, 1994a, 1994b). (See also Shattock, 1994, on the financial fiasco at University College, Cardiff, in 1986–7.) In the wake of the resultant media coverage, universities, colleges and their representative associations issued guidance for members of governing bodies (CUC, 1995; CEF, 1995; AfC, 1995), codes of conduct and ethics, and other governance advice, while the funding councils tightened their disclosure requirements for the purposes of financial accounting. However, it must be recognized that despite all this action some damage was inflicted on the reputation of universities and colleges by the media treatment of these *causes celebres*. Whether or not one considers that such treatment was overblown, the public is not accustomed to thinking in terms of its universities as tainted by 'sleaze'. In seeking to explain those cases, it has been suggested that the constitutional structure of the statutory universities, with its stress on corporate managerialism, a mainly 'lay' board, and optional staff and student board members, make those institutions particularly susceptible to misgovernance. There has been a pejorative reaction on the part of some critics of the statutory university management style (Warren, 1994;

Ryder, 1996). This response is probably unwarranted and it detracts from a cogent argument that the governance systems of all universities, chartered and statutory, need to be reviewed.

For example, at the University of Oxford the Commission of Inquiry established under the chairmanship of the Vice-Chancellor, Dr P. North, has issued a consultative paper on the university's objectives, structure, size and shape (Oxford, 1995). Consultants, Coopers & Lybrand, have prepared a detailed report into the university's decision-taking systems (Oxford, 1996, see also Franks, 1966.)

It is too easy to dismiss the ancient universities of Oxford and Cambridge as unrepresentative of their pre-1992 counterparts. There is justifiable concern that many chartered universities are operating inefficiently because of a participative committee structure which is unwieldy and wasteful of academic time, and that governance and management in HE is often conducted by a small *cadre* of senior university officers in a manner which is not provided for by charter, statutes or regulations. Expressed another way, there is a surrealistic detachment between, on the one hand, what the constitutions of many chartered universities provide *de jure* and, on the other, how in practice, the governance and management of those universities are conducted *de facto*. It is outside the scope of this chapter to describe the different types of governance models in HE or to explain how they evolved (see Farrington, 1994; Bargh *et al.*, 1996; Warner and Palfreyman, 1996; Gray, 1997; Warren, 1997). Suffice it to say that many of the chartered universities have developed historically in such a way as to render aspects of their constitutional structures, at best, outmoded and, at worst, misleading. Thus, if some statutory universities resemble giant tower blocks with design faults caused by the speed of their construction, many of their chartered counterparts give the appearance of labyrinthine mansions, built to a specification of another age and now requiring comprehensive replumbing and rewiring.

The premise on which this chapter is based is, therefore, very simple. Notwithstanding the importance of HE for economic growth and social development, investment in UK HEIs is in crisis, as it is in other industrial and developing countries throughout the world (World Bank, 1994). In response to this crisis and the challenge of how to preserve or improve the quality of HE as budgets are squeezed, the Government has decentralized key management functions to HEIs in order to promote funding diversification and a more efficient use of resources. This increased autonomy makes it more important than ever for HEIs to have decision-taking structures which work efficiently and effectively, contain safeguards against impropriety and command public confidence.

Although there are other important ways in which the decision-taking process at HEIs can be improved (for example, by promoting more effective leadership at all staffing levels – Dearlove, 1995a, 1995b), HEIs might take a fresh look at their constitutional structures and ask themselves the following simple questions.

- What are the structures intended to achieve?
- Do they promote or impede effective decision-taking at a time when HE is faced with an investment crisis?
- Are the constitutional structures sufficiently explicit to be understood by members of the governing body, staff, students and other members of the university in addition to the general public which has a legitimate interest in the well-being of HEIs as part of the fabric of our national life (whatever the level of public funding)?

The premise of this chapter is that, despite the undoubted strengths of the UK HE system and the need for continuing diversity, there is an alarming lack of coherence across the sector with regard to governance structures. In the spotlight of public scrutiny, many HEIs feel uncomfortable when compared with other corporate models which have more coherent and clearly-defined constitutions. HEIs and FE institutions find themselves part of a broader canvas in which corporate governance itself, in the UK and worldwide, is under scrutiny.

This chapter will now consider how, by returning to some simple constitutional basics and drawing on the political theory of earlier generations, guidance can be gleaned which may help to answer the questions just posed.

Back to constitutional basics

Governance and effective governance

Governance in the HE sector is essentially the process whereby independent corporate enterprises which conduct teaching and research take collective decisions. Typically, such decisions should cover the following three main areas.

1. The planning and determination of strategy – this function focuses on the goals of a corporate enterprise.
2. The implementation of planning and putting into effect of strategy – this function focuses on the objectives and means of achieving an enterprise's goals, and it consists of executive day-to-day decisions taken when managing an enterprise.
3. The monitoring and supervision of the executive management of the enterprise, and the evaluation of management decisions against goals. Supervision may lead to decisions being taken by the corporate enterprise to modify its strategy or the means of implementation.

Of these three elements, 1. and 3. are often described as board functions, exercised by simple majority decisions at quorate meetings of the governing body of an enterprise or by delegation to a board committee or officer. Item 2., however, is usually allocated to the enterprise's management, often in the person of the most senior manager or chief executive. The means whereby the governing body controls executive management (2.) is by exercising the sole authority to appoint, appraise and, if necessary, dismiss the most senior manager or chief executive. In the context of HE it is important not to confuse the determination of strategy, which is a board function, with the method whereby the strategy takes shape and is proposed to the board. In practice, of course, strategy will often be based on or shaped by the vision of the academic staff whose views will be put to the governing body via the chief executive or senior staff.

Having identified what governance is, or should be, the next step is to identify what makes one decision-taking process more efficient and effective than another. In answering this question, much will turn on the particular circumstances of an HEI, its culture and history, rate of growth, main sources of funding and tradition of democratic accountability to its own members. However, at the risk of over-generalization, it is possible to discern certain dynamic qualities which, when properly harnessed, seem to promote a decision-taking process which is more effective in coping with the planning, management and supervision of change and the associated problems.

In particular those qualities include:

1. the encouragement of leadership and the sharing of an institution's vision throughout its staff, in contrast to 'command and control' management from top down
2. striking the right balance of experience, skills and expertise on the governing body, and ensuring that there are sufficient numbers of 'lay' persons on the governing body who have relevant experience of business (and hence the planning and use of business resources) and the necessary enthusiasm, commitment and understanding of their responsibilities *and* of public sector values
3. reducing the size of governing bodies to enable members to participate more actively in the decision-taking process, coupled with controlled delegation to fewer committees and a greater use of full-time managers. (See The Report of the Dearing Committee (Dearing, 1997) which follows the appointment of a majority of 'lay' members to promote governing body effectiveness, and a reduction in the membership of governing bodies to a ceiling of 25.)

It is axiomatic that, for the decision-taking process of a corporate enterprise to be effective, it must also command the confidence of all those who have a stake in the enterprise's business. In the case of companies registered under the Companies Acts, it is the trust and confidence of the shareholders that matter. With regard to HEIs, the constituency of persons who have a legitimate interest or stake in the well-being of a particular university or college is much greater, embracing not only the members who normally comprise the corporate body of the institution (i.e. lay members of the Court and Council, academic staff, graduates and students), but also the tax payer and the wider community – the general public. Accordingly, there must be mechanisms to:

1. provide safeguards against impropriety, especially in relation to the mis-application of public money
2. establish clear lines of accountability in the sense not only of giving a financial account upwards to the ultimate paymaster, but also encouraging a genuine responsiveness to all those persons who have a stake in the enterprise.

Dark forces

In order to understand what constitutional safeguards (checks and balances) should be put in place to safeguard against impropriety, one needs to ask the question: what are the main obstacles to propriety? This requires an understanding about the flesh and blood of human nature, and in particular three 'dark forces', which have manifested themselves throughout human history and at least as early as the third chapter of the Book of Genesis. The first dark force is power or, more specifically, the abuse or misuse of power either as a result of its exploitation by one person or a group of persons working in concert, or as a result of the abandonment of power. Throughout history, whether in relation to the governance of states or social and business organizations, the abuse or misuse of power has proved to be a corrupt and corrupting crown – the outward manifestation or, in legal terminology, the *actus reus* of misgovernance. ('Power tends to corrupt and absolute power corrupts absolutely'.) The second dark force is greed or, to put it another way, self-interest, which may be either individual or collective self-interest, seeking to misuse positions of authority and power for self-advancement. This provides the motivation for misgovernance or, in legal terminology, the *mens rea*, of the offence. The third dark force is secrecy, which provides the opportunity for the abuse or misuse of power and the advancement of self-interest. Secrecy offers an environment in which misgovernance is likely to thrive. The sum total of these three dark forces produces the following simple equation:

abuse or misuse of power + self-interest + secrecy = corruption, dishonesty and tyranny.

In safeguarding against impropriety, it should, therefore, be the aim of every enterprise (and so of every HEI) to ensure that its constitution, in whatever form prescribed by law, contains the mechanisms to neutralize or at least control these destructive elements.

Controls

Most of the essential constitutional safeguards against impropriety were identified at least as early as the eighteenth-century 'Enlightenment'. Unfortunately, we seem to have lost sight of the lessons which the political thinkers of that time taught. They are straightforward.

First, to counter the abuse of power, there should be a separation of powers, namely a system of checks and balances designed to safeguard against the concentration of power, especially (but not exclusively) in the executive (or, in business terminology, 'executive management'). This can be viewed as a system of mutual restraints, whereby responsibility for different but complementary functions in the decision-taking process is split between different persons so as to ensure a balance of power and authority. Second, to counter self-interest, there should be a duty of good faith and a well-developed rule against conflicts, so that persons charged with the governance of corporate enterprises should avoid putting themselves in a position where personal interests conflict with public duty. Third, to counter secrecy, there should be openness and this should be articulated through policies of transparency and disclosure, particularly in the manner in which decisions are taken, recorded and made known publicly and in the financial reporting of an enterprise. ('The most powerful tool for ensuring that public business is transacted with propriety is openness', Nolan, 1996.)

In the context of the eighteenth-century Enlightenment, these controls could be said to produce the following equation:

separation of powers + duty of good faith + openness = accountability and liberty.

How can this theory then be applied to HEIs so as to promote more effective governance, rather than become so much chasing after the wind? How can the three main control mechanisms against impropriety be improved?

Improved controls

1 – checks and balances

Many of the recent governance problems in the HE and FE sectors can be traced to a breakdown in the system of checks and balances. Frequently, this occurs because the checks and balances are not clearly understood or respected by management or the board of governors. The situation at the University of Portsmouth was clearly complex and, in his Independent Inquiry Report to the board of governors, Mr J. Lever QC (Lever, 1995) acknowledged that, had the events occurred in any comparable organization, they would have placed considerable strain on the direction and management of that organization. Nevertheless, in respect of the deputy vice-chancellor's agreed departure on payment of a severance package, the chairman of the board of governors was criticized for imprudence in not having obtained board approval in advance for the course that he was proposing to follow. Similar criticism was levelled at the presentation to the board of governors as a *fait accompli* the *de facto* abolition of the post of deputy vice-chancellor and the restructuring of the directorate without giving the board the opportunity to debate the relevant issues of principle.

The committee system of an HEI should also operate as part of a system of checks and balances. Thus, the role of the audit committee is to act independently and authoritatively in examining an institution's financial affairs (in particular, the internal financial controls) more rigorously than the governing body as a whole. Its conclusions should be reported formally to the board of governors so that any important matters can be debated. Similarly, the remuneration committee's function is to advise the governing body in relation to the remuneration packages of the vice-chancellor and other senior members of staff, including, where appropriate, severance payments. This will also call for an approach which is both independent and robust. The Universities of Portsmouth and Huddersfield were criticized because certain committees did not appear to work effectively. Thus, at Huddersfield the original severance package proposed to the retiring vice-chancellor (totalling £411,493, plus a continuation of health insurance and car benefits) was plainly not subjected to the careful scrutiny of an independent remuneration committee which had access to appropriate professional advice. It was left to the Higher Education Funding Council (HEFCE) to be subsequently advised by leading counsel that the original package 'appeared to be excessive' and that, by agreeing to it, the university might have acted *ultra vires*. At the University of Portsmouth, it was the audit committee which was found wanting by the Lever Inquiry in one respect. In relation to its investigation into expense claims by the vice-chancellor, it made the mistake of communicating its conclusions to the governors informally, rather than by way of a formal report including the necessary supporting papers. The board was thereby deprived of an opportunity for formal discussion that could have led to further investigation.

Among FE colleges there is also evidence that roles and responsibilities have been misunderstood so as to result in the meddling of governors in management and by the principal in governance (Hall, 1994). Two polarized viewpoints can often be detected.

The first is that governors overreach themselves and meddle in management. Here the mistaken view is that governors have a discretion over what management powers should be delegated to the principal and that governors should be using specialist skills and experience in the management of their institution. It is also thought that they should exercise interventionist powers so as to manage an institution directly when they think things are going wrong. Typically, in this situation the relationship between the chairman and principal will be poor, the principal may lack confidence and management may be weak.

The second viewpoint is that the principal usurps the governors' role. There is the mistaken view that the principal, as chief executive, should have a free rein to manage both the institution and the governing body to achieve business goals. It is thought that, in the real world, 'lay' governors have insufficient understanding of the college, or time available, to determine strategy and that their role should be to ensure public acceptance of decisions which are, in reality, those of the principal and that active governors are an obstruction to effective governance. Typically, in this situation the relationship between the chairman and principal will be strong, and the principal will dominate the institution by force of personality.

The experience of FE colleges is of direct relevance to those HEIs which are HE corporations. Their constitutional structures are very similar, for example, in the way in which the articles of government allocate responsibility for strategy and oversight to the governing body, and for executive day-to-day management to the head of the institution (i.e. the college principal or university vice-chancellor).

Turning to the chartered universities, the constitutional drawing of checks and balances is much less clear. Thus, the university council is often described as the 'executive governing body' responsible for the management and administration of revenue and property and the general control over the conduct of the university's affairs, and yet is often too unwieldy because of size to be able to carry out this function effectively without significant delegation to an inner 'cabinet'. The vice-chancellor is typically described as 'the principal academic and administrative officer', being generally responsible to the council for maintaining and promoting the efficiency and good order of the university. Constitutionally, the vice-chancellor may lack the clearly defined responsibilities of his or her counterpart in a statutory university as 'chief executive'. The vice-chancellor's *de facto* role will thus frequently exceed the *de jure* job specification.

Doubtless, the failure in many chartered universities to set out explicitly the respective roles and responsibilities of the council (for strategy and oversight) and the vice-chancellor (for day-to-day executive management) flows from the historical separation of powers between the council (for managing resources) and the senate (as the supreme academic authority). The weakening of the senate's powers post-Jarratt should prompt a reappraisal of the system of checks and balances, and the redrawing of responsibilities between the council and the vice-chancellor and between the council and the court. Hence the Dearing Committee of Inquiry in its report (1997: 79) recommended that: 'the Government, together with representative bodies, should, within three years, establish whether the identity of the governing body in each institution is clear and undisputed. Where it is not, the Government should take action to clarify the position, ensuring that the council is the ultimate decision-making body, and that the court has a wide representative role, to inform decision-making but not to take decisions.'

There is plainly room for improvement. With regard to the statutory universities, it is submitted that the existing corporate structure, with the different but complementary roles, provision for delegation of certain functions and the listing of other 'reserved' functions which may not be delegated, is a strong model which should be reinforced.

Ways in which the model could be strengthened include the following.

- Developing the role of the secretary and clerk to the governing body to ensure that procedures are followed and that independent and authoritative constitutional advice is offered to the board – particularly to the chairman and vice-chancellor – so that the interface between governors and management is harmonious and effective.

- The use of codes of conduct and ethics which have a very important role to play in promoting a better understanding of the responsibilities of governors, their accountability and the duty to safeguard public funds, and the need to promote high standards of behaviour.
- Improved training for governors. There has perhaps been too ready an assumption in the HE sector that governors sufficiently understand their role and responsibilities, and that the need for formal training has been exaggerated. This is mistaken. Particularly at a time of financial crisis, HEIs need 'lay' governors who understand precisely what is expected of them. Better governor training should lead to a more effective operation of the constitutional checks and balances.
- Independent advice procedures. These should be adopted by governing bodies to enable governors to take independent professional advice where appropriate.
- The careful review by boards of what responsibilities they are prepared to delegate, what responsibilities should be 'reserved' as non-delegable because of their significance, and the number, purpose and terms of reference of all standing committees.

2 – safeguards against conflicts
In its Issues and Questions paper, the Nolan Committee observed that the mechanisms operated by local public spending bodies for identifying and resolving conflicts of interest 'do not appear to be as extensive as those employed by other branches of the public service, such as local government or non-departmental public bodies'. Considerable variety of practice was noted.

Central to this issue is the need for HEIs to establish a coherent framework within which members of governing bodies are restricted or prohibited from participating in certain decisions in which they have some financial or other interest and which permits them to make a voluntary public disclosure of relevant interests. The articles of government of statutory universities and the standing orders of many of their chartered counterparts commonly require board members to declare any 'pecuniary, family or other personal interest in any matter under discussion' and to take no part in the consideration of, or voting on, the matter. However, such rules often do not require a member who has an interest to withdraw (i.e. physically) from that part of the meeting in which the interest is discussed, and there is commonly no provision which permits board members who have declared the nature and extent of any material interest and withdrawn from the meeting subsequently to be a party to the transaction or arrangement in which they have an interest.

Many HEIs have already adopted, or are in the process of doing so, a register of members' interests which is open to public inspection (Nolan,

1996: 37: 'all institutions should have publicly available registers of interests'). Various models exist, but a particular difficulty is how to define the 'relevant interests' which should voluntarily be disclosed. It is submitted that the guiding principle should be the voluntary disclosure of any interest, financial or otherwise, which is likely to interfere with the exercise of a board member's independent judgement or which, if publicly known, would be perceived as likely to influence that judgement. A secondary principle is that a board member should be invited to provide the same information, if known to him or her, in respect of his or her spouse, partner, children or other close relatives (for example, persons living in the same household or as a dependant). According to this test, a board member should ask him or herself whether members of the public, knowing such information, would reasonably conclude that the relevant interest might influence his or her judgement.

As a support for rules relating to non-participation and voluntary disclosure, codes of conduct and governance training programmes also have important parts to play in reminding board members and managers of the importance of demonstrating high personal standards of integrity and independence.

3 – openness, transparency and disclosure
Governing bodies in the HE sector have, with some justification, been criticized as self-perpetuating and made in their own image and, therefore, at risk of appearing too inward-looking. The process whereby the composition of boards is reviewed and replenished by the filling of vacancies has prompted some debate. Two recommendations made outside the education sector have particular significance. First, the Cadbury Committee (1994) urged that:

> Given the importance of their distinctive contribution, non-executive directors should be selected with the same impartiality and care as senior executives. *We recommend* that their appointment should be a matter for the board as a whole and that there should be a formal selection process, which will reinforce the independence of non-executive directors and make it evident that they have been appointed on merit and not through any form of patronage. We regard it as good practice for a nomination committee . . . to carry out the selection process and to make proposals to the board.
>
> (Cadbury, 1994: 17)

This theme was picked up by the Nolan Committee in its First Report (Nolan, 1995) which included a recommendation that appointments to non-departmental public bodies should be made 'on the basis of merit' with the aim of achieving 'a balance of relevant skills and backgrounds'. The Nolan Committee also recommended that all appointments should be made after advice from a panel or committee 'which includes an independent element', and that the appointments process should be open and subject to external supervision. Adapted to meet the needs of HEIs this seemed to suggest that governing bodies should establish search or nomination committees which include a significant non-governor element, and that the committee should trawl for candidates from a wide field, by making appropriate use of advertising, executive search, consultation with interested bodies, and maintaining and using databases of interested and appropriate candidates.

It was, therefore, not surprising that in its Second Report the Nolan Committee (1996: 21) recommended that 'appointments to the governing bodies of universities and colleges should be made on the basis of merit, subject to the need to achieve a balance of relevant skills and backgrounds on the board'. However, the report declined to recommend external scrutiny by the use of non-governor members on nomination committees, although such mechanisms were clearly favoured by the Nolan Committee and there is some evidence of an increasing use in higher and further education of non-governors in the selection of governing body members.

If HEIs are expected to operate openly and 'in the public gaze', so as to make it difficult for the dark forces of power and self-interest to take root, the lines of public accountability need to be examined. In the sense of 'giving a financial account', HEIs are subject to an upwards accountability to Government through the funding councils, and to Parliament through the Public Accounts Committee. The essential framework is that the Public Accounts Committee is responsible for scrutinizing public expenditure. Under the National Audit Act 1983, the Comptroller and Auditor General is appointed by the Prime Minister with the agreement of the Chairman of the Public Accounts Committee. The Comptroller and Auditor General reports to the Public Accounts Committee and is head of the National Audit Office. He or she has power to carry out investigations into the economy, efficiency and effectiveness of HEIs. The head of institution of each university or college is its accounting officer and may be required to appear before the Public Accounts Committee, together with the chief officer of the relevant funding council. This framework, although commendable in establishing national lines of accountability upwards, does little to promote responsiveness in a horizontal direction to the local community. Although the constitutions of chartered universities provide for the establishment of the Court as a large representative forum for receiving a university's annual report and financial statement, the statutory universities lack an equivalent statutory mechanism for making their governing bodies more responsive to the local and regional communities which they serve. Middlesex University (a post-1992 university) has established its own Court with the purpose of supporting the university as an advisory body 'in the achievement of its stated objectives and to reflect upon its progress'. Many FE corporations have begun to hold annual public meetings for the purpose of presenting their annual reports and accounts and encouraging a dialogue with interested members of the public. It remains to be seen how effective such action will be in promoting genuine responsiveness of a horizontal nature.

The contents of the annual reports received particular attention in the Second Report of the Nolan Committee (1996), which encouraged greater openness in the way in which key information about the governing body, governance structure and policies, objectives, and performance criteria is made available to the public. The Nolan Committee also recommended that a standard of good practice should be developed to limit the extent to which FE colleges and HEIs can withhold information from the public on the grounds of commercial confidentiality.

The proper role of staff and student 'representatives' on governing bodies has sparked some controversy among statutory HEIs and FE and HE colleges (Hall, 1990). It is submitted that, although staff and student board members may play an important role by subjecting management to critical scrutiny, their primary function should not be that of 'watchdogs' or 'whistle-blowers' (i.e. so as to make an institution more accountable upwards to the Government or its agencies), but as shapers of an institution's character and mission. By contributing to the decision-taking process, they are well placed to enhance the responsiveness of an institution to its staff and students as participants in a collegiate body. Accordingly, the view has been expressed that each HEI should be free to choose whether and, if so, to what extent, staff and student board members should be appointed and whether this should be by a process of election or cooption, and that such a choice will be influenced by the tradition and needs of each institution. In other words, the case for compulsion has not been made out (but see the Report of the Dearing Committee (Dearing, 1997) which recommended that governing bodies should be 'required' to appoint staff and student members to ensure 'legitimacy').

Potential personal liability

This chapter concludes on an ironic note. Persons who offer their services voluntarily (i.e. in an unpaid capacity) as members of HEIs' governing bodies are expected by the public to conduct themselves in accordance with standards which are open, clear and fair. They are entitled to expect similar treatment under the law. Instead, there has been some obfuscation in relation to the issue of potential personal liability. Concern has been expressed that this issue has been conveniently 'swept under the carpet', although there has recently been official recognition that a potential problem may exist and that board members of non-departmental public bodies should be indemnified as follows:

> The Government has indicated that an individual board member who has acted honestly, reasonably, in good faith and without negligence, will not have to meet out of his own personal resources any personal civil liability which is incurred in execution or purported execution of his board function.

> (Cabinet Office, 1996: 23)

In particular, unfavourable comparisons have been made about the relative positions of corporation members (of statutory and chartered bodies), company directors and trustees. It is submitted that the law is most unsatisfactory in imposing a range of different standards, in relation to personal liability, in a haphazard and illogical manner. Thus, board members of corporate governing bodies do not enjoy the right to claim relief from the Court against personal liability in circumstances analogous to those which are available to trustees in the strict sense and those available to company directors (see Section 61 of the Trustee Act 1925 and Section 727 of the Companies Act 1985). This confusion is compounded by the fact that it can be argued with some force that trustees of those institutions which are unincorporated have greater personal risk (for example, in the event of an institution's insolvency) than company directors who will have the benefit of limited liability, unless wrongful or fraudulent trading can be proved.

Heads of potential liabilities

Statutory offences

There are many statutory offences which can be committed by corporations and which can result in criminal liability for both corporations and their members. Liability for corporation members is usually (but not exclusively) confined to the situation where the breach is attributable to some act or neglect on the part of the corporation member concerned. Examples include breaches of the legislation relating to health and safety at work, data protection, and environmental protection. Statutory offences can result in fines for members of corporations and, in the most extreme cases, imprisonment.

General criminal liability

Members of corporations are clearly potentially liable under the general criminal law for their activities in the course of their duties. Any fraudulent activity which is detected would be likely to lead to criminal charges. The common law offence of 'misconduct in a public office' could also be used in relation to any dishonest behaviour by corporation members. (See also the proposal of the Nolan Committee (Nolan, 1997) on its third report to introduce a new statutory offence called 'misuse of public office' and its application to all holders of public office.)

Joint civil liability

A person suing a corporation (for example, for personal injury caused by the negligence of the corporation) may seek to include individual board members in the action as joint defendants with the corporation. This would not be regarded as normal practice, but should be considered as a possibility, particularly in the context of arranging insurance cover.

Breach of duty

Members of corporations may find themselves the subject of proceedings for breach of duty. Board members have fiduciary and other duties to the corporation. These include the duties to act in the best interests of the corporation, not to allow personal interests to conflict with the interests of the corporation, and to exercise reasonable care, diligence and skill in carrying out their functions. With regard to the statutory HEIs, there are also the specific responsibilities conferred on corporation members by the articles of government, such as ensuring the solvency of the corporation and the safeguarding of its assets. There is a wide variety of situations in which breaches of duty could arise, but two specific examples (misapplication of funds and insolvency) will be used here to illustrate instances where personal liability may become an issue.

Liability in relation to misapplied funds

HE corporations   There are three main ways in which it may be argued that the governors of statutory HEIs could be liable to the corporations of which they are members in respect of a misapplication of funds. These are:

1. as quasi trustees
2. as fiduciaries
3. by analogy with the liability of directors of companies established under the Companies Acts.

These three possible arguments will now be considered in turn.

   1. **Liability as quasi trustees**   Since HE corporations are usually regarded as existing for exclusively charitable purposes, it seems clear that this type of corporation should be treated as an exempt charity. A Court would view HE corporations as exempt charities only if it thought that their purposes were exclusively charitable. Schedule 2 of the Charities Act 1993 provides that HE corporations are exempt charities 'in so far as they are charities'. Paragraph 64 of Schedule 12 to the Education Reform Act 1988 and paragraph 69 of Schedule 8 to the Further and Higher Education Act 1992 (repealed by the Charities Act 1993) provided expressly and without qualification that the corporations were to be exempt charities. The corporation holds its property 'subject to a binding legal obligation to apply it for charitable purposes only' (Tudor on Charities, 1995: 159). The authority on which this proposition is based is *Liverpool and District Hospital for Diseases of the Heart v Attorney-General*, and it fully bears it out. The somewhat fuller discussion in Picarda, 1995: 383–6, is to the same effect. The safer view, however, is that it holds its property otherwise than as a trustee in the strict sense. On this basis, it cannot be said that the managers or governors of the corporation are charity trustees as such even though they are clearly charity trustees for the purposes of the Charities Act 1993 (Section 97(1) provides:

'In this Act, except in so far as the context otherwise requires . . . "charity trustees" means the persons having the general control and management of the administration of the charity'). It is at least arguable, therefore, that they should be treated as if they were trustees, and, therefore, subject to the control of the High Court in the exercise of the Court's jurisdiction with respect to charities. (*Harries v Church of England Commissioners*; see also Vol. 5(2) of *Halsbury's Laws of England*, 1993: paragraph 375, Note 2. For a fuller discussion of this question, see Hyams, 1994). This proposition is supported by the fact that, if there could be no personal liability on the part of governors in respect of a misuse of the property of a corporation, then in practice there would be nobody in relation to whom the jurisdiction of the Court with respect to these charities could be exercised!

Trustees in the strict sense can rely on Section 61 of the Trustees Act 1925 to limit their liability for breach of trust, which provides:

> If it appears to the court that a trustee, whether appointed by the court or otherwise, is or may be personally liable for any breach of trust, whether the transaction alleged to be a breach of trust occurred before or after the commencement of this Act, but has acted honestly and reasonably, and ought fairly to be excused for the breach of trust and for omitting to obtain the directions of the court in the matter in which he committed such breach, then the court may relieve him wholly or partly from personal liability for the same.

The problem is that, although governors might be regarded by the Court as being in the same position as trustees, they will be unable to rely on Section 61 if this section only applies to trustees proper.

2. **Liability as fiduciaries**   It seems clear that a governor is in the position of a fiduciary towards the corporation of which he or she is a governor. The position is well within the principles indicated in Underhill and Hayton (1995: 16). Furthermore, the case of *Attorney-General v De Winston*, where a borough treasurer was held to be in a fiduciary position towards the borough council of which he was the treasurer, supports the proposition that governors of HE corporations are in a fiduciary position as regards the corporations of which they are governors. However, that may not in itself mean that a governor would be liable in damages to the corporation if the governor participated in an *ultra vires* act. The principal obligation of a fiduciary is generally merely to return property or its equivalent value to that body from which the property was obtained by a breach of the fiduciary duty in question. It seems that, as a matter of principle, a fiduciary is not liable to compensate the body in question for a loss caused as a result of his or her breach of fiduciary duty (see Underhill and Hayton, 1995: 826–9, for a strong disapproval of the case of *Re Leeds and Hanley Theatres of Varieties*, CA). As a consequence, a governor who obtains property in breach of fiduciary duty, will have to return it or compensate the corporation for its loss – and no more.

3. **Liability by analogy with that of directors of companies established under the Companies Acts**   That a director of a company established under the Companies Acts may be liable to the company of which he or she is a director is clear, but the director's liability may be limited under Section 727 of the Companies Act 1985, which applies not only to actions against directors for breach of trust, but also to proceedings for negligence, default or breach of duty. Section 727 of the Companies Act 1985 provides:

(1) If in any proceedings for negligence, default, breach of duty or breach of trust against an officer of a company or a person employed by a company as auditor (whether he is or is not an officer of the company) it appears to the court hearing the case that that officer or person is or may be liable in respect of the negligence, default, breach of duty or breach of trust, but that he has acted honestly and rea- sonably, and that having regard to all the circumstances of the case (including those connected with his appointment) he ought fairly to be excused for the negligence, default, breach of duty or breach of trust, that court may relieve him, either wholly or partly, from his liability on such terms as it thinks fit.

(2) If any such officer or person as above-mentioned has reason to apprehend that any claim will or might be made against him in respect of any negligence, default, breach of duty or breach of trust, he may apply to the court for relief; and the court on the application has the same power to relieve him as under this section it would have had if it had been a court before which proceedings against that person for negligence, default, breach of duty or breach of trust had been brought.

(3) Where a case to which subsection (1) applies is being tried by a judge with a jury, the judge, after hearing the evidence, may, if he is satisfied that the defendant or defender ought in pursuance of that subsection to be relieved either in whole or in part from the liability sought to be enforced against him, withdraw the case in whole or in part from the jury and forthwith direct judgement to be entered for the defendant or defender on such terms as to costs or otherwise as the judge may think proper.

Section 727 does not have to be specifically pleaded by a director who is seeking statutory relief: see *Re Kirbys Coaches Limited.* Relief is only available in respect of actions brought by or on behalf of the company: see *Customs and Excise Commissioners v Hedon Alpha Limited.* The Court is less disposed to grant relief to a director who is paid for his or her services rather than one who has acted gratuitously: see *National Trustees Company of Australia v General Finance Company of Australia.* There is substantial case law regarding Section 727, including a number of recent decisions, although each case tends to turn on the particular facts – see *Claridge's Patent Asphalte Company Limited; Re Duomatic Limited; Re Welfab Engineers Limited; Re Home Treat Limited; Zemco Limited v Jerrom-Pugh; Bishopsgate Investment Manage- ment Limited (in liquidation) v Maxwell (No. 2); Target Holdings Limited v Redferns*

(A Firm) and Another; *Re D'Jan of London Limited*; *Copp v D'Jan*; *Framlington Group PLC and Another v Anderson and Others* .

A failure to comply with the duty placed upon an HE corporation in its standard articles of government for 'the effective and efficient use of resources, the solvency of the institution and the corporation and for safeguarding their assets' could be regarded as giving rise to a personal liability on the part of the governors, if the Court were to regard governors analogously to directors. It is submitted, however, that it is inappropriate to equate the position of governors of HE corporations with that of company directors. This is not least because the duties of the two are fundamentally different. In addition, a company director can usually be expected to be paid for his or her duties whereas, in contrast, the governors of HE corporations are unpaid volunteers.

Generally In order to avoid the current uncertainty with regard to governor liability, it would be preferable for Parliament to make specific provision (probably in primary legislation) to regulate the situation. Such provision could simply apply Section 61 of the Trustee Act 1925 to relevant governors. Alternatively, Parliament could enact that the governors of HE and FE corporations have the right to apply to the Court for relief from personal liability in terms similar to Section 727 of the Companies Act 1985. As a result, governors would be entitled to no less protection than that which is presently available to company directors.

It has been suggested that governors could become liable to an HE corporation in respect of an act which was *ultra vires* the corporation (i.e. beyond the corporation's statutory powers and, therefore, unenforceable) merely because they had caused the corporation to act *ultra vires*. Such a view is probably mistaken, despite what is said in Vol. 9 of *Halsbury's Laws* (4th edition, 1974): paragraph 1344, in reliance on the case of *Young v Naval, Military and Civil Service Co-operative Society of South Africa.* In that case, the company directors whose liability was in issue acted *ultra vires* in voting that certain payments be made to themselves, with the result that the case is adequately explained by the principles governing fiduciary duties of directors. Before liability to the corporation can arise, there would have to be a breach of some duty owed to the corporation. Unless it were possible to establish liability as a fiduciary, a trustee or by analogy with company directors, or unless there were some other way in which a Court might determine that governors could be held liable to the corporation, a decision by governors which causes the corporation to act *ultra vires* cannot properly be said, without more, to give rise to potential liability to the corporation.

It has also been suggested that governors could be liable for a breach of warranty of authority to a third party with whom the corporation entered into a contract, where the corporation did not have the power to enter into the agreement, or alternatively, where some condition binding the corporation (such as funding council approval) had not been complied with. If the corporation had no power under its constitution to enter into the contract, then a person in the position of a governor could, in theory, be liable and such a claim is one against which it might be thought to be desirable to provide some measure of protection. It would be possible that the claim would fail on the basis that the warranty was a representation of law if an alleged implied warranty is determined by a Court to have been a representation with regard to the law. In that case, it will not give rise to liability on the part of the warrantor. If the warranty were one of fact, the claim would be successful. Liability could arise, for example, if it were held by a Court that a governor had impliedly warranted that a procedure required by the articles of government to be followed had indeed been followed, when in fact it had not. In contrast, if the warranty were determined to have been that the corporation had the power to enter into a contract, when its statutory powers did not in fact allow it to do so, then it would, it seems, be a warranty with regard to the law.

Chartered corporations   The exposure of a governor of a university incorporated by royal charter to potential personal liability is at least similar to, if not the same as, that of a governor of an HE corporation. This is subject to the *caveat* that the charter may make provision to the contrary.

Limited liability companies   The liability of a director of a limited liability company is well described elsewhere in the text books on company law (Charlesworth and Morse, 1995; Lai *et al.*, 1996; *Tolley's Company Law Handbook*, 1997). However, it is helpful to examine the manner in which liability might arise for a director of a limited liability company which has the conduct of an HEI. As indicated earlier, the director of a company is not to be regarded as a trustee proper. However, according to Boyle (1990), 'a director is answerable as a trustee for any misapplication of the company's property in which he participated and which he knew or ought to have known to be a misapplication'. On this basis, governors who are company directors are in the same position as trustees, albeit they are not trustees in the strict sense. In addition, it should be noted that a director can be liable to a company for negligence. In this sense, a company director is exposed to a greater potential personal liability than a trustee proper.

Liability in the event of insolvency and dissolution

HE corporations   An HE corporation can only be dissolved by order of the Secretary of State for Education and Employment and, in that event, the Secretary of State may transfer the liabilities of the corporation to another educational body or one of the funding councils. (Statutory provisions which apply to the dissolution of an HE corporation are contained in Section 128 of the ERA 1988.) A failure to transfer relevant liabilities would be judicially reviewable. However, if it were held to be lawful to decline to transfer relevant outstanding liabilities, then it seems that the liabilities would remain outstanding, but that the members of the corporation would not be personally liable to third parties, such as creditors. According to *Halsbury's Laws:* 'If a man trusts a corporation, he trusts that legal person, and must look to its assets for payment; he can only call upon individual members to contribute if the Act or charter creating the corporation has so provided,' (Vol. 9, 1994: paragraph 1209). In fact, none of the relevant statutes so provide. In addition, it seems clear that Part V of the Insolvency Act 1986 (which applies to the winding up of 'unregistered companies') would not apply. Thus, the best view is that the governors of an HE corporation would not be liable on dissolution of the corporation to meet the liabilities of the corporation. In addition, unless the Secretary of State transferred the right to enforce a breach of a governor's duties owed to the corporation (assuming there is such a right) under the relevant statutory provision, the governor's liability in respect of that breach would cease to be actionable.

However, the position is unclear and untested in law, where a corporation has become insolvent or where its assets have been seriously prejudiced as a result of mismanagement and the Secretary of State declines to dissolve it. In such a situation, governors would be vulnerable to the argument that they had breached their duty under the articles of government to ensure solvency and safeguard the assets of the institution, and potentially liable to the corporation for the resultant financial loss. It is conceivable that in such circumstances a corporation might wish to take legal action against those governors who were regarded as wholly or mainly responsible for the insolvency.

Chartered corporations In Farrington (1994), it is stated in relation to a university conducted by a chartered corporation that 'Unless the charter provides otherwise, the members of the corporation are not liable for its debts' (paragraph 2.84). Although no authority is given in support of this proposition, it is consistent with the quotation from *Halsbury's Laws* set out earlier. In addition, 'Where a corporation has been dissolved, its members, in their natural capacities, can neither recover debts which are due to the corporation nor be charged with debts contracted by it' (*Halsbury's Laws*, Vol. 9, 1994: paragraph 1398).

However, the authority is so old – *Naylor v Cornish* and *Edmunds v Brown and Tillard* that the proposition itself might be regarded as suspect. If the proposition is correct, then a governor's liability for the outstanding liabilities of a chartered corporation, in the event of dissolution, is likely to be the same as that of a governor of an HE corporation. It is unclear, however, what the position is with regard to a governor's liability *to* a chartered corporation in the event of its dissolution, but, if governors would remain liable in respect of a breach of their personal obligations owed to a chartered corporation, then an action to enforce such liability would require the joinder of the Attorney-General. This is because of the corporation's charitable status.

Limited liability companies   The position of a board member of a limited liability company in the event of its dissolution is relatively clear and well catered for in the textbooks on company law. However, it is worth noting that, although third parties cannot sue the directors for debts of the company, in the event of its insolvency, the liquidator of the company can pursue a director for compensation for a breach of a director's duties. In that event, the director may be able to rely on Section 727 of the Companies Act 1985 for protection.

Avoidance of personal liability

Practical steps
There are a number of practical steps board members can take to avoid suffering personal liability. These include:

- being aware of the limitations on the powers of the corporation and the terms of reference of all committees
- being aware of the duties and responsibilities of board members
- ensuring that sufficient information is available to the governing body
- ensuring that all personal, financial and other interests are declared and are routinely recorded in a register
- ensuring that the governing body takes professional advice wherever appropriate
- ensuring that meetings are fully and properly minuted
- in particular, making any dissenting views known and ensuring that they are minuted
- if things appear to be going seriously wrong, taking personal advice at an early stage.

The adoption of a well-drafted code of conduct (to which individual board members are required to subscribe) can be a useful means of achieving many of these steps. However, it should be noted that merely voting against a course of action will not necessarily absolve a member of liability. Similarly, resigning or threatening to resign may not be enough. For example, some positive action to safeguard the corporation's assets may be required in exceptional circumstances. (See Chapter 4 on the similar duties of care and diligence imposed upon charity trustees.)

Insurance
HEI constitutions normally allow corporations to insure their members against liabilities incurred arising out of membership and to pay the associated premiums. Indeed, the CVCP recommends it. Insurance should very much be regarded as a safeguard of last resort, especially since it is not possible to insure against all liabilities. In particular, insurance against criminal liabilities (whether statutory or under the general criminal law) is not possible.

In addition, insurance policies inevitably exclude various heads of liability. These vary from policy to policy and the exclusions should always be carefully scrutinized. Liability arising out of deliberate acts or where the person concerned knew that the act was a breach of duty, or was reckless as to whether it was a breach of duty or not, may be excluded. This type of exclusion may mean that, in circumstances where advice should have been (but was not) taken in relation to whether a course of action was in breach of duty or not, the insurer may refuse cover. Liability for defamation is very often excluded, as is liability in connection with environmental pollution.

Invariably, there will be a cap on the amount of cover provided by an insurance policy and frequently there will be an 'excess' provision, which means that below the level of the specified excess, there is no cover. The levels of excess in some local government insurance policies, for example, have been as high as £100,000 or more. Board members should accordingly not allow the existence of an insurance policy to lull them into a false sense of security: an insurance policy will not assist with the inevitable trauma of a legal action or with the possible damage to reputation.

Conclusion

An inescapable conclusion is that, in order for HEIs, schools and other bodies which provide public services to attract and retain volunteers of calibre for public service, legislation should be introduced which will clarify their potential liability and make available a similar range of protections to those which are available to company directors and charity trustees. It would be a valuable addition to the statute book for there to be a simple formulation which would define the limits of personal liability for all those persons who are charged with responsibility for conducting bodies which provide public services in an era when corporate governance occupies centre-stage.

Editors' note: Hence, it is noted with interest that the Nolan Committee has announced (November, 1996) that, with the agreement of the Government, it will commission a study into the issues of personal liability and insurance. Otherwise the liability position remains uncertain and, in the absence of appropriate legislation as mentioned earlier, only litigation will begin to clarify the extent of personal liability. Meanwhile, governors of statutory HEIs and members of councils of chartered HEIs clearly need to ensure that they comply with good practice as set out in the various guides now emerging (CUC, 1995; CEF, 1995; AfC, 1995), in the well-trodden territory of charity law concerning the duties of trustees (Palfreyman, 1995–6; Chapter 4), in the area of company law concerning the fiduciary duty of directors (Chapter 12), and in relation to the proper conduct of meetings (Chapter 5). Certainly, as stated earlier, it should not be assumed that purchasing an insurance policy will compensate for ignorance and neglect!

Further reading

Bargh, C., Scott, P. and Smith, D. (1996) *Governing Universities: Changing the Culture?* Buckingham: SRHE/Open University Press.

Evans, G. R. (forthcoming) *Accountability in Higher Eduction.* Buckingham: SRHE/Open University Press.

Farrington, D. J. (1994) *The Law of Higher Education.* London: Butterworths.

Hyams, O. (1996) Higher and further education dismissals and redundancy – problem areas and their consequences for corporations and governors, *Education and the Law,* 8(2), 137–52.

Oakley, A. J. (1996) *Trends in Contemporary Trust Law.* Oxford: Oxford University Press.

Shilling, A. and Sharp, T. (1997) *Corporate Governance.* London: Butterworths.

Warner, D. A. and Palfreyman D. (1996) *Higher Education Management: The Key Elements.* Buckingham: SRHE/Open University Press.

4

Charity Trusteeship: Unlimited Personal Liability, Again?

Emma Chamberlain (Cole and Cole)

Editors' introduction

This chapter links to the one on governance and explores the duties and powers of charity trustees. It will often not be appreciated that some individuals within a higher education institution (HEI) are functioning as trustees, either by the HEI itself as the trustee or by the individuals themselves being the trustees. There are 150,000 charities in England and Wales, with an annual income of approximately £12 billion, run by one million trustees – of whom it is estimated that a third do not realize they are trustees, let alone properly understand the legal obligations of being a trustee.

What is a charity? What is an exempt charity? What is the exemption from? Who/what is a trustee? What are the duties, powers and liabilities of a trustee? Does incorporation protect the trustees from personal liability? Are HEIs much different from other charities? Are those running the HEI also trustees with the same personal liabilities as for charity trustees in general? Who polices an exempt charity? Can trustees insure against their potential personal liability, in the same way company directors can? (See Chapter 3 concerning Lord Nolan's (1995) call for 'publicly available registers of interests' in relation to members of council/governing body.)

For an interesting discussion of the Royal Holloway and Bedford New College sale of its Turners and other pictures, see Charity Commission (1993), Sheridan (1993/4) and Phillips and Claricoat (1995), and more generally, Palfreyman (1997).

Charity trusteeship

This chapter examines the following basic concepts of charity law. What is a charity? What is an exempt charity? Who or what are charity trustees? What are their general powers, duties and liabilities? These concepts are considered in the context of HEIs and we discuss some practical problems that can arise.

What is a charity?

The legal concept of charity has been developed by the Courts over several centuries. There is still no statutory definition of charitable purposes, although the possibility of introducing one was discussed before the passage of the Charities Act 1992. In the end, it was decided that the benefit of flexibility, which allowed the scope of charitable activities to keep pace with changes in society, outweighed the advantages of certainty and clarity which a statutory definition might be expected to provide. To understand the word 'charitable', it is necessary therefore, to fall back on an Elizabethan statute and case law. (See also the annual *Decisions of the Charity Commissioners*, HMSO.)

The famous statute of Elizabeth I (preamble to the Charitable Uses Act, 1601) contains a list of purposes which were at that time considered to be charitable. Some of the purposes sound odd to modern 'ears:

> The relief of aged, impotent and poor people; the maintenance of sick and maimed soldiers and mariners, schools of learning, free schools and scholars of universities; the repair of bridges, ports, havens, causeways, churches, sea banks and highways; the education and preferment of orphans, the relief, stock or maintenance of houses of correction; the marriages of poor maids; the supportation, aid and help of young tradesmen, handicraftsmen and persons decayed; the relief or redemption of prisoners or captives; and the aid or ease of any poor inhabitants concerning payments of fifteens, setting out of soldiers and other taxes.
>
> (Charitable Uses Act, 1601)

The Charitable Uses Act, 1601 has now been repealed, but has been influential in developing the modern concept of charity. Subsequently, Lord MacNaughton gave an important definition of charitable purposes in the case of *Income Tax Special Purposes Commissioners v Pemsel*. He said, 'Charity in its legal sense comprises four principal divisions: trusts for the relief of poverty; trusts for the advancement of education; trusts for the advancement of religion; and trusts for other purposes beneficial to the community not falling under any of the preceding heads.'

Education and charity

We are concerned here particularly with the second head of charity – that is the advancement of education. The origins of this are found in the references in the preamble to the Elizabethan statute to 'schools of learning, free schools and scholars of universities'. HEIs broadly comprise universities and colleges which may be established directly by Royal Charter (although they are not subject to Crown control) or by Act of Parliament. HEIs obviously come within the second head of charity – the advancement of education – although they may also become involved in other charitable purposes (for example where they have been left a legacy in a will which is to be used for charitable but not primarily educational purposes). Problems of receiving such gifts are discussed later.

It is well established that education need not be provided free of charge in order to be charitable. Education is itself charitable whether the beneficiaries are rich or poor and whether or not fees are paid. Thus, schools in the private sector which charge fees may be charitable provided they are not run purely as profit-making ventures. Education is not confined to the provision of formal instruction. It is wide enough to cover the promotion of conferences devoted to academic subjects or to advance public knowledge of and interest in the Arts. It is also not limited to instruction in academic subjects, so trusts to promote sport at schools and universities have been held to be charitable. The establishment and support of colleges, professorships, schools of learning and fellowships are all charitable.

An educational charity must be established for the benefit of the public or a sufficiently important section of the public, rather than for the benefit of individuals. In addition, if it is to be charitable, the subject matter of an educational charity must be of sufficient value to benefit the community. A leading case here is *Re Pinion*, where the testator left his pictures, furniture and other objects to trustees to be maintained as a collection. Most of the items were of poor quality and the Court decided that since there was no evidence that the gift would benefit the public it was not charitable. Generally, HEIs do not have to address the question of whether what they do or are is charitable. However, an HEI may on occasion receive a gift subject to a binding trust which is not actually charitable (e.g. 'to the Master and Fellows of X college to use for research into the advantages of a revised alphabet and informing the public'). A similar bequest in *Re Shaw's Will Trusts* was found to be non-charitable.

While individuals may derive benefits from an educational charity, the main purpose of the charity must be for the benefit of the public. The line can often be quite finely drawn here. Gifts for the education of limited classes of persons who constitute a sufficiently important part of the community have been upheld. Scholarship funds, for example, exist primarily to encourage high standards of learning which is clearly of public benefit, the advantage to the individual recipient being incidental to the primary purpose. However, a scholarship fund for the benefit of the descendants of certain individuals would not now be charitable nor generally is an educational fund for the benefit of the children of employees.

Although gifts solely to educate a founder's kin at a college have not been regarded as charitable, a trust where only *preference* is directed to be given to the donor's descendants is charitable. The question is whether there is a mere expression of preference or whether it amounts to a positive obligation.

Legacies from wills

HEIs may have to consider issues arising from the advancement of education in the context of legacies from wills. The following two issues arise here.

1. Whether the gift is charitable at all. For example, does the gift *require* the HEI to use the money for too limited a class of beneficiaries to be charitable or is this a mere expression of wish?
2. If it is charitable, is it educational? An HEI may be left a legacy subject to a binding trust which is charitable within the terms of the *Income Tax Special Purposes Commissioners v Pemsel* case but not in connection with any special purpose of the HEI. If the HEI accepts the legacy it is obliged to follow its trusts, but, unless the HEI can broadly show that such a trust is established in connection with the purposes of the HEI, that legacy trust will not be an exempt charity within Schedule 2, Charities Act 1993.

However, provided the gift itself is charitable, there do not seem to be any rules requiring the trust to be consistent with the original foundation, although some HEIs may not be able to accept gifts to their foundation without the consent of the Visitor. Conversely, an HEI is not bound to accept a gift to its foundation or property which is subject to a special condition. If it does so, the trust or condition must be performed whether the property given is adequate for the purpose or not. Care is needed, therefore, when deciding whether to accept legacies and lifetime gifts. The terms of any such gift should be examined to determine whether there is a binding trust or merely a wish, and whether the binding trust is sensible for the HEI to take on. Once the HEI accepts the gift, it has to carry out the obligation and cannot subsequently disclaim the benefit. The question of what constitutes acceptance of a trust is one of fact.

What are exempt charities and who regulates them?

The Charities Act 1993, Section 96(1), defines charity as 'any institution, corporate or not, which is established for charitable purposes and is subject to the control of the High Court in the exercise of the court's jurisdiction with respect to charities'. Note, therefore, that ecclesiastical corporations are excluded from Section 96 (since the ordinary Courts have no jurisdiction over their property), as is the corporate property of Oxford and Cambridge. Although the Courts have jurisdiction over HEIs, the Visitor has exclusive jurisdiction to determine disputes arising under the domestic law of the HEI. Judicial review lies against the Visitor only if he acts outside his jurisdiction or abuses his powers in a manner wholly incompatible with natural justice. Thus, the Courts have no jurisdiction to review the Visitor's construction of university statutes. (For more on the Visitor, see Chapter 8 and the bibliographical essay on the Visitor.)

Many charities are 'registered charities', which generally means that they are under the jurisdiction of the Charity Commission. However, HEIs are not registered but exempt charities under Schedule 2 of the Charities Act 1993 in 'so far as they are charities'. The latter words take account of the fact that the Universities of Oxford and Cambridge, in so far as they are civil corporations, are the owners of corporate property which is not by its nature subject to any trust. (Individual colleges within Oxford and Cambridge *are* subject to Section 96, like all other HEIs except Oxford and Cambridge.)

Under category (w) of Schedule 2, any institution which is administered by or on behalf of an HE charity and is established for the general purposes of or for any special purpose of or in connection with the institution is also an exempt charity. The word 'institution' includes any trust or undertaking and, therefore, covers a wide variety of purposes subsidiary to the HEI itself such as scholarships, the endowment of lectureships or chairs in specific studies, libraries and funds for the provision of equipment and the maintenance of buildings. The words 'on behalf of' allow different types of educational bodies (for example, an FE (further education) corporation and an HE (higher education) corporation or a statutory corporation and a chartered corporation) to set up together an independent body established for the purposes of both institutions which, as such, would be an exempt charity.

As exempt charities, HEIs are generally not subject to the supervisory jurisdiction of the Charity Commission although they are subject to the jurisdiction of the Court via the Attorney-General. The Charity Commission's powers to institute an inquiry (for example, to ensure that the property is being applied for the purposes of its trusts) under the Charities Act 1993, Section 8, do not extend to an exempt charity. Consequently, the Charity Commission's powers under Section 18 to act for the protection of charities (for example, by suspending trustees) are not available in respect of exempt charities. Similarly, the restrictions on sales, leases, mortgages and other disposals of land held in trust for a charity imposed by the Charities Act, Sections 36 and 38 do not apply to exempt charities. As far as land is concerned, HEIs (whether created by statute or charter) can generally do anything that an individual can do – there is no need to give public notice or obtain a surveyor's report (although the latter may be sensible as 'good practice').

On the other hand, the enabling powers of the Charity Commission (for example, its power under the Charities Act 1993, Section 26, to authorize a particular transaction with charity property which is expedient or to make schemes and orders under Sections 13 and 16) *are* available to exempt charities on request of the charity or on an order of the Court. (Note that Section 16(5) which gives power for the Charity Commission to make schemes on the application of one or more trustees or persons interested does not apply to exempt charities. The application must be made by a majority of the governing body of the HEI itself or by Court order.) HEIs who hold old legacies subject to outdated trusts where the purposes cannot be carried out any longer may well want to make a cy-pres application under Sections 13 and 16 of the Charities Act 1993 to the Charity Commission to alter the original purposes.

The rationale for the exemption from Charity Commission supervision is that Parliament has been satisfied that satisfactory arrangements already exist for carrying out the objects of HEIs and safeguarding their property, (for example, through the Secretary of State for Education). An exempt charity cannot, therefore, register with the Charity Commission, even voluntarily. Quite apart from the Secretary of State for Education, there were originally also quite extensive statutory controls exercised by the Ministry of Agriculture over the landowning aspects of college management – primarily Oxford and Cambridge colleges, but also including the University of Durham, although the extent of these controls was reduced by the Universities and Colleges Estates Act 1964. The educational aspects of HEIs – what courses they actually run and their content – are subject to direct controls (e.g. in terms of funding and accreditation).

However, the controls on management of HEIs at least until the passing of the Education Reform Act (ERA) 1988 were generally less onerous than those imposed on non-exempt charities by the Charity Commission. Until then, control was exercised over HEIs through the power of the purse and in the giving of advice to the University Grants Committee. The ERA 1988 replaced the University Grants Committee by a Universities Funding Council extending the legal controls exercised by the Secretary of State. In addition, University Commissioners were given substantial powers to change the nature of academic tenure and to amend the statutes of HEIs to enable redundancies and dismissals to be made. The Visitor in the chartered HEIs also has a role in settling disputes between members of a corporation and inspecting and regulating the corporation.

The Inland Revenue acts as a controlling and supervisory body over exempt charities by examining claims for tax relief by charities and donors. In recent years, the Inland Revenue has examined the activities of HEIs closely to ensure that funds are being used for charitable objects and has looked at a number of trading activities of HEIs (for more on trading, see Chapter 12).

Finally, the National Audit Office has access to HEIs' books and any member of the public has the right to see an HEI's accounts on payment of a reasonable fee (Charities Act 1993, Section 47(2)). Note also that, although the requirements on accounts and annual reports imposed by Charities Act 1993, Sections 41–5, do not apply to exempt charities, under Section 46 charity trustees of an exempt charity are required to keep 'proper books of account with respect to the affairs of the charity' which must be preserved for at least six years (something the HEI should be doing anyway for tax purposes).

Charity trustees

Who are charity trustees?

The term 'charity trustees' is defined in the Charities Act 1993, Section 97, as 'the persons having the general control and management of the administration of a charity'. The expression is not, therefore, confined to trustees of charitable trusts, but includes the directors of charitable companies and members of committees of management of unincorporated charitable associations. If, as is argued later, members of governing bodies are charity trustees within Section 97, then the restrictions in Section 72 of the Charities Act 1993 would appear to apply to them in addition to any other conditions imposed on them by the particular charter of the HEI. Under Section 72, certain people are disqualified from acting as a charity trustee (for example, if they have been convicted of an offence involving dishonesty or deception, adjudged bankrupt or disqualified from acting as a director). It is generally accepted that, although a charitable corporation such as an HEI does not hold its property as trustee in the strict sense, it does hold it subject to a binding legal obligation to apply it for charitable purposes only and, therefore, its position is analogous to that of a trustee. But this would not make the HEI as such the charity trustee within the meaning of Section 97.

Although the managers or governors of the corporation are not strictly trustees, their role is similar to the boards of NHS trusts holding charitable trust funds. In this instance, the NHS trust is itself the sole corporate trustee of the charitable funds – the individuals who are responsible for the management of the funds are the directors of the NHS trust or other officers and are not themselves trustees of the charity. The duties, responsibilities and liabilities of the trusteeship lie with the body corporate. However, that body must act through individual persons in order to express its will. If the body corporate commits a breach of its duty as trustee, it will have done so only as a result of a breach by its directors or other individual officers of their duties towards the body corporate.

The practical reality, therefore, is that the governors of an HEI are likely to be treated as if they were charity trustees and are subject to the control of the High Court. For example, in the case of *Harries v Church of England Commissioners* the governors of the Church Commissioners, a corporate charity, were nevertheless treated as charity trustees in respect of their powers of investment.

What are the duties of charity trustees?

In the most general sense, the duty of any charity trustee is to promote the interests of the charity and to ensure that its assets are applied only for its charitable purposes. The first duty of any charity trustee on appointment is to understand the terms of the governing instrument (whether the constitution is set up by charter or statute). The governing body must ensure that all the assets of the HEI are under its control and that all sums due to the HEI are recovered. This raises a number of practical issues common to all charities in relation to *ex gratia* payments.

From time to time, the governing body may conclude that it is in the interests of the HEI to apply funds for furthering purposes which, strictly speaking, are not educational. For example, it might wish to add to the pension of a long-term employee on his or her retirement or give an extra redundancy payment. The governors are not legally required to make these payments, but wish to do so. These are *ex gratia* payments and not *prima facie* within the objects of the HEI (since, although an HEI may have the power to undertake such acts, those powers have to be exercised in furtherance of the objects). The governing body will only be able to make such payments and provision if it can justify that in these particular circumstances the long-term interests of the HEI will be well served and, therefore, the educational objects furthered.

Wherever there are *ex gratia* payments, the question of personal interest must be closely watched since there have been a number of cases in the HE and FE sectors (discussed in Chapter 3), in which conflicts arose in connection with severance pay to members of a corporation.

Sometimes, HEIs may feel that there is a moral claim on them either to make a payment where there is no legal obligation to do so (e.g. when they have inherited under a will, but the relatives of the deceased are in need) or to waive their entitlement to receive property. However, like any other charity, HEIs should not apply their funds for purposes outside their objects. Previously, a charity needed the authority of the Attorney-General to make an *ex gratia* payment. Now the Charity Commission also has the power (subject to the supervision of the Attorney-General) under the Charities Act 1993, Section 27, to authorize charity trustees (including governing bodies of HEIs) to apply charity property or to waive a right to receive property in pursuit of a moral obligation. Applications must be made to the Charity Commission, setting out the circumstances and why the trustees feel they are under a moral obligation. If the Charity Commission refuses to give the necessary authority an application may then be made to the Attorney-General (Section 27(4)).

The trustees must seek to preserve and maximize the assets of the charity. This includes taking professional advice on investment decisions and ensuring that the best possible price is obtained when charity assets are sold. An HEI must ensure that its investment policy maintains a reasonable balance between income and capital, and that the investments are not unduly hazardous. Investment should not be unduly influenced by non-financial or ethical considerations. Thus, a governing body must not allow its own personal opinions or moral judgements to affect investment decisions. *Harries v Church of England Commissioners* held that it is proper for the trustees to take non-financial considerations into account only where this still allows an adequate spread of investments. Problems have arisen for HEIs where students and members of the governing bodies have not wanted the HEI to invest in a particular company or accept money from a company with a bad labour record or with links to a poor human rights regime. HEIs have very wide powers to delegate administration to officers, committees or sub-committees and also to allow for delegation to external bodies. Indeed, the committee system can act as part of a system of checks and balances but must itself be properly supervised.

The liability of charity trustees of HEIs

Governing bodies of HEIs are usually interested in knowing the extent of their personal liability for breaches of trust. Unfortunately, this issue is not straightforward (see Chapter 3). There is no specific provision in the charters or statutes of HEIs for personal liability of a governing body and, therefore, no specific provision regarding the protection in certain circumstances of governors from such liability. Thus, there is nothing to relieve an individual governor of a corporation from liability along the lines of Trustee Act 1925, Section 61, or the Companies Act 1985, Section 727.

Even if there is a general presumption against the personal liability of governors of HEIs on the basis that express words are needed to impose such liability, it does appear from cases that the Courts may hold governing bodies accountable where there has been misuse of property on the basis that, if there can be no personal liability of the governors in respect of a misuse of property, then there would in practice be nobody in relation to whom the jurisdiction of the Court could be exercised. However, the precise formulation of that personal liability is not straightforward. Although they might be regarded in the same position as trustees, it seems to have been accepted that governors of HEIs cannot rely upon the Trustee Act 1925, Section 61, because that section only applies to trustees proper. (Section 61 empowers the High Court to excuse from personal liability a trustee who has acted in breach of trust, if the trustee has acted honestly and reasonably and ought fairly to be excused.)

Governors of HEIs have fiduciary duties towards the HEI. They are under a duty to further the objects of the HEI and not to place themselves in a position where a conflict of interest may arise. If a governor has obtained property by breach of fiduciary duties (for example, a personal interest has not been declared), it is unclear whether that governor merely has to return the property or must go further and compensate the HEI for any loss caused by the breach of trust. It is likely that a Court would decide that the governor should make some reparation for the loss. By analogy, a director of a company who acts in breach of his or her fiduciary duty (for example by using the company's assets to procure a benefit), will be personally liable for any losses to the company which may result. The Courts, therefore, may regard governors of HEIs in the same light as company directors on the basis that the governors of an HEI have a duty to safeguard the HEI's assets.

Ultra vires

A trustee commits a breach of trust if he or she acts in a way which is not authorized by the terms of the constitution. Whether this means that the governing body of an HEI could be personally liable if it had caused an HEI to act *ultra vires* is debatable. Unless there had been some breach of fiduciary duty (e.g. it had obtained some personal benefit from the *ultra vires* act), it is thought that the governing body does not have personal liability. Personal benefit is, however, likely to be widely construed.

Third parties

Governors of HEIs do not (*prima facie*) have personal liability to third parties, but can governors be liable to third parties with whom the corporation entered into a contract where the corporation did not have power to enter into such a contract? Again there is some debate about this, but the third party might claim for breach of warranty of authority. If the warranty given by the governors was one of law (i.e. that the HEI did have power to enter into a contract when in fact its statutory powers did not permit this), then no liability arises. However, if the warranty were one of fact (i.e. a governor had warranted that a procedure required by the articles of government had been followed, when in fact it had not), then the claim might well be successful.

Charity commission advice

If individuals are concerned about a particular course of action, there seems no reason in principle why the governing body of an HEI could not apply under the Charities Act 1993, Section 29, to the Charity Commission for advice or an opinion on any matter affecting the performance of duties. If the governors act in accordance with such advice, they will be protected against any allegation that they have not acted properly or have not complied with the terms of the governing instrument. However, the Charity Commission is empowered *but not obliged* to advise charity trustees and may refuse to do so if an HEI requests advice on a particular matter which the Charity Commission considers could be better dealt with elsewhere.

Criminal offences

There are a number of statutory offences which can be committed by corporations and which can result in criminal liability for both the corporations and their members. Liability is usually, but not exclusively, confined to the situation where the breach is attributable to some act or neglect on the part of the corporation member concerned (for example, breach of the legislation relating to health and safety at work and data protection).

Insurance

In the context of liability, insurance may be appropriate. Certainly, occupiers liability and employers insurance will always need to be taken out. But wider insurance against breach of trust should not be seen as a panacea and generally has quite a limited use. HEI constitutions normally allow corporations to insure their members against liabilities arising out of membership and to pay the associated premiums. However, insurance against criminal liabilities is not possible. Insurance policies also exclude various heads of liability, such as liability arising out of deliberate acts or where the person concerned knew the act was a breach of duty or was reckless as to whether it was a breach of duty or not. (Taking advice from the Charity Commission on a particular point under the Charities Act 1993, Section 29, can, therefore, help to protect the trustees.) In addition, some liabilities (such as liability for defamation or environmental pollution) are excluded from some policies. Quite apart from any exclusions, there is often a cap on the amount of cover provided by an insurance policy and there is frequently an excess provision.

(**Editors' note**: with reference to the discussion both in this chapter and the previous one concerning whether the governors of an HEI are to be judged by the court as effectively charity trustees or rather as company directors, and hence whether they may in certain circumstances incur personal liability, it is interesting to note the US experience as recounted in Kaplin and Lee (1995, Chapter II). They refer to the leading case of *Stern v Lucy Webb Hayes National Training School for Deaconnesses and Missionaries* aka the *Sibley Hospital* case, which reviews the obligations of the governor of charitable corporations, interpreting them in the context of corporate law rather than trust law with its higher level of judiciary duties (see also *Corporation of Mercer University v Smith* which echoed the *Sibley Hospital* case in applying the laxer corporate law standards to the governors rather than trust law). As noted in Chapter 4, the matter is yet to be tested in English law: if ever it were, the US case-law would be of interest. Palfreyman (1995/6) argues that at least for Oxbridge college Fellows, given their custody of permanently endowed, perpetual, eleemosynary institutions, a fiduciary duty closer to trusteeship rather than company directorship is appropriate.)

Further reading

Cairns, E. (1996) *Charities: Law and Practice.* London: Sweet & Maxwell.
Charity Commission (1993) *Decisions of the Charity Commissioners* (No. 6, Royal Holloway and Bedford New College). London: HMSO.
Claricoat, J. and Phillips, H. (1995) *Charity Law A to Z: Key Questions Answered.* Bristol: Jordans.
Cracknell, D. (ed.) (1996) *Charities: The Law and Practice.* London: FT Law and Tax.
Dale, H. P. and Gwinnell, M. (1995/6) 'Time for change: charity investment and modern portfolio theory', *The Charity Law & Practice Review*, 3(2), 65–96.
Farrington, D. J. (1994) *The Law of Higher Education.* London: Butterworths.
Harbottle, M. (1995) *Investing Charity Funds.* Bristol: Jordans.
Harrison, J. (1992) *Charity Investment Matters.* London: Lazard Investors Limited.
Harrison, J. (1994) *Managing Charitable Investments.* London: ICSA.
Oakley, A. J. (1996) *Trends in Contemporary Trust Law.* Oxford: Oxford University Press.
Palfreyman, D. (1995–6) 'Oxbridge fellows as charity trustees', *The Charity Law & Practice Review*, 3(3), 187–202.
Palfreyman, D. (1996–7) 'The Oxford colleges and their college contributions scheme', *The Charity Law & Practice Review*, 4(1), 51–65.
Palfreyman, D. (1997) Gift horses – with strings attached! A guide to the use of benefactions or donations, *Perspectives: Policy and Practice in Higher Education*, 1(4), 124–6.
Pettit, P. H. (1993) *Equity and the Law of Trusts.* London: Butterworths.
Phillips, H. and Claricoat, J. (1995) 'The sale of chattels held on charitable trusts', *Christie's Bulletin*, Summer 1995, 1–9.
Picarda, H. (1995) *The Law and Practice Relating to Charities.* London: Butterworths.
Quint, F. (1994) *Running a Charity.* Bristol: Jordans.
Richens, N. J. and Fletcher, M. J. G. (1996) *Charity Land and Premises.* Bristol: Jordans.
Sheridan, L. (1993/4) 'Cy-près application of three Holloway pictures', *The Charity Law & Practice Review*, 2(3), 181–4.
Tudor on Charities (1995) London: Sweet & Maxwell.
Underhill, T. and Hayton, D. J. (1995) *Law of Trusts and Trustees.* London: Butterworths.
Warburton, J. (1992) *Unincorporated Associations.* London: Sweet & Maxwell.

5

The Law of Meetings

David Palfreyman

No book aimed at the managers of HEIs (higher education institutions) could possibly be complete without something on meetings, and, in this case, their legal context. The law of meetings is determined mainly by common law, but also by statute (e.g. the legislation controlling limited companies which prescribes the format of annual general meetings (AGMs), meetings of boards of directors, etc.). Procedure at meetings and the conduct of them is often based on convention, which sometimes is not supported by common law (for example, common law does not require that a motion has a seconder before it can be put, but convention does).

In the case of HEIs, the charter, statutes, ordinances, regulations, standing orders or whatever, will often prescribe in detail the arrangements for meetings, covering areas on which the common law is silent. The HEI manager needs, first and foremost, to be familiar with the institution's governing instrument and what it says about the convening of meetings, the election of chairs, the quorum for a meeting, voting at meetings, etc. Second, he or she needs to be familiar with the common law as applicable to meetings for circumstances where the HEI's rules are ambiguous or unhelpfully silent.

Helpful texts

Farrington (1994: 209–17) summarizes well the issues covered in detail within the main legal texts, as do Farrington and Mattison (1990: 34–45). The definitive authority (in print) is *Shackleton on the Law and Practice of Meetings* (1997) and also in print is Burton and Patfield (1994). Shaw and Smith (1979) and Moore (1979) are also comprehensive. Somewhat dated is Powell-Smith (1967). For a handy summary of the role of the committee secretary, see Joynson and Wood (1987). There is also much on the psychology of meetings, including the justly famous *Meetings, Bloody Meetings*, a video by John Cleese/Video Arts – see also Sharman (1993) and Stratford

(1988), together with texts on team-building such as Belbin (1989) and Fraser and Neville (1993).

The essential elements
The role of the chair

The chair must conduct the meeting in a proper and orderly fashion, allowing fair opportunity for all members to contribute to discussion and ensuring that the meeting is clear about what is being voted on. In an HEI the threat of disorder in a meeting is remote, but still possible (for example, in a meeting about student discipline, student accommodation charges or staff redundancies). The chair may use or (more likely) permit porters or security staff to use, *reasonable* force to remove a person from a meeting, *if* the meeting has first voted to exclude that person because he or she is disrupting the meeting *and* after that person has refused the option of going voluntarily. If that person's behaviour is so blatant, the chair will probably adjourn the meeting for, say, 15 minutes and then, if circumstances are still chaotic, the chair may order the removal of the person without a proposal for exclusion being put to the meeting. That person may find him or herself in breach of the peace and subject to criminal proceedings in certain circumstances. The chair can be removed by the will of the majority at a meeting (subject to the charter and statutes, or similar) if there is reasonable evidence of corruption, gross partiality, or sheer incompetence. If the chair unilaterally departs, the meeting can legitimately continue after electing itself another chair. Subject to the charter and statutes, the chair is the creature of the meeting, not the other way around! The chair has a vote, simply as a member, but a casting vote as chair only if the charter and statutes specifically permit it – there is no casting vote in common law. If the chair has no casting vote or decides not to use it, the *status quo* applies in that there will have been no majority reached for the proposal. A chair can vote one way using the personal vote, but another way using the casting vote. For example, some chairs might use the casting vote to maintain the *status quo*, after having personally voted for change, on the basis that change should come about only if there is significant support for it, not just by scraping through on a casting vote. (Hence, the lack of a casting vote under the common law is sensible – it means that the *status quo* prevails in the event of a tied vote and is not to be altered by one member who happens to be chair and in effect has a chance to vote twice according to his or her personal views.)

Notice of meetings

In the unlikely event that *all* members were present and *all* agreed to an instant meeting, then at common law a legitimate meeting can take place, but the charter and statutes for an HEI will usually specify how to convene a meeting (even an urgent one) and common law requires reasonable notice to be given, unless *all* members agree to waive the notice period in the circumstances just suggested. Such notice must, as a judge commented in one case cited in *Shackleton on the Law and Practice of Meetings* (1997) be 'a fair and candid and reasonable explanation of the purpose or purposes of the meeting'. Care is needed to ensure that nobody can argue that the notice given was 'not frank, not open, not clear and not in any way satisfactory – it was tricky'. Hence, care should be taken over use of 'any other business', using this agenda item only for minor matters needing urgent attention and not for major matters, even those in need of urgent attention, unless it is *really* safe to assume that the irregularity inevitably arising with regard to the lack of notice can be covered over by the fact that the majority of members will be present for the any other business item and will vote for it (see later, 'Dealing with irregularities'). Some statutes may specify that, for example, no proposal concerning the expenditure of money shall be considered at a meeting without notice of it having been explicitly given on the notice/agenda sheet.

The quorum for meetings

Unless the charter and statutes specify a different arrangement, the common law quorum is half plus one of the membership and the quorum must be maintained throughout the meeting, not just achieved at the beginning. The quorum is of voting members. Non-voting members, observers, etc., do not count and nor, for specific items, would a voting member who is disbarred from voting on that particular matter because of having to declare a personal or financial interest in the item due to be discussed and voted on, not least because convention requires that he or she should absent him or herself from the meeting while the item is discussed and voted on.

Voting at meetings

At common law voting is by show-of-hands of those entitled to vote (see 'the quorum for meetings'), unless a poll is called for by a member. A poll is a written vote, with members signing their names against a list or on a poll-slip. Thus, it is not the same as a secret ballot, which is a permissable variation of the show-of-hands. There is no provision at common law for a proxy vote, but it may be allowed for in the charter and statutes of a particular HEI. A simple majority is required to decide a matter, unless the HEI's rules require, say, a two-thirds majority to change by-laws, amend standing orders, etc. In this way, a governing body of, say, 20 can function in common law with 11 present, and its own statutes or similar may require the 11 to be present only at the start of the meeting, in which case a matter can be decided not only by those among the 11 who actually vote on it (and several could abstain) but, later in the meeting as people leave, by a simple majority of, say, the five members who vote on it (while one other might abstain). Hence, three out of 20 can bind the rest, unless the chair suggests, and the meeting accepts, that:

- it is inappropriate to reach a decision at such an ill-attended stage of a meeting (perhaps leaving the opportunity for discussion to continue, but without the intention of reaching a vote or decision);
- the rest may rescind any decision that is reached at the next meeting;
- the decision is challengeable by the absentee majority on the limited grounds set out as follows (see 'Dealing with irregularities') (for example, because improper notice was given or because the decision was *ultra vires* or in breach of trust).

Discussion, debate and motions

There are conventions about how to conduct the debate and, sometimes, the charter and statutes specify the procedures (often in the form of standing orders). If they do not, the common law requirements are that matters be conducted in an orderly and reasonable way. It is to be noted that there is no requirement at common law for a motion to be seconded before it can be put, although the convention is that it should be. Hence, a chair would be safer to accept such a motion from an insistent proposer, even without a seconder, than to rule it out of order (presumably, it would stand little chance of being approved and a quick vote would dispatch the proposal into oblivion).

Minutes

The minutes are a record of who was present (ideally, they should also record departures of members during a meeting) and of decisions taken. There is no legal duty to record discussion and to explain how and why a certain decision was reached, unless the matter relates to an individual (discipline or grievance) and it is appropriate to show that the requirements of natural justice (see 'The rules of natural justice') were complied with in reaching the decision. The 'house-style' varies from HEI to HEI as to how detailed the minutes are, but most HEIs use minutes to record just the decisions (with reference to supporting papers) rather than the nuances of debate. The decision is valid in law from the time it has been taken and the approval or confirmation of minutes at the next meeting is merely a recognition that the minutes are accurate, and *not* a chance to debate again whether X or Y should have been decided. Where there is a controversial matter, the chair will normally take care to make clear the exact wording of the motion being voted on, and that wording will duly appear as the resolution in the minutes.

Ultra vires and intra vires

Any decision or action reached by a committee has to be within its power or authority (*intra vires*) and not beyond its remit (*ultra vires*). This means that care needs to be taken that a decision is within the terms of reference for a committee or that there is an appropriate power under the charter and statutes for the governing body of the HEI to do X or Y.

Dealing with irregularities

In the event of dispute as to whether a meeting was properly convened, whether decision X was really reached and whether the meeting was conducted badly, etc., the High Court will issue an injunction prohibiting the consequence of the irregular proceeding being put into operation only if a majority of the members seek it. A minority will suffice only where the body concerned has *deliberately* tried to exclude certain members from the decision-making process or is taking an *ultra vires* (see earlier) decision, or is in breach of trust (for more on trusteeship, see Chapter 4). As Shaw and Smith note:

> If the majority at the meeting would be competent to do regularly that which has been irregularly achieved and they approve it, it would be futile for the minority to seek to impair the results of the proceedings; for the same results will ultimately be achieved by the will of the majority with due regard to the formal requirements of the [presumably, next] meeting. Accordingly the Courts will give no remedy upon the application of an individual member or even a number of members if they comprise only a minority of those present at the meeting.
> (Shaw and Smith, 1979: 179)

But, since a quorum might be only half plus one of the members, and since a decision may be reached by just a simple majority of those present *and voting* (i.e. many could abstain), an action *could* be approved by a very small section of the membership, and hence a judicious chair will ensure that potentially controversial matters are not decided when the number of members present has declined steadily as the meeting has progressed (see 'The quorum for meetings' and 'Notice of meetings', especially in relation to any other business items).

The rules of natural justice

Clearly, committee procedures, especially in relation to disciplinary and grievance processes dealing with the rights of the individual, need to follow the rules of natural justice – the *audi alteram partem* rule (need to provide a fair hearing) and the *nemo judex in causa sua* rule (a process which is impartial and free from bias).

Defamation

The making of comments in writing (libel) or orally (slander) at meetings which, allegedly, damage an individual's reputation is clearly a risk in the committee process. The defence against a writ for defamation is likely to be either that the comments which were made were indeed true (justification) and/or that the statements concerned were made in the context of qualified privilege (i.e. if they were made in a meeting where it was appropriate and legitimate to be discussing such a matter in that way in front of relevant interested parties). Such a defence as qualified privilege could be defeated if there was undue publication of the statement (for example, if it was made orally before people who had no relevant interest in the matter and who just happened to be present, or if it was circulated more widely in writing than it need have been – except that dictating a letter to a secretary or having a paper typed by a secretary is not undue publication). Similarly, qualified privilege is no defence if it can be shown that the making of the statement had been motivated by malice and not on the basis of an honest belief that it was true and relevant to the matter concerned. Malice might encompass a reckless indifference to the truth, where a damaging statement was made or repeated without considering its validity. Shackleton (1997) has a useful summary of the law relating to defamation, and most texts on tort cover the topic – see Markesinis and Deakin (1994) or Winfield and Jolowicz (1994). Definitive works are Carter Ruck (1991), Scott-Bayfield (1996), Clarke-Williams (1997).

Company law relating to meetings

The HE manager of today is likely to be *de facto* and *de jure* the Company Secretary of the HEI's trading company. Hence, he or she will need to be familiar with the legislation governing the conduct of meetings of boards of directors and the convening of AGMs, as based partly on the common law already discussed but mainly set out in relevant legislation. There are numerous standard texts on company law and on the role of the Company Secretary, including Marshall *et al.* (1995), Cheffins (1996), Lai *et al.* (1996), Sparrow (1996), and *Tolley's Company Law Handbook* (1997). (For more on trading companies, see Chapter 12.)

Part 3

The Higher Education Institution and its Staff and Students

6

The Higher Education Institution–Student Contract

Simon Arrowsmith and Nicola Hart (Martineau Johnson)

Editors' introduction

Perhaps the most likely area for legal confrontation is to do with the relationship between the HEI (higher education institution) and its students or potential students (applicants). This is not surprising since there are many students, who as they are paying more and more towards their education, are likely, especially in an age of consumerism, to become increasingly demanding of value-for-money and to resort to law if they feel thwarted. Perhaps this is why, as the Oxford Proctor is quoted in Chapter 1, the majority of complaints originate from dissatisfied overseas students (they are likely to have paid out more of their own money than home students funded by the UK taxpayer, whose fees are lower anyway). Another factor might be the increasing maturity of the average student. A *Times Higher* report (31 May 1996) noted that nearly half of US college students are over 24, whereas less than one-third were in the 1970s – a trend which is 'changing the face of many campuses'. A US commentator is quoted as having remarked, 'This is a different population from your passive 18-year-old who comes in and is more accepting and less demanding.'

The education experience

The student–HEI confrontation used to be mainly in the context of discipline, especially in the late 1960s and early 1970s. Now it is about the appropriateness of 'the educational experience'. Can there be clear norms of what a reasonable HEI should supply by way of the educational experience to a reasonable student? What is a reasonable student? What happens if the product falls below normal standards or the standards explicitly set by an HEI? What must the student do to prove that there is in tort a duty of care, or a contractual duty to provide a reasonable educational package?

How does the student show that the package is inadequate? Even if these two legal hurdles are overcome, what can be demonstrated as the damage suffered by the student? If there is damage, how can compensation be calculated? In short, will the concept of 'academic negligence' develop in the same way that medical negligence has evolved in recent decades? To what extent can an HEI rely on hiding behind the protective veil of expert academic judgement, whereby, providing there is no obvious neglect of its procedures or of the basic rules of natural justice, the court will not peer behind the veil to ask whether the academics were competent as examiners or teachers, or, in the case of applicants, in terms of how they decided to whom to offer places and whom to reject? How wide a definition of the educational experience might the courts set? Is pastoral care covered? Should an HEI be expected to sort out personal problems among its students? Has it a greater duty of care while the student is under 18 (as a few might be, and as most applicants are)? If the 17-year-old applicants drink to excess when attending for interview, is the HEI liable if one chokes on his or her vomit during the night?

Not even US courts assume that an HEI has an all-encompassing duty to supervise adult students in their private activities, as opposed to official organized games, field trips, laboratory practicals, etc. Kaplin and Lee quote a case where 'the court held that the university's *power* to regulate student conduct on campus did not give rise to a *duty* to regulate student conduct on campus or to monitor the conduct of every student on campus . . . no duty to supervise social activity was found' (Kaplin and Lee, 1995a: 97, emphasis added). But perhaps where known risky fraternity rituals routinely take place an HEI should take steps to enforce its rules:

> The court determined that the university's own policy against hazing, and its repeated warnings to students against the hazards of hazing, 'constituted an assumed duty' . . . amounted to an undertaking by the university to protect students from the dangers related to hazing, and created a duty to do so.
>
> (Kaplin and Lee, 1995a: 98)

In general, however, the student doing stupid things, if aged 18 or over, will be assumed to have appreciated the risks and the HEI is safe (no longer being *in loco parentis*). In this way, an HEI cannot and has no strict duty to protect students from the consequences of heavy drinking – 'The prevalence of alcohol consumption on the modern college campus would make compliance with such a duty almost impossible' (Kaplin and Lee, 1995a: 109, citing a 1979 case). In 1997 there were three alcohol-related student deaths on just two US campuses, while in 1996, eight members of one fraternity were charged with manslaughter in an alcohol poisoning case. Yet an HEI needs to be careful not to give itself a duty by virtue of making the issue of drinking 'a big issue' and making it seem that the HEI is assuming control. Indeed a 1971 US case, *Hegel v Langsam*, is noted with approval in a standard English law textbook, *Winfield and Jolowicz on Tort* (1994, 103), as confirming: 'A university incurs no liability for failing to control the private lives of its students, allowing them to be seduced, become associated with criminals, or become drug addicts'!

Protecting an HEI

What can an HEI do to protect itself? Should its regulations be as detailed as possible to legislate for anything and everything, or should they be general so as not to create hostages to fortune? What should be the procedure for dealing with student complaints, especially if the student starts to talk of going to law? There is no underestimating the management time likely to be taken up by such a case, and the potential cost not only in working through internal procedures but also of any court actions (especially if the complainant receives Legal Aid). One case reported in the *Times Higher* (31 May 1996) had been dragging on since 1993. It involved a claim for the refund of overseas fees amounting to £20,000 and has led to the National Union of Students (NUS) Scotland commenting, 'We do not believe the present procedure [at university X] constitutes an appeals procedure . . . It does not conform to natural justice [in not allowing the appellant to appear in person before the Appeals Board].' An article in the *Times Higher* of 12 July 1996, 'Complaints cost hard cash', refers to 'a rising tide of student complaints', dealing with which 'can cost an institution up to £50,000 a year' and to a report of the Higher Education Quality Council (HEQC) prepared by D. Farrington which noted that many universities had no formal complaints procedure. Articles on the same page describe a Visitor case at Birmingham University lasting eight years and a threat of legal action from students at Westminster University over alleged course disruption caused by building work (the students are seeking legal aid to sue for loss of earnings from part-time jobs which they would have worked at but for needing to do extra academic work).

Dearing (1997) largely echoes the report from the Nolan Committee on *Standards in Public Life* which recommends that:

> Students in higher education institutions should be able to appeal to an independent body, and this right should be reflected in the Higher Education Charters. The higher education funding councils, institutions, and representative bodies should consult on a system of independent review of disputes.
>
> (Nolan, 1996: 83)

It is not yet clear whether this simply means extending the Visitor chartered university model to all HEIs, an enhanced version of the Visitor model binding arbitration, or a completely new appeals quango of some kind (see also Chapters 8 and 9, and the bibliographical essay on the Visitor, especially the section on 'The Visitor post-Nolan', plus Farrington, 1997 and CVCP, 1997.

The US perspective

Kaplin and Lee (1995a) in the USA devote over 250 pages (a quarter of the volume) to 'The college and the students'. They trace the evolution of the student as a person with enforceable Federal, State and contractual rights, rather than being on the receiving end of *in loco parentis* and the 'privilege' of being admitted to membership of the groves of academe. Even so, on the whole, 'courts have applied the contract theory to postsecondary institutions in a deferential manner . . . Nor have institutions been subject to the rigors of contract law as it applies in the commercial world' (Kaplin and Lee, 1995a: 374; see also NACUA, 1989).

Thus, higher education (HE) used to be seen as:

> a unique enterprise that could regulate itself through reliance on tradition and consensual agreement . . . The judiciary also was deferential to higher education . . . courts accepted the proposition that attendance at a public postsecondary institution was a privilege and not a right . . . The institution was given virtually unlimited power to dictate the contract terms, and the contract, once made, was construed heavily in the institution's favour.
>
> (Kaplin and Lee, 1995a: 374)

All this has changed as the HE system, post-World War II, has moved from elite to mass in the USA (and, recently, in the UK). The new players in the game were not necessarily prepared to accept the cosy old rules: 'The notion that attendance was a privilege served as an irrelevant nicety in an increasingly credentialized society. To many students higher education became an economic professional necessity . . . One major trend is student (or educational) consumerism' (Kaplin and Lee, 1995a: 217). In the USA, students have sued after being 'accused' of plagiarism, after being barred from the campus computer network, after being dropped from sports teams, after suffering violence on campus as the result of alleged inadequate security, after being given low grades . . .

Kaplin and Lee note that:

> Another potential source of tort liability, albeit a generally unsuccessful one for plaintiffs, is the doctrine of 'educational malpractice' . . . Although they often sympathize with students who claim that they have not learned what they should have learned, or that they, their professors, were negligent in teaching or supervising them, courts have been reluctant to create a cause of action for educational malpractice . . . The judge disagreed, ruling that the student was ultimately responsible for his academic success.
>
> (Kaplin and Lee, 1995a: 375)

So, even in the USA, the land of the medical negligence suit and no win–no fee ambulance-chasing lawyers, the concept of 'educational malpractice' has not taken off. There is the difficulty of proving the damage (unlike, say, a patient with the wrong leg hacked off as a result of medical negligence) and the difficulty of calculating the damages due – 'If I'd been allowed to get a First rather than a 2:1, I'd now be a rich City lawyer and not a poor university administrator', or perhaps it should be 'If I'd been allowed to get a Third rather than a First, I'd now be a merchant banker and not a university professor'!

Much of the litigation focuses on the HEI's reservation (by way of using disclaimers) of the right to change course structures and the aggrieved student's attempt to 'get what he or she thought he or she signed up for'. As Kaplin and Lee state:

> The contract theory is still developing. Debate continues on issues such as the process for identifying the terms and conditions of the student–institution contract, the extent to which the school catalogue [prospectus] constitutes part of the contract, and the extent to which the institution retains implied or inherent authority not expressed in any written regulation or policy.
>
> (Kaplin and Lee, 1995a: 375)

There are aspects of 'unconscionable' (unduly harsh) contracts clearly unfair to the student and 'contracts of adhesion' (take it or leave it) weighted in favour of the HEI. The moral is that:

> administrators should be sensitive to the language used in all institutional rules and policies affecting students. Language suggestive of a commitment (or promise) to students should be used only when the institution is prepared to live up to its commitment . . . should consider the adoption of an official policy, perhaps even a 'code of good practice', or fair dealing with students.
>
> (Kaplin and Lee, 1995a: 376–7)

Kaplin and Lee argue that 'The judicial trend suggests that most rules and regulations will be upheld', providing they are not arbitrary and capricious, they are reasonable, they are clear and there is no malice or bad faith in their application in the case of student X. Even fewer legal constraints:

> pertain to an institution's application of academic standards to students than to its application of behavioural standards. Courts are more deferential to academia when evaluation of academic work is the issue, believing that such evaluation resides in the expertise of the faculty rather than the court.
>
> (Kaplin and Lee, 1995a: 465)

Thus, the US courts will not readily lift the veil of expert, academic judgement: 'The courts are not equipped to review academic records based upon academic standards within the particular knowledge, experience, and expertise of academicians' (from a 1975 case, Kaplin and Lee, 1995a: 467); 'Courts are particularly ill equipped to evaluate academic performance' (a 1978 case, Kaplin and Lee, 1995a: 467); 'judicial review of grading disputes would inappropriately involve the courts in the very core of academic and education decision making . . . in the absence of demonstrated bad faith, arbitrariness, capriciousness, irrationality or a constitutional or statutory violation, a student's challenge . . . is beyond the scope of judicial review' (a 1990 case, Kaplin and Lee, 1995a: 474). (Indeed, a 1997 English case follows this line, the court in *Thirunayagam v London Guildhall University* refusing to supply the aggrieved student with an injunction instructing the University to award him a first class degree in law!) But an HEI must stick to the rules. One lost a 1989 case for failing a student nurse who was deemed too fat to be an effective nurse, rather than not intelligent enough to pass the academic content of the exams.

On the admissions process, Kaplin and Lee note that the benefit of the doubt also lies with the HEI, the applicant having to demonstrate that the HEI had been 'arbitrary and capricious' in decision-making over his or her application – 'a formidable barrier for disappointed applicants to cross' (Kaplin and Lee, 1995a: 379). The HEI must, however, abide by any legislation concerning discrimination on grounds of race, age, sex and disability, and it must honour its published admission and selection criteria. Once an offer has been made and accepted, the HEI must honour the admission contract and have available the promised course for when the student arrives.

As for the even wider duty of care, a recent US Federal Law (1990 and 1992) requires HEIs to provide data on the numbers and types of crime on and near the campus, especially in relation to sex offences. Such legislation was a response to the increasingly violent nature of US HEIs, not least arising from 'acquaintance rape' ('date rape' as it is also known) among students. Clearly, the collection and publication of such data puts the HEI on notice as to its security problems and it then risks incurring liability if it fails to provide *reasonable* security measures and does not give 'timely warning' to its employees and students of growing security problems. But, as stated earlier, at least the HEI's duty of care does not, usually, extend to monitoring the student every hour of the day – they are adults!

Back to the law of England . . .

A *Times Higher* article ('Ill-starred treks') stated:

> A spate of high-profile expedition disasters has unleashed a wave of role-tightening across campuses and is endangering the future of a brave tradition . . . These disasters highlight the fact that blame, and possibly litigation, may fall on a university if its name is associated with a botched expedition. A student at Queen's University in Belfast had an accident while on a field trip a few years ago and sued the university, leading to an out-of-court settlement.
>
> (*Times Higher*, 5 July 1996)

The issue is, of course, the duty of care owed by the HEI to its students, not just in relation to formal field trips as part of the course but perhaps even to inadvertently 'blessing' in some way a student-organized and -led expedition: 'You older and wiser people at the University of Barset should have told me it was dangerous to try and tag crocodiles . . . to visit malaria zones without medication . . . to travel in war-torn Zarland' or whatever.

On the matter of student sport there is potential liability for the HEI if it is in breach of its duty of care to ensure that student sport is organized with safety in clear focus. There is a statutory (Health and Safety at Work Acts and Regulations, plus possibly the Occupiers' Liability Act) and common law (the rules relating to negligence) matrix of responsibility falling upon the HEI to do all that is 'reasonably practicable' to put in place safe procedures and practices which are known about and used. It concentrates the mind to recall that health and safety legislation can now bring criminal penalties to bear on individuals who have neglected safety issues. See the CVCP (Committee of Vice-Chancellors and Principals) Report on *Sport in Higher Education* (CVCP, 1996) and also *Smolden v Whitwirth (The Times*, 18 December 1996) concerning a 17-year-old seriously injured in a rugby scrum collapse and the negligence of the referee in failing to control the game: in an HEI context the referee might be a member of staff from the HEI's sports centre for whose negligence the HEI would be vicariously liable!

There is also the issue of references for students (and indeed for staff) in which there may be statements which are difficult to sustain. A 1996 House of Lords' judgement led to an out-of-court £35,000 settlement from an HEI to an ex-student for lost wages after her prospective employer cancelled a job offer on receipt of a reference referring to her 'personal attitude and emotional stability'. So, who owes what duty of care to whom when supplying a reference?

So what's new?

Lest, however, one should think awkward students are only a recent creation:

> Many of the southern [European] students were recruited from wealthy backgrounds, and a good number were of noble origin. A sizeable proportion of them were in their twenties or even older, and some came straight to university from holding positions of responsibility in society. Students of this type had a more legalistic, contractual view of university life than was prevalent in England. In the southern environment, students were accustomed to regard the universities and lecturing staffs as agencies to be used and hired so as best to serve the students' own convenience and future professional interests. This kind of thinking would have struck few chords in the English students, who accepted their role as academic apprentices.
>
> (Cobban, 1988: 21)

Would the modern-day equivalent of 'the southern students' be self-financing mature MBA students?

Introduction

This chapter deals with the legal nature of the relationship between the HEI and the student. The title describes this relationship, for convenience, as a contract. Whether there is such a contract in legal terms will be the first substantive question to be considered. The chapter analyses the nature of the relationship, the status of the two parties and their obligations towards each other, the ways in which the relationship is entered into and may be terminated, and what consequences follow from that analysis in terms of legal redress for parties considering themselves to have been wronged.

The chapter is also concerned with the part played in the relationship by outsiders – in particular the roles of the courts and the Visitor and the effect of the intervention of UCAS (Universities and Colleges Admissions Service) in admissions procedures, and in general the extent to which the relationship is regulated through UK statutory and European law.

Some preventive and remedial suggestions are offered, designed to protect the interests of the HEI by discouraging the making of claims and minimizing their chances of success if made.

The nature of the problem

An understanding of the legal foundations of the HEI–student contract and the principles which will be applied by those sitting in judgement is increasingly important as challenges multiply in number and in range. Students are encouraged in today's individualistic culture to view themselves as consumers of the HEI's educational services. They are armed with charters setting out what many see as their rights (see *The Charter for Higher Education*, DfEE, 1993). There are many more mature students than ever before. They are more likely than the traditional school-leaver to have a financial stake in their degree qualification, possibly having given up employment for the privilege of entering on an HEI course. Students come now from a wider variety of cultural and racial backgrounds, bringing different expectations and perceptions of the educational experience. HEIs are eager to encourage the growth of the market for their services overseas and promises made in the sales-drive abroad may turn out not to be matched by the reality of the UK student experience. There are quite simply more students than ever before. This on its own is likely to result in a rise in the incidence of claims and complaints.

There is a long history of student challenges before the courts and the Visitor in the reported case law. While it is probably true that more have been imaginative than successful, dealing with those claims and complaints has been and continues to be a significant drain on resources for the HEIs facing them, in terms of expense and management time.

New types of challenge develop as our culture and society's expectations change. It is worrying to observe the emergence of a concept which might loosely be labelled educational negligence, arising perhaps out of the common perception that these days almost any accident or failure must be laid at somebody's door. There is an increasing amount of statutory regulation of relationships with individuals, whether it is for their protection as consumers or visitors to premises, or on grounds of their race, sex or disability. HEIs, as institutions with a public role, have suffered too as a result of the rise in popularity of judicial review of administrative decisions in the High Court – perceived unfairness is less likely than ever to go untested. Underlying all of these is the HEI–student contract and the scope which that provides for challenge in various interesting ways.

Is there a contract?

It appears now to be generally accepted law that the relationship between the HEI and the student is based in contract (see *Moran v University College, Salford (No. 2)*). There has been considerable academic debate on the subject which has arisen out of the need to label the relationship in order to determine the mutual obligations of the parties, or indeed whether there were any obligations. The difficulty of categorizing the relationship arises partly from the fact that it is not recorded or documented conventionally as a contract. Nevertheless, the contractual analysis is the one which seems to match most closely the actuality of the relationship and which provides a structure appropriate to what are generally seen as the obligations of each side. Therefore, the relationship will be referred to in this chapter as the HEI–student contract. Historically it has not been seen as necessary or appropriate to document the relationship explicitly as a legal contract, which would require the identification of the parties, the terms of the contract and what each of them was to gain from it and was required to perform under it. Of course, these elements are present in various forms in the documentation which passes between the two parties and goes to make up the contract without explicitly stating that. The content and effect of the various parts of the documentation which go to form the contractual nexus will be considered later.

The question to be considered, in connection with documenting the relationship, is whether it would be a different kind of relationship and perhaps a better one if the terms were not quite so extensively and copiously recorded in the form of rules and regulations. The inevitable concomitant obligation of creating regulations is that of abiding by them oneself – those who live by the regulations should expect to die by the regulations.

More than one contract?

The case law on the subject of the HEI–student contract generally falls into two categories in terms of the stage of the relationship under consideration. These two stages are referred to in Farrington (1994) as the contract for admission and the contract of matriculation, the former covering the stage from pre-entry agreement up to registration and the latter from the point of registration onwards, when the student enters and becomes part of the HEI community. The reason there are two contracts may be because the courts generally have analysed the obligations arising in one or other of these two phases – not crossing over the boundary between them.

There clearly are different obligations and types of obligation at each stage of the relationship, but that does not necessarily lead to the conclusion that there must be two contracts. It may be more helpful and practical to consider the relationship as taking the form of a rolling contract which matures and changes shape in the course of its life, with both parties apprehending from the start the prospect of the introduction of new terms as the contractual relationship develops. This analysis has the advantage of making more sense of the early (pre-entry) phase of the relationship, where the weight of the obligations are otherwise very heavily on the side of the HEI.

A possible partial analogy for this approach can be found in the employment relationship. An offer of employment on particular terms to start work on a certain future date is made by the employer and accepted by the prospective employee. From that stage, both sides are bound by the terms of the accepted offer and if the employer seeks to withdraw from the arrangement before the employee starts work, he or she will be obliged to give due contractual notice of termination or else be liable for damages for breach of contract to the extent of paying the employee in lieu of notice.

Who are the parties?

Clearly the HEI and the student are parties. The question arises of whether there are any other parties to the arrangement. UCAS is involved in the role of what might be described as a broker in the pre-entry stages. What is its status and could it be claimed to have any contractual responsibilities?

UCAS processes applications. That function does not make it an agent of the HEI in the relationship with the student. Therefore, the HEI is unlikely to be fixed with responsibility for a mistake made by UCAS, whereas it would be likely to be liable to the student for the consequences of a mistake in the information it disseminated or any offer it made through UCAS (see *Moran v University College, Salford*). On the other hand, UCAS does enter into a form of contractual relationship with each individual student (who pays a sum of money with an application) and, accordingly, has contractual responsibilities to that student at least to the extent of handling the application with a reasonable degree of care and skill. UCAS enters into an individual relationship with each of the HEIs which is also of a contractual nature and carries similar obligations. The global relationship between UCAS and all the institutions whose applications it processes is more difficult to define, but it seems that there may be an implied contract arising out of the informal negotiations between all of those bodies which result in their agreeing to abide by the UCAS scheme rules in the interests of maintaining the system.

How and when the contract is made

In broad terms, the contract comes into existence between the HEI and the student when an offer is made and accepted, specifically when the acceptance is transmitted to the HEI. That simple position is slightly complicated by the involvement of UCAS and by the fact that many offers are conditional. (See the Appendix page 95, mainly based on information kindly supplied by UCAS.) In the case of a conditional offer, the obligation to admit the student comes into effect at the point at which the condition is fulfilled. Both parties are contractually bound from the moment of acceptance, but if applicants fail to satisfy the conditions within the prescribed period, the HEI is not obliged to register them as students. From the HEI's point of view, it is clearly important to monitor the making of offers to avoid becoming bound to provide places in situations where it does not wish to be bound. The centralized admissions service provided by UCAS goes some way towards standardizing the applications and admissions process and, therefore, making it easier to monitor. There are, however, certain relatively common practices that may result in the HEI becoming contractually bound to provide places it may not have to students it may not wish to admit. For example, one of the points at which a contract may be formed is at the stage where an informal offer is made to a prospective student (see boxes 10 and 11 in the flow chart, Appendix). An informal offer may be made by a member of the HEI staff who has no authority to do so. Unless it can be shown that the student could not reasonably have believed that person had authority, the HEI may be bound by the offer.

Regulating the practice of making informal offers is difficult from the HEI's point of view. There are some practical steps which can be taken to ensure that the HEI does not become fully legally committed at too early a stage. One method would be to require that all prospective students who visit tutors or lecturers at the HEI should be sent a simple standard letter making clear that any discussions or offers made are informal, in principle only, and that the student will have to go through UCAS procedures before any binding commitment is made. The HEI should then keep a record of all students who visit or attend the HEI, detailing who they see and that a standard letter was sent out.

As HEIs are increasingly seeking to recruit international students, the problems surrounding informal offers should also be borne in mind in the context of international recruitment fairs. Members of staff attending such fairs may make statements to prospective students ranging from outright offers of a place to a guarantee of accommodation. These statements are capable of forming the terms of a legally binding contract, provided that the person making them has actual or ostensible authority to make such statements. In the case of prospective international students, it may be more difficult to arrange the distribution of a standard letter and it may be that the only practical way to prevent the formation of such contracts is to ensure that the members of staff concerned are fully aware of the risks.

Another situation in which the HEI may run the risk of becoming inadvertently bound to admit students is during the hectic 'clearing' period following the publication of examination results, when HEIs may have to process thousands of applications in the space of a few days. At present, the clearing period seems to be dealt with in a variety of ways by HEIs – some provide staff with formal training and procedures to deal with the applications, whereas others adopt a more *ad hoc* approach. Clearly, a more systematic approach is likely to facilitate control of the offers made during this period.

The procedures for postgraduate admissions may also have potential pitfalls for the HEI, particularly in the case of research degrees where applications are usually made to individual supervisors. The fact that the decision to admit is made by individual academics may make the task of monitoring the number and quality of admissions more difficult. A number of HEIs – in the UK and abroad – have tried to tackle this by establishing committees charged with taking the final decision on whether to admit the applicant in question. The academic who has been approached by the student may submit his or her comments and recommendations to the committee. The committee will then consider these together with the likelihood of the applicant successfully achieving the qualification and whether the HEI is able to make available to the student adequate and appropriate facilities. It is clearly easier for a body that is aware of all the applications that are being made to judge this last point than for an academic (who may only be aware of the applications that have been made to him or her personally). The importance of this consideration to the post-enrolment stage of the contract is discussed in 'The terms and conditions of the contract' later.

The classical elements of a contract: where are they to be found?

The formation of a legally binding contract ordinarily depends on the existence of the following elements:

- offer
- acceptance
- consideration
- capacity and intention to create legal relations.

Capacity is no longer an issue generally because most students and prospective students of an HEI will be aged at least 18 and will, therefore, be legally capable of entering into a binding obligation. The other side of this coin is that the HEI no longer has to consider itself as being *in loco parentis* – an outdated analysis of the relationship now replaced by the contractual one (see Lewis, 1983: 252). Any students who are under 18 will have the capacity to enter into a contract for education as such contracts are considered to constitute 'contracts for necessaries', by which minors will be bound (see *Pickering v Ginning* and *Chapple v Cooper*).

An offer and an acceptance of a place on a specified course are clearly prerequisites at the pre-entry stage. In *Moran v University College, Salford (No. 2)*, the court rejected the argument that the unconditional offer made to Mr Moran was merely an invitation to him to enter into discussions which might lead to an agreement to accept him on a course and provide him with appropriate instruction in return for his promise to arrange for fees to be paid. There must be sufficient clarity and certainty about the terms of both in order to identify clearly what is the subject matter of the contract. Both parties also clearly intend to be bound – the student expects the HEI to provide a place on a course in accordance with its commitment and the HEI depends for part of its funding on admitting students to courses, as well as depending for its reputation on complying with the terms of its offers.

Consideration is more difficult to identify and has given rise to debate on the question of what consideration the student provides. It is suggested that the correct analysis at the admission stage is (according to *Moran v University College, Salford (No. 2)*) that the student provides consideration at the point of transmitting his or her acceptance of the HEI's offer by giving up the opportunity, as required by UCAS rules, of negotiating with other HEIs. At the post-registration stage, it is easier to identify the student's consideration, in a financial form, whether it is paid personally or by some other party on the student's behalf.

How long does the contract last? Does it change or mature?

The contract lasts until it reaches the end of its term (as agreed, whether expressly or impliedly) or until it is terminated earlier by agreement or breach. One of the disadvantages of the two-contract analysis is that it is difficult to account for the transition from one to the other – when does the contract for admission end and the contract of matriculation begin? Is the end of one conditional upon the beginning of the other? If the end of one and the beginning of the other are simultaneous, it is difficult to discern the purpose served by dividing the contractual relationship into two. If the contract is to be considered as a rolling or maturing contract, then from the point of registration onwards the contract can be characterized, presumably, by its essential purpose as the contract to teach. This interpretation has the disadvantage that it is not easily reconciled with traditional contract theories, which may require all the terms of a contract to be certain at the outset. However, it corresponds most closely to the reality of the HEI–student relationship and is, to that extent, a useful concept.

Termination might occur, for example, when one party commits a repudiatory breach which the other accepts as bringing the contract to an end, as when the HEI unilaterally withdraws the promised course and the student decides not to accept the alternative offered. Termination might also occur when the wronged party acts to bring the contract to an end upon the other's breach, as when the HEI removes a student who breaches its disciplinary rules. Following termination for breach, the wronged party may have a right to claim damages or some other remedy, as discussed later.

The terms and conditions of the contract

There will be express and implied terms of the HEI–student contract. The terms at the pre-registration stage are relatively easy to identify, namely the obligation on the HEI to admit the student to the course on which he or she has been offered a place and the obligation on the student to turn up and register. It seems unlikely that an HEI would ever take action to force a student to comply with this obligation, but this does not mean that the obligation does not exist.

Having registered, the contract to teach comes into effect, bringing with it more varied and interesting obligations. The express obligations on the HEI and the student at the heart of the contract will be to provide the promised course and to pay the promised fees, respectively. In addition, the student will agree, usually expressly, to be bound by the terms of the HEI's various rules and regulations in force from time to time. The contractual basis for the incorporation of those rules is discussed as follows.

The implied terms of the contract to teach are more elusive. They change and develop with the case law and with the changing expectations of society as to what HE is about or for. The new implied terms, which it can be argued qualify the basic minimal obligation to teach, arise principally as a result of the increasingly collaborative and interactive processes of today's HE. For example, continuous assessment, open book examinations and the more traditional supervision obligations in respect of postgraduate students could all require the HEI to take a more pro-active approach to guiding its students through the HE experience which will lead them to their degree. Counselling and pastoral care, as well as academic feedback, may be seen in future to form part of the overall teaching-contract obligations.

There are also implied terms regarding quality. The HEI has an obligation to provide the student's education with a reasonable degree of care and skill (see *D'Mello v Loughborough College of Technology, The Times*, 16 June 1970). If the student's course involves outplacement or practical experience, the

quality of that experience is also likely, ultimately, to be the HEI's responsibility and will not be absolutely delegable. There will probably be implied
terms that the HEI will provide appropriate and adequate facilities (such as
library facilities, access to computers, science practicals and laboratory facilities) to give the student a proper opportunity of achieving the required
standard to attain a degree (see *Sammy v Birkbeck College, The Times*, 3 November 1964). Furthermore, the HEI is probably under a duty not to take any
action, such as reducing ancillary facilities of this nature, which would have
the effect in practice of so devaluing the educational experience that the
resulting qualification would be perceived as worth little or nothing in the
marketplace.

(**Editor's note**: *The Times Higher Educational Supplement* (31 October 1997)
reported on the mess at Thames Valley University (TVU) where an instruction from a PVC to assessors to treat 30 per cent or above marks in the
September resits as if they were 40 per cent pass marks led to accusations
of the University 'dumbing down' degrees, and an admission from the VC
that the instruction was 'a mistake made for the best of reasons' (in the
context of administrative chaos). A law student is quoted: 'It's bedlam.
What really worries me is that employers will see TVU as the university that
awards upper seconds to people just for turning up. That's not true, but
who will listen after this? There needs to be some sort of independent
investigation to rebuild confidence inside and outside the university.' In
fact, TVU has invited the QAA (Quality Assurance Agency) to satisfy itself
that the problems are being properly dealt with.)

As it may be extremely difficult to identify with complete certainty the
precise nature and extent of the terms that the courts may be prepared to
imply into the contract, there is a persuasive argument for making aspects
that are of particular importance to the HEI express terms of the contract.
Over recent years, for example, many HEIs have included express provisions in their registration documents to cover the question of a student's
intellectual property (IP) rights. This is covered in more detail in Chapters
10 and 11. Here, it is sufficient to note that IP rights fall into that category
of topics which should not, generally, be left to be the subject of an implied
term.

HEI regulations, rules and procedures also have a place in the contractual nexus. Their exact status is debatable, but it is the essence of the HEI–
student relationship that the HEI must have a right, subject to a requirement
of reasonableness, to regulate the affairs of the whole HEI community. Given that this community will number thousands of people with many
different interests, occupations and relationships within the community, it
would be neither practical nor correct to assert that internal HEI rules and
regulations are contractual in the sense that they cannot be altered except
with the agreement of the individuals affected.

In practice, it is suggested, the HEI has wide powers to regulate and impose
rules, so long as it acts reasonably and brings its regulations to the attention
of the appropriate people at the appropriate times. Their contractual status

is probably best expressed as being a body of rules to which each individual signs up in principle, including variations which may be made by the HEI (impliedly reasonably) from time to time. Thus, the introduction of new rules and regulations during an individual student's course may on occasion be subject to challenge as a unilateral variation of the contract. However, the better argument, as long as the change is reasonable, is that the HEI is not only entitled but under a duty to make rules to regulate and ensure the smooth running of its community. In this sense, the HEI–student contract is different from the employment relationship (for example, where an employer's freedom to change what are known as rules is considerably circumscribed by implied terms and the constraints of a large body of statutory regulation).

What constitutes a breach?

At the admission stage of the contract, a breach can be fairly clearly identified where the HEI refuses to admit the student to the promised course, withdraws or makes changes to the course in circumstances where no effective disclaimer of liability applies.

In the contract to teach, the failure by the HEI to comply with any of the implied terms as to the nature of the teaching obligation and its quality may give the student a right to claim a remedy for breach of contract. Imposing unreasonable rules and regulations might also give rise to a claim, usually of a different kind (an example is discussed in 'Function of and intervention of third parties' later).

What remedies are there?

A student's complaint may, depending on the circumstances, go before the court or the Visitor. If the complaint is to be taken before a court, the student will have to choose between the County Court and the High Court. Experience has shown that students tend to prefer the County Court, because it is cheaper to commence proceedings and because it is a more informal forum than the High Court. In both the High Court and the County Court, students are entitled to represent themselves. The lack of legal representation has a number of implications for the HEI.

If it were necessary for the student to obtain legal advice, the substance of that legal advice would, in many cases, be that the student had no case to pursue, thus sifting out many of the truly unmeritorious claims. In the absence of any such advice, students often try to pursue non-existent or extremely weak claims to trial, which can be an expensive process for the HEI in question. In many cases, the HEI is forced to defend the action through to trial because it cannot, for political reasons, settle the action out of court. In those relatively rare circumstances where the institution is prepared to negotiate with the student, legal advisers would be able to persuade the student to join in such negotiation. Students conducting their own case are frequently incapable or unwilling to try to settle the action.

If students had to secure legal representation, the legal costs they would incur in doing so might encourage them to abandon the idea of proceeding through the courts. At present, the only costs a student is likely to incur are for issuing proceedings and for photocopying and postage. Experience shows that many students who take a breach of contract claim before the courts, have ample time to spend in preparing the case and are not unduly concerned about the hidden costs to them (in terms of lost earning time) in conducting the case. The fact that the student may have plenty of time to devote to the preparation of his or her case means that he or she will usually have an extremely thorough, if somewhat biased, understanding of the case. This can make such students tenacious and difficult opponents and can result in increased legal costs for the HEI as it tries to defend against the student's claim. It is small comfort for an HEI faced with a large legal bill to know that few cases of this nature have, to date, been ultimately successful.

In breach of contract cases, the most likely remedy that students will seek in court is damages. They may seek a discretionary remedy (such as an injunction) to force the HEI, for example, to reinstate a course or part of a course. In practice, it seems unlikely that a court would provide such a remedy where the withdrawal of the course had been as a result of circumstances outside the HEI's control, such as the death of a key person. Presumably, the same principle would apply in the case of a claimant who sought to force the HEI to comply with the terms of an offer made in error – generally, specific performance would not appear to be appropriate.

Where relevant, the Visitor makes a number of remedies available to the wronged student, possibly including damages and a range of types of restitution (see Chapter 8). Public law remedies may also be available to the student by way of judicial review (see Chapter 9). That subject is beyond the scope of this chapter, save to note that students may seek this type of remedy where the claim cannot be brought within the boundaries of contract law. This could be, for example, a challenge by a student that the HEI's procedures are themselves unfair.

It should also be noted that the prospective student may use the judicial route at the pre-contract stage. Applicants who consider that the decision to reject them has been taken on the basis of inappropriate selection criteria might consider applying for this type of remedy. To some extent, the bringing of this type of complaint can be prevented by careful consideration of the way in which the reasons for rejecting an applicant are to be communicated, and, indeed, whether any reasons should be given at all. As a general rule of thumb, it is best to avoid giving detailed reasons in situations where there is scope for the rationale behind them to be misunderstood or challenged on grounds of inherent unfairness. Other complaints by applicants may be related to the manner in which any interview was conducted, where, for example, it was apparent that they were being interviewed by someone who had no knowledge of the subject area for which they were applying.

How remedies are obtained and calculated

In order to obtain damages for breach of contract, the student must first establish in court that the contract has been breached. If damages are claimed, a causal link has to be established between that breach and any loss which the student claims to have suffered. In many cases, this may be very difficult, even where the breach in question is relatively easy to prove. It is, however, possible to envisage circumstances in which the causal link may be more easily established (for example, where a student is offered and accepts a job subject to obtaining a doctorate and the offer of the course leading to the doctorate is subsequently withdrawn by the HEI).

If the student can establish the necessary causal link, the basic principles of compensation apply at both stages of the contract identified in this chapter. In the case of a breach of contract by the HEI in failing or refusing to register a student who has been offered a place and who has fulfilled any conditions attached to the offer, there will be two alternative methods of assessing damages – one based on the proposition that the contract should have been fully performed, the other on the basis that it was not made in the first place.

The first method will compensate the student by awarding him or her damages – essentially on a future basis – calculated to meet the loss incurred as a result of not being able to be in the position the student would have been in had the contract been performed. The measure of damages on a future basis may be quite difficult to calculate, because it will involve a number of imponderable factors, such as the likelihood of the student's surviving the course and passing the examinations at the end of it, as well as the prospects which may result from obtaining the degree. The nature of the breach of contract may be relevant. If the HEI made a clerical error and refused then to honour the offer to an unqualified candidate, it may be possible to argue that damages should be limited by the unlikelihood of the academically weak candidate succeeding in any event. The student will be under a duty to mitigate loss. In many cases, this will mean attempting to find a suitable alternative course or re-entering the system the following year or at the earliest opportunity. If this succeeds, the loss may be minimal. The student must also give credit for the expense which would have been incurred if admitted onto the course (for example, on course materials and books).

The alternative method of calculating damages is to allow recovery of expenses incurred as a result of or in connection with the breach of contract. This may be expressed as the intention to place the student in the position, not as if the contract had been performed, but as if it had never been made. The student cannot recover both lost expenses and damages representing future loss.

In the case of a breach of the terms of the teaching phase of the contract, the same principles apply as described earlier to the calculation of the measure of damages. Establishing a causal link between poor quality teaching or support and failure leading to loss is again likely to be a difficult exercise. It may be possible to use comparative material, drawing from the experience of other students on the same course or from the claimant's results in other papers or examinations.

The emergence of the tort law concept of educational negligence has already been mentioned briefly in this chapter. It is suggested that, in the main, a claim of negligence would be brought alongside a claim for breach of contract, rather than instead of the contractual claim, because the parties involved will usually also have a contractual relationship. The courts have been reluctant, thus far, to award damages in situations in which negligence on the part of the HEI has been alleged, usually because the causal link between the alleged negligence and the loss suffered is as difficult to prove as in the case of a breach of contract. For example, in the case of a student who was a member of the National Front, whose beliefs provoked such extreme reactions on the part of fellow students that he was effectively excluded from lectures and who subsequently failed to obtain the degree he required, the advice from his lawyers was that his case would fail because the causation point could not be proved. Although it was arguable that the institution had acted in a way that was both in breach of contract and negligent, the student was advised that it was impossible to prove that he would have obtained the degree he required had it not been for that institution's action or lack of action.

However, the case of *Smolden v Whitworth and another*, *The Times*, 23 April 1996, where a referee was held liable for the injuries sustained by an amateur rugby player during the collapse of a scrum may be an indication that the courts are not afraid to interpret liberally the causation requirements where the perceived interests of justice demand. It is difficult to envisage a situation, other than one in which personal injury has been suffered, where the courts would be willing to adopt such a broad interpretation of causation requirements, but it is by no means guaranteed that they will not do so in the future, and it is worth noting that personal injury nowadays is quite clearly judicially recognized as embracing the effects of nervous breakdowns (see *Walker v Northumberland County Council*, concerning an employer's duty of care to an employee suffering from excessive stress by overwork).

Function and intervention of third parties

This chapter has already dealt with the function and involvement of UCAS. Other third parties whose functions have an obvious impact are the courts and the chartered university's Visitor. The courts will become involved, not to arbitrate in academic disputes or to impose their academic judgement (the same applies to the role of the Visitor), but to regulate the terms of the contractual and public law relationships (see Chapters 8 and 9, and also *R v HM The Queen in Council*, ex p *Vijayatunga*).

Breach of contract, unfairness (public law) and negligence (in terms of misrepresentation or careless teaching) will all provide the courts with the opportunity to intervene. They will also consider allegations of discrimination on the grounds of race or sex, including in relation to the marking of examinations and the provision of academic feedback and support. Sexual harassment allegations in the academic context will also be a matter for the courts, so that an HEI may find itself vicariously liable in a sex discrimination claim arising out of harassment of a student by a lecturer in the course of his or her employment.

The courts and the Visitor will also be concerned with procedure. Failure by the HEI to follow its own procedures and regulations, particularly where the result is apparently to allow a real danger of bias, will provide clear grounds for the courts to intervene. The jurisdiction of the Visitor in the chartered HEIs and in Oxford and Cambridge colleges essentially covers all matters arising out of the HEI's internal laws. It is less clear that the Visitor's jurisdiction extends to the pre-offer stage to cover application and selection.

Other outside forces which have an impact on the HEI–student contract are the regulatory regimes of consumer law, emanating from UK statutes and European directives. In terms of pure contract law, the parties to the contract have freedom to define its terms by agreement between them. However, the consumer protection legislative framework detracts from the HEI's freedom to set the terms of the bargain, taking into account the disparity of bargaining power in relation to the student. The Unfair Contract Terms Act 1977 deals with contract terms which attempt to exclude or restrict the potential liability of a business in relation to a consumer. The current view is that the Act *does apply to* HEIs. Liability for death or personal injury arising from negligence cannot be excluded, whilst the exclusion of other liability arising from negligence is subject to the requirement of reasonableness. The Unfair Terms in Consumer Contracts Regulations (UTCCR) 1994 came into force in 1995 – see Unfair Terms in Consumer Contracts Regulations (SI 1994/3159) and EC Council Directive 93/13/EEC. The impact of the UTCCR 1994 is on unequal consumer bargains. Their effect is much wider than the Unfair Contract Terms Act 1977, because they apply potentially to any express term of the contract falling within their scope. The better view seems to be that the UTCCR 1994 do apply to the terms of the HEI–student contract. The UTCCR 1994 apply to any term of a contract between a party acting for purposes relating to its business and someone acting outside his or her business, which has not been individually negotiated, that is, in all situations where the consumer is not able to influence the substance of that term. Students are likely to be regarded as consumers when courses, accommodation and materials are supplied to them by HEIs. Those standard terms which create or record a contractual relationship between the student and the HEI, ranging from course prospectuses to disciplinary rules, will be a clear target. The consequences if the HEI's standard contract terms are unfair is that they will be declared void, with the effect that the HEI will be obliged to provide the agreed service without relying on the advantages conferred by the unfair terms.

The requirement of reasonableness essentially applies to both the Unfair Contract Terms Act 1977 and the UTCCR 1994. Its application is not an exact science. The UTCCR 1994 contain an indicative and illustrative list of terms which may be regarded as unfair, helping to clarify the possible criteria which will be applied by the courts (see Schedule 3). A term from this list which is likely to be of particular relevance to HEIs is one which has the object or effect of enabling the seller or supplier to alter unilaterally, without a valid reason, any characteristics of the product or service to be provided. Those terms which define the main subject matter of the contract or concern the price or remuneration are not subject to assessment for fairness, provided that they are in plain, intelligible language (see UTCCR 1994, Regulation 3(2)). At present, the only persons entitled to challenge unfair terms in court are individual consumers, since in UK law there is no general right of representative action on behalf of parties to a contract. However, this position is subject to a challenge in the European Court of Justice, referred from the High Court, as to whether the UK should enact legislation to allow persons or organizations to take action before the courts on behalf of consumers (see DTI Press Release R/96/160, 28 February 1996). If that challenge succeeds (which is very likely as EC Council Directive 93/13/EEC, Article 7.2, provides that member states must ensure that organizations who have a legitimate interest receive the right to take action), student associations might want to perform that role and challenge the terms of the HEI–student contract. In addition, however, both individual students and student associations can make a complaint to the Director-General of Fair Trading that a contract term is unfair (see UTCCR 1994, Regulation 8).

Practical preventive or remedial action

Look at procedures

To avoid legal challenge, procedures must be fair in the way they apply to students and in the way in which they operate. A student may seek to challenge a procedure which denies him or her, for example, the right to put his or her side of the story, as being contrary to natural justice. It is, therefore, important to examine procedures initially to ensure that they are fair. It is also vital to make sure that different sets of procedures (for example, HEI rules and course rules) are compatible, not contradictory.

Follow procedures

Once procedures, policies and codes have been put in place by the HEI, those responsible for operating them must follow them, or risk legal challenge. Therefore, procedures need to be clear, unambiguous and workable in practice. If experience shows problems in any of these areas, the procedures should be reviewed and rewritten as a preventive exercise. This is unlikely to be enough on its own. Those implementing the procedures must understand what they mean and how they work.

Know the policy

It is not sufficient, in cases of alleged discrimination and bias, to point to a documented policy. The courts expect those responsible for operating it to understand and be familiar with it. Again, therefore, this suggests that anti-discrimination policies should as far as possible be simply framed with reasonably memorable requirements, avoiding excessive complexity. There is also an expectation that institutions of the scale of HEIs will invest considerably in training in equal opportunities, and in monitoring and reviewing policies and procedures in operation.

Too many regulations?

As regulations proliferate, it becomes increasingly difficult to put into practice the principles briefly outlined earlier. An alternative strategy is to cut the regulatory regime down to a bare minimum framework and simply attempt to deal with matters such as academic appeals in accordance with the basic requirements of natural justice. The implications of this strategy are that the HEI places greater reliance on its officers to conduct themselves reasonably and fairly without needing to be tied into a restrictive regulatory structure, and that challenges by students would have to be framed either in public law by way of judicial review or on the basis of a breach of an implied term of reasonableness in the way a decision was reached.

Publication and information

The effect of many of the terms of the HEI–student contract, including disclaimers and exclusions of liability, will depend to a large extent on appropriate and timely publication. Disclaimers and exclusions will be ineffective if they are not drawn to the student's attention at or before the formation of the contract. Publications also need to be consistent. The HEI's prospectus should not be inconsistent with the terms of, for example, departmental literature or the HEI calendar. On arrival, the student should not receive a new set of literature in wholly different terms to that which was sent at the time the offer was made.

Anticipating and mitigating strategies

The changing shape of educational provision in the form of more mobile and modular courses provides an opportunity for the HEI to assist the disappointed student to mitigate the possible damage if a course or part of it is withdrawn.

Clarity

Whatever preventive strategies are put in place, clarity as to what is expected of individuals who have a role to play in the relationship will greatly assist their effect. This applies not only to internal HEI procedures, but also to the part played by outsiders (for example, employers who accept students on outplacements for a part of the degree course). Each party should clearly understand the scope and limit of their responsibilities and freedom to act. Clarity in the wording of procedures and regulations will also greatly assist if those documents are challenged under the UTCCR 1994, which contain a general requirement of plain language (see Regulation 6).

Effective complaints procedure

Every HEI should have a complaints procedure in place. If the procedure is operated effectively, it may be possible to prevent at least some of the complaints brought by students from reaching the court. In some cases, sympathetic treatment of the complaint, a clear explanation of the HEI's position and a discussion of what, if anything, may be done to prevent a recurrence of the situation about which the complaint has been made, may succeed in satisfying the complainant. This is in much the same way as complaints within the National Health Service can often effectively be dealt with if handled speedily and openly, but tend to fester and become intractable if the complainant feels that ranks are being closed against him or her.

Conclusions

The HEI's actions and operations seem likely in future to come under increasing scrutiny by outsiders and to be subject to a greater variety of challenges. Establishing and operating a strategy to deal with these challenges depends on individuals understanding, anticipating and taking avoiding action. Their ability to do so depends, in turn, on the framework within which they operate and in particular the clear understanding at all levels of the HEI of the essential and characteristic elements of the contract with the student and of its challenges and opportunities.

A note on references

A former student of the University of Glamorgan accepted £25,000 in settlement of a damages claim for a negligent reference. Staff giving references for students (or employees) should be aware of the basic principles and the possible liability of the institution (or, in some cases, even the individual). The key case is *Spring v Guardian Assurance.*

According to the law, there is no obligation to give a reference or to show the reference to the student. If a reference is given, then defamation, negligence and misrepresentation are possible grounds for action, either by the subject of the reference or by the new employer who relies on it. The institution will normally be liable for the consequences of a negligent/ defamatory reference given by a member of its staff, unless (against the odds) it can establish that the reference was given outside the course of employment (or, as lawyers like to say, on a 'frolic' of the referee's/employee's own). Only *reasonable* exclusions of liability for negligent acts or omissions carried out in the course of a business will stand up in court. The question of what is 'reasonable' in this context has not yet been tested in court, but for now it seems sensible not only to include a disclaimer to the effect that neither the institution nor the referee can be held responsible for any error. That disclaimer should be backed up by following the good practice guidelines for staff.

1. Tell students to seek in advance your agreement to give a reference.
2. If you are unable or unwilling to give a reference but you still receive a request for one from a potential employer, communicate your refusal carefully, without implying a negative reference.
3. Stick to facts and only give opinions within your professional competence (e.g. no medical opinions).
4. Include the institution's disclaimer.
5. Check there are no outstanding disciplinary proceedings/investigations (e.g., cheating).
6. Mark all correspondence 'private and confidential – for the attention of addressee/committee/panel only' and state that the reference is given only for the benefit of the addressee(s).
7. State that the contents of the reference are confidential and not to be disclosed to anyone else without the referee's permission.
8. If a reference is given orally, keep a note of what was said.

This note has been extracted from the regular column in *Managing HE* (Hobsons Publishing plc, Cambridge) contributed by Martineau Johnson, and one of the editors, David Palfreyman.

Further reading

CVCP (1997) *Independent Review of Student Appeals and Staff Disputes: Interim Report of the CVCP Nolan Group.* London: CVCP (N/97/11).

Farrington D. J. (1994) *The Law of Higher Education.* London: Butterworths.

Farrington, D. J. (1997) *Handling Student Complaints.* Sheffield: UCoSDA Briefing Paper 48.

Furmston, M. P. (1992) *Universities and Disclaimers of Liability.* London: CVCP N/92/112 (29/5/92).

Harris, B. (1995) *Disciplinary and Regulatory Proceedings.* Chichester: Barry Rose.

Holloway, J. (1994) 'The rights of individuals who receive a defective education', *Education and the Law,* 6(2), 207–19.

Lewis, C. B. (1983) 'The legal nature of a university and the student-university relationship', *Ottawa Law Review,* 3(1), 77–92.

Lewis, C. B. (1985) 'Procedural fairness and university students: England and Canada compared', *The Dalhousie Law Journal.*

Markesinis, B. S. and Deakin, S. F. (1994) *Tort Law.* Oxford: Oxford University Press.

Parlour, J. W. and Burwood, L. R. V. (1995) 'Students' rights', *Education and the Law,* 7(2), 63–78.

Treitel, G. H. (1996) *The Law of Contract.* London: Sweet & Maxwell.

Winfield and Jolowicz on Tort, 14th edn (1994) London: Sweet & Maxwell.

Appendix: the HEI–student contract (admission stage)

Commentary to accompany flowchart

The flowchart represents the process of one application to one university and shows the different steps that may apply and the various ways in which the process may be concluded.

Box no.	Comments
1.	The flowchart begins at the point where the applicant is considering HE.
2.	He or she may consult a careers advisor to help decide to which course or institution he or she should apply.
3.	The applicant will almost certainly consult the university prospectus and possibly one or more independent guides.
4.	He or she will apply for a UCAS pack, which will include the UCAS handbook for students, the application form and instructions and a copy of the 'Charter for Higher Education'.
5.	He or she may decide that further information is needed.
6.	If further information is needed, the applicant is likely to contact the university for it. This may involve speaking to tutors, accommodation support staff or representatives of the students' union, depending on the nature of the enquiry.
7.	This information may be obtained in oral or written form.

8.   Once the applicant has obtained all the information needed, he or she will decide whether to apply to the university. If he or she does not, the process will end.

9.   Applications are normally made exclusively through UCAS. However, in some cases the applicant may wish to make an informal approach to the university, perhaps to test the likelihood of being offered a place at that university if he or she were to submit a formal application.

10.   If the applicant does want to try an informal approach, he or she will usually send a CV or other record of the details required by the university. This informal approach would most likely be through a course tutor.

11.   The university may respond to the effect that it will not consider applications other than through the UCAS system. In other cases, the university may inform the applicant that it would not be prepared to make any offer to that applicant in any event. However, in some cases, universities are prepared to tell the applicant that if they were to receive the application through UCAS, they would be prepared to make an offer either generally or in terms that are specified to the applicant.

12.   Irrespective of whether or not the applicant makes an informal approach, he or she will have to complete a UCAS application form. He or she may (but need not) select up to six institutions.

13.   The university will consider the applicant's details and decide whether it wishes to make an offer. It may interview the applicant prior to making this decision but is discouraged by UCAS from making offers that are subject to a satisfactory, later, interview. If it decides it does not wish to make an offer, the procedure comes to an end. If the university does make an offer, it may do so in one of two ways.

14.   First, it may make an offer that is unconditional, that is to say there are no conditions attached that relate to examination results.

15.   Applicants are usually advised by UCAS to wait until they have received decisions from all the institutions to which they have applied before accepting offers. At that point (or earlier if the applicant chooses to ignore the advice), the applicant may decide to accept the unconditional offer firmly.

16.   If he or she does accept the unconditional offer firmly, as there is no need to await examination results, he or she is entitled to turn up at the start of the academic year and be enrolled. However, the applicant may have to continue to comply with certain administrative formalities.

17.   Alternatively, the applicant may accept the unconditional offer as an insurance offer. (Applicants are entitled to have an insurance offer in case they do not satisfy the examination requirements imposed on them by the university of their first choice. The insurance offer will, therefore, be lower than the first choice offer.) If the unconditional offer is accepted as insurance, the applicant must wait for the exam results to see if he or she has met the requirements of the 'firm' offer. If the offer is not accepted as insurance, the applications procedure comes to an end in respect of that offer.

18.	Second, if the university does not make an unconditional offer, it will make an offer to the applicant that is conditional on the examination results, which the applicant may accept firmly.
19.	The applicant may accept it as insurance. If he or she does not accept the offer firmly or as insurance, then the application procedure in respect of that offer comes to an end.
20.	For those who have accepted conditional offers firmly or as insurance, publication of the exam results is the point at which the offers 'crystallize'.
21.	Where the applicant has matched or exceeded the offer, the university sends out confirmation that this is the case.
22., 23. and 24.	If the applicant had accepted the offer firmly, he or she is required to confirm that he or she still wishes to take it up within a stated number of days from the date of the university's confirmation. If the applicant does so, he will be entitled to turn up and enrol at the start of the academic year.
25. and 26.	The applicant may not confirm for two reasons. First, he or she may have done better than expected and may want to transfer to another (in his or her eyes, better) university. Alternatively, he or she may have done so much better than expected that he or she wants to withdraw entirely for that year, to reconsider the options for the following year. UCAS purports to give the university the right to block a transfer to another university, but not to prevent a withdrawal.
	If the applicant does not confirm and does not ask for a transfer, the offer lapses. He or she is not entitled to enter the clearing system for that year. Clearing is the system which allows those not holding a place at the confirmation stage to apply for vacant places at other institutions.
27.	Where the applicant had accepted an offer (whether conditional or unconditional) as insurance, he or she is required to confirm that he or she wishes to take advantage of it within a stated period of time prior to enrolment. Failure to do this means that offer will lapse. The applicant will not be entitled to enter the clearing system.
28. and 29.	If the applicant does confirm, he or she will be entitled to turn up and enrol at the start of the academic year.
30. and 34.	If, when the exam results are announced, the applicant has not satisfied the conditions, the university may decide to accept the lower grades. If it does, the applicant is entitled to turn up and enrol at the start of the academic year. If it does not, then the applicant can enter the clearing system or withdraw until the following year, perhaps gambling on being able to get into his or her first choice university with those lower grades.
31.	If the university is not prepared to accept the lower grades, it may be prepared to offer the applicant an alternative (and for the university, perhaps, a more unpopular) course.
32. and 33.	If the applicant is prepared to accept the alternative course, then he or she may turn up and enrol at the start of the academic year. If the applicant does not accept, he or she may go into clearing or withdraw.

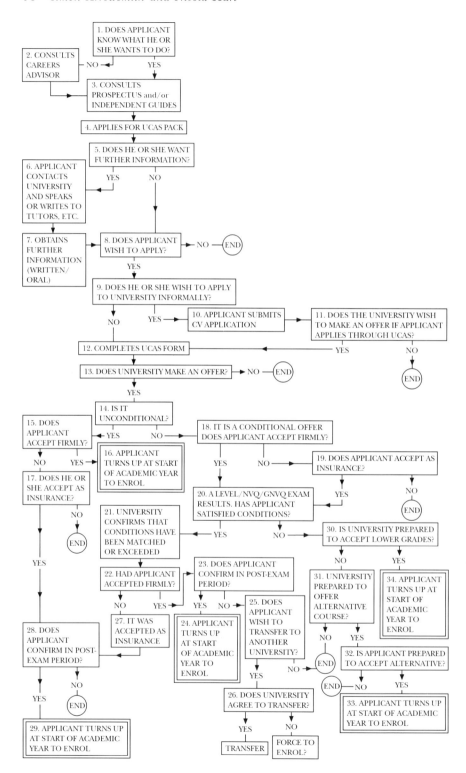

7

The Regulation of the Community: Student Discipline, Staff Discipline, Grievances and Harassment Codes

Simon Arrowsmith (Martineau Johnson)

Editors' introduction

As was stated in Chapter 1, the generality of the employees of HEIs (higher education institutions) are covered by the same basic employment law as any other employee. This is the subject of many textbooks and, hence, there is no need to discuss employment law in this book (other than to note how things are to some degree different for one particular group of staff in many – but not all – HEIs, that is academic staff to whom the so-called 'model statutes' imposed by the University Commissioners under the Education Reform Act (ERA) 1988 apply, and some of whom still retain tenure). This chapter also explores the disciplining of students, which, in the late-1960s and early-1970s, was the main source of case law involving HEIs and of references to the Visitor, but which is now of less prominence than conflicts about the examination of the graduate thesis, for example. The chapter also deals with the emotive and complex area of codes concerning harassment.

Looking as far back as 1910 we find Williams (1910: 182–3) comments: 'There is probably an implied contract that a university or college supplies efficient tuition. An action would lie by an undergraduate . . . for breach of contract to educate . . . [But] a member of a college is bound to conform to reasonable rules of discipline, and if he do not do so, the contract to educate is not broken. In a recent case, a Cambridge undergraduate was expelled for refusal to go to Chapel. He brought an action for breach of contract to educate . . . On the trial at Herts Assizes, Wilts, J. directed judgement for the college on the ground that the relation of an undergraduate to his college was in matters of discipline not a contractual one' (*Green v Peterhouse*, 1896). Farrington (1994) refers to *Green v Master and Fellows of*

St Peter's College, Oxford, both he and Williams citing *The Times* of February, 1896. (The reference in *The Times* in fact refers to St Peter's, *Cambridge* as the full legal title of Peterhouse and anyway, St Peter's Oxford was not founded until between the wars.) As discussed in the bibliographical essay on the Visitor, the contractual dispute envisaged by Williams, and as in *Green,* would for a chartered university (as all were in 1910), be exclusively within the jurisdiction of the Visitor and should not reach the courts.

On the issue of harassment codes, note should be taken of the Protection from Harassment Act 1997 which is intended to deal with 'stalkers', and which may also strengthen the position of an employee facing harassment in the workplace by giving him or her the right to go to the police under the Act's two new criminal offences and to seek civil redress under the Act's new statutory tort of harassment. In the issue of 'stalking' see the book *Being Stalked* written by Robert Fine, a sociology lecturer at the University of Warwick. Fine recounts his experience of being harassed by a mature student and the long legal battle, supported by the University, to obtain an injunction. Note that the Protection from Harassment Act 1997 makes harassment on two occasions a criminal offence and allows a Criminal Court or a Civil Court to make a restraining order/issue an injunction. The test is whether 'the reasonable man' would consider the behaviour and actions complained of to be harassment: this may include 'merely' causing fear of violence by using threatening language and, as mentioned, might apply to bullying within the workplace.

Griffiths (1977) argued that students do not get a sympathetic reaction from the judiciary, especially in the event of disputes about discipline reaching the courts when not automatically falling within the exclusive jurisdiction of the Visitor in the chartered HEIs. Later editions of his well known *The Politics of the Judiciary* do, however, somewhat soften the firmness of the view taken in the first edition, where Griffiths declared: 'Students are not one of the more popular minorities and Her Majesty's judges in recent times seem to have shared much of the prejudice shown by other, equally senior, members of society [167] . . . the courts seek assiduously to find some ground on which to disregard breach of the rules of natural justice [on the part of the university/college authorities in disciplining students,] [169] . . . students are seen essentially as children and sometimes very unpleasant children – above all, as very undisciplined children. And universities and colleges are institutions of the State and so to be upheld [170] . . . The student cases indeed are excellent examples of the judicial obsession with, as they see it, the necessity to protect and preserve the structures of constitutional authority without undue concern for the rights of those who wish to challenge that authority [197] . . .'.

Academic freedom

There is especially the issue of academic freedom, as defined in the ERA 1988, which interacts with the employment contract for academic staff and, indeed, with the contents of Chapters 10 and 11 on such matters as the rights to intellectual property (IP), copyright and the use of the Internet to disseminate material. The ERA enshrining of the principle of academic freedom is in the form: 'academic staff have freedom within the law to question and test received wisdom and to put forward new ideas and controversial or unpopular opinions without placing themselves in jeopardy of losing their jobs'. Also, Nolan (1996) has recommended that:

- HEIs should 'institute codes of practice on whistleblowing';
- HEIs 'should make it clear . . . that the institution permits staff to speak freely and without being subject to disciplinary sanctions or victimisation about academic standards and related matters, providing that they do so lawfully, without malice, and in the public interest';
- 'gagging clauses' should be used sparingly:

> Where it is absolutely necessary to include confidentiality clauses in service and severance contracts, they should expressly remind staff that legitimate concerns about malpractice may be raised with the appropriate authority (the funding council, National Audit Office, Visitor; or independent review body as applicable) if this is done in the public interest.

(Note the critical comments of the Swansea Visitor, Sir Michael Davies, on the use of such a clause – Davies, 1994.)

Moreover, Nolan wishes to see 'a system of independent review of disputes', both for staff and students (possibly by extending the Visitor model in the chartered HEI to the statutory HEI – see Chapters 8 and 9 plus the bibliographical essay on the Visitor and especially the section on 'The Visitor Post–Nolan'). See page 49 above re Dearing (1997) on these issues.

In addition, the concept in the chartered universities of the academic staff (and certain 'academic related' senior administrative staff and library staff) as *members* of the university, rather than simply its employees, has to be taken on board. In the context of Oxford and Cambridge, these staff (as Congregation) *are* the university, there being no equivalent of a lay-member dominated Council which might be said to be the employer of the academic staff. Thus, would a chartered university and its members act so firmly and 'managerially' as in the following recent instances from statutory HEIs? One university (South Bank) threatened an injunction against academics lobbying the university's academic board to protest over proposed redundancies (as reported in *Times Higher*, 28 June 1996). Another HEI (Robert Gordon) was sued by the Educational Institute of Scotland (a kind of NATFHE/AUT) over proposals to change the academic contract (as reported in *The Times*, 18 June 1996).

Yet even the ancient University of Cambridge found itself in the High Court in 1997, facing one of its lecturers seeking judicial review of its internal promotions procedure (*R v the University of Cambridge* ex p *Evans*). In his judgement granting leave for judicial review but staying the matter pending Cambridge rethinking its position, Mr Justice Sedley emphasized the need for HEIs to be very careful in clarifying the degree to which a 'higher' committee can properly delegate its decision-making to a sub-committee, and stressed the appropriateness of an employer giving reasons to successful candidates for promotion. It was recognized, however, that 1997 'good practice' might differ from 1991 'settled law' in the form of *R v Civil Service Appeal Board* ex p *Cunningham*, where Lord Donaldson, MR, had, *obiter*, suggested that an employer need *not* give reasons. Mr Justice Sedley cited several later cases and commented that 'No public lawyer supposes that the last word has yet been said on the duty to give reasons.' The *Oxford Magazine* (No. 145, Michaelmas Term 1997) subsequently carried articles from Dr Evans and the retiring Cambridge Registrary, Stephen Fleet: the latter noted that promotion procedures 'remain under consideration' and 'revised procedures for 1997 will incorporate improvements', but also noted the 'settled law' aspect referred to above. At the time of going to press the latest development is that Dr Evans has also taken the matter of her non-promotion to an industrial tribunal, and the University Chancellor (Prince Philip, Duke of Edinburgh) has appointed a retired Lord Justice to investigate certain allegations made by Dr Evans against the Cambridge Vice-Chancellor. It will be noted from Chapter 8 and the Bibliographical Essay that, being a civil corporation, Cambridge is believed to have no Visitor: hence the Lord Justice will presumably be acting in a quasi-Visitor role (will his report be published as was that of the University College, Swansea Visitor? – Davies, 1994).

The US perspective on academic freedom

Kaplin and Lee (1995a) argue that academic freedom is difficult to define: 'The concept of academic freedom eludes precise definition.' It applies to individual academics in their relationship with the HEI and to the relationship between HEIs and the State. These two aspects may end up in conflict. For example, one 1990 US case involved an academic refusing on grounds of academic freedom to apply the HEI's standardized course evaluation forms to her classes. The courts held that:

> she has no right to evidence her disagreement [with the HEI] by failing to perform the duty imposed upon her as a condition of employment [since the HEI's requirement was] unrelated to course content [and] in no way interferes with . . . academic freedom [and anyway the use of such teacher evaluation] *is part of the University's own right to academic freedom.*
>
> (Kaplin and Lee, 1995a: 420, emphasis added)

The US Supreme Court has generated via case law some degree of protection for academic freedom as a recognized concept in constitutional terms (see the short reference to academic freedom in the ERA 1988 as inserted during debate in the Lords, thanks to Lord Beloff, Lord Jenkins and others, and the lack of UK litigation/case law to date).

The US courts do not interpret 'academic freedom to be a licence for uncontrolled expression at variance with the established curricular contents and internally destructive of the proper functioning of the institution' (a 1972 case quoted in Kaplin and Lee, 1995a). In short, in terms of pedagogy, academics must operate within a management hierarchy. That element of their job is like any other (a 1991 case noted that 'The University's conclusions about course content must be allowed to hold sway over an individual professor's judgements'). Hence the management of an HEI is not able to tell an academic to increase or decrease a mark or grade awarded to student X or Y. That would be violation of academic freedom, a challenge to the academic's professional judgement. However, the HEI's management can *itself* change the grade!

Academic freedom in the context of research and publications, as opposed to curricular content and style, is a more clear-cut matter in US law: 'The classroom is the arena where institutional authority is greatest and courts are most hesitant to enter. Research and publication is the arena where the institution is likely to have least authority' (Kaplin and Lee, 1995a: 328).

Scope

This chapter concerns itself principally with the operation of HEI disciplinary procedures, largely in relation to the student body, although staff discipline is also addressed where relevant to the immediate regulatory theme of the chapter. The regulation of the HEI community involves consideration of the basic relationships between students and/or staff on the one hand and the HEI on the other. However, the probably contractual nature of the HEI–student relationship is the subject of Chapter 6, and the peculiar characteristics of the HEI–staff relationship, whether based on technical issues of membership of a corporate body, the contract of employment or the particular colour given to that contractual relationship by developments particular to the sector (e.g. the 'model statute' and the role of the University Commissioners under the ERA 1988), are outside the ambit of this chapter. It is concerned with the disciplinary jurisdiction and the theory and practice of disciplinary procedures, and is rooted in a discussion of the continuing significance (if any) of the notion of an HEI community.

Why is it an important subject?

In his interesting article on the exercise of university disciplinary powers, Whincup (1993) presented his discussion in the context of an examination of changing social standards over the past 20 or 30 years and seemed to take the view that the changing nature of disciplinary issues between the HEI and the student could usefully be related to the changing social environment, within higher education (HE) and at large. He identified a decline in litigation between universities and their students over a period of time and tentatively attributed this to (*inter alia*) 'some greater appreciation amongst students of their own relatively favoured position in society as compared with that of their many unemployed and poverty-stricken contemporaries who have not had the opportunity of higher education'. He identified the subjects of such litigation as having changed from what he described as 'abstract or cosmic grievances' to more mundane concerns about rooms, rents and jobs.

The timing of his article is illuminating. So are

- the rapid changes in recent years in the constituency of the student body;
- the increase in the number of international students who may be relatively unfamiliar with UK society and the social and cultural preconceptions traditionally underlying its HE system;
- the increase in the numbers of mature students, many of whom may perceive that they combine prior experience of living in the real world with significant financial sacrifice and/or risk in undertaking HE study;
- the changing shape and methodology of structural organization in HE;
- the developing (consumeristic?) concept of the student as customer;
- changing patterns of educational service delivery, stressing greater access, modularity, flexibility, credit transfer, remote study, etc.;
- the rise of 'league tables' and other forms of competitive bench-marking;
- the growing reliance of HEIs on both capital and revenue funding from sources other than the public purse;
- the tendency on the part of so many HEIs to evolve a self-image which deliberately places them in a relationship of active interdependence with a whole range of social and economic constituencies (see almost any university mission statement for the late-1990s).

Many of the traditional principles of the academic world have been based on its organization into structures which are partially closed communities, substantially self-validating in a variety of ways. The previously fashionable conception of HE as a privilege is itself suggestive of access to a world in many ways removed from society at large. This comfortable notion has been supported by the development of (*inter alia*) disciplinary and other regulatory mechanisms largely independent from the corresponding action of society at large, as expressed through the operation of the law courts as the principal mechanism for ordering formal dispute. It has been all very well for High Court judges to insist that 'there shall be no Alsatia in England where the King's writ does not run' (*Czarnikow v Roth, Schmidt and Co.*), but by and large, for more than half a century after that pronouncement, HEIs (in the form of chartered universities) were able readily to defend the privacy and exclusivity of jurisdiction conferred through private charitable foundation by the use of the university Visitor as the final and essentially internal Court of Appeal for disputes of most kinds arising within the university. The public courts have been reluctant to accept challenges to this matrix of extended self-regulation except on the most limited grounds (see *Thomas v University of Bradford* and *R v HM The Queen in Council*, ex p *Vijayatunga*).

Half the HEIs in the sector these days, however, do not enjoy the privilege of such overtly private jurisdiction. Although the world of local authority activity and procedures has always had a logic all its own, it has historically been subject to multi-faceted challenge in the courts. Of course, the Higher Education Corporations founded under the ERA 1988 have departed from the aegis of their former local authority masters, but historically and culturally that is where they came from, and this has left many and varied marks on their cultures. Even for the chartered universities, the operations (based in public statute law) of the University Commissioners under the ERA 1988 have significantly restricted the jurisdiction of the Visitor and have placed areas of HEI operation uneasily in proximity to the quite distinct mechanisms (e.g. industrial tribunals) used by society at large to regulate corresponding activity. More recently, the judicial mauling of King's College, London which resulted in the Report by Zellick (1994) has caused something of a crisis of self-confidence among university managers as regards the competence of their private disciplinary systems to address some of the more extreme forms of student behaviour and the second Nolan Report (1996) has actually recommended the institution of an independent arbitrator as a last port of call for the determination of disputes for HEIs which do not boast a Visitor. In some ways, this may appear a victory for the concept of a 'Super Visitor', and a promising (for conservatives) indication that disputes within HEIs should be settled by an office or service. Some will see this as aping the private jurisdiction, with a promise of avoiding extensive, costly and high profile exposure to the Courts. However, if this proposal were to be adopted, it would have its origins in public statute law and would not emanate from individual private foundations. Alternative dispute resolution, it is suggested, is not a hallmark of a quasi-Alsatia. At every turn, it seems, one may find evidence of the partially-closed and largely self-regulatory community being placed in closer proximity to the public law and legislators. The extent to which, if at all, the academic community at HE level can regulate itself more or less conclusively is being called seriously into question. That must have significant implications for both the design and the operation of the principal emanations of internal regulatory systems, in particular disciplinary and related codes.

Participation in a partially closed community

Whincup (1993) seemed to think that litigation between universities and their students was becoming increasingly uncommon. In my experience this is unlikely, rather the reverse is true. Indeed, irrespective of the number of proceedings issued in the courts, the climate within which those operating HE internal regulatory mechanisms are required to work is becoming increasingly contentious and, prospectively, very much more litigious. When a senior university manager (which she has done recently) volunteers the information that she receives two threats of litigation per week throughout the year, either from students or staff, it may be dangerous to assume that these are merely the untypical fruits of success of a controversial and expansionist HEI.

Staff have contracts of employment. Students probably (it is suggested elsewhere in this book, see Chapter 6) also have a contractual relationship with the HEI. In the case of chartered universities, the contractual matrix is complicated by the status of most staff and students as 'members' of the university. Generally, chartered HEIs also have Visitors. However, the distinction (for disciplinary purposes) between chartered and statutory universities seems of marginal relevance. Membership of a university (where that applies) may facilitate the establishment of *locus standi* for certain procedural purposes, but, having regard to the rise during the 1990s of 'charterism' (arguably an emanation of consumerism from which HE has by no means escaped), it would seem that in the sector generally:

- HEIs acknowledge more than ever before in their day-to-day operations that they take their place in and owe responsibilities to society at large;
- the underlying general social thrust (encouraged by the Government and supported where necessary by legislative action) seems to be towards asserting that almost any constituency of any kind may have either a contract or at least a compact of some description with virtually every other relevant constituency.

Seeking to regulate an interactive and, hopefully, common interest grouping substantially by internal means requires the clearest possible prior thought about how the community is to be defined. Looking at the full range of activities of members of its community, the HEI has to decide:

- what is and is not its business;
- how it is to establish parameters of behaviour by members of or participators in a partially closed community;
- on what precepts this and the disciplinary exercises which flow from it are to be based;
- accordingly, what sorts and degrees of behaviour will be found unacceptable and in what contexts;
- the relative gravity with which the HEI will regard those sorts and degrees of behaviour.

In this respect, there may be lessons to be learnt from current judicial fashion. Some recent experiences indicate that outsiders (for example, the courts and Visitors) have an unnerving habit of taking a narrow and exclusive view of offences as listed in disciplinary regulations, being inclined to extend the list to cover marginal behaviour only under the *eiusdem generis* rule even where the list of offences in the regulations is expressly offered only on an exemplary basis.

One approach which can be adopted in revising lists of offences is to offer a conceptual focus. In Appendix VI to his report, Zellick (1994) offers a definition of the essence of 'misconduct' and lists a series of actions which would constitute misconduct. Some of these (for example, 'behaviour which brings the University into disrepute') have a strong interpretative element which in practice could involve a significant degree of subjectivity in the classification of particular acts. That in itself is certainly not a reason to exclude such general definitions. However, it will require some cultural self-confidence on the part of the HEI to elucidate such a general definition with consistency and success (and the former may well be the key to the latter), usually on the basis of custom and practice. Interestingly, Zellick's misconduct list is not offered as including only examples. Instead, the types of activity listed are placed in the context of earlier paragraphs in the Appendix, which offers an express generic definition of the essence of misconduct as it affects 'the proper functioning or activities' of the HEI and the draftsman goes on to discuss the purpose of the disciplinary code and its status. In future, it is suggested, taking such an approach is likely to be safer than merely offering a non-exhaustive list of what are expressly identified only as examples. Serious consideration should be given to the incorporation of a preliminary statement of regulatory principles (of which Zellick's formulation is an example) as a preamble to all disciplinary and other behavioural and regulatory codes.

The (persuasive) logic of this argument is that the viability of any self-regulating system is better served if it is built on a clear and open explanatory platform rather than merely proceeding by unilateral assertion. That is because the operation of internal disciplinary procedures will be more defensible in an outside forum (in the event of legal challenge) if the person who is the subject of disciplinary proceedings cannot reasonably argue that the (reasonable) principles underlying the disciplinary regime were not drawn to his or her attention upon entry into the community. Instead, any behaviour which might attract disciplinary proceedings will have been generically identified and its unacceptability appropriately contextualized and explained.

Forms of regulation

It is suggested that it will be sensible for any HEI, as and when time permits, to review all relevant codifications of behaviour, from the general and fundamental to the most specific. Ideally, an HEI should be confident that it has rendered consistent in its conception and operation all codes touching upon the regulatory exercise and to varying degrees governing it, as well as examining the ways in which the different codes affect each other, actually or potentially. These may include the HEI's general regulations, its academic and/or examination regulations, disciplinary codes, harassment codes, complaints and grievance procedures, localized or partial rules (those relating to the activities of the students' union, the library, access to and use of the Internet, and so on), residence regulations, charters, contracts of employment and teaching and learning 'contracts', where these exist (see the model in Farrington, 1994: 378).

Is a charter a form of regulation? Following on from the argument that anything which does or could introduce even a general statement of intention and promise performance and mutual obligation might be capable of assuming quasi-contractual force, it seems sensible to examine even charter-style documents as forming part of the matrix of mutual promises about performance and behaviour which touch on (even if they do not legally govern) the totality of HEI–student relationships. (Documents which are not in themselves legally binding could conceivably be adduced as evidence of a tortious duty of care owed by an HEI to its students.)

Such a review would also need to contemplate the relationship between the internal regulatory matrix and outside rules or criteria for behaviour. For example, the HEI needs to be confident that it has considered and knows how to react to the ill-defined and frequently misunderstood relationship between internal disciplinary codes and the criminal law of the land. A major purpose of Zellick's report (1994) was to examine the nature of that relationship on the difficult cusp of more or less serious criminal activity by members of the HEI community. One common conceptual problem on which many HEIs frequently stub their toes is the issue of double jeopardy – Whincup (1993) is only one of several commentators who have illuminated this area helpfully.

Civil 'authorities' beyond the HEI, however, also have an important role in the activities of academic communities. For example, collaborative ventures (e.g. in vocational and professional education) between HEIs and outside bodies have an enormous potential to create disciplinary problems. There is now a variety of courses which have an academic content and are run principally from and by HEIs but which lead (in addition to an academic qualification) to some form of vocational certification enabling the student to practise professionally after graduation. There is an inherent duality in such courses and qualifications. The HEI may be concerned to test the student academically and to procure the student's acceptable behaviour in the context of its own community. The outside body may necessarily have as part of its agenda assessment and arrival at a judgement in relation to the fitness to practise (after qualification) of the student and will have its own approach to the determination of appropriate and inappropriate behaviour or character. That approach may not square with the educational agenda and societal self-image of the HEI. If the partnership (between the HEI and the outside authority or agency) which runs and examines the course is not founded on the clearest possible constitutional and operational framework, then when there are differences of opinion as to the acceptability and 'triability' of the student's behaviour, there may be potentially insurmountable investigative and procedural difficulties for both partners in addressing issues of possible student misconduct. Unfortunately, recent experience suggests that such partnerships are frequently not thought through before they are launched and may have the flimsiest of legal bases for what is essentially contractual activity and will undoubtedly potentially have a disciplinary dimension (for more on franchising, see Chapter 14).

In paragraph 37 of his report, Zellick has some constructive proposals (which every HEI should at least examine) as to the working relationships between different disciplinary regimes within the HEI.

Private/public law

The HEI–staff relationship is principally expressly contractual. It is suggested that the better view is that the HEI–student relationship is principally expressly and/or impliedly contractual. Contracts may be a matter of private law. However, most HEIs are either incorporated under public statute law or, if they originate as private charitable foundations, operate in the public domain to a considerable extent. Most HEIs are charities and true charitable objects require a significant element of public benefit for such organizations as these.

As Whincup (1993) points out, 'in a dispute over a contract, the rules of public law may require more than mere compliance with its terms; they may also require compliance with the requirements of "natural justice" '. What are the requirements of natural justice? A working paraphrase might embrace:

- the right of every person to know the nature of the charge made against him or her;
- the right of every person to have a proper chance to put his or her case;
- the conspicuous absence of bias or prejudice in the operation of the system set up to arrive at a judgement.

In HEIs we see a system for the administration of justice in a partially closed community. This operates in the context of investigative and judicial procedures which will unavoidably fall short of the full rigour of the publicly administered law and its tribunals. Nowadays, and for the foreseeable future, the wider context is provided by the articulation (by the Nolan Committee) of the primacy of principles of public life which include transparency, probity and accountability. That these are (without argument) taken to apply to HEIs is rather obviously confirmed by the express focus of the second Nolan report on (*inter alia*) higher and further education – under the generic heading of 'local public spending bodies'.

Against this background, rendering HEI disciplinary and other self-regulatory procedures consistently defensible against attack in the public courts makes it absolutely essential that the principles of natural justice are built into the design of the system and actively observed in its operation. If this is done, HEIs should not suffer failures of nerve when they contemplate that they do not have the equipment to mimic the public criminal or even civil courts, either procedurally or evidentially. There should be no embarrassment over the design and operation of simple or at least readily comprehensible and expeditious procedures as long as, in both their design and their application, they are not only fair but conspicuously so. This is the best, and in the longer term perhaps the only, way in which the elements of a private jurisdiction at work can expect consistently to survive examination in the courts. Thirty years after the instigation of industrial tribunals, any sensible employer would recognize this principle, embrace it, and order its affairs accordingly. Although there are special circumstances peculiar to HE (it is suggested that these are neither as extensive nor as special as some in HE would think or like), it is difficult to understand why HE administrators should not take confidence from this analogy.

Academic freedom

One of the more obvious examples of special pleading as to the peculiarity of HE is the clarion call in defence of 'academic freedom'. It is not suggested that academic freedom is a ruse or a spurious invention. On the contrary, it now has statutory recognition. Unless academic freedom is recognized and consistently cherished, the conceptual independence and a large part of the purpose of HE is lost. It is, however, important for those who wish to enjoy academic freedom to acknowledge that it is precisely a species of freedom and not of licence – and to act accordingly. Like many so-called freedoms, it arguably represents a privilege and certainly brings with it concomitant responsibilities. There have been isolated cases in which regulatory procedures have been abused to repress criticism of institutional standards, practices and management. From experience, there have been far more incidences of, for example, members of HEI communities assuming that 'academic freedom' will provide a water-tight defence to disciplinary proceedings arising from the issuing of defamatory material via printed or electronic publishing media of which HEIs are the proprietors or in which they will otherwise be legally implicated. To require community members who wish to express controversial opinions to do so with discretion and a sense of their privileges and responsibilities towards the community is not to attack academic freedom. It is, of course, just as important in this as in many other operational areas that HEI administrators should not suffer from failures of nerve and should be capable of seeing the wood for the trees.

Quo vadis

Unfortunately, it seems almost inevitable that where we are going from here is to judicial review, to actions for breach of contract and/or 'educational negligence' in the County and/or High Courts, and to the Visitor or to whatever generically equivalent independent arbitration agency may be legislated into existence for statutory corporations (see Chapters 8 and 9). The way forward is to establish appropriate contractual, substantive and procedural platforms, to render their operation more even-handed and consistent, and to understand and embrace the rules of natural justice and the relevant principles articulated by Nolan (1995). The quasi-private jurisdiction will not survive if it is secretive or inaccessible. A side effect of Nolan is probably also that custom and practice, historically so vital in the operation of closed or partially closed communities, will diminish in importance unless it is consistently and properly documented. Those administering disciplinary and other self-regulatory systems will increasingly have to leave a defensible paper trail to document the conspicuous underlying fairness of their activities. This is a task which may demand a lot of management time, but it is likely to improve institutional self-confidence and save more time and much money in the longer term. Attacking the issue in this way may prove the best form of defence of the viability of any kind of private jurisdiction. Elsewhere in the education sector, there are beginning to appear encouraging signs of judicial recognition of the primacy of the administrative exercise – maintaining the smooth running of a well-ordered institution in the interests of all its participators – in the judicial review of internal disciplinary procedures and proceedings (see *R v Camden London Borough Council*, ex p *H. (a minor)*, *The Times*, 15 August 1996, as discussed also in *Education Law Monitor*, 1996, 3 [10]).

Practical pointers

The following are in no particular order.

1. However great the temptation, do not change either the rules or the procedures to fit the situation. In so many potentially disciplinary circumstances, it is so easy to see that setting about investigation, prosecution or judgement in some way slightly or wholly different from that prescribed by the HEI's own existing rule-book seems much more sensible and fairer to all parties. The temptation is striking. It is also a most widespread and fundamental procedural trap, into which HEI managements still fall with dismaying regularity.
2. Giving reasons for a judicial determination will render the process of forming judgement more transparent. To that extent, it may be more defensible against attack in some other tribunal. However, it may also display the partiality of the internal tribunal or its inability to come to grips with all salient factors in the case. It is at least equally attractive (frequently, more so) for a stated determination to identify those features of the case to which the judges had had regard and those which have been disregarded or allowed a relatively lesser importance.

3. Accommodate public law concerns as far as you can within the limitations of your private/internal procedures and be conspicuously fair (an understanding of most reliable articulations of the rules of natural justice is a good starting point).
4. Be as procedurally bombproof in practical terms as you can (e.g. in ensuring that the regulations are not designed in such a way that the type and severity of the ultimate punishment can be seen to determine which procedure will apply to the investigation and prosecution of the case). Pay particular attention to the classification and description of offences. Make provision for the tribunal proceeding in the absence of the accused. Make provision for reasonable adjournments in appropriate circumstances. Ensure, where you can, clarity of interpretation. For example, in your HEI, what does the phrase 'may be accompanied by a friend' actually mean? Does it always mean the same thing? Can the 'friend' be a solicitor? Probably, the HEI may be obliged to concede, 'yes' (see Harris, 1995: 177–81, re 'the McKenzie Friend' and the 'right' to legal representation if the charge is serious enough. For example, the difference between a fine for a student's minor misdemeanour and the possibility of being expelled for a grave offence.)
5. Think about the operational flexibility your whole regulatory matrix gives you. For example, your constitutional documents may empower someone (perhaps the Vice-Chancellor) to suspend. Why? What does suspension mean? What can it mean? Could it be construed as punishment or is it clear that it is not prejudicial but merely a neutral management operation to preserve the viability of the HEI's activities until decisions can be made about whether or to what extent disciplinary procedures shall apply? What is the mechanism and what are its consequences? Are they flexible enough? Is 'partial' suspension possible? May conditions on use of facilities (for example) be imposed? Are both finite and infinite (in time) suspensions constitutionally permissible? Is there a mechanism for reviewing suspension?
6. Do not confuse the internal tribunal's judicial function with the prosecuting function of the management. Both represent the HEI, but in different ways. The efficacy of internal tribunals is recognized and so the fact that the HEI has this dual function is certainly not fatal, but it is compromised if one function is to any degree procedurally confused with or tainted by the other. If the Registrar is to be Chief Prosecutor, then he or she clearly cannot also be Secretary to the tribunal.
7. Make sure that the management case is thoroughly prepared. Problems frequently arise because those preparing to present the management case either cannot or will not think with sufficient rigour and from the most basic propositions about how the case is to be built, evidenced and argued. It has been known to be fatal to assume that the tribunal's collective knowledge and experience is the same as that of the HEI management, let alone that the managers' cultural preconceptions about

the type of behavioural issue under consideration are shared individually or collectively by the tribunal members.

8. Make sure that the tribunal is clear about its remit, procedures and possible findings. If this involves obtaining genuinely independent advice for the tribunal (as distinct from advice required by the management), do it. Many a good management case has foundered on the jurisdictional or procedural confusion of the tribunal members, however individually gifted or wise they may be as academics.

9. Be clear about the relationship between your different behavioural regulations/codes and their operation in practice.

10. Above all, try always to distinguish between the interests and protection of the HEI community and (on the one hand) those of society at large and (on the other hand) private disputes. This is rarely a straightforward precept to apply in practice. It is also, however, absolutely essential to preserve the integrity and viability of disciplinary codes in organizations which hope to maintain a large measure of self-regulation. In aspiring to effect such regulation, the HEI and its managers wish to do justice and to see justice done by its and their own lights, but above all the mechanisms are in place for, and should be animated with a view to, the defence of the interests of the whole of the HEI community and the preservation of its continuing operational viability.

Further reading

Cane, P. (1996) *Introduction to Administrative Law*. Oxford: Oxford University Press.

CUC (1997) *Advice on Whistleblowing*. Bristol: CUC.

Dearing (1997) *Higher Education in the Learning Society*. London: HMSO. (Paragraphs 15.2 to 15.68 of the main report, pp. 236–47.)

Evans, G. R. (1996) *Raising Concerns and Handling the Consequences in Further and Higher Education: A Handbook*. London: Council for Academic Freedom and Academic Standards.

Farrington, D. J. (1994) *The Law of Higher Education*. London: Butterworths.

Furmston, M. P. (1992) *Universities and Disclaimers of Liability*. London: CVCP N/92/112.

Galligan, D. J. (1996) *Due Process and Fair Procedures*. Oxford: Oxford University Press.

Harris, B. (1995) *Disciplinary and Regulatory Proceedings*. Chichester: Barry Rose.

Holloway, J. (1994) 'The rights of individuals who receive a defective education', *Education and the Law*, 6(2), 207–19.

Lewis, C. B. (1983) The legal nature of a university and the student-university relationship, *Ottawa Law Review*, 3(1), 77–92.

Lewis, C. B. (1985) 'Procedural fairness and university students: England and Canada compared', *The Dalhousie Law Journal*, 7(2), 49–63.

Parlour, J. W. and Burwood, L. R. V. (1995) 'Students' rights', *Education and the Law*, 1, 7(2), 63–78.

Wade, H. W. R. and Forsyth, C. F. (1994) *Administrative Law.* Oxford: Oxford University Press.

Whincup, M. H. (1993) 'The exercise of university disciplinary powers'. *Education and the Law,* 5(1), 19–31.

Zellick, G. (1994) *Final Report of the Task Force on Student Disciplinary Procedures.* London: CVCP.

8

Disputes I: the Role of the Visitor in the Chartered Institutions

David Isaac (Cole and Cole)

Editors' introduction

If the procedures within a chartered university – as opposed to a statutory university or a college of HE (higher education) fail to resolve a dispute between a member of the university (a student, an academic and certain senior managers and librarians, but not other employees) and the institution, then the role of the Visitor can be invoked for all disputes relating to the internal rules (except certain disputes concerning the contract of employment for academic staff).

What is a Visitor? What jurisdiction and powers does he or she have? Is there an overlap between the jurisdiction and powers of the Visitor and the normal role of the courts in relation to the contract between the student and the chartered university? How does the university or, indeed, the aggrieved student, actually make contact with the Visitor? If the Visitor is the Queen (or some other great dignitary), who will actually handle the matter on her behalf? What does it cost to have the Visitor visit? Can the Visitor award damages? Is there any appeal against the decision of the Visitor? This chapter explores all these issues and notes the recommendation of the Nolan Committee (1996) that:

> Students in higher education institutions should be able to appeal to an independent body, and this right should be reflected in the Higher Education Charters. The higher education funding councils, institutions, and representative bodies should consult on a system of independent review of disputes

> (Nolan, 1996: 28)

The question arises whether a revised Visitor model would meet with approval from Nolan, both for continued use in the chartered HEIs (higher education institutions) and for extending to the statutory HEIs.

There are many Visitor cases from the eighteenth and nineteenth centuries, mainly in relation to Oxbridge colleges (**Note**: not in the University of Oxford or the University of Cambridge, neither of which, unusually amongst the 'old' universities, have a Visitor: but see 'A Bibliographical Essay on the Visitor', for a discussion of whether Oxford and Cambridge do or do not have a Visitor.) In addition, there are a few rather famous recent ones, including the only one which has ever been widely published (Davies, 1994). Here the Visitor, on behalf of the Queen, was Sir Michael Davies, a retired High Court judge, who produced a superb report which silenced five years of squabbling at University College, Swansea, and which superseded several earlier enquiries (and all at a cost of several hundred thousand pounds). It is noted from the *Times Higher* (31 October 1997) that a postgraduate student at UEA (University of East Anglia) has been granted £1000 from the NUS (National Union of Students) to help him take a case for damages against the university to its Visitor. As discussed in this chapter there has been doubt whether the Visitor can award damages, but it is now clear that damages can be awarded (see the bibliographical essay and *Thomas v University of Bradford*) and perhaps aggrieved students will increasingly seek them in the content of becoming personally liable for tuition fees post-Dearing.)

The legal oddity of the visitorial function is interesting. It is an area of law left over from the canon law and the Middle Ages (like a Consistory Court or a Court of Chivalry) and, as such, only in very limited circumstances does the ordinary court exercise a supervisory check on the Visitor via the mechanism of judicial review. The Visitor cannot be challenged on the ground of error of fact or even of law – only where he or she has acted outside the Visitor's jurisdiction (e.g. no power under the university statutes to be involved, behaving contrary to the rules of natural justice or if refusing to act when clearly the Visitor should). Similarly, there is no appeal beyond the Visitor – the visitorial court is the *forum domesticum* of the university (Farrington, 1994, quotes one case referring to the Visitor having 'untrammelled power to investigate and right wrongs arising from the application of the domestic laws of the chartered institution' and sums the role up as 'an Ombudsman with teeth'). Williams (1910) quotes Lord Camden, remarking of the Visitor function in an eighteenth-century case: 'a despotism uncontrolled and without appeal, the only one of the kind existing in the kingdom'.

The author of this chapter concludes by putting forward an innovative elaboration of the visitorial system which could be used by all HEIs, statutory and chartered. This is a matter for consideration and debate and there is some doubt as to the virtues of extending the system, even in this modified form. Perhaps, however, some kind of unified system will emerge as a result of the Nolan Committee's interest in HE or as a follow-on from any post-Dearing-style 'marketization' of UK HE which leaves the Government feeling that the student needs consumer protection in a competitive marketplace. One notes in the USA the existence at many HEIs of the entity known as the 'Ombudsman of the University' to whom students and staff can complain.

The Visitor is alive and well in English and Welsh chartered HEIs, and also in Australia, New Zealand, Canada, but is, of course, missing in the statutory HEIs, in Scotland's HEIs, and in the USA: where the Visitor is not to be found, there is usually discussion of whether something similar should be created. A bibliographical essay on the Visitor by David Palfreyman, at the end of this book, reviews the literature and key cases.

Introduction

The Visitor has traditionally provided an important forum for independent scrutiny in Oxbridge colleges and chartered universities. Statutory limitations have now been imposed on the role and criticisms of the concept have increased. Lord Nolan (1996) has also commented on the role of the Visitor in HEIs in his investigation of standards in public life (1996). It is timely, therefore, to ask whether or not the visitorial concept is worth maintaining in HE.

In this chapter it is hoped to show that despite some drawbacks in the way in which the visitorial process currently operates, the concept of the Visitor is one that has significant advantages for universities, which could be developed for all HEIs. Frequent reference is made to 'universities', by which is meant all chartered universities and, perhaps unusually, the term is also used to include Oxbridge colleges, all of which have a Visitor.

Background

The concept of the Visitor is an unusual one and has its origins in Canon Law (see Picarda, 1995: Chapter 41). A Visitor is a person who has domestic judicial authority over 'eleemosynary, lay, and ecclesiastical corporations for the correction of the life and conduct of the members and the adjudication of disputes between them' (Mitcheson, 1887). In practice, Visitors have a role principally in religious and educational contexts. The theoretical justification for the appointment of a Visitor has always been that the founder of an institution should have the authority to determine disputes arising within that institution.

The precise identity of the Visitor varies from institution to institution. It is frequently the case that the Visitor is The Queen or the Archbishop of Canterbury or some other lay person, in which case a Commissary will be appointed to act in her or his place. Indeed, unless the Visitor is a lawyer, and one with sufficient time and inclination, a Commissary will almost invariably be appointed to undertake the task. Such a Commissary will usually be a QC or perhaps a retired judge. The precise role of each Visitor depends very much on the institution concerned and its instrument of government, which usually sets out the identity of the Visitor, the terms on which matters must be referred to him or her, and his or her visitorial rights.

Instruments of government usually provide that any domestic issue (i.e. one which relates to internal university management, abuses of management or other conduct concerning the government of the university) should be adjudicated by the Visitor. As a result, disputes about the running of the university and grievances raised by members of the university (from the Vice-Chancellor and lecturers to any student) must be referred to the Visitor. If an internal grievance procedure exists, a complainant must usually exhaust this route first. If a complaint is referred in this way, the Visitor will determine how the matter is to proceed and, if it cannot be settled, he or she will be required to hear the case.

The Education Reform Act (ERA) 1988, Section 206, has diminished the role of the Visitor insofar as employment matters are concerned, because any dispute relating to the appointment, employment or termination of academic staff is deemed to be outside his or her jurisdiction. The rationale for this was to allow academic freedom (by providing for access to the Courts), but this change has significantly reduced the arena in which the Visitor can operate.

What are the benefits of the visitorial system?

Sir Robert Megarry identified many of the advantages of visitorial proceedings in *Patel v University of Bradford Senate*, primarily informality, privacy, reduced expense and the finality of any decision given. Many of Sir Robert's observations are still relevant today. The following are the principal benefits of the visitorial system.

Informality

A member of a university who has exhausted any relevant internal grievance procedures can still ask that a matter be referred to the Visitor by lodging a complaint. It is unusual for a fixed procedure to exist. On the appointment of the Visitor, the complainant will be asked to set out his or her case in writing and the university will have an opportunity to respond. Rarely do further exchanges take place on paper. The next stage is for a hearing to be fixed and this usually takes place at the university. This relatively simple procedure tends to make for considerable informality, even if the involvement of lawyers does sometimes tend to encourage increasingly formal pleadings. Every Visitor conducts cases differently, but proceedings are always held in private and are generally less formal than court hearings. The fact that complainants do sometimes appear in person encourages this approach.

Reduced cost

A direct consequence of the relative informality of the visitorial system is a reduction in costs for all concerned. This is due to the fact that cases tend to be heard faster than in legal proceedings and that preliminary hearings rarely take place. As a result, the risk of running up large legal and other costs is reduced. This is good news for universities as they invariably meet the fees of the Visitor and all other costs attached to the hearing. The Visitor does have the power to award costs and damages against a party. Despite the rarity of this actually happening, this fact can be a disincentive to staff or student complainants for whom such an award would result in financial disaster. Nevertheless, such a possibility may discourage frivolous claims.

Speed

It is undeniable that, if a matter can be brought to a hearing with fewer procedural requirements, it will inevitably be adjudicated faster. As a result, visitorial proceedings are speedy when compared to the hearing of a non-urgent case in the High Court. Delays, of course, sometimes occur even in visitorial proceedings. Depending on the identity of the Visitor or his Commissary, fixing a date can be far from easy. Demands on the time of a high-profile Visitor (or, indeed, a high-profile Commissary) often result in the deferment of cases. The complexity of a case, the volume of papers and a large number of witnesses can also make it difficult to fix an early date. Such difficulties, however, are minor compared to the fact that it may take at least two years before a case is brought to trial in the High Court (for more on the process of litigation, see Chapter 20).

Privacy

There is no doubt that the fact that visitorial hearings are in private does encourage greater confidence on the part of the complainant. Not only is the risk of adverse publicity removed, but a complainant may feel that he or she can air grievances in a way which would not be possible in a public arena. The only drawback is that, since the results of Visitor hearings are rarely (if ever) published, there is potential for inconsistency between hearings – even in the same university. Hence, the noteworthy publication of the Visitor's report relating to an enquiry at University College, Swansea (Davies, 1994).

Impartiality

The fact that an internal hearing provides the opportunity for adjudication by someone completely removed from the running of a university is a unique feature of the visitorial system. This aspect, more than any other, does generate great confidence in the forum provided by the Visitor. Although Visitors are sometimes criticized for being too partial to the administration of a university, this criticism is usually unfounded as Visitors are all too keen not to be identified with the institution.

Finality of the decision

Another feature that is unique to the visitorial system is the fact that there is no right of appeal. Unless a Visitor exceeds his or her power, a decision given by a Visitor is final and cannot be challenged. This situation reinforces the speediness of the decision-making process and generally inspires greater confidence. It also ensures that long-term disruption in the life of the university is kept to a minimum.

A useful resource

In addition to the points already given, there is one further advantage which is presented by the role of the Visitor. This arises because a Visitor can provide a useful resource to a university by adjudicating informally on points of interpretation or areas of uncertainty even if they are not central to a live dispute. A Visitor can be in an excellent position to determine uncertainties arising over the meaning of a statute. He or she can also be used as an arbitrator when members of a university (including the governing body) cannot agree on a particular issue of importance when all other avenues have failed. This facility is often used by universities in practice.

Drawbacks to the visitorial process

Notwithstanding the benefits just described, there are some problems in the way in which many visitorial proceedings are processed and heard. The most significant are as follows.

Jurisdiction

Real problems can arise in identifying whether the Visitor actually has jurisdiction in a matter. Determining this issue alone can take many months, especially if it can be argued that the matter falls within areas that are now excluded under the ERA 1988. Problems have arisen as to whether a referral to the Visitor has occurred before the date on which recommended grievance and complaint procedures have been formally adopted. If the complaint was made before the 'relevant date' in the ERA 1988, Section 206(4), the Visitor should still have jurisdiction.

Other jurisdictional issues relate to whether or not a case falls squarely within those matters which are capable of being heard by the Visitor (which will depend on the instrument of government in question) or if an individual is eligible to bring a complaint. The latter issue has now been largely clarified as a result of 1980s case law. The reality, therefore, is that in some cases what will eventually be a very swift hearing can be delayed for some time until these matters are determined.

Procedural issues

Even if it has been agreed that the Visitor is to be involved in a complaint, important preliminary issues of procedure can often arise and must be determined. These usually relate to questions about the identity of the Visitor's Commissary (if the Visitor is not to sit him or herself), the form which the pleadings should take and whether or not there should be oral evidence. Frequently, the nature of a complaint is not entirely clear and it is essential that the Visitor or the advisors seek clarification from the complainant as to the precise nature of the matter in dispute. These matters can cause delays, which will hold up an early hearing date.

In some cases, there are so many procedural issues in dispute that it is necessary to hold a preliminary hearing or for a written judgement to be delivered by the Visitor on these issues alone. Disputes of this kind also arise between parties in the context of legal proceedings, but since legal procedures are more prescribed and well established, there is greater certainty in the procedural requirements demanded of the parties. Furthermore remedies exist when a party fails to heed directions.

Insufficient knowledge of the institution and HE

Although an historical connection often exists between a university and its Visitor, some Visitors do not have any particular knowledge of the institution in question. Such criticisms are made less frequently where a named individual is appointed to the post. Experience shows that these Visitors often build up an excellent knowledge of the institution, its personnel and its statutes. This is not always the experience of those universities who have Visitors appointed by virtue of their office. Invariably, these Visitors appoint Commissaries who have no connection at all with the institution and who vary from matter to matter.

As the issues within universities become more complex, some understanding of HE is an increasingly important requirement for a Visitor – particularly so when no other forum exists in which grievances can be properly aired. Indeed, one of the major criticisms made to the Nolan Committee by unions representing university teaching staff was that Visitors often lack an understanding of the increasingly commercial world in which academics are now required to function.

Inconsistency of decisions

As each visitorial case begins from scratch, without access to previous decisions, there is a risk that cases may be decided differently from earlier cases or that an instrument of government may be interpreted in a new manner. Decided case law relating to Visitors can provide some guidance, but the ultimate authority is always the Visitor (who has the potential to be very subjective). The private nature of the proceedings also means that there is no opportunity for a Visitor to create precedents to be used by other HEIs.

Preferred rights

Some opponents of the visitorial system base their criticisms on the fact that the very concept of the Visitor affords preferred rights to academics and students. Such critics argue that the existence of a quasi-judicial forum in HEIs epitomizes the unworldliness of universities. They are keen for HEIs to become as commercial as possible and believe that there should be no jurisdiction which governs the resolution of academic affairs other than the courts. To the extent that redress does not exist in law, a hearing should be denied.

What is the alternative to the visitorial system?

Before assessing whether or not visitorial proceedings should be abolished, it is interesting to compare the experience of the 'new' universities and designated institutions that came into existence under the ERA 1988 and the Further and Higher Education Act 1992. Neither category, as yet, has any formal concept of the Visitor.

Much depends upon the nature of the complaint that arises. The majority of claims are resolved by means of an internal disciplinary complaint under the terms of the university's disciplinary or complaints procedure. Such procedures usually provide for the board of governors to be the ultimate arbiter. If the problem is an employment-related issue, the ultimate forum will be an industrial tribunal. Other remedies available to students and members of staff alike are judicial review (although this is seldom used in relation to employment matters) and breach of contract claims in the County or High Courts. (For more on judicial review, see Chapter 9. For more on the HEI–student contract, see Chapter 6.) For those who cannot secure legal aid, the cost of funding actions in the High Court can be high. Save in the case of industrial tribunals, high costs make anything but threats to issue proceedings a virtual impossibility. In addition, delays in getting a matter to the High Court can be serious and the industrial tribunal can sometimes be a slow route. In all but the most extreme cases, matters are settled out of court.

So do the statutory universities and designated institutions have any greater problems in resolving internal disputes than other universities? In practice, matters are frequently resolved informally as a result of the intervention of the governing body. Only if that fails will the case end up in the public forum of the industrial tribunal or the County or High Courts. Problems of partiality do arise and often there can be disaffection amongst both the student and academic bodies because of the perceived lack of impartiality of the governing body. This fact alone has led some statutory universities to consider the appointment of a Visitor (or a person of similar standing) who would be able to determine internal disputes. The University of Teeside, for example, has appointed a Visitor to provide guidance for the university and advice to its board, and the University of Portsmouth has produced the concept of a Chancellor's Court. This deals head on with the difficulty that otherwise arises when the ultimate arbiter of internal disputes is the governing body or the Vice-Chancellor, both of whom are seen as part of the university management. The other major reason is the cost of legal proceedings. A cheaper and impartial system of review which reduces the necessity for legal proceedings must be in the interests of most HEIs.

Should the Visitor be abolished?

The current debate about the role of the Visitor is taking place against a background of increasing commercialization in the HE sector, at a time when fundamental questions are being asked about HE in general. Such developments will inevitably have some impact on the manner in which disputes are resolved in universities. On the commercial front, if students are required to pay for their education, they may demand more for their money, including greater rights of redress. In addition, as universities compete with one another for students and funds there may be additional incentives to provide effective dispute resolution procedures. Student charters may not in themselves be enough. In an increasingly litigious society, any alternative to legal action must generate confidence and be seen to work.

The ability to resolve matters without recourse to law is a desirable objective for many organizations – especially those which are run other than for profit. The concept of a non-legal external dispute resolution procedure is very valuable. Whilst the present operation of visitorial proceedings has some drawbacks, there are significant advantages in the concept which continue to make it desirable for universities to maintain the practice. The disadvantages are matters which can easily be overcome.

The Nolan Committee

In its investigations (Nolan, 1996) the Nolan Committee has turned its attention to HE and further education (FE). Among the areas of specific

examination were independent review and the resolution of disputes. In
this context, the Committee has considered the role of the Visitor in universities. Although stressing that the 'visitorial system of hearing appeals is not
by any means perfect', the Committee has recommended that it is 'essential
to look for a system of scrutiny that has a clearly-defined remit; involves
minimum cost; and deters malicious or vexatious complainants'. Nolan rejects
the idea of a full-time ombudsman, but does not recommend any particular
route forward: the National Audit Office has, however, recently supported
the concept of an HE/FE ombudsman. Instead, Nolan encourages institutions, representative bodies, and funding councils to cooperate on agreeing
a detailed solution. The report does refer to a specific suggestion made to
the Committee, which consists of the establishment of a standing panel
of senior persons experienced but no longer involved in education, from
which conciliators or arbitrators may be drawn. He also lays down a number of helpful guidelines. These are primarily to encourage conciliation, to
exclude personal grievances and employment related matters, and to focus
on maladministration and malpractice, academic standards and freedom.
With this impetus, it is clear that further consideration must be given to
establishing an appropriate independent forum which could be used by
all universities. Indeed, the CVCP (Committee of Vice-Chancellors and Principals) in its response to the second Nolan Report said that it would be
giving 'urgent attention' to the form and nature of the new mechanism to
be established – see the Committee of Vice-Chancellors and Principals
(CVCP, Press Release, 16 May 1996) and pp. 354–6.

A new model?

To encourage further debate about the means by which disputes in universities are to be resolved, the following matters are put forward for
consideration.

1. The identification of a group of potential HE commissioners – a group
   of eminent men and women (including lawyers) with experience of the
   HE field and of dealing with disputes, from whom each HEI could
   appoint a Commissioner when appropriate. (For example, Queen's University in Belfast amended its statutes in 1983 and has established a
   panel of four Visitors, including a lawyer and an academic.) A Commissioner would not be appointed for all time since different Commissioners would be experienced in different areas. As such, an HEI could
   take advantage of the different skills available and relevant to each case.
   It might also be possible to appoint both male and female representatives. Suitable training for all Commissioners would be desirable.
2. All existing avenues of internal complaint within an HEI should be
   exhausted before a referral to an external adjudicator is possible. If
   this route has been followed, the matter should always be within the

jurisdiction of the Commissioner, unless the issue does not relate to the HEI and its members and lies within the remit of another representative body.

3. Both the HEI and the complainant should have an opportunity to make representations on the appointment of a Commissioner to resolve a dispute. However, in the event that the parties cannot agree the chair of the Commissioners should decide.

4. The Commissioner should follow an established procedure for hearing and determining cases. The system should cover cases of maladministration and malpractice and questions of academic standards and freedom. It might include employment matters, since an effective dispute resolution procedure outside Industrial Tribunals and the Courts could deal adequately with most of the employment matters in HEIs and at considerably less cost.

5. Detailed rules should be set out in a model constitution, which would form an annex to each HEI's instrument of government. There should be an agreed form of complaint and a right to reply. Standard forms might be used. The emphasis in these procedural steps should be on clarity, informality and speed. A Commissioner should also have the right to dismiss frivolous or vexatious complaints.

6. Hearings should take place in private, but decided cases should be made public. This would establish a body of precedent which could help in the determination of disputes in other HEIs and provide an important means of sharing valuable experience.

7. There would be no right of appeal, although it might be difficult to exclude entirely the possibility of challenge in the form of judicial review proceedings if a Commissioner exceeds his or her powers.

8. Whenever possible, the Commissioner should act as a mediator and/or conciliator. The benefits of such a role were demonstrated by Sir Michael Davies when he acted as Visitor to the University College of Swansea (Davies, 1994). Nevertheless, it is clear from his report that no matter how hard a Visitor might try, it is sometimes impossible to achieve a negotiated settlement.

9. The cost of the Commissioner should be borne by the HEI. Depending on the time spent by the Commissioner, this might be significant. However, to demand that a complainant should contribute or run the risk of paying all the costs is a considerable deterrent. The disadvantages of vexatious and frivolous claims are outweighed by the provision of an accessible system which ensures the smooth running and good health of the HEI. In addition, there would be no right to award damages. The only exception to this might be in the arena of employment matters.

10. There should be an agreed timetable, specifying that issues in dispute should be determined quickly and, if possible, within three months of the complaint being lodged.

11. Commissioners could be used as a point of reference for the determination of issues with which the HEI needs assistance but which do

not amount to a dispute. The wisdom of a Commissioner could be a valuable sounding board for an HEI.

Conclusions

This chapter has sought to identify the benefits and some of the drawbacks which exist in the present role of the Visitor. While accepting that there are some aspects which cause difficulty, an independent forum for the adjudication of disputes in universities is a valuable one which should not be abandoned. The current manifestation of the concept in the form of the Visitor generally works well. Rather than being abolished, the visitorial system should be developed further and extended to all HEIs. On closer scrutiny, surprisingly few of its features are anachronistic. The majority of criticisms lie in practical considerations where new procedures and experienced personnel could straightforwardly minimize current problems. The debate has already recently moved on because of the recommendations of Lord Nolan (Nolan, 1996). Indeed, it will now move faster in the light of the CVCP's response to his report.

To contribute to this debate, a possible alternative model to the existing visitorial system has been proposed. These proposals might not satisfy all critics. Nevertheless, the model sets out some useful ideas based on practice in this area in an effort to establish an improved system. Its basis depends on the commitment of people with experience relevant to HE today. If the current debate results in an effective, economic and trusted dispute resolution procedure for all HEIs, it could improve morale, help and encourage committed staff and students, and create more time for teaching and research.

Further reading

Farrington, D. J. (1994) *The Law of Higher Education*. London: Butterworths.
Harris, B. (1995) *Disciplinary and Regulatory Proceedings*. Chichester: Barry Rose.
Picarda, H. (1995) *The Law and Practice Relating to Charities*. London: Butterworths.
Tudor on Charities (1995) London: Sweet & Maxwell.
(See also pages 340–60 of 'A Bibliographical Essay on the Visitor'.)

9

Disputes II: the Scope for Judicial Review in the Statutory Institutions

Paul Pharoah (Martineau Johnson)

Editors' introduction

The statutory universities and colleges of higher education (HE) do not have the Visitor as a means of dispute resolution (see Chapter 8). They rely on the courts to interpret the contract between the higher education institution (HEI) and its students or its staff (whether academics or other employees) (see Chapters 6 and 7). There are circumstances, however, when the law might be invoked by way of judicial review (JR), in order to clarify whether the HEI has fair and proper procedures, whether it is applying them in a reasonable way, whether it might be exceeding its powers (acting *ultra vires*), etc.

JR has become something of a growth industry in recent years, but, although more JR cases than ever before are being heard, many of them do not get the result the seeker of JR hoped for, and many other seekers of JR do not even get past the first hurdle of an initial hearing to decide whether there really is a case to be heard. Very few JR cases have yet involved HE disputes. The threat of JR is, therefore, like a dog's bark being worse than its bite. Yet JR is a 'heavy' and fast-moving legal process which can be used, or threatened, as an aid to concentrating the mind of an HEI as to whether it really does appreciate the legal position and feel secure in defending it.

This chapter explores the circumstances where JR might be sought of an HEI's actions (or even of its inactivity), the likely defences for the HEI, the possible remedies if the seeker of JR succeeds in persuading the court that something is wrong, the possible overlap with other kinds of court involvement and the very limited circumstances in which a chartered university (or even its Visitor) might be subject to JR.

Note the Nolan Committee's recommendation that:

> Students in higher education institutions should be able to appeal to an independent body, and this right should be reflected in the Higher

Education Charters. The higher education funding councils, institutions, and representative bodies should consult on a system of independent review of disputes.

(Nolan, 1996: 17)

This may mean the Visitor model (or something similar) is extended to statutory HEIs (see Chapter 8), although in January 1997, a Committee of Vice-Chancellors and Principals (CVCP) Working Group has come up with the concept of binding arbitration as a last resort for dealing with student complaints and appeals (CVCP, 1997). The National Union of Students' (NUS) immediate response was to oppose the idea, its President commenting that, 'In no other sector are people expected to make the kind of investment they make in higher education without having the ability to take legal action if necessary.' (See the section on 'The Visitor post-Nolan' in the bibliographical essay on the Visitor.)

From a US perspective Kaplin and Lee (1995a) note the difference in the USA between a *public* HEI (one that is funded by the State) and a *private* HEI. The former is like a UK statutory HEI, its actions are 'State action', are subject to control under relevant public law legislation concerning 'due process' (the rules of natural justice). The latter is like a chartered university in the UK (although, of course, a chartered university in the UK does receive public funding just like a UK statutory HEI). If, however, the US Government is so heavily involved in directly funding part of a private HEI's activities as perhaps to make the activity concerned *de facto* a publicly provided and funded operation, then the HEI may have to comply with relevant State law as if its actions were 'State action'. It has, in effect, become an extension of State bureaucracy for the purposes of providing State-subsidized academic programme X or Y, or whatever.

Introduction

This chapter gives an outline of the present scope and application of JR, with examples in the context of education where possible. It then considers the subject in relation to the statutory HEIs and their contractual relations, and finishes with some general points which are worth bearing in mind when administrative decisions are being made in order to make them as review-proof as possible. The application of judicial review to the visitorial jurisdiction in the chartered universities is dealt with in Chapter 6. This book does not cover JR in other parts of the educational system such as the funding councils, or educational institutions themselves other than HEIs established under the Education Reform Act (ERA) 1988.

Development of JR

The role of the courts in reviewing administrative acts and decisions has expanded very considerably during the last 30 years. JR is currently rather popular:

- with lawyers, as a burgeoning and glamorous area of work;
- with constitutionalists, or at least those who favour the curbing of executive power by the judges;
- with academics, turning out a growing volume of books and papers;
- with the public, as an effective method of enabling the 'little man' to question or overturn acts of powerful and often faceless public bodies.

Although almost all JR cases are dealt with by the High Court, the procedure is relatively straightforward. Oral evidence is not heard and, although major points of principle may be at stake, the form of application, affidavits in support or in response, and the judgements are often quite brief. Proceedings must be commenced promptly, and in any event within three months of the decision complained of, and may be concluded within a shorter timetable than for other litigation. Discovery and interlocutory proceedings are rare. There is an expeditious procedure for especially urgent cases. High profile cases, such as the Home Secretary's frequent appearances in the courts on issues involving immigration or homelessness, or heavy commercial matters such as Virgin's challenge to the award of the Channel 5 franchise, attract much publicity. This increases awareness of what JR can achieve and stimulates further recourse to the courts.

There were only 160 applications in 1974, but by 1994 the number had increased to 3208, 'although only 1260 of these survived the first hurdle of gaining leave to proceed and only about 30 per cent of those were ultimately successful'. Another reason for the growth of JR is the expansion since 1979 of the number of public bodies whose decisions and procedures may be subject to it. There are now about 3000 of these – many of them no doubt do not share the popular enthusiasm for JR.

However, the impact of JR on HEIs should be kept in perspective. Only about 3% of all applications relate to the whole education sector, and of these the majority involve admissions to or special educational needs in secondary schools, rather than HEIs. The number of HE cases where leave to proceed has been granted by the court is small, and the number where the applicant is ultimately successful is even smaller. The courts are not yet, as some newspapers have suggested, overflowing with litigious students or schoolchildren, egged on by predatory lawyers.

Nature of JR

Hardly a news bulletin seems to appear without someone who is disappointed about something saying that he or she will be 'going for a judicial review', using the term for almost any referral of a civil dispute to a court. The correct application is far more specific. Essentially, JR is a means of ensuring via the courts that public bodies have acted lawfully, reasonably and fairly. In ordinary civil litigation, the courts are required to decide on the merits of the case, as between competing parties. In JR, the courts will not normally substitute their own judgement for that of the body which has made the decision. The judge has only to ask whether a lawful power exists to make the decision which has been made by the decision-maker, whether that power has been abused and whether it has been used unfairly. If none of these requirements has been breached, the decision-making body will be left to get on with its own business. The courts have consistently refused to trespass on the particular expertise of the original decision-maker or to apply a restrictive approach to construction of its regulations. Sir John Donaldson MR said in *R v Panel on Take-overs and Mergers*, ex p *Datafin*:

> When it comes to interpreting its own rules [the Panel on Take-overs and Mergers] must clearly be given considerable latitude both because, as legislature it can properly alter them at any time, and because of the form which the rules take, i.e. laying down principles to be applied in spirit as much as in letter in specific situations.

The higher the degree of expert or professional judgement (rather than the application of objective criteria) required from a decision-maker, the less likely the Courts will be to uphold a challenge.

So the courts are not concerned either to rewrite HEIs' disciplinary, still less academic regulations, or to take the interpretation of them out of their hands, provided that lawful powers are applied in a fair and reasonable way. See *R v Higher Education Funding Council*, ex p *Institute of Dental Surgery*, where the HEFCE's decision to reassess the Institute of Dental Surgery's research was a matter of academic judgement and not one for the courts. (Although contrast *Reilly v University of Glasgow*, where, although a challenge to an admissions decision was unsuccessful, the Scottish Court of Session did consider the case on its merits.) Even if an applicant for JR is successful in challenging a decision in the courts, it may ultimately be unchanged. Once any defect in the original decision-making process has been identified and remedied, a new decision taken by the correct route may still turn out to be the same. JR is, therefore, a hollow victory in some cases.

JR is regarded by the courts as a last resort as a means of challenge, at least in the absence of exceptional circumstances. If alternative means of redress are available, such as an unexhausted internal or statutory right of appeal from the original decision, the applicant must satisfy the court as to why review is appropriate. The lack of a visitorial jurisdiction in the statutory HEIs has exposed them to JR more than the chartered universities, which have this additional level of appeal mechanism which provides a *final* arbiter for most conflicts (see Chapter 8 on the Visitor). The courts have declined to define what 'exceptional circumstances' in this context are. However, review may be appropriate where the urgency of the situation requires faster action than the normal timetable of an internal appeals system permits – see *R v London Borough of Newham*, ex p *X*, a school exclusion case, where 'bearing in mind how critically important every day and certainly every week was in the education of a child', interlocutory relief was appropriate so the child went back to school three weeks before the normal statutory appeal was heard. In *R v Manchester Metropolitan University*, ex p

Nolan a student successfully challenged disciplinary proceedings, without first having gone through the university's review procedure, because he could not obtain confidential minutes containing evidence of material irregularity without going to the Courts.

Grounds and remedies

There are three principal sets of grounds for challenge by JR of decisions of public bodies.

The first is illegality, including *ultra vires* (the exceeding of jurisdiction), error of law (e.g. misinterpretation of regulations) and unlawful delegation of the decision-making function. The second is the abuse of powers, including irrationality, failing to take into account relevant facts or taking into account facts which are not relevant, bad faith, improper motive and the fettering of discretion. The third set of grounds is procedural unfairness, including bias, failure to provide a proper hearing and material irregularity in the decision-making process. Some particular applications of each of these are considered later in this chapter.

JR has its own category of remedies, the prerogative writs, in addition to the remedies generally available in litigation. All relief in JR proceedings is at the discretion of the Court – no particular finding guarantees any particular result. The Courts may decline to interfere, or do so minimally, if the wider public interest so requires, or if intervention would be futile or inappropriate – see *Moran v University College Salford* (*No. 2*), where the persistent Mr Moran established a contractual right to be admitted to a course, but had to be content with damages rather than a mandatory order enabling him to take it up.

The courts may quash an administrative decision or action by a public body (*certiorari*), leaving it to be taken again. They may direct a public authority to comply with a particular obligation by doing something (*mandamus*) or prevent it from taking a decision which would be unlawful (prohibition). The legal position may be clarified by declaration. Injunctions to prevent unlawful action may be granted in JR, but damages for wrongful administrative action are available only where there is also some established cause of action in private law, (e.g. negligence or breach of statutory duty). The House of Lords has now set down guidelines for the rights of private individuals to claim damages from public authorities for breach of statutory duty and/or negligence in failing to perform a statutory function – see *X (Minors) v Bedfordshire County Council*. As a result of the decision of the European Court of Justice in *R v Secretary of State for Transport*, ex p *Factortame Ltd*, a member state may be liable for loss and damage caused to individuals as a result of breaches of Community law, whatever the organ of the State whose act or omission was responsible for the breach. Whether HEIs are to be regarded as organs of the State for this purpose remains to be determined.

JR is available only in respect of decisions made by public bodies. University Visitors are specifically excluded except on very limited grounds – see *R v Lord President of the Privy Council*, ex p *Page* and also Chapter 6. The two tests which determine whether a decision-making body is judicially reviewable, set out in *R v Panel on Take-overs and Mergers*, ex p *Datafin* are operation in the public sphere, or in pursuance of statutory powers. It was argued in that case that a statutory source of power was essential for making the decisions of an organization liable to JR. The court disagreed, saying the nature as well as the source of the power had to be considered. If the body in question was exercising public functions, or if the exercise of its functions had consequences in terms of public law, that could be sufficient. Although further widening of the scope of JR was resisted by the Court of Appeal in *R v Jockey Club*, ex p *Aga Khan*, the courts have had no hesitation in identifying both the chartered and the statutory universities as public law bodies.

If a contract has been entered into between the applicant and the decision-making body, the courts are likely to find this to be a private rather than public law relationship, which makes JR inappropriate. So in *R v Fernhill Manor School*, ex p *A*, a private school was held not to be a public law body, even though it operated within the statutory framework of control of the Education Act 1944. Further, the relationship between a private school and its pupils was founded on the private contract between the school and those who paid for their education. Therefore, even though the rules of natural justice had not been followed in an exclusion, the public law remedy of JR was not available. The position would have been different if, as in *R v London Oratory School*, ex p *Regis*, the school's articles and instrument of government had been made under powers contained in the Education Acts and no private contract had been involved. See also *R v Haberdashers' Aske's Hatcham College Trust*, ex p *T*, where City Technology Colleges established under the ERA 1988, Section 105, were held to be public law bodies subject to JR. The judge in *R v Fernhill Manor School*, ex p *A* quoted Wade (1988):

> Where a disciplinary body has no statutory powers its jurisdiction will normally be based upon contract. Members of trade unions, business associations, and social clubs and also students in universities and colleges have . . . contractual rights based on their contracts of membership, with implied terms which protect them from unfair expulsion. In these cases declaration and injunction are the appropriate remedies. *Certiorari* and prohibition are quite out of place, since the Crown's supervisory powers over public authorities are not concerned with private contracts.
>
> (Wade, 1988: 603)

As we have seen, declaration and injunction are remedies generally available in litigation, but *certiorari*, *mandamus* and prohibition are peculiar to JR. In the *R v Panel on Take-overs and Mergers*, ex p *Datafin*, the court was clear that if the source of power of the decision-making body was contractual, then JR was not available. The essential distinction is between the individual and consensual relations implied by a contract, and the general and involuntary liability to public law. So attempts to secure JR by employees of a health authority (*R v East Berkshire Health Authority*, ex p *Walsh*) and a county council (*R v Derbyshire County Council*, ex p *Noble*) were unsuccessful, even though these were undoubtedly public law bodies, because an employment contract is a private law matter.

The same reasoning was applied in *R v University College London*, ex p *Riniker*. Mrs Riniker, who had already secured an admission of unfair dismissal and an offer of compensation from University College London (UCL) in an industrial tribunal, asked the court for mandatory reinstatement and striking out of a condition of re-employment which banned her from entering or being involved with a language centre. She said this was a restriction on her right of free speech, confirmed by the Education (No. 2) Act 1986, Section 43. The court accepted that Section 43 was justiciable by JR in an appropriate case. (For such a case, see *R v University of Liverpool*, ex p *Caesar-Gordon*). UCL was a public law body, even though it is a non-statutory chartered institution. However, the restrictions imposed by UCL on Mrs Riniker were found to be administrative matters linked to her private contract of employment, not an attempt to interfere with her public law right of free speech. Leave for JR was, therefore, refused.

If a contract of employment is a private not public law matter outside the scope of JR, what about relations between universities and their students, particularly the procedurally difficult areas of disciplinary and academic regulations, in the light of the contract of admission or matriculation? Farrington (1994: 367) states that the legal basis of the disciplinary powers of HEIs established under the ERA 1988 and the Further and Higher Education Act 1992, whose students are not members of a corporation, rests in the voluntary subscription of the individual to the rules of the institution, which become part of the contractual terms binding on both parties. See Chapter 4 for a detailed consideration of contractual issues.

There are some older cases of JR in universities which pre-date both the establishment of the statutory HEIs and any recognition of the student contract, but these are not now of much relevance. In *R v Aston University*, ex p *Roffey*, where the Visitor's jurisdiction was not invoked, the court refused to become involved in procedural matters when students were excluded for failing exams, principally because of the applicants' delay, saying that insistence on the rules of natural justice would be 'a useless formality'. In *Glynn v Keele University*, about a student who sunbathed nude on campus, the court accepted jurisdiction (despite the existence of a Visitor) and that there had been procedural unfairness, but again exercised its discretion against becoming involved in disciplinary proceedings. In *Herring v Templeman*, a case involving expulsion from a non-statutory teacher-training college, there was criticism by the Court of Appeal of the court's willingness in *R v Aston University*, ex p *Roffey* to entertain the application and support for Wade's view that the contractual nature of the relationship should have been considered (and the Visitor route explored).

The state of student–HEI relations and English administrative law had moved on considerably by the time of *R v Manchester Metropolitan University, ex p Nolan*, a case about a bar student who took notes into a Common Professional Education (CPE) exam. There had been procedural irregularities in the subsequent disciplinary proceedings and some confusion between the faculty disciplinary committee and the CPE exam board. The case is described (Carroll, 1994) as the first occasion on which a student in the UK has been able to persuade a court of an abuse of academic disciplinary power sufficient to warrant JR and to establish that statutory universities without Visitors owe their students the full range of public law obligation, enforceable through applications for JR.

In fact, the judge (Sedley J.) dealt with the jurisdictional point very briefly, saying:

> The respondent is a body corporate by virtue of Chapter II of the Education Reform Act 1988. As a public institution discharging public functions, and having no visitor, it is subject to judicial review of its decisions on conventional grounds. It is not disputed that the applicant has sufficient interest to bring the grounds upon which he relies before this Court.
>
> (Carroll, 1994: 72)

The contractual/consensual argument for the basis of disciplinary rules appears not to have been considered. So far as I am aware, it has not yet been argued in any of the recent JRs of decisions by HEIs (for example, *R v University of Cambridge*, ex p *Evans*, 1997).

Carroll (1994) concludes that the enforcement of student rights in academic and disciplinary matters remains within the law of contract for chartered institutions, whose powers are not underpinned by statute. The same view was taken by the Irish High Court in *Rajah v Royal College of Surgeons of Ireland*, although in Scotland there seems to be a greater willingness to allow JR of matters arising from a contractual relationship – see *Joobeen v University of Sterling*. Carroll questions however whether a student can be said freely to enter into a balanced contractual relationship with an HEI which admits him or her, and suggests that the limited application of JR to Visitors should be broadened, in order to provide the same degree of protection for students in chartered universities as *R v Manchester Metropolitan University*, ex p *Nolan* indicates are available in the statutory sector of HE. There are few reports so far of cases of JR involving statutory HEIs since that case. In *R v University of Humberside*, ex p *Cousens* a student claimed that refusal to exercise a discretion to condone a part failure was irrational, in view of his otherwise satisfactory performance. The Court of Appeal did not agree. The question of contractual relationship does not seem to have arisen.

In *R v Sheffield Hallam University*, ex p *Rowlett* a student was suspended for drug-taking after a university investigation and expelled after a subsequent disciplinary hearing. She appealed unsuccessfully to university governors and then applied for JR. Sedley J. allowed the application because Ms Rowlett had not been given prior warning of all the charges against her. He rejected the arguments that there was a real danger of bias because of private knowledge of the chairman of the disciplinary committee, and that adequate notice of the evidence against Ms Rowlett had not been given. He found that the appeal panel had addressed irrelevant issues. Again, no reference to contract was made.

Reducing the risk of JR

As the possibility of JR is a fact of life for statutory HEIs and there is scope for conflict with contract, how can they avoid falling foul of the courts? The following suggestions may help.

The decision-making body must be properly constituted

Clearly, the body which produces the decision must be correctly convened and made up according to the relevant constitutional provisions. See *R v Secretary of State for Education*, ex p *Prior*, where a grant-maintained school got into a tangle over the respective roles and composition of its governing body, staff committee and appeals committee. But contrast *R v de Montfort University*, ex p *Cottrell*, where although the university had imperfectly applied its own academic appeals procedures, leave for review was refused on the grounds that this did not result in any unfairness to the applicant.

The body responsible for making the decision must not delegate it

The general rule is that a body to which decision-making powers are formally delegated may not in turn delegate them further. Particular care is needed if, as with many committees, certain powers are delegated to the chairman. It is wise to confine delegated decisions to minor or emergency matters, and to ensure that major or permanent ones are decisions of the whole committee. (See page 101 re *R v University of Cambridge*, ex p *Evans*.)

The decision must be intra vires

A decision is *ultra vires* not only if there is no express power to make it in the constitution, statute or regulations concerned, but also if a decision-making power is not used either in the way intended by Parliament, or on the correct legal basis. If a decision is reached on a basis erroneous under the general law, then it is outside the parameters of permissible use and, therefore, *ultra vires*.

The decision must exercise the mind of the decision-making body

There must be an exercise of discretion which shows that the decision-maker's mind was not closed to the circumstances of the individual case. In *R v Warwickshire County Council*, ex p *Collymore* the council's decision to refuse a discretionary grant to a Legal Practice Course student was quashed because a general policy to refuse such applications had been applied without proper consideration of the individual circumstances. However, the use of a standard letter for the notification of decisions, with variations for individual cases, is not in itself evidence of failure to give proper consideration to the case – see *R v Lancashire County Council*, ex p *Maycock*, a schools admissions case.

The decision-making body's discretion must not be fettered

A balance must be struck between the obvious desirability of achieving consistency and even-handedness in decision making, and following policy guidelines or precedents so slavishly that no discretion is exercised in the individual case, or allowance made for what might be the exceptional case. There have been a number of JRs of schools' admissions policies on these grounds. There is no objection to the formulation or publication of guidelines, provided that discretion in applying them is not eliminated.

All relevant evidence must be considered

Reasonable enquiries to obtain the relevant evidence must be made before a decision is made. Irrelevant considerations must not be taken into account. What is relevant or irrelevant may often not be defined in rules or regulations and, therefore, be open to interpretation by the decision-making body and subsequently by the courts. If further relevant evidence emerges, the decision should be reconsidered.

The decision must accord with the evidence

This is the famous test of 'Wednesbury reasonableness' (*Associated Provincial Picture Houses Ltd v Wednesbury Corporation*). A decision is reviewable if it is manifestly absurd, irrational or perverse and one which no reasonable body properly directing itself could have reached. This is difficult to prove. A partner in the City law firm Allen & Overy is quoted as saying, 'You have to establish that the decision-makers were on the verge of being carried off by the men in white coats'. The courts resist being drawn in to considering the merits of the case under the guise of being asked to find a decision irrational.

A decision must not be in pursuit of an improper purpose

Administrative powers may only be exercised for the purpose for which they are granted. Decisions which have an ulterior motive, seeking to achieve a certain result merely by using powers directed at other considerations, are reviewable.

The effects of a decision must be proportionate to the legitimate objectives of making it

Proportionality is a European concept only beginning to be applied by the UK courts. In *R v Manchester Metropolitan University*, ex p *Nolan* the judge held that failing a student permanently could be a proportionate response to the offence of seeking an unfair advantage by taking notes into an exam, even though this fell short of the more serious offence of cheating.

The legitimate expectation of the individual who is the subject of a decision must be taken into account

This is the equivalent of estoppel in private law and rests on the assumption that public law bodies will consistently apply known procedures in arriving at administrative decisions, particularly the practice of consultation before rules are changed. In *R v Rochdale MBC*, ex p *Schemet*, parents had a legitimate expectation that free bus passes would continue to be issued for travel to school until some rational grounds for changing the policy were given and they had an opportunity to comment.

It is sometimes argued that statements made on behalf of a public law body, about the effect of its regulations in a particular case, establishes a legitimate expectation on the part of the person to whom the statement is made. The courts are wary of this approach, particularly if the alleged statement is unclear or vague in its content – see *R v Coventry University*, ex p *Ali*.

The individual who is the subject of a decision must first have the opportunity to put his case to an unbiased decision-maker

It is a fundamental requirement that the decision-making body should hear both sides of the story, so that the individual's response to matters raised in respect of him or her is taken into account. This extends to the opportunity to comment on all the evidence against him (but not necessarily to a right to see in-house advice to the decision-making body – see *R v Secretary of State for Education*, ex p *S*).

There must be a fair hearing

Provided that there is an adequate opportunity for the individual to put his or her case, the requirements of a fair hearing are not fixed. The courts recognize that a full-scale adversarial hearing, importing all the rules of judicial proceedings, is often not practical in terms of resources, expense and delay. There is no absolute requirement for an oral hearing if all the relevant evidence can be adequately considered in written form. The form of the hearing may be less important than the requirement that it should be balanced and thorough. See *R v London Borough of Camden and Governors of Hampstead School*, ex p *H*, where the Court of Appeal stressed the governors' obligation to decide the factual issues to be resolved and the inquiries which could reasonably be made to resolve them, rather than the necessity for calling bodies of oral evidence. Affected parties must have adequate notice of all the matters to be raised against them – see *R v Sheffield Hallam University*, ex p *Rowlett*.

Reasons for a decision may be required

Failure to give reasons is not necessarily a ground for JR, but a person affected by a decision must be able to rationalize it in order to determine whether to accept it, appeal or apply to the court. If reasons are given, they must be intelligible. The amount of detail which the courts require for the supporting of administrative decisions varies according to the gravity and frequency of the type of decision involved and the severity of its effect on the person subject to it, but the requirements of the courts may be increasing in this respect – see *R v Higher Education Funding Council*, ex p *Institute of Dental Surgery*, *R v Lancashire County Council*, ex p *Maycock* (a school admissions case) and page 101 re *R v University of Cambridge*, ex p *Evans*. A decision which is unusual or at odds with the most obvious conclusion should be explained by reasons which may be unnecessary in a more straightforward case. However, in *R v University of Humberside*, ex p *Cousens* the need for any more detailed reasons than were contained in the University's decision letter was emphatically rejected.

The decision-maker must be unbiased

An assessing person or body who is in some way linked with the proceedings may be disqualified from making a proper decision. In *R v Gough*, the House of Lords said that where an adjudicator had a direct pecuniary interest in the outcome of the proceedings, the court would assume bias and disqualify him or her automatically. Otherwise, the test to be applied in all cases of apparent bias was whether there was a real danger of bias, in the sense that a decision-maker might unfairly have regarded with favour or disfavour the case of any party to the dispute – see also *R v Sheffield Hallam University*, ex p *Rowlett.*

Procedure and costs

Applications for leave to seek JR are normally dealt with, on paper or at an oral hearing, without the respondent having been either notified or represented. Only if leave is granted, does the respondent become a party to the litigation. Initially, it is up to the judge considering leave to decide whether the applicant's case has a reasonable chance of success. If there is an arguable case, leave will be granted.

However, in *R v Horsham DC*, ex p *Wenman*, the court said that it should be standard practice for an applicant to send a letter before action to a prospective respondent, before applying for leave. Further, there are some cases where the respondent is represented at the leave stage: if the respondent's presence has been requested by the court, if notice has been given or if the respondent has found out what is afoot and decided to be involved at an early stage. The detail of procedure and tactics in JR is beyond the scope of this book and institutions will wish to consult their legal advisors at the earliest opportunity.

Leave may be granted on certain grounds but refused on others, in which case the unsuccessful grounds cannot be reopened at the full hearing – see *R v Staffordshire County Council*, ex p *Ashworth.*

A high proportion of all applications are settled either before the application for leave is dealt with, or after it is granted. Negotiations leading to settlement may take many forms, but it is always worth considering whether a re-determination of the decision to which the applicant objects should be offered, without prejudice to the determination of the original challenge. This may short-circuit expensive and time-consuming proceedings, and may be useful later in relation to costs, even if the offer is declined. If leave is granted, the courts certainly expect public law bodies to take a good look at the decision under question. As applications for leave to proceed are normally dealt with in the absence of the respondent, institutions will usually not incur costs at that stage. If leave is granted, the question of costs will be reserved to the substantive hearing and may be a factor in subsequent negotiations. Should a full hearing take place, costs will follow the event in the usual way subject to the over-riding discretion of the court.

If the respondent is represented at the stage of application for leave and successfully resists it, the court has discretion to award costs against the applicant. This is more likely if the applicant has failed to send a letter before action, or has not made full and frank disclosure of all the circumstances to the court. Since the Court of Appeal's decision in *R v Secretary of State for Wales*, ex p *Rozhan*, orders for the costs of successful respondents are being made if the court considers the applicant has caused unreasonable expense by making a hopeless application. If the applicant is receiving legal aid, his or her liability to pay the other side's costs if the application is unsuccessful is limited by the Legal Aid Act 1988, Section 17. This means that in practice, no order for costs will normally be made against a legally aided applicant, leaving institutions to pay their own legal costs even when successful. However, the court still has a discretion to order costs against an unsuccessful legally-aided applicant, even though there may be no immediate prospect of those costs being paid. This is the so-called 'football pools' costs order, which could be enforced at some future time, when the applicant's financial circumstances have improved. This might be especially relevant in the case of legally-aided student applicants who later move into employment.

Further reading

Cane, P. (1996) *Introduction to Administrative Law*. Oxford: Oxford University Press.
Clayton, R. and Tomlinson, H. (1993) *Judicial Review: A Practical Guide*. London: FT Law & Tax.
de Smith, S. *et al.* (1995) *Judicial Review of Administrative Action*. London: Sweet & Maxwell.
Farrington, D. J. (1994) *The Law of Higher Education*. London: Butterworths.
Fordham, M. (1995) *Judicial Review Handbook*. London: Wiley.
Gordon, R. (1996) *Judicial Review: Law and Procedure*. London: Sweet & Maxwell.
Gordon, R. and Barlow, C. (1996) *Judicial Review Deskbook*. London: Wiley.
Harris, B. (1995) *Disciplinary and Regulatory Proceedings*. Chichester: Barry Rose.
Manning, J. (1995) *Judicial Review Proceedings: A Practitioner's Guide*. London: Legal Action Group.
Public Law Project (1994) *Is it Lawful? A Guide to Judicial Review*. London: Sweet & Maxwell.
Public Law Project (1995) *Applicant's Guide to Judicial Review*. London: Sweet & Maxwell.
Supperstone, M. and Goudie, J. (1992) *Judicial Review*. London: Butterworths.
Wade, H. W. R. and Forsyth, C. F. (1994) *Administrative Law*. Oxford: Oxford University Press.

Part 4

The Higher Education Institution and its Academic Activity

10

Intellectual Property, Copyright and Trade-Marks

Alasdair Poore (Mills and Reeve)

Editors' introduction

Apart from Research and Development activity within industry, the software industry and perhaps certain aspects of management consultancy, the issue of intellectual property (IP) is largely otherwise only to do with the world of higher education (HE). However, it is an increasingly important issue for higher education institutions (HEIs) and for individual academics (both in search of a Patent fortune) and it is an area throwing up an increasing amount of legal activity, as is identified in the survey of HEIs described in Chapter 1.

This chapter also explains the basics of copyright. This, again, is of growing significance in the contractual relationship between HEIs and their academics and it covers the concept of trade-marks. For example, the old University of Oxford shield was not a registered trade-mark and it appears worldwide on T-shirts at no profit to the University, whereas the more elaborate 1980s version is very definitely registered and clearly intended as a money-spinner – it was the basis of a joint commercial venture with Liberty of London whereby Oxford Ltd had sales of some £4 million projected for 1997, prior to Liberty's recent financial problems which have brought about the closure of its 'Oxford Collection Shop', (in fact, the University has opened its own shop, see Chapter 12 on Trading). Why else might an HEI bother to register its crest/logo? We commend to HEIs the suggested scheme for the management of IP issues set out at the end of this chapter.

Introduction

IP is an area of very substantial importance in the business community. The accelerating pace of technological development, in terms of articles and goods that are traded and the way in which individuals and businesses operate, means that the relevance of IP will increase further. Examples are the use of Internet, the use of increasingly powerful computers and electronic communications, and the distribution of information and publications electronically. This development is one which is evidently key to HEIs. They are institutions at the heart of the development and dissemination of information and knowledge. Through research or teaching, they are involved in areas where IP is important. In addition, as pressure to look for further assets or marketing opportunities rises, intellectual property will need to play a greater role.

When looking at IP, one must not over-emphasize the prospect of a major development which may transform the finances of an HEI. They arise rarely and usually unpredictably. Nevertheless, it is important to be aware that IP issues arise throughout the business of an HEI, and to ensure that, if the right framework exists, the framework will support the small and great alike. This chapter aims to give an overview of IP so that these issues can be addressed.

IP is made up of many different types of rights. The rights are relevant to different aspects of the business of an HEI. This chapter gives an overview of some general issues, a summary of the main IP rights which are relevant, and a discussion of ownership and acquisition, transfer and exploitation, third party rights and management of IP.

What is IP and why is it important?

Most people know, in general terms, what IP is. Patents, copyright, trademarks, rights in designs and confidential information are examples. They protect subject matter as different as drugs and computers, software, books, sculptures and musical performances, names such as Coca-Cola or the BBC, wallpaper, furniture and dress designs. IP is an umbrella term used to cover a very wide range of rights. Some of these rights have statutory origins and some arise from history. Some must be registered, whereas others subsist without any formal steps being taken. Some relate to new technology, others to brand identity or image and some to artistic expression. It is important to be aware of the diversity of IP. In detail, the rights are very different and must be handled in very different ways. However, they still often fit together to provide a broad umbrella of protection; and they also have common elements which mean that they are often discussed together.

Three general concepts

Scope of protection

The essence of any IP right is that it can be used to stop other parties from carrying out an activity. It allows the owner to prevent others from:

- using an invention which has been patented;
- making copies of a text or issuing those copies to the public;
- using the mark a trader has used or intends to use to identify its business.

However, the type of protection depends on the type of right.

'Reproduction' rights   Some rights can be used to prevent third parties *copying* the owner's work. They can be used to prevent the creation or distribution of copies or derivative works. In this way, they protect the investment in effort made by the owner. However, they do not act as a complete bar on making a similar product or one which satisfies the same need. If there is no copying, a third party cannot be restrained by this type of right. These rights do not create a complete monopoly. If the owner identifies a market opportunity, others may still be able to take advantage of it provided they do not copy. Rights which fall into this category are copyright and unregistered design rights.

Monopoly rights   These rights can be used to exclude others absolutely. It does not matter whether the third party obtained the idea from the owner or independently. An example is a patent on a drug. Here, other parties can be prevented from making the drug even if they discovered it through independent research.

There are two advantages:

1. an absolute monopoly is much more valuable because the owner can ensure that only he, she or it benefits from the exploitation of the resulting product;
2. it is much easier to prove infringement because it does not matter how the third party came to do the infringing activity.

Narrower rights   Protection for confidential information depends on the relationship between the 'owner' and the person using it. That relationship may be based on contract (e.g. a secrecy agreement) or on some implied duty of confidence.

Registrability
The second general concept is registrability. Some IP rights arise automatically, or with no steps being taken by the owner. In other cases, some formal steps may be required to 'register' the right, usually with a national or transnational authority. Usually, to obtain registration an application must be made, accompanied by an appropriate fee. In most cases, the authority reviews ('examines') the application in order to see whether it meets the formal and substantive requirements. If it does, the application will be granted. Most registrable rights correspond to the monopoly rights. Examination of the applications sifts out those which *prima facie* do not justify a monopoly, and so prevents a person from obtaining an unfair advantage in the market. The main registered rights are patents, registered designs and registered trade-marks.

Intangibility
The third aspect of IP rights is that they are intangible. Unlike physical objects, you cannot pin them down. You cannot prevent a third party using the subject matter just by keeping possession yourself. This is also what makes the rights so valuable. Once done, the work can be used again and again. For example, a piece of software, once written, can be duplicated many times for use by others. The value in the rights can be very considerable, because it reflects the possibility of repeated use. Conversely the possibility of replication makes IP relatively difficult to protect. In many cases, a third party can make the same use of IP as the owner. Moreover, the third party can change or even improve the subject matter. This mutability of subject matter often makes IP rights much more difficult to enforce.

National character

Almost all IP rights arise under national laws, which are specific to the country in question. However, in most cases now there are international conventions which mean that the elements of the rights are very similar in each country. A few countries (such as Taiwan and some South American countries) are outside this international regime. National character does mean that where registration is required, the right must be registered in each country.

Types of intellectual property

The principal IP rights are patents, design rights, copyright, confidential information and trade-marks. Design rights and trade-marks can each be in two types, registered or unregistered. There are other significant rights in particular fields, such as semi-conductor topography rights, performers' protection, plant breeders' rights and the database extraction right. Table 10.1 summarizes a selection of important rights with notes of their main characteristics and subject matter.

Patents

Criteria
The criteria for a patentable invention in the UK are set out in the Patents Act 1977 (and the European Patent Convention) and case law. The three principal criteria are as follows.

Novelty　The invention must not have been described or used in public by the inventor or anyone else before the application is made. The most important consequence of this is that the inventor and anyone else knowing of the invention must not talk about it before obtaining protection, unless any disclosure is in confidence. Even confidential disclosures should be made only with care as confidentiality is rarely perfect. This is particularly significant in HEIs where students and researchers often have a primary aim of securing publication. In particular, in fast moving fields where patent protection could be most important (such as genetic engineering) fast publication is a prerequisite. Consequently, it is important to set up a framework for providing advice on such inventions and, if appropriate, authorizing and obtaining protection as rapidly as possible.

Not obvious   The invention must be inventive or not *obvious*. It is obvious if a person (or research group) of average skill working in the field would have thought of the invention (based on their knowledge and what similar people would be expected to know, and on publicly available information). In practice, it is quite an easy test to pass.

Capable of industrial application and other policy exclusions   Essentially this test has two functions:

1. to separate out technical from aesthetic and similar innovations;
2. to avoid giving protection where, for policy reasons, this is thought inappropriate.

   Important examples are computer programs *per se* and methods of treating humans or animals, although in practice the restriction on patentability can often be circumvented.

Seeking protection
An application must be filed in respect of each country where protection is sought. It could be very difficult to file the large number of applications which might be required in a short time. Fortunately, international conventions overcome this.

The Paris Convention   An applicant can file an application in one country. Provided other applications are filed within a year of the first application, they are deemed to be filed on the same date as the original application. A very large number of countries are party to this convention.

Patent Co-operation Treaty   A single application can be made designating a large number of countries (including most of those which are most economically important). This progresses as a single application for up to two-and-a-half years, after which it is transformed into a number of national applications.

European Patent Convention   A single application to be made for a number of European countries, including all the European Union (EU) countries.

Table 10.1 Intellectual property rights: characteristics

Right	Registered/ unregistered	Scope	Requirement	Exceptions	Term	Examples
Patent	Registered	Monopoly	New, not obvious, industrially applicable	Application of drugs or surgical techniques, plant and animal varieties, software per se, methods of doing business	20 years from application Renewal fees annually	New articles: corkscrew, computer equipment, biro, gear wheel, hovercraft, flow meter New substances: drugs, plastics, insecticides, toothpaste formulations, solvent mixtures New methods: polymer manufacture, cleaning method, opening a bottle, flying an aircraft, detecting an enemy ship
Registered design	Registered	Monopoly	Shape or configuration, pattern or ornament, appeal to eye, new, not commonplace	Not sold as an article, functional or method of operation, must match, must fit	25 years from application Renewal fees	Television monitor, armchair, telephone handset, perfume bottle, motor car, motor mower, electrical terminal, car hub cap, licence disc holder, fabric design, decorated teapot, jewellery, furniture, clothing design
Unregistered design	Unregistered	Not copy	Shape or configuration, recorded, original work	Method of operation, must match, must fit	10/15 years; last 5 licensed	Car, steering wheel, book-end, gear wheel, electrical terminal, clothing design, circuit board

Copyright	Unregistered	Not copy	Recorded, original	(Fair use exceptions) Making articles to designs	70 years (after death of author in most cases)	Books, lists, tables, computer software, drawings, diagrams, pictures, sculpture, engraving, printed circuits, photographs, music, plays, films, buildings, broadcasts
Trade secret	Unregistered	Unconscionable or contract	Not known (relatively)	Employee issues	Indefinite, for ever	Customer lists, client preferences, pricing strategy, financial performance, secret formulae, product developments, research results
Passing off	Unregistered	Confusion	(*De facto* distinctive)	(Descriptive)	Indefinite	Jif lemon, Macdonalds stores, Jaffa cakes, BCCI
Registered trade-mark	Registered	Monopoly/ confusion in some cases	Distinctive, not the same as another mark	(Descriptive) honest use provisions, comparative advertising	Indefinite, forever, renewal every 10 years	Names: Coca cola, Wranglers, Quaker, The Times, logos, packaging, shape of goods (coke bottle), jingles (First Direct), smells (rose scented tyres, Chanel No 5), textures
Others						Semi-conductor topography rights, plant breeders' rights, petty patents, geographical origins, (trade libel)

Copyright

Criteria

Copyright protection is given to any original artistic, literary or dramatic work and to cinematographic and broadcast works. In the UK 'original' means, broadly, that if effort has gone into making the work, copyright subsists in it. In practice, in the UK this is a very low threshold. Before copyright arises, the work must be recorded in a material form. If it is recorded in writing or electronically (even transiently, such as in computer memory), the recording does attract copyright. There are also certain qualifying requirements which are rather technical (based on first publication and the nationality or residence of the author). They are unlikely to be of significance here.

Seeking protection

In the UK no steps are required to obtain protection. Copyright arises automatically when the relevant work is created. Copyright does not need to be registered. In many other jurisdictions, similar protection is obtained under two international conventions – the Berne Convention and the Universal Copyright Convention. Copyright works are customarily marked with © or 'Copyright', the year of publication and the name of the copyright owner. In most cases this is no longer required, but it is still valuable as an indication that the copyright owner claims rights.

Multiple rights

One consequence of the simple manner in which copyright arises is that many works may be subject to several different levels of copyright or similar protection. For example, each version of a piece of software may fall within the scope of copyright in all the earlier versions of the software. This is of particular significance in relation to multimedia works, where there may be several different layers of protection available (and if a work is being prepared, several different consents required).

Related forms of protection

The following two additional rights also relate to copyright and should be mentioned briefly.

Moral rights

These arise under the Copyright Designs and Patents Act 1988. There are two important rights:

1. the right to be named as author;
2. the right to prevent your work being subjected to derogatory treatment.

As a result of the uncertainty about the problems which may arise with moral rights, it is common to require a waiver from authors. This prevents them asserting the right in the future against the person to whom the waiver is given.

Database extraction right

This is a new right introduced under EU law. It gives certain rights in relation to the extraction of information from a database, so that the owner of the database can prevent further dissemination of that information. In the UK it is similar in impact to copyright protection for databases. However, in most other countries copyright cannot be used to protect many databases.

Designs

Unregistered designs are very similar to copyright, except that the duration is only 10 years. Registered designs can be used to protect features of shape configuration, pattern or ornament which appeal to the eye. The design must be new (i.e. not used or published as an industrial design previously).

Trade-marks

Trade-marks are used to protect trading reputation. They are intended to identify goods and services and act as a sign that they come from the same source as other goods and services. Examples are the trading name or logo of an HEI. When used on textbooks, on examination papers, in conferences or for consultancy, it suggests to the customer that the same quality of goods or services are to be expected as were previously provided. They can form the basis for identifying that source to third parties who have not encountered it before.

Unregistered trade-marks

Protection arises from use of a name, logo or image. In due course, customers come to associate that name with a particular organization or goods or service. The courts will prevent a third party using the mark in a way which confuses or is likely to cause confusion. For example, use of the name 'de Montfort' in a way which suggested (incorrectly) an association with de Montfort University would be an infringement.

Registered trade-marks

Registration permits a party to specify the trade-mark in which it wishes to claim exclusive rights.

Distinctiveness

The trade-mark must be something which can serve to distinguish products or services from each other. It must be a 'sign' and that sign must be capable of being used as a trade-mark (i.e. it must be capable of acting as an indicator that goods or services come from one source as opposed to another).

Protection will not be given for marks which are very descriptive until they have been used for a significant period of time. An example is the use of a geographical name or a surname, which might be used to describe the origin of goods. A leading case involved the name 'Yorkshire' for trailers. Without use, it would not be registrable. In fact, the mark had been used for many years and was well recognized by those in the trade. This is clearly a common problem for HEIs which will often be called by geographical names.

No conflict
No one else can have prior rights.

Foreign applications
There are several routes for foreign protection:

• the Paris Convention (as for patents, but the priority period is six months);
• the European Trade Mark Convention (a single application is effective through the whole of the EU);
• the Madrid Protocol and Madrid Agreement (these allow single 'umbrella' applications to be made in respect of certain countries).

Creation and acquisition

Within HEIs, IP or the subject matter of IP is being created all the time. Staff who write lecture notes or prepare texts for teaching generate copyright works. Researchers create know-how directly as a result of their research, they generate copyright works in the data they collect and in the papers they write. They might make inventions.

It is widely recognized that often the most important issue in HEIs is recognizing the IP which arises and identifying the elements which are valuable. This is important for two reasons. Clearly, for those rights which require registration, the essential ingredient must be spotted before registration is no longer possible. However, even for rights which do not require any formal steps to protection, unless they are recognized it is unlikely any use will be made of them. The step of identifying and recognizing IP is discussed later at greater length in 'Management of intellectual property'.

Ownership

Ownership of IP arises either through its creation (or registration) or by transfer. The former is most important for an HEI acquiring rights. Table 10.2 identifies the 'original owner' in respect of a number of IP rights.

Table 10.2 Ownership of intellectual property rights

Right	Original owner
Patent	Inventor or inventor's employer if created in the course of special duties or normal duties which would be expected to give rise to an invention
Copyright: literary, artistic and dramatic works	Author or author's employer if created in the course of employment
Copyright: sound recordings or films	The person/organization making arrangements for the recording or film to be made
Copyright: broadcasts	The person/organization making the broadcast
Unregistered design rights	The author or the author's employer if made in the course of employment, or the person commissioning the design from the author or employer
Registered design	The same as for unregistered design or a person who has acquired the right to apply the design
Unregistered trade-mark	The person/organization generating the goodwill
Registered trade-mark	The first applicant, unless the application is made in bad faith

Variety of sources or creators?

In HEIs there will usually be several different potential sources of IP rights each with a different status: students of the HEI, lecturing and research staff, general staff, consultants and outside contributors (such as external supervisors and industrial participants). Ownership issues will depend on who the creator was and in which circumstances the right was created. In some of these cases, an express contract will govern the relationship between the HEI and the creator (for example, the staff will be under a contract of employment and consultants may have specific consultancy agreements). In general, HEIs will wish to address the question of ownership expressly and in advance. Therefore, they will seek to set up some contractual arrangement.

Lecturing and research staff

In general, such staff will be employed on contracts of employment. If there are no express terms governing IP, the position will usually be governed by implied terms. Rights other than rights in inventions will belong to the employer if they were made by the employee in the course of his employment. Rights in inventions will generally be governed by the Patents Act 1977 (see Table 10.2).

The question arises as to whether the IP was created in the course of employment when it was outside normal hours of work or at home. In practice, this will depend on whether it was part of work being carried out within the framework of the HEI and whether out-of-hours work is usual.

In relation to patentable inventions, some staff (e.g. administrative staff and arts research staff) are not in a position where inventions are likely to arise so as a result the inventions made by them belong to them. The argument has also been raised that lecturers in some HEIs are not 'paid to invent' on the grounds that they do not have a contractual obligation to do research. However, in most cases some element of research will form a part of their job, and if they carry out some research functions those will probably be regarded as part of the job.

The provisions normally implied by statute or general law can be varied (although, in relation to employee inventors, only in favour of them). Variation can be made by an express agreement or by an express IP policy which is effectively incorporated into the contract of employment. However, it can also arise by an established custom which has become part of the pattern of working. Although most HEIs will not have established such a pattern in relation to inventions, there might be arrangements in relation to copyright works such as books written by lecturers. Similarly, software written by lecturers and research staff may 'habitually' have been freely exploited by the staff. If there are such customs, then these may need to be addressed in a specific policy, taking care that when the policy is introduced it does not amount to a breach of the employee's contract of employment.

In order to clarify the position, HEIs should adopt a general policy on IP applicable to staff, which is incorporated into the staff contracts.

Students
As discussed in Chapter 6, students may be subject to a special contract. Preferably, this should include provisions relating to IP. Alternatively, it may be possible to bind the student under a suitable IP policy. In the absence of a special arrangement, IP created by students will usually belong to the student. In some cases, it will be important for the HEI to own the IP. Students may contribute an idea which is important to the results of the research and be patentable or produce copyright works of value (for example software, datasets or written works). In other cases, such as music performed or written by students, it may be very appropriate that the student retains ownership, although the HEI may wish to have rights, for example, to use it as teaching material or to publish.

Contract staff and consultants
There will often be a written contract under which such persons serve. However, unless this addresses IP specifically, the HEI may still not acquire all relevant rights. The courts will imply the minimum necessary to give business efficacy to the contract. For example, if a contract author assists in writing teaching materials, the copyright in that work will remain with the author with only a licence in favour of the person commissioning the work. If an invention is made, the invention will, in the absence of any express provision, belong to the consultant. Again, the court may imply a limited

licence in favour of the HEI in order to use the results of the consultant's work.

Outside contributors
The general rule is that what they contribute, will, in the absence of any agreement (possibly implied), belong to them.

Mixed sources
Another complication which may arise in HEIs is that a number of different people, with different positions, may create IP. It is particularly important to have a framework for resolving issues of ownership and use of the rights, otherwise disagreements over this may affect the whole project.

Creating an express contract in relation to IP

The contract of employment, consultancy agreement or Research and Development agreement, can contain specific terms dealing with IP. This is likely to be the most common course where the arrangement is a reasonably formal one with an outside party, such as a consultant or research collaborator.

Alternatively, the contract may make reference to an IP policy. This would be quite common in relation to staff. A similar arrangement may be used in relation to students, if there is a contractual relationship between the students and the HEI (see Chapter 6). The advantage of such an arrangement is that, if properly implemented, it allows the HEI to change the detail of the policy without reaching agreement with each member of staff or each student. For example, any share given to relevant staff of the revenues of exploitation of IP generated by them might be changed from time to time, or the terms on which academic staff are permitted to publish might be altered.

In addition, in considering what should be included in such a contract or rules it is clearly important to consider how to handle different forms of IP or IP which arises in different circumstances. The contribution made by a student acting as a research assistant on a scientific project might be treated very differently from that made by a musician recording music in conjunction with the HEI.

The issue of IP may be addressed in a contract relating specifically to IP (e.g. in a confidentiality agreement or a specific agreement where a student is helping in a research project and there is no other policy arrangement which would apply).

Additional terms
At the same time, other relevant terms should be addressed, for example the right each party has to use the IP and whether there is to be any reward or inventor compensation for the creator, the assistance in securing protection and publication and confidentiality.

Assignments, transfers, exploitation and licensing

Exploitation is fundamental to the ownership of IP. If the rights are not exploited, there is little point in having them. Exploitation can be carried out in a number of ways. For businesses the main way is by carrying on, themselves, the activity protected by the rights. For a drug company this will be manufacturing and marketing the drug. For a software company it will be issuing copies of the software. In practice, HEIs are less likely to be involved in such direct exploitation. In most cases, exploitation will involve selling the rights to a third party or licensing a third party to use them.

Sale or licensing

These are two fundamentally different ways of giving others the right to use IP. The important difference is in control of the IP rights after the transactions. In a sale, the rights are transferred to the purchaser and, if there is a breach of the agreement or the purchaser becomes insolvent, the seller may have fairly limited recourse. In a licence, the licensor may be able to terminate the licence and find an alternative partner. There will usually be other substantial differences. For example, a licence is often subject to periodic payment of a royalty and issues such as maintaining and enforcing the rights will be in the hands of the licensor. Sale payments, however, will frequently be one-off or over a limited time, and enforcement will be in the hands of the purchaser. In addition, a purchaser might want some guarantees of the rights he or she is purchasing. These types of issue are not, however, fundamental. There is considerable flexibility in the way in which they can be handled and often an agreement begins to look like a mixture of licensing and sale.

Formal requirements

There are relatively few formal constraints on how the licensing or sale of IP is carried out.

Content of the agreement

Most IP can be transferred or licensed without restriction. In practice, agreements for trade mark licensing should include certain requirements (relating to control of use of the mark and the quality of products or services to which it is applied). Failure to do so may lead, in due course, to the mark becoming unenforceable. In addition, any agreement must clearly comply with any competition law requirements. For example, there are specific provisions relating to tying supplies to patent licences. There are more general requirements under UK and EU competition laws in respect of provisions restricting competition (such as price fixing or territorial limitations).

Formalities

Certain types of agreement or assignment must be in writing and might need to be signed by one or both parties. The main agreements covered are assignments and exclusive licences in respect of patents and applications (signed by both parties) and in respect of trade-marks, copyright and design right (signed by the assignor).

Stamp duty

Stamp duty applies to written assignments and irrevocable exclusive licences of IP rights (other than know-how). A document which is not stamped cannot be used in evidence in a UK court and (subject to registration) there is no other consequence. However, if it is necessary to rely on a document in court, and if the document is stamped late, penalties may be payable.

Registration

Transactions relating to UK patents, registered designs and trade-marks must be registered in the UK Patent Office. Failure to register means that a subsequent transaction may take priority over the earlier one. In addition, if the transaction is not registered within six months (without a proper reason) the ability to recover damages for infringement of the right may be impaired. The Patent Office is required not to register a transaction unless any appropriate stamp duty has been paid on it. HEIs will not usually be so concerned with stamp duty or registration issues, because they will usually be licensing or selling rights, rather than acquiring them. However, where they are building up a portfolio of rights for sale or licensing to a third party (for example, in an ongoing development project with other parties or through their exploitation companies), they will want to make sure those rights are effectively established.

Formal assignments

One other area of assignments and transfers should be mentioned. Often parties do not want full details of a licence or transfer available publicly. Registration of the transaction involves providing a copy of the document, which will usually be publicly available. In addition, if there is a need to rely in court on a transaction, this may receive wider attention. For these reasons, it is often the practice to execute a formal assignment or licence, which is in short form, confirming the rights granted. This can then be registered or shown to third parties. Inventors are commonly asked to execute an assignment particularly as it might be required for US applications. Copyright is also important. Often copyright works are prepared on a consultancy arrangement in which copyright does not belong to the commissioning party. It is very desirable to obtain a short form of copyright assignment from all authors of any work which may be exploited so that these can be relied on in any sale or dispute.

Infringement of third party rights

Businesses generally have to consider whether the products they manufacture or the name they use infringes third party rights. These issues are
not, in most cases, so pertinent to HEIs. There are, however, areas of importance such as the conduct of research, the use of software, the use of
copyright works (e.g. as texts in teaching or illustrations in books) and any
business activities of an HEI.

There is no exception for infringement of IP rights by HEIs. The fact that
use is in an academic environment will not avoid infringement. In practice,
owners of IP rights may take less interest in the activities of an HEI, because
they do not represent a competitive threat. In other cases, special arrangements have already been reached to address the needs of the academic
community. However, where infringement represents a threat or loss of
custom, action may be taken.

Exceptions

Experimental and research use
Generally, an HEI carrying out research is in the same position as other
businesses. Consequently, if an HEI uses a patented technique for gene
sequencing, it will usually need a licence. A body which is carrying out
experimental work related to the subject matter of the invention does not
infringe a patent covering that invention. Thus, where a research team is
experimenting with a patented drug to examine how it acts, making the
drug for that purpose would probably not infringe the patent. However, the
exception is very narrow. For example, carrying out clinical trials for a
competing manufacturer would not be covered. In relation to a copyright
work, fair dealing for the purpose of research or private study is not an
infringement of copyright. In order to qualify as fair dealing, the copying
which is carried out must not substitute significantly for original sales of the
copyright work. Consequently, rules such as copying no more than 10 per
cent of a journal and then only a single copy are sometimes applied.

Software/database
Most use of software and copying of databases will infringe copyright and
the HEI or the relevant individual needs to be licensed. HEIs can benefit
from some centrally negotiated licensing arrangements, which can significantly reduce the cost and administration associated with such licensing.

Copyright licensing arrangements
In addition to arrangements relating to software, there are also general
copyright licensing schemes in relation to copyright in literary and artistic
works (see Farrington, 1994: 8.23–8.54).

Management of IP

Understanding the issues involved in IP is a small part of having a successful approach to IP in any organization, including HEIs. The most important element is managing the IP. This falls into several areas:

- creating awareness;
- identifying and 'capturing' IP;
- selecting viable IP;
- protecting;
- creating a strategy for exploitation and managing exploitation.

In most cases, it is recognized that the most difficult steps are the first three.

Creating awareness

This can be achieved by a mixture of education and dissemination of success stories or disasters, usually combined with accessibility of advice.

Capturing IP

There are a number of mechanisms which HEIs use for identifying IP rights and 'collecting' them under central control. These include carrying out IP audits, improving awareness by briefings or by inclusion of IP teaching within the teaching of a wide range of courses and award schemes. In each case, these are likely to be fairly resource-intensive. The most effective method of capture is to have staff dedicated to monitoring what is going on in the HEI and who discuss IP issues with staff of the HEI on a regular basis. Most HEIs are unlikely to have the resources to employ a person full-time in this role. In that case, a part-time research manager may be effective. Alternatively, outside bodies, including firms of patent agents, will be prepared to carry out the same job, in the expectation of obtaining some spin-off. Implementation of a general policy relating to IP might also be effective. If effective and well publicized, this will reduce to some extent the necessity of searching for IP.

Selecting viable IP

This creates particular difficulties. Decision-making can be helped by knowledge of the potential for exploitation and the field in which exploitation will be carried out. Many inventions can be sifted out on the basis that they have no commercial potential. Nevertheless, many usually remain. HEIs can sometimes be in a better position to assess these inventions than outside businesses. Although HEIs do not necessarily have the exposure to the commercial market place, they do often have much readier input to academic advice on the issues involved. If the HEI is not able to form a view, there are a number of outside exploitation organizations which have now established a reasonable reputation in identifying suitable partners.

Summary

The principal element of managing IP is to be aware of it and to create awareness of it. In doing so, it may be desirable to adopt a policy covering IP specifically (including ownership, handling and rewards for innovators) and to implement that throughout the HEI. It will also probably be desirable to provide a focal point for information and advice as well as control (e.g. of Research and Development contracts), by creating an IP responsibility or unit or by contracting with an outside party to provide that service.

Further reading

Bainbridge, D. (1996) *Intellectual Property*. London: Pitman.
Brooke, M. Z. and Skilbeck, P. M. (1994) *Licensing*. London: Gower.
Chartered Institute of Patent Agents (1995) *CIPA Guide to the Patents Acts*. London: Sweet & Maxwell.
Chartered Institute of Patent Agents (1996) *European Patents Handbook*. London: Longman.
Chartered Institute of Patent Agents and Institute of Trade Mark Agents (1996) *The Trade Mark Handbook*. London: FT Law & Tax.
Cornish, W. R. (1996) *Intellectual Property*. London: Sweet & Maxwell.
Drysdale, B. and Silverleaf, T. (1994) *Passing Off*. London: Butterworths.
Farrington, D. J. (1994) *The Law of Higher Education*. London: Butterworths.
Flint, M. J. (1997) *User's Guide to Copyright*. London: Butterworths.
Holyoak, J. and Torremans, P. (1995) *Intellectual Property Law*. London: Butterworths.
Inglis, T. and Heath, S. (1997) *Using Trade Marks in Business: Commercial Guide to Trade Marks Law*. London: John Wiley.
Laddie, H., Prescott, P., and Vittoria, M. (1995) *The Modern Law of Copyright and Designs*. London: Butterworths.
Michaels, A. (1996) *Practical Guide to Trade Mark Law*. London: Sweet & Maxwell.

11

The Internet: a Modern Pandora's Box?

Stephen Dooley (Manches & Co.)

Editors' introduction

Extensive use of the Internet is less than five years old, but already in the USA and in the UK there have been libel actions for alleged defamation (between academics). In the UK, a Government Minister has 'invited' a Vice-Chancellor to 'deal with' a student allegedly disseminating defamatory material about the said Minister over the Internet. Some higher education institutions (HEIs) have now posted warning notices by their e-mail terminals.

The ever-growing use of the Internet raises other problems of copyright and protection data. What are the likely legal issues to do with the Internet? What duty of care does an HEI have in terms of responsibility for attempting to control use of the Internet by its students and its staff? How can the HEI discharge that duty and avoid liability (if any)? What should it do if the Minister rings up, if thereby it is put on notice of a likely abuse of the use of the Internet? Are there any legal issues involved in, as the University of Oxford has done, cutting off the institution's users from accessing certain salacious areas of the Worldwide Web?

Controversy at Cornell University, USA, over students disseminating politically incorrect statements over the Internet, has led to a debate about free speech in Cyberspace, about how much responsibility an HEI can be reasonably expected to take for such infringements and about the HEI's duty to provide a non-threatening environment in which students can study and be protected from receiving offensive e-mail (the latter less a matter for the law and more about social conventions).

This chapter explores the legal interface between the HEI and the Internet – a fast developing area of law. Hence, this chapter will inevitably 'date' faster than others in the book. This 'shelf-life' issue and the fact that the extent of and type of Internet use will vary from HEI to HEI means that we have deliberately *not* added to this chapter any suggested form of words whereby an HEI may attempt to limit its liability for breach of copyright, for defamation, for Data Protection Act (1984) problems, etc. We urge each HEI to establish its own policy and to keep the policy under constant review.

Introduction

The Internet appears to pervade throughout the academic community – many HEIs have web-pages, some offer distance learning courses and give tutorials over the Internet, colleagues discuss research projects by e-mail, and staff and students use Internet search engines to gather information from any part of the world. A popular view amongst many of the Internet's users is that because it is not located in any one country, it is an electronic wild frontier and not subject to any country's laws. In reality, however, the Internet has a presence in almost every country in the world and all of these countries wish to regulate the use of the Internet in accordance with their national laws. The Internet is subject to more legal rules than any other structure on Earth. Consequently, an HEI manager needs to consider the risks to which the HEI, its employees and its students may be exposed through use of the Internet, not only arising from UK laws but, potentially, from the laws of every country in the world. This chapter is designed to identify some of the risks which are most likely to arise and to suggest possible strategies to minimize these risks.

Copyright

Copyright is the right of protection which, in the UK, arises automatically on the creation of any original literary, dramatic or artistic work, original sound recording, film, broadcast, cable programme or original typographical arrangement. This right also extends, in the UK, to less obvious forms of original work such as computer programs and databases. All of these types of works are found on the Internet. Copyright protection arises only when the work has not already been copied and when the author of the work has been creative in some way. A mere recitation of data is not creative, but the skill exercised when compiling a database may well be sufficiently creative to merit the protection of copyright (see *Waterlow Directories Ltd v Reed Information Services Ltd*).

   The author or creator of copyright work will normally be the owner of the copyright in that work. If there are joint authors, and their work is not distinguishable, they will own the copyright jointly. If, however, the author created the work in the course of the author's employment then, in the absence of an express agreement to the contrary, ownership of the copyright will automatically belong to the author's employer. It is a moot point whether this includes the copyright in works created by members of an HEI's teaching faculty. Convention holds that copyright does not pass to the HEI in these circumstances, but this is discussed in more detail in Chapter 10. Some jurisdictions, such as in the USA, go further and hold that, if the author was a contractor or consultant, then copyright will vest in the person commissioning the work, whereas in the UK copyright remains with the work's author in these circumstances.

There are two types of rights associated with copyright. The first is moral rights. These are:

- the author's personal right always to be identified as the author of his or her work if he or she asserts this right;
- the author's right to object to the derogatory treatment of his or her work;
- the author's right not to have the work falsely attributed until 20 years have passed since the death of the author;
- the right of a person commissioning photographs to forbid the issuing of copies to the public.

These rights apply to material on the Internet as well as to conventional media and should be borne in mind by everyone placing material on the Internet.

The second and more widely known type of right is associated with copyright. These are the exclusive rights to copy, reproduce, publish, transmit, adapt or broadcast the work, or to give others permission to do so. In the UK, these rights last for 70 years from the date of the author's death (or the last author's death if there is more than one) for literary, dramatic, musical or artistic works. Copyright in sound recordings, broadcasts or cable programmes lasts for 50 years from the end of the year of initial transmission. In typography, copyright lasts for 25 years from the year of first publication. The copyright in films expires 70 years from the end of the year in which the last of the director, screenplay author, dialogue author or music composer for the film dies. Computer-generated works (e.g. fractal patterns) are protected for 50 years from the year of first publication. The same periods of protection apply to works originating from within the European economic area (EEA), and works originating from outside the EEA are given the same protection in the UK if the country of origin is a signatory to the Berne Convention (which almost all of the industrialized countries are). It is very important to bear in mind that a broadcast over the Internet may contain work by various authors and may include, for example, a sound recording and a literary work, and that the two works are given different periods of copyright protection.

If anyone copies, performs, adapts or translates a copyright work without permission from the copyright owner, they are committing an infringement of copyright. It is also an infringement of copyright knowingly to sell, distribute, import or possess for business purposes an unauthorized copy of a copyright work. The consequences of infringing copyright are described in Chapter 10.

Problems

The first problem concerning copyright in the context of the Internet is how to protect an HEI's copyright in material which it puts on the Internet. Except in very limited circumstances, copyright material may not be used without the permission of the copyright owner or of someone the owner has authorized to grant that permission. However, that permission may be given by implication. If material is put on a web-page it is almost certain that the courts would hold that this constitutes an implied permission to other users of the Internet to transmit that material across computer networks and to hold copies on computer hard-disks. It is not clear what other rights might be given by implication to a user who downloads material from an HEI's web-site. It seems likely that the user would, by implication, be allowed to print a copy of the material and to include it in a project or study. It is less likely that the user would be allowed to produce multiple copies of the work – see *Aztech Systems PTE Ltd v Creative Technology Ltd.* The user would almost certainly not be allowed to use the material for commercial gains – see *Banks v CBS Songs Ltd and Others.* Rather than relying on implication, an HEI should state in clear, non-technical language what it is prepared to allow a user to do with the HEI's material. It might, for example, allow students to use its material on its web-pages for research or private purposes subject to a proper acknowledgement of the HEI's copyright in the form '© HEI's name 199X' being given, but forbid any use for commercial purposes. This would not, of course, prevent a user from reading or viewing the HEI's copyright material and then using the information contained in the material (as opposed to the material itself) for commercial purposes.

The second problem is how to avoid infringing other people's copyright. If any copyright in material on an HEI's web-site does not belong to the HEI, it must make sure that it obtains permission to use that material and to allow others on the Internet to use that material. The publishers of several journals are now finding that, although they have obtained permission from authors to publish their articles in conventional journals, they have no permission to publish them on the Internet. The result is that they, and everyone transmitting or downloading those articles, is infringing the authors' copyrights.

As well as putting information on the Internet, HEIs will certainly take information from it. Potentially an HEI could infringe copyright when an employee or a student stores material from the Internet on the HEI's computers. Although, as mentioned earlier, the copyright owner may have given an implied permission to do this by putting the material on the Internet, this is not the case if someone has put a copyright work on the Internet without the owner's permission. If this happens, the individual who downloaded the material and the HEI on whose computer it is stored will have committed a copyright infringement. If, and only if, the HEI can show that it had no knowledge of this infringement, is it likely that the courts will award no damages against the HEI. Even so, the court is likely to order that the offending material be removed at once. There is US case law which suggests that in such circumstances, the HEI, as the innocent storer of the information, has not committed a copyright infringement, but that, having been made aware of the infringing material and continuing to hold it will constitute an infringement – see *Religious Technology Center v Netcome Online Communications Services.* The Court's decision in that case is questionable because the question of whether a copyright infringement occurs does not require knowledge on the part of the guilty party. Much like breaking the speed limit, an infringement has either happened or not, and the perpetrator's state of mind is an issue only in relation to the sanctions imposed.

It will be sensible for an HEI to institute guidelines for users of the Internet. It should, among other things, make users aware that they should put another author's work on the Internet only if they have express permission to do so, or if the work is out of copyright. Additionally, the HEI should immediately investigate any use of its computers which it suspects may involve copyright infringement. If it fails to do so, then, in the event of a serious copyright infringement, the courts might take the view that the HEI's degree of ignorance is culpable and award damages against the HEI. It is also possible that the HEI would be regarded as condoning copyright infringement were infringing material to be found on web-sites hosted by its computer systems and had it taken inadequate supervisory steps.

It is also worth pointing out that an HEI could be liable for copyright infringement if its web-sites connect to sites which are known or believed to carry infringing material, or if the means of linking the page to the HEI's web-sites bypass or delete copyright notices which would otherwise have appeared to the viewer. These connections should be monitored to ensure that no pirate sites are linked to the HEI's site.

Confidentiality and patents

The Internet is an open structure and sending any form of confidential information over it may rob the sender and recipient of any right to claim that the information be treated as secret, in much the same way as would happen if a confidential agreement were sent by postcard. Although not a perfect solution, encryption of information does minimize the risk of information being intercepted and used. It certainly indicates that the sender regarded the information as confidential. However, it does not mean that the courts will necessarily agree that the information deserves to be treated as confidential. No one can successfully sue for breach of confidence unless the information was in some way secret and was also known by the recipient to be confidential. Merely encrypting data does not mean that it must be treated as confidential, but if an HEI receives information which appears to be sensitive or which it is told is confidential, it should take appropriate measures to avoid disclosing the information.

Another precaution which all HEIs should consider adopting is to attach a footer to any e-mail message stating that the information attached is confidential and only for the use of the addressee. This should stop others claiming that they thought information received from the HEI could be disclosed freely.

Encryption and confidentiality notices are absolutely vital in the context of patents. If information relating to an invention enters the public domain before a patent application has been filed then the invention cannot be patented. Transmitting information in an unencrypted fashion by e-mail will amount to putting it in the public domain. It should also be pointed out that, whereas (normally) only addressees will open their conventional mail, an e-mail is liable to be opened by anyone sitting at the recipient terminal.

Staff and students must be made aware of the unprotected nature of the Internet and advised not to send sensitive information over the Internet, or they should ensure that appropriate precautions are taken. It would be extremely inadvisable for an HEI to hold confidential records, e.g. exam papers or financial information, on machines accessible via the Internet. At the very least, those machines should be protected by professionally installed software. If confidential information is copied and disseminated, the HEI could be sued unless it can show that it has taken appropriate precautions, including the education of its staff and students. There is also a risk that any information relating to national security, foreign policy or police matters which is placed on an HEI's web-site could result in a breach of the Official Secrets Act (1919). The best defence is to maintain a reasonable level of monitoring of the HEI's web-pages and to remove any potentially sensitive information immediately.

Data protection

In October 1995, the European Union (EU) issued a directive on data protection which aims to harmonize the rights of individuals concerning the processing of data relating to them. This directive must be implemented by the members of the EU by October 1998. Until then, every European country will apply its own data protection legislation which, in the UK, is the Data Protection Act (DPA) 1984. The DPA 1984 applies to any information relating to a living individual by means of which the individual can be identified either by the use of that information alone or in conjunction with other information held by the same person and where information is stored in a form which allows automatic processing. All information held on computer is capable of being automatically processed and everyone holding data on a computer should consider the effects of the DPA 1984.

If personal data is held, the data user must register with the Data Protection Registrar. Failure to do so is a criminal offence punishable by a fine.

The registration must contain correct details of the type of data held and the use to which it may be put. Anyone involved in the processing of such data must provide adequate security measures. Anyone who controls the content of the data must also ensure that all the data is:

- obtained and processed fairly and lawfully;
- held for specified and lawful purposes (registered as described earlier);
- not used or disclosed in any manner incompatible with those purposes;
- adequate, relevant and not excessive in relation to the purposes;
- accurate and up-to-date;
- not kept for longer than is necessary.

In addition, any individuals making enquiries are entitled to be informed if data on them is held, and they must be given reasonable access to that data and the opportunity to correct any error. These requirements are known as the 'data protection principles'.

Information covered by the DPA 1984 may pass along the Internet by means of e-mail communication or it may be found on web-pages or online services such as bulletin boards or databases. Because the pathway information takes to reach a destination on the Internet is an unpredictable one, information may pass through countries whose laws differ considerably from those in the UK. If information covered by the DPA 1984 is to be made available over the Internet, then the HEI's registration with the Data Protection Registrar must make clear that the information is to be made available on the Internet and consideration must be given as to whether it is possible to adopt adequate security measures. In the past, the Registrar has proved reluctant to accept such registrations, but they are necessary and so the Registrar is now more amenable than previously.

Thought should also be given as to whether information has been obtained fairly. Obviously this depends on who put the information on the Internet and the nature of the information. Personal data which individuals put out about themselves is fair game for anyone seeking information on the Internet, but personal data put out by a third party should be treated with extreme caution. Personal data which is incidental to the documents in which it is contained (e.g. news reports) are exempt from the DPA 1984. E-mail addresses are, however, subject to the DPA 1984.

If an HEI or its employees and students, hold personal data and disclose that data without having properly registered their use of the data, the HEI will have committed an offence as the party responsible for controlling the equipment on which the data is held, unless the data was of a type exempt from registration or unless the disclosure was made with the concerned individual's consent or in an 'emergency' situation, such as when the disclosure is to save the data user's life or to prevent the commission of a crime. There is no need to register data, nor is the subject able to gain access to it if, for example, the data is held purely for personal use or is data held only for payroll purposes. However, it is unlikely that data of this type would be transferred across the Internet.

HEIs should establish if they, their staff or their students, hold personal data on the HEI's computers which is connected to the Internet. If personal data is held, and is not exempt, the HEI must register its use and ensure adherence to the data protection principles.

The EU data directive is, potentially, going to have an extremely restrictive effect on the Internet and may cripple the use of online databases which contain personal data. The directive forbids the transfer of personal data outside the EU unless the recipient's country has equivalent data protection laws to those of the EU. Of the 160 or so countries in the world outside the EU, there are only about six with equivalent data protection laws. Not only does the directive have the potential to turn Europe into an information black hole on the Internet as far as the rest of the world is concerned, it will also stop the transfer of personal data within Europe because the network path which an Internet transmission from the UK to Belgium may take could involve a route through China and Ghana. It is to be hoped that the directive will be considered carefully in the light of what is feasible in relation to use of the Internet when members of the EU implement the directive.

Pornography and offensive communications

This topic has probably accounted for most of the literature devoted to the Internet in the newspapers and it is a fact that in 1995 'adult' web-sites were four times more popular than the next most popular type of web-site (business and financial sites). Many of the reported cases have involved caches of pornographic materials maintained on HEI computer equipment by staff or students. To date only the individuals concerned have been prosecuted – the HEIs involved have not been charged.

One area of potential risk has been the transmitting of obscene material from the UK to areas with more restrictive obscenity laws (e.g. the USA). Under UK law, these risks are really those of service providers such as UKERNA, Demon or Pipex rather than HEI hosts. However, this is not necessarily the case in other jurisdictions which may impose liability on an unwitting HEI host, but there is the difficulty of a prosecution brought in a third country being able to affect an HEI host directly. It is more likely that pressure would be brought on the Internet service provider to disconnect a host which was not keeping a clean house. For example, to deal with this problem in December 1995, the Bavarian Federal Prosecutor's office found it impossible to pursue the hosts of various obscene bulletin boards and instead threatened to prosecute the service provider, CompuServe, unless it cut off the offending web-site.

Within the UK, it is an offence under the Obscene Publications Acts (1963 and 1984) to distribute material by the transmission of electronically stored data which, on resolution into user-readable form, is obscene. This means that not only could the sender of the obscene material be prosecuted, but so could the HEI whose computers were used to transmit the material. It is a defence to any prosecution to show that the HEI did not examine the obscene material and had no reasonable cause to suspect that the material was of such a nature that its publication might lead to liability.

It is also an offence if an HEI transmits or possesses any indecent pseudo-photography of a child. This means any indecent picture of a child which has been created by electronic or any other means. If charged, in order to have a valid defence, an HEI would have to demonstrate that none of its officers had seen the image and that the HEI had no knowledge or suspicion that the image was indecent. It is also a defence to show that the image was needed and used only for legitimate purposes such as research.

In order to be obscene under UK law, something must be so appalling that it is likely to deprave or corrupt those viewing it. Where images of children are concerned, standards of what is proper are high, and an image involving an adult which might have been risqué will be viewed as indecent if a child or childlike images are portrayed. Any material involving suggestive pictures of children should be excised from an HEI's computer network unless they are present on the network for a legitimate purpose.

There have also been cases in the USA involving students sending obscene and threatening e-mail messages. Under UK laws, it is conceivable that if a recipient of such messages suffers emotional harm then the sender could be prosecuted for causing actual bodily harm – see *R v Ireland*. An HEI could also be prosecuted if it were shown that it had been reckless in permitting the transmission of such messages.

To avoid any potential liability, an HEI must prove that its supervision of those using the Internet was not reckless. This will require the HEI maintaining some form of supervisory role of its computer networks. The extent of this supervision will, chiefly, depend on the resources available to it and the degree of perceived risk. The HEI should also take steps to ensure that its users are told clearly what type of behaviour is not permitted when using the Internet via the HEI's equipment.

Defamation

Defamation is a serious concern in the academic community because individual academics and students tend to have strong views and sometimes express them with a certain lack of regard for the consequences. The range of people and organizations who may be sued for defamation is very wide and an HEI will almost certainly find that it is potentially liable for a defamatory statement made by a student or a member of staff on the Internet. It should also be remembered that the aggrieved party may well prefer to sue the HEI in preference to an individual who, even if identifiable, might not have the funds to pay any damages – the HEI will probably have the deepest pocket if the writs start to fly. A defamatory statement is one which lowers the reputation of the person against whom it is directed in the eyes of others, and an action may be brought against anyone involved in the publication of that statement. This includes any party on whose web-page or bulletin board the statement appeared, as well as anyone involved in the transmission of that material.

The normal rule of law is that an action for defamation may be brought wherever the defamatory material appeared. The nature of the Internet means that a defamatory statement which is placed on a web-site located at, say, a UK HEI may be viewed in Pakistan and an action brought under that country's laws. In practice, however, it is likely that most actions against a UK HEI will be brought in the UK, as this country has defamation laws which tend to favour a plaintiff, and because it is difficult to enforce a foreign court order against an HEI based entirely within the UK. For an action to be brought in a particular country, publication must have occurred in that country, but in the case of the Internet this simply requires a plaintiff to instruct his, her or its lawyers in the chosen country to view the offending material via their personal computer before preparing the writ.

The other main risk for an HEI and any other defendant in an action for defamation is the amount of damages which might be awarded against them. Damages for defamation are based on the degree of harm suffered to the plaintiff's reputation and this depends on the number of people seeing the defamatory comments and the value of the plaintiff's reputation. Although there has been a tendency to curb the extortionate damages awarded against newspapers, the risk of damages being awarded against defendants in a defamation case involving the Internet is considerable. Newspapers tend to have a circulation in only one country, but the Internet is accessible worldwide. This means that the courts would consider whether a plaintiff had a worldwide reputation which had been damaged by a defamatory remark. They may also have to consider the popularity of the relevant web-site or bulletin board. If the number of viewers is small, the damages awarded will reflect this, but some sites and boards are extremely popular and attract thousands of visitors daily.

Minimizing risks

Leaving aside the international angle, there is a need to consider how an HEI may minimize its risks and those run by its staff and students in relation to a defamation action brought in the UK. It must be emphasized that what constitutes sensible and prudent action under UK law may be viewed as an assumption of responsibility in another country. An HEI will have to consider what the most sensible approach is given its potential risks, but, as a rule, it is probably best to observe the law in this country before worrying about actions brought abroad.

Parliament enacted the Defamation Act in 1996 which deals specifically with remarks put out across the Internet. It does not, however, make the position of an HEI which hosts web-pages or a bulletin board any clearer.

Traditionally, the law has provided that anyone involved in the publication of a defamatory remark may be sued, but it has distinguished between primary and secondary publishers. A primary publisher has no defence, even if it did not know the statement was defamatory. A secondary publisher, on the other hand, can escape liability if it can demonstrate that it did not know of the defamatory material, had no reason to suppose defamatory material might exist in the publication, and that this ignorance was not as a result of it failing to take reasonable and sensible precautions to avoid publishing defamatory material.

If an HEI is responsible for deciding what appears on a bulletin board or a web-site, it will clearly be a primary publisher and liable for any defamatory material originating from its Internet connections. If, however, it does not control the content of the site then it may be able to claim to be a secondary publisher and to rely on the defence just described. Examples of sites where an HEI might be a secondary publisher include sites run by students or other individuals at an HEI or sites connected to the HEI's sites. There is very little scope for claiming to be a secondary publisher in respect of sites which are maintained as the official HEI sites.

If an HEI wants to plead the defence available to a secondary publisher it needs to show that it has behaved responsibly. At the very least, this will involve vetting postings on the computer systems about which it has cause to feel suspicious and, depending on the resources available to the HEI and the amount of traffic it has on its system, perhaps demanding some monitoring. The HEI should also ensure that all users are aware that it reserves the right to edit material and even to disconnect users if that becomes necessary. At the same time, it should also make it very clear that individuals are responsible for the contents of their own web-sites and personal communications and cannot abrogate responsibility to the HEI. If this point is not made, the HEI may find itself liable for any defamatory remarks posted by any of its students or staff.

If an HEI is involved in a claim for defamation, it may find that not only are damages awarded against it, but the court could also order that material be removed and that the HEI disclose the identity of any relevant party, even if the HEI has been found to be an innocent party.

Related to defamation is the issue of free speech. The German authorities famously put pressure on an Internet service provider to close the account of a leading US neo-Nazi. Under US laws his rhetoric, although patently offensive, was protected in the USA as an exercise of his constitutional right to exercise free speech. His actions were illegal under the German constitution, but the web-site was based in the USA and not subject to German law. It is understood that the Internet service provider did terminate access to the neo-Nazi web-page.

The UK Government, on the other hand, took no such approach over criticism of the Saudi Government by dissidents from that country. In March 1996, Ian Taylor, the then Science and Technology Minister, stated that the Government favoured Internet service providers and hosts developing codes of practice covering not only what is illegal on the Internet, but also what is unacceptable. This approach has been the preferred choice of the companies who are active on the Internet. The Labour Party, on the other hand, has joined the calls for international regulation coming from Governments, including those of China, France, Singapore and, by implication, the USA (given its hastily conceived and apparently unconstitutional telecommunications bill).

Conclusions

To avoid liability for the use which it, its staff and its students make of the Internet, an HEI should take several steps. Such steps might avoid the sort of recent problem faced at the University of Melbourne where a member of staff has been sacked for using the Internet not only to download pornography, but also to breach copyright on software.

It should consider whether its employment contracts and staff procedures make clear what can and cannot be done on an HEI's computer network. In particular, it should consider instituting an Information Technology Security Policy based on BS5799, available from the British Standards Institute, laying down the procedures staff should follow when using or supervising the use of information technology. It should adopt a policy of training its staff and students on the security risks which may be encountered on the Internet and should consider adopting a monitoring and supervision policy appropriate to the HEI's resources, the amount of use made of its computer networks and the type of use to which those networks are put. Most importantly, every user should, before being allowed access to the Internet, be given a (hopefully) short document spelling out those actions which are prohibited for users of the HEI's Internet terminals. The JANET 'Acceptable Use Guidelines' are a good example of the sort of guidelines which an HEI might wish to place on its staff and users. Obviously, risks vary according to circumstances and some terms may not seem appropriate whilst, in other cases, it may be necessary to focus on a particular risk and draft user guidelines so that certain types of behaviour are clearly forbidden. It is also advisable for HEIs to ensure that each user signs a form agreeing to be bound by these guidelines before being allowed access to the Internet.

Further reading

See the further reading section for Chapter 10, and also Gringas, C. and Nathanson, N. (1997) *Nabarro Nathanson: The Law of the Internet.* London: Butterworth Law.

Part 5

The Higher Education Institution as
a Business

12

Trading Companies

John Boardman (Eversheds)

Editors' introduction

A few higher education institutions (HEIs) have run all their commercial activities through a wholly-owned subsidiary trading company for over 25 years. More have established such companies only recently and others have not (yet) seen the need to have a company at all. Some HEIs use such a company only for very specific trading activities.

This chapter explores the reasons (tax, commercial and legal) for creating a trading company. It looks at the structure of such a company and the degree to which it really can protect the 'parent' HEI from liability if there were major problems and extensive damages to be paid. There is an exploration of the duties of the HEI staff, who will also be the directors of the company, and whether they can be left, in certain circumstances, with personal liability or whether their personal position is always protected by their being employees of the HEI and by being directors only because they are required to be so by the HEI as part of their jobs. In which case, might not the HEI be vicariously liable for those employees via the well-established route of employer's liability even when those employees are functioning as the supposedly independent directors of the trading company? The chapter also deals with the routine demands of company law imposed on the running of the company, including the need to have annual general meetings (AGMs), the need for meetings of the board of directors to follow a certain format and the need to file company accounts annually.

From a US perspective Kaplin and Lee (1995a) noted in a new chapter to the Third Edition, ('The College and the Business/Industrial Community') that 'Entry into the world of business and industry exposes higher education institutions to a substantial dose of commercial law . . . contract law is the foundation.' (Kaplin and Lee, 1995a: 911). They comment that income-generating activities have increased significantly in recent years: 'With increasing frequency and vigour, postsecondary institutions have expanded the scope of "auxiliary" enterprises or operations that involve the sale of goods, services, or leasehold (rental) interests in real estate.' (Kaplin and Lee, 1995a: 929) As early as 1940, a US case concerned an HEI operating an airport to support its course in aeronautical engineering. A case in 1957 concerned the HEI running a TV station. Later cases concerned a laundry, a residential conference centre and the sale of hearing aids.

Often the issue is allegedly unfair competition for local business arising from the use of State-subsidized HEI premises from which to run a similar operation. Some US States forbid publicly-funded HEIs from engaging in certain competitive commercial transactions. There are also relevant Federal anti-trust laws (e.g. the case of an HEI in an undergraduate textbook price war, the HEI bookshop and a local one in fierce competition). The US laws are similar to those in the UK in relation to the taxing of profit-making trading activities. Also increasingly common are research collaboration projects, partnerships, joint ventures and sponsorship arrangements.

> Virtually all such arrangements, involving either institutional or faculty relationships, with industry, have the potential for creating complex combinations of legal, policy, and managerial issues. Perhaps most difficult are the potential conflict-of-interest issues arising from arrangements that precipitate split loyalties, which could distract attention and drain resources from the academic enterprise.
>
> (Kaplin and Lee, 1995a: 947–8)

Great care and skill is needed to protect the HEI's interests. They 'should make sure that they are served by legal counsel with expertise in the complex problems of technology transfer and the starting of commercial ventures' (Kaplin and Lee, 1995a: 948). (For more on intellectual property, see Chapter 10.)

See especially the February 1997 Charity Commissioners' booklet CC35 *Charities and Trading*, and the Inland Revenue's C52 *Trading by Charities – Guidelines on the tax treatment of trades carried on by charities*. The former can be obtained by ringing 01823 345427; the latter on 0151 472 6038. The Charity Commissioners state in paragraph 68 of their booklet that their guidance on good practice in relation to trading is based on 'our experience of cases, where substantial amounts of a charity's money have been lost as a result of ill-considered investments in subsidiary trading companies . . .'. (See also Customs & Excise booklet VAT Notice 701/1 *Charities*.)

Introduction

Trading companies are set up for a variety of reasons and can be a useful vehicle for an HEI to use. In 1996 the Higher Education Funding Council (HEFC) produced a report on such companies. However, some questions remain. Why is the company being set up in the first place? Does the HEI have the power to set up the company? What continuing liability will the HEI and its officers have and what are the responsibilities of the directors of the company? What are the disadvantages of having other shareholders in the company? Other models such as partnerships are possible, but they are often unsatisfactory from a legal point of view and are seldom used.

The reasons for setting up a trading company

Essentially, trading through a separate trading company has a number of benefits.

1. Charitable status and taxation:
   - it is encouraged, and may be necessary, under charity law;
   - it has tax advantages – profits derived from the activity may be taxable if carried on by the HEI. Although, in principle, taxable in the hands of the subsidiary, the extraction of the profits via Gift Aid or a deed of covenant eliminates the tax charges and there may be VAT savings too.
2. Commercial:
   - the subsidiary company will be a separate entity from the HEI, with the benefit of limited liability and perhaps having a more entrepreneurial environment;
   - the powers of the HEI may not allow it to carry on the desired activity – companies can have much wider powers.
3. Tax schemes:
   - some companies are set up, not strictly for trading purposes, but for the purposes of tax saving schemes. However, most of the principles in this chapter apply to such companies as well, so they will also be considered here.

Charitable status and taxation

HEIs usually possess charitable status either as an exempt charity or, exceptionally, as an excepted charity. The significance of their being exempt or excepted charities is that the Charity Commissioners have little jurisdiction over them and many of the regulatory provisions of the Charities Act 1993 do not apply. However, most of the information and guidance published by the Charity Commission expounds charity law in general (which does apply to exempt and excepted charities) and good practice, which all charities should generally follow. Some HEIs are charitable companies limited by guarantee and are subject to the direct control of the Charity Commissioners. (For more on charity trusteeship, see Chapter 4.) The Charity Commissioners have stated that, where a charity wishes to benefit largely from permanent trading for the purpose of fund-raising, it should do so through a separate non-charitable trading company so that its charitable status is not endangered (see Leaflet CC35, a Charity Commission publication on trading). If the HEI is not aware of the consequences of trading, it could by trading be putting at risk its status as a charity for tax purposes. The purpose of trading is usually to generate income and profit, but it must be extremely careful if it is to avoid paying tax on that profit. It is a common misconception that charities, and hence HEIs, are automatically exempt from tax. A charity is still, in principle, subject to tax on the profits of any trade activities. Although there are exceptions to this rule, they are restrictive and the conditions are often difficult to satisfy. Before an HEI establishes a subsidiary trading company for tax purposes, it should first consider whether this is actually necessary. The activities which the HEI proposes to carry on may be covered by a statutory tax exemption contained in the Income and Corporation Taxes Act (ICTA) 1988, Section 505.

Section 505(1)(*e*) provides that income from trading activity is exempt if the profits are applied for charitable purposes and:

- the trade is exercised in the course of the actual carrying out of a primary purpose of the charity – as in the case of the provision of education training and research by an HEI;
- the work in connection with the trade is mainly carried out by beneficiaries of the charity.

An Inland Revenue Extra Statutory Concession C4 further states that tax will not be charged on profits made at bazaars, jumble sales, gymkhanas, carnivals, firework displays and similar activities arranged by voluntary organizations or charities for the purpose of raising funds for charities, subject to certain restrictions. The difficulty here is that all the conditions of the concession must be met and there is no right of appeal if the Inland Revenue refuses to grant the benefit of the concession. In any event, these may not be of much help to an HEI. The Inland Revenue has also agreed to a special *de minimis* exemption in cases where a primary purpose trading activity which falls within the ICTA 1988, Section 505(1)(*e*), may include an element of some non-exempt trading. However, it will establish first whether the non-exempt activity can be assessed as a separate trade in its own right. It is a difficult task to fall into these statutory exemptions.

Charitable status confers a number of tax benefits. It allows the HEI to be exempt from capital gains, income and corporation taxes on income arising from the carrying on of the HEI's primary purpose. Further, any receipt of money by way of inheritance is exempt from inheritance tax. HEIs are also eligible for other benefits, (e.g. business rates relief) and are not liable to pay stamp duty. However, by directly carrying out non-exempt trading, charitable status and its consequent tax benefits may be lost.

Commercial

An HEI might want to devolve certain activities away from its core for commercial reasons. This may be the case for certain money-making activities (such as the exploitation of inventions and know-how). The setting up of a trading company could be to provide a focus for a commercial enterprise with a different culture from that of an HEI. The separation of 'pure' charitable activities from those which are essentially commercial is sometimes seen as desirable. Using a trading company could also facilitate the setting up of a joint venture. A company structure is often a sensible way to effect this. The establishment of a trading subsidiary will benefit the HEI by providing it with limited liability. This allows for trading which is considered more speculative or risky to be isolated from the assets of the HEI. However, the HEI should be aware that this advantage might be lost in certain circumstances.

Tax schemes

Many companies have been set up by HEIs as part of 'off the shelf' tax schemes. These are established primarily to avoid tax and often have little or no commercial justification. Many of these companies were set up to avoid substantial amounts of VAT on building works, but some of the loopholes which they sought to exploit have now been blocked and the use of subsidiary companies for such a purpose is less common. However, more complex schemes are now being sold.

Conclusion

The real purpose of a trading company is not always clearly thought out and, in practice, it can often be difficult to know what its true purpose is.

Taxation

As mentioned previously, taxation is one of the reasons trading companies are used. The establishment of trading subsidiaries for charities is a well-recognized practice, which is not classified as tax avoidance. There are a number of taxation consequences which are dealt with as follows.

Financing the trading company

One challenge is to provide adequate working capital without prejudicing the benefits of limited liability. However, this only becomes a real problem in the case of very substantial operations and is usually soluble. The important aims should be:

- to make sure that all dealings between the HEI and the trading subsidiary are on an 'arms' length' basis and properly documented;
- to pay before the subsidiary's year end a generous estimate of its trading profit, less income tax at the basic rate, to the HEI.

Loans

Where there is a decision to establish a subsidiary, the charity will often own all the shares in the trading company. The trading company will require funding which could be made available by:

- borrowing from a commercial source;
- borrowing from the charity;
- the issue of share capital.

(Lai *et al.*, 1996, 550–1)

The Charity Commissioners have stated that capital required for the expansion, or even the survival, of a trading subsidiary should come from a commercial source and not divert the charity's resources from its charitable activities. However, there are difficulties with this proposition. First, a commercial source will usually require a guarantee to repay any loan from the charity itself, so removing much of the protection of any limited liability for the charity. Second, the subsidiary will usually have to pay a higher rate of interest on a loan obtained from a commercial source than the charity would. This will benefit neither the subsidiary nor the charity. Accordingly, the solution that most charities adopt is to provide the trading subsidiary with a secured loan at a market rate of interest. The provision of working capital to trading subsidiaries is a considerable practical difficulty especially as they grow in turnover. All realized profits must be paid to the charity each year, so if tax is to be avoided, they can only accumulate reserves by means of unrealized gains and they frequently have insignificant fixed assets.

The ICTA 1988, Sections 505 and 506 broadly state that the charity could lose a tax exemption already obtained if it uses the profits for non-qualifying purposes. A list of qualifying investments and qualifying loans is contained in Parts 1 and 2 of the ICTA 1988, Schedule 20. That list does not specifically include investment in, or loans to, subsidiary companies. However, a charity can make a claim to the Inland Revenue to ensure that it will treat such loans or investments as qualifying on the basis that they are made for the benefit of the charity and not merely for the avoidance of tax. Both the Inland Revenue and the Charity Commissioners expect transactions with the trading subsidiary to be on an 'arms' length' basis. In other words, the investment must stand up to commercial scrutiny. This will be tested in the case of a loan by the rate of interest payable, the terms of the repayment and the security.

Extraction of profits

Once the subsidiary begins to make a profit, it needs to adopt an effective method of passing that profit onto the HEI without incurring any liability to tax. There are three basic ways of doing this:

1. by deed of covenant;
2. by Gift Aid;
3. by dividend.

A payment under a deed of covenant is a charge on income. As such, if a company makes a profit and properly covenants all of its profits to a charity there will be no charge to tax. The amount covenanted and paid during the relevant accounting reference period will be tax-free in the hands of the HEI and tax-deductible for the subsidiary. The trading company does not make a gross payment to the parent HEI. It must deduct income tax at the basic rate from the covenanted amount, pay the net amount to the HEI, and pay the tax to the Inland Revenue. On receiving the net payment, the HEI can reclaim the tax deducted from the covenanted payment.

Under the ICTA 1988, Section 338(1), the payments made under deed of covenant are only deductible in computing taxable profits if there are profits chargeable to tax in the year in question. This often creates a problem since the actual taxable profits of the accounting period are not usually known until after the end of the accounting period. To overcome this difficulty, the deed of covenant will usually allow the trading subsidiary to make an estimated payment with the facility that any over-payments are returned by the HEI once the taxable profits of the subsidiary are agreed. This is specifically allowed by the Inland Revenue. However, this facility will not allow a trading subsidiary retrospectively to top up its covenant if the covenant payment is below the taxable profits. Therefore, it is better to over-estimate the taxable profits of the accounting period.

Gift Aid provides tax relief for single tax donations made to a charity (the ICTA 1988, Section 339). The trading company should deduct basic rate income tax when it makes the payment to the charity and pay the tax to the Inland Revenue. The charity then reclaims the tax from the Inland Revenue. The gross amount of the payment is the charge on income. It is allowed as a deduction against the company's profits for corporation tax purposes for the accounting period during which the payment is made.

It is a matter of choice whether the payment is made under a deed of covenant or Gift Aid. Neither is automatic. Certainly Gift Aid is effective if a payment needs to be made urgently and there is no covenant in place. A deed of covenant has two advantages:

1. the HEI is assured that the net profits of the subsidiary will be paid to the HEI and this provides additional justification for providing finance and facilities to the subsidiary;
2. in the deed of covenant it is possible to provide a mechanism so that if the annual profits are over-estimated, the excess can be returned to the subsidiary. This cannot be done so neatly with Gift Aid.

Another option is to pay a dividend (Lai *et al.*, 1996: D75/1). Paying a dividend can offer some degree of flexibility if the company wants to retain some income to expand its functions, although any income retained would be subject to tax. The dividend route is really only appropriate if the company is liable to pay tax at the small companies rate. When paying the dividend, the Company will have to account for advance corporation tax (ACT), but the HEI should be able to recover the basic rate tax under the ICTA 1988, Section 505. (**Editors' note**: the Finance Act 1997 contains provision to allow trading companies to make their 'donations' to the 'parent' charity up to nine months *after* the end of the company's tax year, thereby alleviating some of the problems about the timing of such payments and the predicting of profits as discussed above.)

VAT

As charities, HEIs are subject to VAT administration that is extremely complex. It consists of aspects of standard-rated, zero-rated and exempt supplies, and involves questions of business and non-business activities. A detailed analysis of the nature of VAT can be found in *Halsbury's Laws*, 4th Edition, Volume 5(2), paragraph 360.

HEIs may apply for voluntary registration if their taxable supplies do not exceed the threshold, but those HEIs whose activities are either wholly non-business or wholly exempt, cannot register for VAT. This can be a disadvantage since, if you cannot register, you cannot reclaim input tax. In practice, almost all HEIs' supplies are exempt and so they are able to recover input tax only on purchases for the purpose of non-exempt supplies which they are making. It is important that the trading subsidiary only carries out taxable activities, which means that it should ensure all activities are run for a profit. As such, all VAT charged to the trading company should be reclaimable, and it will account for output VAT on all its standard rate supplies and on any zero-rated supplies also made by the trading company. Businesses which make only taxable supplies and recover all their VAT inputs will only have regard to the cost of an item excluding any applicable VAT. Education and training delivered by an HEI will be exempt from VAT, but that supplied by its trading subsidiary will not. Equally, the HEI will not be able to recover VAT on its inputs for this activity, but the subsidiary will be able to do so. If, for a given course of education and training, there are significant inputs which are taxable for VAT purposes, it is possible (for the same net cost to the VAT-registered customer) to recover these inputs by delivering the training by the trading subsidiary. If the course is provided by the HEI, the VAT on the inputs will be irrecoverable.

Powers of the HEI

As charities, HEIs must apply property and income only for their defined charitable purpose. In addition, the instruments which contain the constitution of the particular institution will need to be looked at to ensure the HEI has the power to form and, if necessary, to fund the particular subsidiary, and also which body within the HEI has the power to make the decisions in relation to it. For example, statutory HEIs will have their powers limited by the provisions of the Education Reform Act (ERA) 1988. An HEI would have to carefully consider what it was allowed to do under its constitution before embarking on any such arrangement. Particularly difficult decisions will need to be taken in relation to companies formed as part of tax saving schemes.

The use of a subsidiary to avoid the problems is, as mentioned previously, encouraged by the Charity Commissioners and the Inland Revenue, but at the end of the day the subsidiary is doing something the charity often cannot. It will often be the case that there will be a fine line between what is *ultra vires* the institution and what is not. On the one hand, a training subsidiary will doubtless not cause any concerns. On the other, purely money making operations may do. Particular problems will also occur with companies where the HEI does not have a 100 per cent stake. For example, guaranteeing the bank borrowing of such a company may be *ultra vires* – see *Rosemary Simmonds v United Dominions Trust and Partners*.

Relationship between HEI and the trading company

There will often be an agreement between the HEI and its trading company dealing with the relationship between the two. The trading company may need to use various resources of the HEI. This can include the secondment of employees and management charges, and there may be a need for an agency or licensing agreement to allow the subsidiary to market the name and logo of the HEI. Such an agreement will be required particularly if the company is not a 100 per cent subsidiary. Reporting structures from the trading company to the HEI are sometimes very unclear. It is important that these are defined so that clear lines of responsibility exist between the trading company and the appropriate body of the HEI.

Liability

In theory, the establishing of a limited liability trading company has the potential to reduce the liability of the HEI. Establishing a trading company allows for trading which is more speculative – giving rise to the possibility of greater profit without risk to the assets of the HEI. If the trading company fails, the HEI can walk away. However, in practice, the position is often different and for legal and commercial reasons the HEI may still find itself liable.

Legal reasons

- If the HEI provides a guarantee, for example to the bank.
- Shadow directors and wrongful trading.
- Lifting the corporate veil.

Wrongful trading

If a company becomes insolvent, there is a potential liability for wrongful trading. The directors can be made personally liable for liabilities incurred by the company after the directors knew *or ought to have known* that an insolvent liquidation was inevitable (see the Insolvency Act 1986, Sections 213 and 214). For this purpose, 'directors' includes *de facto* directors (i.e. those who act as directors but are not formally recorded as such) and shadow directors. If an officer of an HEI regularly attends meetings or is involved in the strategic planning for the trading subsidiary and acts in a way which a director would, he or she may be a *de facto* director. All liabilities incurred by the other directors will thus be shared with any *de facto* directors as well. A shadow director is a person in accordance with whose instructions the actual directors of the company are accustomed to act. This may be the HEI itself or officers of it – see *Re Hydrodam (Corby) Ltd (in Liquidation)*. The effect of this is that in the event of insolvency, the HEI and its officers may be held liable as shadow directors for the debts of the company. The status of both *de facto* directors and shadow directors is, by its very nature, determined after the fact. Consequently, any HEI may be acting in such a manner without realizing it. For this reason, great care is required to ensure that no body or person is acting in a way that could possibly be interpreted as incurring liability.

Lifting the corporate veil

The courts also have a general power to look behind the separate and independent nature of a subsidiary company in certain limited circumstances (for example, fraud). This is called 'lifting the corporate veil' – see *Halsbury's Laws* (1996), Volume 7(1), paragraph 93.

Commercial reasons

In addition, HEIs may feel they simply cannot let a subsidiary of theirs fail and will support it in any event. If they let a subsidiary fail, it could damage their reputation.

Starting the company

General

The same practical considerations which would be required for any limited company will also usually apply to a trading subsidiary. A business plan should be prepared, which should contain details of the objectives of the company, the management structure, the requirement for financing, an assessment of risks and a discussion of the constraints which will or may be placed on the activities of the subsidiary. Consideration will need to be given to the effect which the establishment of a trading company will have on the charitable status of the HEI and whether a company is the correct vehicle for trade, rather than a partnership or joint venture (for more on partnerships, see *Halsbury's Laws*, 4th Edition, Volume 35).

Incorporation

Every company will be different, although generally they will have the same basic aim which will be to trade. Companies can be incorporated as companies limited by guarantee or shares – see *Halsbury's Laws* (4th Edition) Volume 7(1), paragraphs 103–10. Companies are either purchased 'off the shelf' from a law stationers or can be newly incorporated. They are usually bought 'off the shelf' as it is often easier and quicker to purchase a ready-made company and adapt it, rather than incorporate a new company. Following incorporation, the company is given a unique company number which will not change, even though its name may.

Once the company has been issued with the necessary constitution documents, it is ready to hold a board meeting of the directors. They should be appointed either at the first board meeting, or, if a company has been purchased 'off the shelf', directors will already have been appointed. At this meeting, a Company Secretary will also need to be appointed. The Company Secretary will act under the instruction of the company to file all documents required by the Companies Registrar and keep the statutory books up to date. Failure to file these documents and to file them in time could result in a company being fined or struck off and can give rise to fines for the directors. Finally, a chairman should be appointed to run the meetings of the board. This should be one of the directors. The directors will have to decide on and appoint the auditors (if needed) of the company, its accounting reference date, the address of its registered office and matters such as insurance and bank accounts (see *Tolley's Company Law Handbook*, 1997).

The board will also need to grant service contracts to its directors and decide on their terms of employment, including remuneration. The service contracts can be awarded for a maximum of five years. A longer term must be agreed by the members in a general meeting by ordinary resolution.

Types of companies

Company limited by shares
If the HEI decides to set up a trading company limited by shares, it must decide who will have the shares and in what proportion. It may wish to take 100 per cent or it may wish to allow other bodies to be involved. The extent to which the HEI will be able to control the company will depend on the amount of shares it holds. If it holds over 75 per cent it will have the power to pass special and extraordinary resolutions of the company and, with

51 per cent, ordinary resolutions. The effect of minority shareholdings will be dealt with later (the Companies Act 1985, Sections 370, 378 and 379A).

Where the HEI does not have a 100 per cent holding in the company, there will often be a shareholders agreement. This is a contractual document signed by all the shareholders which details what agreements have been reached between the shareholders outside of and in preference to the memorandum and articles. This document should be used to protect the HEI's and other shareholders' positions within the company.

Company limited by guarantee
Companies limited by shares are commonly used where no profits are to be produced, (for example, a charitable subsidiary or a non-profit-making research association). A company limited by guarantee has no share capital. The members all agree that on dissolution they will pay in an amount, commonly £1 by way of guarantee. They are generally a less flexible vehicle than a company limited by shares.

Public limited companies (Plcs)
It is perfectly possible to form a subsidiary company as a Plc. This is sometimes done to give it greater credence and marketing appeal. There are downsides, such as the requirements for a greater share capital. There are also an increasing number of restrictions which apply to Plcs and not other companies which can make them traps for the unwary and reduce their flexibility.

Memorandum and articles of association

Companies have memorandum and articles of association as their constitution. These are usually standard documents, tailored to meet the individual requirements. The memorandum states the main purpose of the company and its powers – what is and is not permitted. Although the company could be stated in its memorandum to be a 'general commercial company', the memorandum usually contains specific provisions defining the activities of the company. Where these provisions are not sufficiently thought out and do not enable the company to fulfil its aims, the efficient running of the company will be affected. If the company does something beyond its defined powers, this will be *ultra vires* and so void. In particular it will, therefore, be vital that the memorandum provides the power to enable the company to pass its profits to the parent HEI.

The articles state how the company is run, what its internal procedures are and, in particular, they will deal with members' and directors' rights and obligations. The usual changes from the standard articles will be in relation to companies with more than one shareholder and will deal with such matters as the allotment and transfer of shares, share rights and the appointment and removal of directors.

Members

Members of a company, called 'shareholders' in a company limited by shares, ultimately control the company. However, most of their powers are delegated down to the directors and their real power lies in appointing and removing the directors (see the Companies Act 1985, Sections 292 and 303). Meetings of members are called 'general meetings'. Any meeting other than an AGM is called an extraordinary general meeting (EGM). The AGM usually consists of formal business such as receiving the accounts and appointment of auditors and directors. There are procedures for dealing with matters by written resolutions as opposed to formal meetings. If a formal members meeting is held, the HEI will have to appoint a corporate representative to act on its behalf at the meeting. Although it is possible to have a private limited company with one shareholder (see The Companies (Single Member Private Limited Companies) Regulations 1992), it is still common for 100 per cent wholly owned subsidiaries to have two share-holders – the HEI and a nominee.

The directors

The board of directors will normally take the strategic management deci-sions in a company, with implementation being delegated down from the managing director to the rest of the executive. There are two sources of directors' duties. Under statute, directors have certain liabilities (for example in relation to health and safety legislation and environmental legislation). They will, therefore, be liable *directly* if things go wrong. Although it is possible to have insurance cover for negligent acts, it is not possible to get insurance cover for criminal penalties such as fines for a health and safety offence.

Under common law, directors are also under a duty to act in good faith and in a fiduciary capacity. This means they should act above all in the best interests of the company. These duties are owed to the company and *not* to the nominating HEI. Difficult questions of conflicts of interest can arise in this way. The directors must also exercise reasonable skill and care in relation to the conduct of the company's affairs. Failure to do this could lead to the director being ordered to compensate the company for any loss incurred and account for any profit made. Directors have a duty to declare any interests they have in the company's contracts and property transac-tions (see the Companies Act 1985, Sections 317 and 320).

The Cadbury Report (Cadbury, 1994) gives guidelines on how directors should act, recommending divisions of responsibility on the board and clearly laid down, effective procedures. It also recommends that all dir-ectors should be allowed to seek legal and financial advice at the expense of the company. Although not required by law, many private companies follow the Cadbury Code as guidelines of good practice.

The company secretary

The company secretary is normally responsible for detailed compliance with the relevant legislation. This means that he or she must ensure notices of meetings are prepared and distributed correctly, the meetings themselves are conducted correctly and that resolutions passed by the company are filed if necessary. The minutes of all meetings must be entered in the statutory books, which must be kept accurate and up-to-date, particularly in relation to the Register of Directors and Secretaries, the Register of Members, the Register of Interests and the Registers relating to the allotments and transfers of shares. Failure to do this can result in fines (the Companies Act 1985, Section 288).

As a board, the directors and company secretary must ensure that accounts and directors' reports are kept and filed when appropriate. The company will be required to make an annual return, stating the identity of the members and their shares in the company, together with a list of the directors' details. Further, the requirements relating to the publishing of the company name, registered office (a sign must also be displayed at that office) and company number on stationery must all be complied with. Failure to comply results in a fine (see *Tolley's Company Law Handbook*, 1997).

Minority shareholdings

Many companies owned by HEIs will be 100 per cent wholly owned subsidiaries. Some will have minority shareholdings held by other shareholders. This is often the case with companies beneath the main parent subsidiary. Sometimes, HEIs themselves may have a minority stake. Occasionally, the other shareholders may be staff at the HEI and this can give rise to difficult questions of conflicts of interest. It is important to understand the rights and obligations of other shareholders. Members of the company act by passing resolutions. There are four types of these – special, extraordinary, ordinary and elective. The special and extraordinary resolutions require 75 per cent of those present to be in favour. Ordinary resolutions require more than 50 per cent of those present to be in favour and elective resolutions must obtain unanimous consent. Ordinary resolutions are usually all that are needed, with special resolutions being reserved for more fundamental changes (for example changes to the articles). However, as most decisions are in fact taken by directors or other executive staff, additional restrictions are commonly found in the articles or shareholders agreement ensuring that certain decisions must have the agreement of all, or a specified percentage, of the shareholders.

Minority shareholders have rights and remedies for the breach of those rights (e.g. under the Companies Act 1985, Section 459, they have the right not to be oppressed by the majority). This would mean, for example, the majority shareholder is not entitled to pay out large salaries to staff, thereby completely using up all the profits available for distribution by way of dividend. The articles will also deal with transfer of shares, usually with preemption rights giving the other shareholders the right to buy the shares of the transferor at an agreed price. Unfortunately shareholders frequently fall out. The legal mechanisms in articles and shareholders agreements will not make shareholders work together – at the most, they deal with a mechanism for splitting up the company on a fall out. Any structure which involves other shareholders must, therefore, be thought through very carefully.

Further reading

Charlesworth, T. and Morse, G. (1995) *Company Law*. London: Sweet & Maxwell.

Cheffins, B. R. (1996) *Company Law*. Oxford: Oxford University Press.

Goode, R. (1995) *Commercial Law*. London: Penguin.

Lai, J. P., Martin, S. and Cranidge, C. (1996) *Tolley's Company Secretary's Handbook*. London: Sweet & Maxwell.

Shackleton on the Law and Practice of Meetings, 9th edn (1997) London: Sweet & Maxwell.

Sparrow, A. P. (1996) *The Role of the Company Director*. London: Technical Communications (Publishing) Ltd.

Sparrow, A. P. (1997) *The Responsibilities of Company Directors*, (FT 'Management Briefings' series). London: Pitman.

Tolley's Company Law Handbook, 3rd edn (1997) London: Tolley.

Treitel, G. H. (1996) *The Law of Contract*. London: Butterworths.

See also the booklets from the Charity Commissioners, Customs and Excise and the Inland Revenue mentioned in the Editors' Introduction.

13

Mergers and Acquisitions

Simon Arrowsmith (Martineau Johnson)

Editors' introduction

The current system of further and higher education in the UK is one that has 'grown like Topsy'. It seems to owe nothing to rational planning and design, but everything to chance, politics and history. There is hardly a city in the country which does not have two or more higher education institutions (HEIs) and a sprinkling of further education institutions (FEIs). Sometimes those institutions have even grown up on adjacent sites, separated in one instance by only a low copper beech hedge and, in another, by grassed areas. It would seem extremely likely, therefore, that as financial pressures increase (as they surely will), there will be more and more mergers. These will not only take place between institutions from the same sector, but also between sectors. Even before the Dearing Committee met, several mergers between FEIs and HEIs had already been agreed in principle by the appropriate governing bodies. It would seem most probable that by the millenium the first 'regional' or 'community' universities will exist in the UK, encompassing the complete spectrum of what is now designated as further education and higher education (HE) work.

It is important to note that during the last 20 years there have been many mergers. There is now hardly a single free-standing institution left from the hundred or so teacher education and art and design monotechnics of the early 1970s. They have all combined, been merged with larger institutions or simply disappeared.

This chapter is, therefore, most timely and the proposed list of questions for a due diligence report will, no doubt, be referred to on frequent occasions. The section 'Practical tips' is also extremely helpful. To it, we would like to add the following two points from our own experiences.

- If at all possible, do not use the term 'merger' in public and certainly not 'acquisition' or 'takeover' in public. Such words invariably cause low morale and even panic. Euphemisms such as 'partnership' are preferable.

• At an early stage in any discussions, agree the future of the two heads of institution involved. (See Palfreyman *et al.*, forthcoming on *Managing Mergers.*)

As this volume goes to press, we note reports of the first ever proposed FE/HE merger to be cleared by the FECE for further negotiation: High Peak College and Mackworth College with Derby University, creating, possibly by 1 August 1998 an institution with 19,000 FE students and 12,000 HE students.

Introduction

The following (summarized) extracts come from trade press coverage of HE finances during the summer of 1996.

> A university calls in accountants to help draw up a recovery plan. Staff replacement is frozen and compulsory redundancies are contemplated to supplement previous programmes of voluntary redundancy and early retirement. Residential areas are sold and leased back. Offers to overseas postgraduate students double. An outpost of two university departments is closed and the operations contract into the core campus. The CVCP contemplates large-scale student loans to cover maintenance and a proportion of tuition fees. A university principal warns that cash pressures could force universities into 'privatization'. A university contemplates a wave of compulsory redundancies, trying to soften the blow by proposing as an alternative transfer of some of those lecturers affected to another HEI. HEFCE publishes details of its holdback methods designed to penalize both under-recruitment and over-recruitment of students. Admissions tutors are accused of poaching students during 'Clearing' to meet targets and avoid revenue funding cuts. Ballots of academic and ancillary staff are promised with a view to strike action in protest at funding cuts and pay offers. Proposals to limit funds allocated after the RAE to units of assessment graded 3 and above are criticized. FE Colleges make refunds to hundreds of students because of the closure of business-related courses, accusing universities of 'nicking our clients'. Universities face cuts of 30 per cent in funding for buildings and equipment in the current financial year, and 50 per cent in the next three years. The Secretary of State receives a report from the sector stressing the importance of achieving and/or preserving levels of surpluses and reserves 'appropriate for a commercial organization'.

Another summer is over and a new academic year begins!

HEIs face increasing competition to secure revenue funding from the public purse. Almost all need to cut revenue expenditure as far as they can without compromising operations. Tax-saving schemes put forward by thoughtful accountants are in vogue. The race has long since been on to maximize income from non-exchequer sources. In a private report, one HEI is characterized as the country's 'most successful university', the index of success being its alleged achievement of the lowest level of reliance on public revenue funding. The Committee of Vice-Chancellors and Principals (CVCP) takes legal advice as to whether 'top up' fees can be introduced without breach of contract. For some years, there have been experiments with 'cheap money' capital funding schemes involving innovative use of private sector finance. Not every HEI which got involved in the old business expansion schemes is equally pleased with the results. Some who considered the possibility but did not take the plunge are now glad that they did not bother. As yet, the private finance initiative does not seem to have taken off across the sector. Some lawyers active in both education and banking observe greater difficulty in setting up appropriate loans for capital developments. Not all HEIs seem equally adept at understanding and exploiting the possibility of European grant funding. Wholesale defections of prestigious research units are contemplated as a real threat.

The context in which to consider this chapter is that of an HE (and FE – in many areas the distinction is becoming increasingly blurred) sector in which public sector funding and regulation both appear to be driving institutions towards permanent strategic consideration of operations and options which are traditionally associated with private sector enterprises. A recognizable competitive educational market-place has formed and is developing rapidly. Among the characteristics of the market-place for which the winners (or perhaps the survivors) are already planning is its present and likely future fluidity. The model is not simply corporate. However, a comparable reconfiguration of the existing or traditional operating units in the market-place seems inevitable. Which HEIs will go bust? Will any be allowed to go bust in a sense recognizable in the corporate world? How would this happen? What corporate recovery strategy might be pursued locally or centrally? If traditional ideas about the education services to be delivered and their modes of delivery are undergoing radical change, how would this not involve a reconsideration of the number, size and nature of the operational vehicles – in short, merger/acquisition/takeover?

What is happening and why?

A serviceable legal definition of what is happening in merger/acquisition/takeover is that it is a transfer of activities which requires transfer of an HEI's assets, staff and third party rights and responsibilities. One party to the transaction may or may not disappear. Usually, there will be no direct equivalent of the purchase by a company of the share capital of another, in which the latter becomes a subsidiary of the former, but keeps its status as a separate legal entity. The emerging model for a full merger is usually one of the following:

1. the transferring entity ceases to exist, with all its assets and liabilities being vested in the transferee;
2. some, but not all, of the activities, assets and liabilities of the transferor are acquired and the transferor remains in existence independently with its operations reduced.

HEIs can and do acquire the assets and liabilities of other institutions and merge with them in that the two become one. An HEI can also acquire part of the operation of another institution. Many chartered universities have the requisite (private) statutory powers. The statutory universities, as higher education corporations (HECs) exist in a public statutory context which expressly recognizes the possibility of such transactions. Recent examples include an HEI acquiring the HE operation of an FE corporation, with the latter retaining its independent existence as a provider of FE.

The starting points in strategic management terms of this type of transaction are as follows:

1. Operationally, what is happening and intended to happen?
2. Why?

Both of these questions need to be answered confidently and clearly as a prerequisite to taking the appropriate structural decisions and pursuing the transaction to an effective conclusion. In general terms, managers may be quite clear on what they are acquiring, but the nature of the operations of the 'target' institution (or its relevant part) must be analysed and understood, as must the legal and constitutional basis on which the target operation is presently conducted.

The acquiring HEI's reasons for the merger will also determine both structure and procedure. For example, a takeover which is only one element of an HEI's overall acquisitive strategy will most likely (and most easily) be structured and followed through according to a preplanned pattern also used in other transactions. Is the merger aggressive or defensive? Is it largely designed to improve the acquiring HEI's future position in relation to funding? Does that relate to teaching, research, overseas students and/or other revenue sources? Is the potential for saving overheads by joining forces a major factor? Is it that the integration of the two operations will offer another potential and substantial saving? Is the proposed merger driven by synergy, quantifiable efficiency gains or benefits derived from combining or complementing existing operations? Does the acquirer know of the circumstances which have led to the target contemplating the merger? An understanding of these issues needs to be complemented by a detailed appreciation of the political context in which both operations work. By their nature, HEIs cater for a variety of constituencies at a variety of levels and are dependent on those constituencies to varying degrees. Contemplating any merger without understanding potentially adverse responses from all those constituencies will tend to stall or undermine the transaction.

Which route?

The transaction might be either statutory/constitutional or contractual, or it might have elements of both. The first question for managers is 'Can the HEI do what is proposed?'. Can the parties point to express powers in their constitutions or under relevant public statutes to enable them to carry out the transaction? If not, then revision of constitutional documents may be needed. This will tend to make for a long 'lead time' before the transaction can be completed because of the formalities and third-party approvals involved in fundamental constitutional change for HEIs. If there is no constitutional bar, then the parties will need to give thought to whether the legal framework for the merger will be exclusively constitutional or whether it may include elements of contract between the parties. If both parties are to survive the transaction as independent entities, there is some point in contracting, because there is some prospect (at least in theory) of the transferee being able to exercise contractual rights against the surviving transferor.

Precedents for exclusively constitutional mergers exist in, for example, the dissolution of FE corporations and the transfer of their assets, undertakings and staff to an HEC, and for exclusively contractual mergers in the acquisition by various HEIs of colleges of nursing and midwifery training from regional health authorities.

When either a part or the whole of an operation is transferring, it has been a frequent concern that the native characteristics or integrity of the transferring operation will be compromised or lost when it is subsumed into a larger legal whole. Such concerns tend to lead to exploration of quasi-autonomous structural options, such as the vesting of the target operations in a subsidiary company of the transferee, which will operationally direct the subsidiary while the transferor survives and retains some responsibility for, or stake in, the transferred activity. Although it is possible in theory to contemplate the sub-contracting of educational provision in this way, it is open to the objection that transferred operational control does not sit well with the retention of ultimate responsibility. In practice, there seems to be no advantage beyond what can be achieved by:

- a fully transferred and merged operation appropriately divisionalized within the transferee's organization;
- the admission by the transferee of a formal consultative role for the transferor or interested constituencies, and/or legally binding agreements made by the transferee to guarantee levels or areas of provision for specified periods, and to preserve the target's underlying asset base against depletion without replacement.

The subsidiary option also carries with it additional layers of bureaucracy because of the companies legislation regime, taxation issues and questions of employment (e.g. will employees transfer to the subsidiary or be employed by the transferee to do the subsidiary's work?). Unless the particular transaction suggests compelling reasons for using a subsidiary, it usually seems much more straightforward to follow a simpler structural route (the simplest available in any particular case) and then to make practical adaptations in the transferee's management structure to create the environment within which the merged institution (or the relevant part of it) can operate most satisfactorily.

There is, of course, a political dimension. It is frequently found that the prospect of wholesale dissolution of one party meets with significant resistance. If this issue is insurmountable, that in itself may be a signal that (perhaps for a probationary period) the parties should be contemplating some form of engagement which falls short of complete merger from the first day. Such possibilities are explored briefly later in this chapter.

In the event of wholesale dissolution, is it a matter of concern that the disappearance of one party to the transaction will (except in extreme cases, such as fraudulent misrepresentation) effectively destroy the transferee's ability to obtain recompense if the operation acquired proves in due course to be falling sadly short of legitimate expectations at the time of the merger in circumstances which involve breach of contract by the transferor? In practice, both the transferee's governing body and the relevant funding council(s) will simply need to be as confident as possible that the affairs of the target operation have been thoroughly investigated and the feasibility of the merged operation extensively justified by a thorough due diligence exercise prior to approval of any merger plans.

If the nature of the transaction is such that a specific matrix of contractual obligations governing the merger can be used, that is to be recommended. If nothing else, it will have the effect of focusing both parties on the nature of the transaction. The contract will set out:

- the basis on which the target operation is to change hands;
- when that will happen;
- precisely what will be transferred in terms of assets, liabilities, staff, etc;
- what residual liabilities and claims (if any) can be fixed on the transferor;
- the price to be paid (which may take the form of payment and/or the assumption of the liabilities of the target).

What is being transferred?

The question of whether an acquisition is something which the HEI ought to be entering into as a matter of strategy is one for the transferee's governing body to consider, taking into account the funding and commercial implications against the background of the institution's perceived role in the wider community. Policy and strategy need to be separated from operational responsibility. Although the governing body may be called on to take certain decisions or to resolve a negotiating impasse with strategic implications, it should delegate the responsibility for managing the transaction through to completion to the senior executive team. The governing body may also be called on to deal with and resolve political issues both external and internal to the HEI. The executive needs to identify with as much precision as possible what is being transferred, how operationally the transfer is expected to take place and how the new merged operation will work.

Is the whole operation being transferred – will or could some obligations remain with the transferor? If, for example, the chosen route to transfer is via statutory dissolution, then (in the absence of exclusions or special provisions) the whole of the real and personal property and the people and all liabilities may transfer, but that will not obviate the need to investigate the position thoroughly. If the transfer is to be contractual, then all issues of identification and appraisal of assets and staff must be addressed by the transferee with the assistance of the transferor before any contractual commitment is accepted. If the transfer is to be of part of the operation only, then it is likely that there will be shared assets and provision. The feasibility of dividing them up or continuing to share them, needs to be evaluated so that appropriate contractual arrangements can be made where probably none have existed before. Many examples of this type of process are to be found in the wake of statutory assets/undertakings transfers under both the Education Reform Act (ERA) 1988 and the Further and Higher Education Act 1992.

What are you getting?

In a traditional corporate acquisition, the transferee will commission a due diligence enquiry into the operations of the transferor, covering such matters as finance, personnel, assets, debts, outstanding or potential litigation and property. This will serve a number of purposes. It may bring to light matters of which the transferee was unaware and which could make a material difference to whether the transaction proceeds at all or the basis on which it goes forward. It will give the transferee a clearer picture of what it is acquiring. In corporate contractual terms, the transferor will usually give warranties about the state and condition of its business. Although the promises (of continuing effect) which comprise these warranties will invariably be qualified by disclosures against each or all of the warranties, the surviving promises will provide the transferee with a remedy under the contract if, after the acquisition, it turns out that material facts were not revealed.

In a merger in the HE sector, the significance of due diligence will vary according to whether the transferor survives or disappears. If the transferor survives, the acquiring HEI should ideally adopt the traditional corporate position of requiring and relying on warranties provided by the transferor. The transferee will still want to undertake a detailed due diligence exercise, but the transferee may not rely on the results of the due diligence *per se* but on any contractual warranties provided by the transferor, qualified by disclosures against those warranties. For a merger involving an HEI, there is the additional need to confirm the power of the transferor to give warranties. Transactions are not always between parties of equal bargaining power. That factor or the political climate surrounding the transaction may militate against the giving of any warranty, and there may be no choice but to accept this if the transaction is to proceed. In these circumstances, due diligence assumes an even greater importance than would be usual in a corporate transaction.

If the transferor is disappearing as an independent legal entity, there is unlikely in practice to be any body against whom the acquiring HEI can claim if the acquisition does not meet expectations. In theory, the acquiring institution could require warranties personally from members of the target's governing body. Leaving aside the question of whether the courts would enforce personal liability arising from breach of warranty, most transactions are unlikely to be effected in such a pitch of financial desperation that the transferee will both seek and be able to obtain such warranties. Nor is the transferor likely to favour giving warranties. Nevertheless, experience suggests that the possibility of a requirement on a governing body to provide warranties on a disposal can be used as a bargaining tool in improving other terms and conditions surrounding the transfer, and will at the very least serve to concentrate the minds of both the governing body and the executive of the transferor on the importance of providing a detailed and accurate representation of the state and condition of the target operation. It is suggested that, whether or not promises of warranty status can be obtained, there is a vital role to be played by professional advisers in obtaining and verifying as much detailed information as possible.

It would be pointless to try to identify in detail a full range of questions comprising the due diligence enquiry which will be equally relevant to all transactions. However, what follows will provide a flavour of the kind of subjects to be investigated.

1. Is all of the property actually owned by the target?
2. Are there any constraints on the use of any of the properties which would inhibit further alternative use and/or development?
3. Is there any property occupied by anyone else? If so, on what terms?
4. A detailed investigation of the planning history and prospects for the properties is recommended.
5. Investigate all employment and consultancy arrangements and consider whether existing pension structures can be accommodated.
6. Obtain full details of all employees and confirm that they can continue to be employed on their existing terms having regard to the requirements of the Transfer of Undertakings (Protection of Employment) Regulations 1981.
7. Are there any leases or occupational interests yielding rental stream or other investment return?
8. Any existing valuations should be checked and their underlying assumptions tested where possible.

9. New and recent buildings should be investigated to establish the contractual arrangements made with developers, builders and others at the time.
10. Possible contingent or other residual liability should be investigated (e.g. under former leases or in respect of environmental issues).
11. The extent and nature of the target's bank facilities need to be considered. How would they be affected by the merger?
12. The full range of the target's contractual commitments (and relevant documents) needs to be reviewed for (*inter alia*) any particularly onerous terms and for assignability.
13. Are there any outstanding issues relating to any recent or threatened Health and Safety Executive inspection or action?
14. Are all necessary liquor and other licences subsisting and valid, and are they subject to any terms and conditions which could be affected by the merger?
15. Review the list of items on lease, hire purchase, etc., and consider assignability. In the event of the merger, will there be any automatic terminations and possible consequent penalties?
16. Is the scope of your insurances likely to cover all assets and activities of the target?
17. Check the terms of any historic gifts or donations which may be subject to any conditions which may impact on the future activities of the target when under your control.
18. Check the terms of any Business Expansion Scheme or continuing capital scheme used to finance previous development projects.
19. Have any services been contracted out? Review the relevant documents and consider the employment position.
20. Obtain and appraise copies of any funding council or other relevant third party report on the target and its operations.
21. If the target is particularly specialized in its activities (e.g. an agricultural college), consider engaging specialist surveyors or other experts to ensure that the activities comply with all UK and other relevant regulations.
22. Consider whether environmental issues need any enquiries or other investigation.
23. Consider the constitutional basis of the target itself and the basis on which it regards itself as empowered to enter into the transaction.
24. Review key operational records, which might include minutes of meetings of the governing body, any executive body, the finance and general purposes committee, and the personnel/employment committee.
25. Obtain and appraise details of any subsidiary companies.
26. Consider any relevant external validation relationships and whether they will be affected by the merger.
27. Consider any franchising arrangements of the target, either as franchisor or franchisee.

28. Establish whether there are any charitable or other trusts technically independent from, but associated with, the target. Review the implications of the merger on these arrangements.
29. Investigate whether the target has complied and continues to comply with the terms of revenue or capital grants from any public or private source.
30. If relevant, review the assets transfer position of the target and establish whether there are any formal declared or possible pending disputes.
31. Take tax advice, especially in relation to any subsisting VAT-saving or deferral schemes.

It will be appropriate to identify key office holders/executives at the target and to make sure that successive drafts of the due diligence report (as it develops) are reviewed regularly by them as well as by your own executives. When the report reaches its final form, try to fix the governing body of the target with whatever degree of responsibility it will accept for the accuracy and completeness of the report. If possible, written confirmation as to its accuracy to the best of the governing body's knowledge and belief should be obtained. If this is not possible, at least seek confirmation that the governors have read it and see their comments on it.

Other options

Without wishing to be defeatist, it is essential at the planning stage and subsequently that HEIs look carefully at the widest possible range of contingencies. It does not undermine the process of successful negotiation carried out with a full merger in mind to reserve one's position on whether outcomes other than immediate full merger may turn out to be more desirable or, realistically, possible within a limited time scale. A further constitutional mechanism for demerger will be possible, but backing out (after the event) will always be more expensive, painful and demoralizing than experimenting with new operational arrangements during a finite transitional or even probationary period. Unravelling such a probationary arrangement will, in turn, be less difficult (structurally and culturally) than dissolving what was originally contemplated and initially carried out as a full eternal marriage.

Whatever their status – purposive, probationary or merely an experiment in ever closer association – transitional arrangements will require careful focus on:

• the working relationship between originally different sets of disciplinary and other procedures and regulations;
• a clear examination of a variety of exit contingencies and their implications;
• an investigation and assessment of all associated operations (including subsidiary companies, joint venture and franchising or other partnerships);
• clear decisions on where responsibilities for contingent and/or continuing liabilities will rest until each critical point in the process;

- evaluation of any subsisting and incomplete transfers of assets and liabilities into either party to the merger;
- preferably, a cautious approach to leasing and other contractual arrangements with any third parties which will or may survive the merger.

Practical tips

The range of legal, fiscal, accounting and other aspects of any form of associative or merger project will require outside professional advice, for two obvious reasons.

1. However substantial and multi-talented the in-house management teams on both sides may be, they will continue to have their independent day-to-day responsibilities for the running of their own institutions to attend to. The focus of the project and the efficiency with which it is driven forward are likely to be compromised if it is ever assumed that the particular project can simply be bolted on to existing management responsibilities. The range of investigative, analytical and negotiating jobs to be done will, however, probably also involve expertise outside the normal experience of even the most accomplished management teams.
2. Ultimately, merger proposals will require presentation to, and some form of validation by, a variety of outside bodies and the governing bodies of the institutions themselves. The resulting decision will be of critical and continuing importance. To arrive at the best informed decisions, and to be perceived as having prepared for those decisions in the most responsible way, will demand careful evidence of independent external investigation and assessment. There is a real as well as a perceived need for disinterested professionals in a variety of disciplines who will bring expertise, varied experience and real independence of judgement to all aspects of any merger process, and who will accept responsibility to the governing bodies and perhaps also third parties for the results of their work.

Within each institution, there needs to be a clearly defined and focused project team with an identified leader and a variety of clear roles and role-players. There should be a designated contact for all advisors. The contact may be inside the organization or one of the outside professional advisors. The coordinating function of that person will be of vital importance. It should be quite clear who is the main negotiator in each area. Ideally, following the corporate model, this should not be the same person as the principal decision-maker in the team. Communication within the team is important. Each member needs to be clear about his or her role. The team leader should ensure that important questions are asked early enough of team members. Communication with outside advisors is essential. It is not a good idea to work on the basis of providing the minimum amount of information necessary – the people handling the legal structure of the transaction will need to know almost everything. Get good outside advice early. You are more likely to achieve a satisfactory deal (and show your own governing body, auditors and the world at large that you have done so) if both sides have proper advice throughout. Otherwise, problems will only become apparent at the last moment or after completion. Although this type of transaction has become more common, it could still be a once-in-a-lifetime experience for the managers of the HEI concerned. Experienced advisors should be able to bring a variety of relevant and complementary experience. Your team will be well prepared and briefed, both internally and by external advisors, with a great deal of mutual communication. Do not expect that the other side will be similarly well placed. Try to identify at an early stage what are likely to be the major issues and stumbling blocks. These are not always immediately apparent. Bringing fresh and experienced perspectives to this kind of crucial analysis is another important contribution of outside advisors. It is very helpful if principles and pressure points can be identified and agreed early on in the process. When dealing with the other party or its advisors, it is important to deal with people who are empowered to take decisions. Do not waste time talking to people at low level who do not have the authority to reach agreement. It is also sensible to establish and observe protocol and reserve your own top decision-maker for the equivalent person on the other side.

Perhaps the single biggest contributing factor to a successful transaction will be an early and accurate but flexible and imaginative critical path analysis – identifying the major issues to be addressed and when and in what order the process is to be moved forward and the desired result achieved. The analysis will always include minimum and maximum timings where these appear and can be defined. If the merger is being driven by a public statutory framework, some actions and timescales will be laid down by law, including, for example, set periods for consultation with interested parties. In any type of merger, there might need to be periods of time set aside for matters such as obtaining a landlord's consent to assign a lease or consultation with trade unions about the transfer of employees.

The future?

A phase of mergers and acquisitions in any particular sector is quite likely to be followed by disposals or divorces. Some of the mergers and associations carried out in recent years may well come apart in due course. Where possible, the planning process should try to embrace contingencies and build in flexibility for further development. There should be nothing surprising or frightening about the idea that a merged entity will be subject to further dynamic development. Disposals of unsuccessful ventures are possible, but full formal divorce after a full marriage and integration will be far more cumbersome and difficult to manage in the HE (and indeed FE) sector than in the corporate sector. We might start to see the continuing dynamic of merged organizations developing in a different way – possibly by further transactions in the style of corporate management buy-outs (in effect the hiving off of distinguishable divisions of activity and/or resource). For example, schools of agriculture or other divisional entities with a clear identity of their own might start to be more assertive about negotiating their own future. The successful strategic HEI management of the future may well require an acknowledgement of this further dynamic principle, rather than seeking to repress or ignore its operation. The future may see the social function of and governmental/public sector stake in HEI organization and activity being played down in favour of more nearly naked economic logic and the desirability of organizing units which deliver educational services more clearly and frequently by reference to the principle that the ultimate end user (frequently employers) will need to pay for the delivery of the service and will expect an ever greater stake in the formation and re-formation of the organizational units which deliver the service.

Further reading

See the further reading for Chapters 12 and 14, plus the HEQ (1991) volume on Mergers in Higher Education (which includes several case studies).
See also Palfreyman, D. *et al.* (forthcoming) *Managing Mergers*. Leeds: Heist Publications.

14

Franchising

Nigel Sternberg and Michael Smith (Eversheds)

Editors' introduction

Once the commercial concept of franchising was confined primarily to fast-food outlets; now we are seeing some higher education institutions (HEIs) allowing other HEIs and further education institutions (FEIs) to deliver their academic courses (or parts of them) not only elsewhere in the UK but also in other countries. This process is as commercial as expanding the chain of fast-food outlets, but the delivery of the product is somewhat more complex, as is the measurement of the quality of the product.

This chapter explores the legal relationship between the franchisor HEI and the franchisee institution. Just what is being franchised and under what terms and conditions? How does the franchisor control quality of delivery? In the event of dissatisfaction, against which institution might the unhappy student have legal redress? If there is such a complaint (or even a dispute between the two institutions) and the student and 'parent' HEI are in different countries, under the legal system of which country is the matter to be addressed? Indeed, is there a choice to be exercised by one party or another? If staff are being exchanged, which institution is responsible for the care *and* the good conduct of such staff when not in their employing HEI?

It is quite probable that some of the franchising arrangements so far reached between institutions (especially between institutions in different countries) have not adequately dealt with these matters. It is also probable that they are based on the initial surge of enthusiasm and 'an exchange of letters'. What then happens in the event of the two institutions falling out? What contractual terms might the law assume within ('imply' into) the non-existent formal contracts?

The *Times Higher* on 14 June 1996, contained the headline (concerning difficulties at Swansea Institute of Higher Education) 'Franchise row rages at Swansea'. The story concerned the problem of balancing entrepreneurial endeavour with the careful maintenance of quality-control procedures, especially at a distance from the home HEI. Indeed, a Swansea MP referred the issue at the Swansea Institute to the National Audit Office (NAO), and the principal of the Institute resigned over the matter (as did two of the governors). The NAO January 1997 Report identified 'a breakdown in both governance and management', while at the same time an HEFCW audit report raises concern over a lack of control of overseas activities, for example, travel costs for visits abroad as a substantial chunk of any fee income being achieved, and 'an unknown stock' of blank degree certificates being held by one of the Institute's foreign agents. The NAO Report floats the concept of an HE Ombudsman (see Chapter 3 on governance).

A further *Times Higher* article, on 26 July 1996, told of the franchising of an MBA from a UK university to a German private school. Despite careful vetting mechanisms and strong controls on the part of the UK HEI, the whole thing was an educational disaster.

A *Financial Times* article, on 14 October 1996, explored the 'unfettered proliferation' of MBA courses in South-east Asia, offered by UK HEIs through partnerships and franchising which 'by common agreement are substandard'. The article talks of 'bad apples in the barrel [which] will rot the whole system', and notes that auditors from the Higher Education Quality Council (HEQC) had visited the region. The British Council is also concerned at the potential damage being done to the image of UK HE.

In November 1995, the Committee of Vice-Chancellors and Principals (CVCP) and the HEQC each published complementary codes of practice aimed at helping HEIs maintain and reinforce the standards of service they offer to international students (whether studying at the HEI itself or abroad under partnership/franchise operations). The CVCP's code (1995) concentrates on the HEI at home. The HEQC's code (1995) concentrates on collaboration with institutions abroad.

What is franchising?

'Franchising' is a much used term within education. It is also loosely used, embracing a variety of activities. It can mean franchising in the sense that retailers would understand, something more akin to sub-contracting or simply the transfer of intellectual property (IP) in teaching materials. It can also refer to operations within the UK and worldwide.

The essence of franchising within education is some form of collaboration or cooperation between two or more institutions, in order to facilitate the delivery of education or training to students. For ease of reference, two basic models of franchising will be used as the basis for discussion in this chapter. These models are simplified and the distinctions made between the two may not always be valid. Nevertheless, there is a practical value in identifying the following types of franchising.

Figure 14.1 UK HE–FE franchise

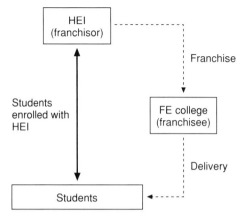

Figure 14.2 International franchise

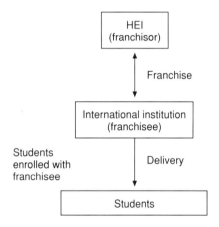

1. UK-based HE/FE franchise (See Figure 14.1.)
   Under an arrangement such as this, an HEI (the franchisor) enrolls a cohort of students as it would any other, but arranges for the delivery of teaching to those students to be performed by and at an FE college (the franchisee). The arrangement might not apply to all the teaching which the students are to receive under their arrangement with the HEI. Typically, the FE college may be responsible for the delivery of the first year of a three-year course.
2. International franchise (See Figure 14.2.)
   In this model, a UK HEI (the franchisor) enters into an arrangement with an institution in another country (the franchisee), whereby attendance by students at the overseas institution leads ultimately to an award of the

UK HEI. The arrangement might involve little more than the validation of an existing delivery of education, or, at the other end of the spectrum, the wholesale transfer of know-how and course materials to the international institution specifically for the purposes of the franchise.

Many of the points raised in this chapter will apply to other types of arrangement which may often be labelled franchises, such as pure validation agreements, accreditation agreements and educational consultancy agreements. It is probably fair to say that franchising within education generally and within HE particularly has not always enjoyed the best of reputations over recent years. Arrangements have often been poorly documented, with the result that institutions on both sides of the equation have suffered. There has also been media attention, particularly in relation to international franchises in Greece and South-east Asia, where concerns have been voiced about the quality of delivery. Although HEIs should be sensitive to some of the political and other issues which have surrounded franchising, the most important legal consideration (and, perhaps, the most important management issue) is the nature of the contracts which surround the franchise and the terms of those contracts. If the issue of contracts can be addressed successfully, it is arguable that many potential problems will be prevented. This chapter will, therefore, focus very deliberately on points to be considered in negotiating and drafting franchise agreements.

The contractual structure

There are two distinct strands which require analysis. First, there will be a contract between the HEI (the franchisor) and its partner institution (the franchisee). Some of the legal issues which arise from this are discussed in more detail later in the chapter. Second, the question of student contracts must be considered. The students to whom the franchised training or education is delivered will be in a contractual relationship with the franchisor, the franchisee or possibly both.

The student contract

Although for some time there has been a degree of uncertainty as to the nature of the relationship between students in HE and the institutions which they attend, it is now widely accepted that a contract lies at the heart of that relationship (see Chapter 6). The contract may come into existence at a very early stage and forms the basis of the institution's authority to apply disciplinary regulations, academic procedures and appeals mechanisms. There may be additional, incidental contracts between institution and student (for example, in connection with the provision of accommodation).

A noticeable feature of HE over recent years has been a greater willingness on the part of students to assert themselves as consumers of education,

Figure 14.3 Potential problems of the UK franchise relationship

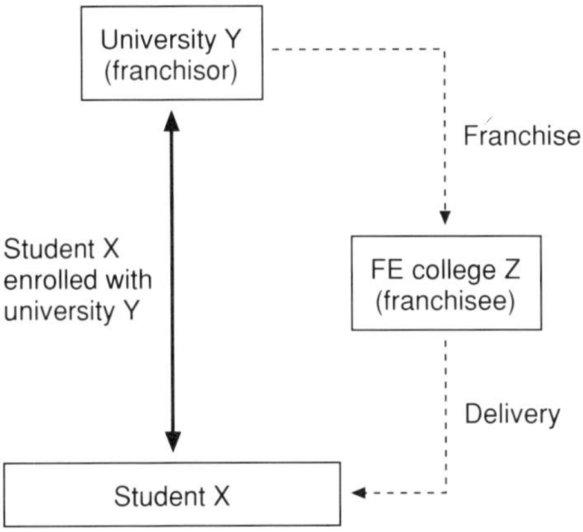

with legal rights against providers which they are increasingly willing to enforce. The process has arguably been accelerated by the introduction into HE of student charters, as part of the citizens' charter initiative. This has serious implications for HEIs, both in terms of exposure to compensation claims and legal costs and in terms of management time. Universities and colleges are rapidly having to reassess the management arrangements which govern their relationship with their students and to overhaul these where necessary. These matters are brought sharply into focus in a consideration of a franchise relationship. Consider, for example, some of the questions which will arise in the context of a domestic HE or FE franchise, where student X enrolls with university Y for a three-year course, the first year of which is to be delivered at and by FE college Z (see Figure 14.3).

- Does student X register as a student of FE college Z as well as of university Y?
- What happens if the student charter of university Y contains commitments (perhaps relating to residential accommodation or access to information technology), which FE college Z is simply unable to deliver?
- If student X behaves in a way which is contrary to the disciplinary regulations of FE college Z but not to those of university Y (whether because of an oversight or a different approach to such matters), does FE college Z have the necessary authority to instigate disciplinary proceedings?
- Which institution is liable if student X is dissatisfied with the quality of the education delivered and threatens legal action?
- How is the situation altered (if at all) if FE college Z has underperformed because of failures on the part of university Y (e.g. a failure to provide proper course materials)?

A closer understanding of the contractual structures is required if these questions are to be answered (see Treitel, 1996).

Figure 14.4   Potential problems of the overseas franchise relationship

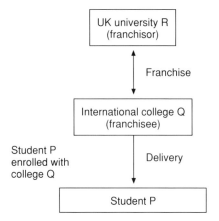

Privity of contract

In the three-way contractual relationship between franchisor, franchisee and student, it is necessary to pay some attention to the doctrine of privity of contract. Under English law, only those who are parties to a contract may enforce its terms (*Tweddle v Atkinson*). This is a firmly entrenched principle, which means that if A agrees to provide services to B, C cannot take action against A for any failure by A to perform.

In the context of HE franchising, this may have a number of implications. For instance, in the example just given, the contract for the delivery of education may exist between student X and university Y. FE college Z, which is actually responsible for delivery, may find, therefore, that it has no contractual basis for attempting to enforce its disciplinary regulations against student X. The matter needs to be addressed in the contract between university Y and FE college Z. For example, university Y might agree to take action against student X if he or she were to infringe the college's disciplinary code. Also student X might be required as a term of his or her contract with university Y to adhere to the disciplinary code of FE college Z. There may be other implications if the contractual structure is different – for example, in an international franchise, in which student P enrolls as a student of overseas college Q, with education to be delivered under a franchise arrangement with UK university R (see Figure 14.4). If student P is dissatisfied with the quality of education delivered and wishes to take legal action, then, on the face of it, the rules of privity of contract suggest that student P can take action only against college Q.

It is not possible to predict whether the effect of the principles of privity of contract will be to the advantage of a franchisor or a franchisee, and those involved in franchising should not be complacent in assuming that the doctrine will provide a shield against liability, for the following reasons.

- The UK courts have shown some willingness to introduce an element of flexibility into the doctrine of privity of contract (see *Jackson v Horizon Holidays* and *Norwich City Council v Harvey*).
- The difficulties raised by privity of contract may be avoided by other means (for instance through the application of the principles of the tort of negligence). Also, just because the doctrine may seem to operate to protect a franchisor against claims from students, it will not necessarily prevent claims being brought directly by the franchisee.
- The doctrine may not operate as rigidly in foreign jurisdictions as it does in the UK (see Whittaker, 1995).
- It cannot be assumed that just because student P enrolls with overseas college Q, there will under no circumstances be a contract between student P and UK university R. A contract is easily formed. A contract does not depend on being reduced to writing, nor does the existence of one written contract (for example, the enrolment form between student P and overseas college Q) preclude the creation of a further oral contract between other parties. Depending very much on the terms of the franchise and the circumstances which surround it, it might be that a student of overseas college Q could overcome the apparent difficulties created by the privity of contract doctrine by establishing a direct contractual relationship with UK university R. Alternatively, principles of agency may apply (see Markesinis and Munday, 1992).

The practical lesson which emerges from these considerations is a principle which will be repeated. In order to avoid being drawn into some of the difficult technical arguments which might be thrown up by the privity of contract doctrine in the context of liability, and in order to find a route around some of the difficulties of the enforcement of disciplinary regulations which the doctrine might create, the parties *must* deal clearly with all relevant matters in the contract between themselves.

Matters to be addressed will include the following.

- There should be terms which deal expressly with the application of student charters and disciplinary codes.
- There should be clear statements as to where the parties expect liabilities towards students to lie. These may be entirely with one of the parties or they may be divided between them. For example, the franchisee might accept responsibility for matters directly within its control (for example, for the provision of accommodation). Similarly, the franchisor might retain responsibility for, say, the quality of the teaching materials (if the arrangement is that these will be produced by the franchisor and distributed to the franchisee). It is important that any division of liability be clearly expressed. Too often, agreements of this type refer to nebulous principles, rather than readily identifiable heads of liability.
- It may be appropriate for any apportionment of liability to be supported by contractual indemnities.

- Where contractual indemnities are used, the parties should consider the inclusion of provisions allowing the party which will ultimately be responsible for accepting liability to have conduct of any claim. This is to avoid the situation in which the party against whom the claim is actually brought settles too quickly or too generously, safe in the knowledge that it has the protection of an indemnity.

There are circumstances in which the contractual structures may be different from, and indeed more complex than, those set out above. For instance, it is not unknown for UK institutions to work jointly (through some joint venture or partnership arrangement) to franchise to an international institution. Whatever the practical arrangements, it is important that full consideration is given to the contractual structures. It is also important to consider carefully some of the individual terms of the contract.

Funding, payment and principal obligations

It is demonstrative of the wide range of arrangements which are caught by the term 'franchising' in HE that payment streams can operate in two entirely different directions, according to the nature of the arrangement. In a domestic HE–FE franchise (see Figure 14.1), the HEI will make payments to the FE college in return for the college delivering educational services which would otherwise have been the responsibility of the HEI. In other types of franchise arrangement, the payment stream will be reversed. Where an HEI simply makes teaching materials available to another institution, whether in order to save development costs for the franchisee or because the franchisee does not have the requisite time, knowledge or experience to develop the courses itself, the franchisee will make payments to the franchisor. This will generally apply in the case of international franchises, where the overseas institution will pay a franchise fee to the UK HEI in return for (perhaps) the provision of educational materials and endorsement of the final award.

Whatever the structure adopted, it is important that the written agreement between franchisor and franchisee should record precisely the practical arrangements which the parties intend. The payment provisions should also make reference to:

- the milestones against which payments are to be made, if there are to be staged payments;
- any external conditions which apply to payment (e.g. the receipt of funding from a third party);
- the applicability of taxes, particularly (but not exclusively) in relationships with commercial providers and/or overseas institutions;
- the treatment of students who drop out of courses part way through a year, provisions to deal with increases in enrolment numbers and the fee payable where the arrangement runs for more than one year.

IP rights

Most franchise arrangements will involve some transfer of teaching materials from franchisor to franchisee. Exceptions to this include arrangements which are in fact no more than validation arrangements and/or where the yardstick for delivery is the achievement of a specific qualification, for which the franchisee develops its own material. Where there is to be a transfer of teaching materials, the question of IP rights needs to be considered (see Chapter 10). In particular, the franchisor will need to assess:

- its own ability to make the necessary teaching materials available to the franchisee without infringing the IP rights of any third party;
- the use which the franchisee will be permitted to make of the teaching materials provided under the franchise arrangement.

Ownership of IP rights

If an HEI, as franchisor, transfers materials to a franchisee which it does not own or which it is not otherwise entitled to transfer, it exposes itself to the risk of actions for infringement of copyright or other IP rights. There are two main areas of exposure – in relation to third-party owned materials and in relation to the rights of academic staff.

Third-party owned materials

Teaching materials have always drawn on third-party sources, such as original text, photographs and musical works. There has been statutory recognition of this through the permitted acts set out in the Copyright, Designs and Patents Act 1988. These provide some protection for the educational use of third-party materials against actions for infringement of copyright. The protections include those which relate to research and private study, activities for the purposes of instruction or examination and anthologies for educational use. However, it should be understood that these exceptions are narrow in their scope and that separate consideration will have to be given to licensing schemes.

If materials which are the copyright of third parties are included within a teaching package without permission and are not caught by the permitted acts, their inclusion will constitute copyright infringement. The chances of the copyright owner taking action may be increased where the infringement is compounded by further dissemination of those materials to a franchisee under arrangements which may be to the financial benefit of the franchisor. Care should be taken, therefore, to ensure that unlawful copying does not take place.

IP rights and academics within HE

The HEI will also need to consider the extent to which it can rightfully claim ownership (for the purposes of exploitation) of the materials which have been produced by its own teaching staff. Teaching materials are likely to attract copyright protection as literary works under the Copyright, Designs and Patents Act 1988.

The first owner (the person entitled to enjoy the benefits of copyright protection) of the copyright in a literary work which is made by an employee in the course of his or her employment will be his or her employer. It would, therefore, seem that teaching materials produced by an academic as part of his or her teaching duties will in fact be the property of his or her employer, the HEI. However, there are arguments to suggest that the situation is not as straightforward within HE. There is a long-standing custom and practice within HE that lecturers are permitted to take their lecture notes with them as they transfer employment from one HEI to another. It is possible that this custom and practice may create some modification to the basic statutory principles of copyright law (some support for this suggestion is found in *Noah v Shuba*).

It would seem, therefore, that an HEI cannot assume as a matter of course that it is entitled to make teaching materials produced by its academic staff available to its franchisees. How then should the HEI deal with this situation?

- The situation may, of course, be clarified through contracts of employment. Although policies vary from institution to institution, a number of HEIs have clauses in their employment contracts with lecturers which expressly reserve ownership of IP rights in teaching materials (and more widely) to the institution, sometimes in return for a share of the fruits of any exploitation. Such a policy can, however, raise potentially difficult considerations.
- In the absence of any express provision in the employment contract, the HEI might take the view that lecturers may have copyright in teaching materials and ask for specific consent for the use of those materials in franchise packages.
- Alternatively, the HEI might try to clarify the position in its favour by ensuring that the copyright in all relevant materials does in fact rest with the HEI. This might be achieved by commissioning lecturers, as part of their employment duties, to produce teaching materials *specifically for franchise packages*. The individual lecturers will need to take the decision as to whether they produce new materials or simply rely on their existing material. Either way, if the situation is spelt out with clarity, the doubts as to ownership in copyright set out earlier are likely to be resolved.

Licence terms

One of the factors to influence the discussions between the HEI and its staff with regard to the inclusion of teaching materials in franchise packages is the purposes to which those materials are to be put. That, in turn, leads to a discussion of licence terms as they apply between franchisor and franchisee. For example, if the intention of the franchisor is that materials are to be used by the franchisee only for its own internal purposes and not for dissemination to other institutions, the franchisor will need to ensure that it has the ability to enforce any such restrictions through its agreement with the franchisee. That agreement will need to include, or to make reference to, a licence of IP rights.

Such a licence should deal *inter alia* with the following matters.

- (As discussed earlier) the uses to which the materials can be put (restrictions might be based on geography, types of student or types of course).
- Use outside the agreed parameters should be prohibited, as should any copying or distribution to third parties other than as is strictly required for the permitted uses.
- Clarification as to which of the parties will own the IP rights in any newly created materials.
- There may be a need to deal with matters other than copyright. For example, franchise arrangements may permit the franchisee to use the trade-marks and logos of the franchisor, in which case the limits upon such use should be clearly stated. Also, there may be a need to refer to IP which does not enjoy any formal protection (such as know-how).
- The licence will also need to deal with what happens to the IP rights in the teaching materials and the physical copies of those materials, when the franchise comes to an end.

The treatment of IP rights within HEIs has historically concentrated on the exploitation of patentable inventions. There has generally been little examination of the IP rights in teaching and research materials. Consequently, there has often been a failure to deal adequately with IP in franchising and other related agreements.

Control over the quality of delivery

The wide variety of arrangements which fall within the generally understood meaning of franchising in HE means that there are also differences in the extent to which the franchisor will seek to control the delivery of teaching or training. In some cases, the only test may be the achievement of a specific award, as verified by external examiners. In other cases, there may be arrangements more akin to a retail franchise, where delivery has to take place strictly in accordance with a manual of instructions. The issues which flow from this go to the heart of much of the controversy which has surrounded educational franchising, both within the UK and overseas. Where franchising has attracted adverse comment, it has often been because of a perceived lack of control by the franchisor over delivery of teaching or training carried out in its name by the franchisee. In particular, this has been an issue with regard to franchising in FE.

The determination of what is an appropriate level of control by a franchisor over the activities of a franchisee is a management/academic issue. However, the legal documentation will need to capture accurately the respective obligations of the parties in this context, and there are at least three important issues which need to be considered by franchisors in putting together documentation.

1. Exposure to costs

It is a pre-requisite of any properly regulated franchise arrangement that there be contact between the staff of the two institutions. However, the franchisor needs to be sure that the franchise agreement does not allow the franchisee to dictate how much contact there should be. The contract should define in precise terms the commitments of the franchisor and should provide for an ability to levy additional charges and/ or terminate the arrangement if demands are made in excess of those commitments.

2. Liability to students

Whilst there are many good reasons why a franchisor should reserve the ability to exercise close control over delivery of materials by the franchisee, it should be noted that this may increase the exposure of the franchisor to liability to students. If, by exercising close control, the franchisor is in effect accepting ultimate responsibility for determining how teaching or training is delivered, and delivery is unsatisfactory, the franchisor may find itself the target of legal action, either by students or by the franchisee.

Depending on the relative strength of bargaining positions and the circumstances of the franchise, it may be possible for the franchisor to protect itself against this by way of contractual indemnity. However, there is a very fine balance to be struck between the need to achieve control and possible exposure to liability. There is also a need to consider the issues relating to contractual structures discussed earlier.

3. *Ultra vires* – to provide or to procure?

In any consideration of franchising, it is necessary to make brief reference to developments which took place during 1996 in the FE sector. This, in turn, requires an understanding of the specific form of franchising in which FE colleges are widely involved as franchisors.

Franchising within FE has generally involved a collaborative arrangement between FE colleges and other existing training providers. These other providers include professional training organizations, the internal training departments of companies and charitable organizations. Under the franchise arrangement, the training which those organizations deliver to their students is brought within the aegis of the FE college, so that it qualifies for funding from an appropriate funding body and leads to a college award.

The FEFC has increasingly sought to regulate such activities. This culminated in the publication of Council Circular 96/06, which questioned whether the type of franchise just described fell within the statutory powers of FE corporations to 'provide further and higher education' (under the Further and Higher Education Act 1992, Section 18), and suggested that if the college did not in fact have sufficient control over the ultimate provision of training to students, it might be operating outside its statutory powers.

These provisions do not translate unchanged into HE. Much (but not all) franchising within HE is of a different type. Furthermore, the powers of HEIs are not uniform in the way that those of FE corporations are. As well as the distinction between chartered universities and HE corporations incorporated under the Education Reform Act (ERA) 1988, there are many local variations in the constitutional documents of universities.

However, there are analogies to be drawn and lessons to be learnt. In particular, the experience of the FE sector draws attention to the fact that all publicly funded education institutions have duties to ensure that quality of delivery is preserved, as well as legal obligations to act within their powers (statutory or otherwise) and to exercise a proper degree of care over their stewardship of public funds. In particular, these points should be borne in mind in the context of innovative or speculative schemes.

The whole area of the control over quality of delivery is difficult and there are fine balances to be struck between potentially competing forces. Much will depend on the practical arrangements which the parties envisage and their relative bargaining strengths. However, it may be helpful to consider including within the franchise agreement:

- a clear indication as to how it will be determined whether delivery under the franchise is at an acceptable level;
- a requirement that the franchisee should comply with any reasonable request which the franchisor may issue from time to time concerning the manner of delivery;
- an ability for the franchisor to have some input into the selection of staff who are to be responsible for the delivery;
- provisions which deal fully with the ability of either party to terminate the arrangement (particularly in this context where performance is not up to standard) and the consequences of any such termination.

Termination and consequences of termination

Early termination of a franchise arrangement is likely to be harmful to both franchisor and franchisee. It is, therefore, important, as with any commercial agreement, to ensure that the circumstances in which early termination may take place are properly documented. Particular care will need to be taken to ensure that the termination provisions tie in properly with the provisions relating to the quality of delivery. For example, a franchisor may wish to be able to terminate the arrangement if the franchisee commits a significant number of relatively minor breaches of the quality standards applicable to the arrangement. The contract will need to provide expressly for this. There are also some consequences of early termination which are particular to an educational franchise.

Responsibility for completing delivery of training

If any agreement for the provision of education or training services is terminated early (whether it be a franchise agreement or some other form of agreement), there will be students left who will not have completed their programme of study. The parties may anticipate dealing with this in a variety of ways. The franchisee might continue to deliver training, with that delivery funded from another source. On the other hand, the situation may be more difficult. For example, in a UK-based HE–FE franchise (see Figure 14.1) university Y may decide that part way through an academic year it has no option but to terminate its franchise arrangement with FE college Z. University Y will be left with a cohort of students to whom contractual promises have been made regarding the delivery of education and will have to make alternative arrangements. This could be extremely difficult and lead to significant expense.

It is not suggested that wording in a contract can solve these problems. However, what the contract can do is to make provision for the franchisor to be reimbursed any additional expense which it suffers (whether by having to re-arrange the courses or as a result of claims made against it by the students). There will also be merit in including clauses requiring the franchisee to cooperate fully in such alternative arrangements as the franchisor may wish to make. The situation will be somewhat different with an overseas franchise, where the UK HEI would not expect to be in a direct contractual relationship with the students. However, the UK HEI should still seek to protect itself through the contract against any claims brought by students as a result of termination.

Staff and the Transfer of Undertakings (Protection of Employment) Regulations 1981

It is possible to envisage circumstances which might arise on the termination (or indeed the expiry) of a franchise arrangement, in which the Transfer of Undertakings (Protection of Employment) (TUPE) Regulations 1981 would apply. The TUPE Regulations 1981 give effect to European Council Directive 77/187 (the Acquired Rights Directive). Where there is a relevant transfer of an undertaking the TUPE Regulations 1981 will apply, with the following consequences.

- The transfer will not operate so as to terminate the contract of employment of any person employed by the transferor in the undertaking. Any such contract of employment will be transferred to the transferee together with all rights, powers, duties and liabilities under or in connection with it (the TUPE Regulations 1981, Regulation 5).

* Where any employee of the transferor or transferee is dismissed, that dismissal will be treated as automatically unfair if the transfer or a reason connected with the transfer is the reason or principal reason for the dismissal (Regulation 8(1) applies), unless it can be established that the reason or principal reason for the dismissal was an economic, technical or organizational reason entailing a change in the workforce (Regulation 8(2) applies).
* There will be duties to inform and consult employee representatives (Regulation 10).

There has been a significant volume of case law relating to the interpretation of the TUPE Regulations 1981. Much of this has centred upon the definition of a 'relevant transfer' of an 'undertaking'. The approach in European cases has been to look at 'economic entities' rather than 'undertakings'. An economic entity may consist of merely the provision of services and there is no requirement for there to be a transfer of property. The decisive criterion is whether the economic entity retains its identity, so it is necessary to determine whether what has been transferred is an economic entity which is still in existence. This may be apparent where its operation is continued or renewed by a new employer with the same economic or similar activities (see *Spijkers v Gebroeders Benedik Abbattoir CV*).

A related issue may be whether a particular individual is employed in the undertaking in question so as to fall within the scope of the TUPE Regulations 1981. Where a part of an undertaking is transferred the TUPE Regulations 1981 apply to any employee who is 'assigned' to that part (see *Botzen v Rotterdamsche Droogdok Maatschappij BV*). This means that if employees are dedicated to a particular function and/or spend a substantial part of their time engaged in it, they are likely to be subject to the TUPE Regulations 1981. There is no precise guidance as to the meaning of a 'substantial part of their time', but a rule of thumb would seem to indicate something in the region of 80 per cent.

If the TUPE Regulations 1981 did apply to a franchised activity, then following termination or expiry of the franchise for any reason, the employees of the franchisee engaged in the delivery of education under the franchise might claim to be transferred if the activity were transferred (whether to another franchisee or back to the franchisor). For this to be the case, the franchise would have to be arranged in such a way that those employed in connection with it formed a distinct and identifiable unit, devoting a substantial part of their time to the delivery of education under the franchise. Furthermore, it would require the franchised activity to be transferred, rather than simply discontinued. Note also that the TUPE Regulations 1981 apply only to 'an undertaking situated immediately before the transfer in the United Kingdom' (Regulation 3(1) applies), although the Acquired Rights Directive will of course be applicable throughout the European Union

(EU). The potential effect of the TUPE Regulations 1981 should not be overstated, but franchisors should be aware that there are circumstances in which it can apply.

It will be sensible to include in the contract requirements that the arrangement be structured so that the conditions just described are not satisfied. If there is any risk that this cannot be achieved, the franchisor may wish to consider some involvement in the selection of staff (on the grounds that they may eventually become its own employees) and seek indemnities from the franchisee (particularly if termination occurs because of the franchisee's breach of contract).

Dispute resolution

Although this is not the place to undertake a full and detailed examination of the very complex provisions which apply to choice of law and jurisdiction clauses in international contracts, it is important that some of the basic principles be understood, particularly in relation to overseas franchises. Even the most cordial and well-documented relationship between two independent parties has the potential to lead to disagreement, and it is important that the parties should address how such disagreement should be resolved. In order to do this, it is necessary to consider two questions.

1. What is the preference of the parties with regard to the method of dispute resolution?
2. According to the laws of which country do they wish any dispute to be resolved?

Methods of dispute resolution

Parties can choose from a variety of methods of dispute resolution. These include a structured form of negotiated resolution, determination of certain matters by an expert, arbitration and the jurisdiction of the courts. A favoured matter of dispute resolution within educational franchises would seem to be a reference in the first instance to a structured negotiation, backed up by an arbitration clause. Of course, other possibilities are available. Whatever method is chosen, there are some critical drafting and practical points to consider (for more on litigation, see Chapter 20).

Structured negotiation

A clause which provides for a structured negotiation will typically state that the parties will attempt to resolve any dispute under an escalated procedure, with discussions taking place, for example, first between course leaders and then (if agreement is not reached at that level) between those at a more senior level of management. The clauses setting out such an arrangement should ideally contain the following provisions.

- A statement that any negotiation will take place in good faith, with a *bona fide* attempt to resolve the dispute in question.
- There may be circumstances in which it is quickly apparent to both parties that the problem in question is of a nature or a magnitude which renders resolution under this procedure unlikely. The procedure should, therefore, be capable of being abandoned by mutual consent.
- As with any clause which provides for a matter to be referred to a party or parties, the clause should be checked carefully to ensure that it does not contain the possibility of deadlock. In particular, it should not require there to be mutual agreement before the next stage of the procedure is invoked, nor should it contain open-ended periods of time.
- There may be occasions when one of the parties needs to take rapid action against the other, without being hindered by a negotiated dispute procedure. For example, litigation relating to copyright infringement is often conducted through injunctive proceedings, where time is of the essence. The clause should, therefore, make provision for such steps to be taken without the need to go through the full discussion procedure first.

Expert determination

There are certain disputes which are most appropriately resolved by an expert (rather than an arbitrator). This may be particularly relevant where the dispute is of a technical nature. This method of determination might have advantages in terms of time and cost, and might sometimes be appropriate in a franchise agreement (perhaps in connection with technical issues where a franchise is heavily dependent on electronic teaching materials). If so, the following points should be considered.

- The range of issues which can be referred to an expert must be clearly set out and should be limited to matters within his or her expert knowledge.
- The way in which the expert is identified and appointed needs to be made clear, taking care once again to avoid any possibility of deadlock.
- The costs of employing the expert should be dealt with. A common provision is for the costs to be borne equally by the parties, unless the expert determines that the conduct of one party has been such that that party should bear all of the costs.
- It should be stated that the decision of an expert will, in the normal course of events, be binding upon the parties (unless there has been a manifest error in the decision-making process).

The use of an expert may be attractive, but its applicability to franchise arrangements should not be over-estimated. For example, it may be difficult to find somebody with the appropriate experience and expertise.

Arbitration

Although there are undoubtedly some attractive features for using arbitration (rather than the jurisdiction of the court) as the final method of determination, there would seem to be a tendency to assume that arbitration is quick, cheap and easy. This is not necessarily so. Arbitration proceedings can turn out to be more time consuming and expensive than court proceedings. Any decision to include an arbitration clause should, therefore, be made carefully, with all relevant matters covered in the clause. In addition to the issues concerning the appointment of the arbitrator, the costs of the proceedings and the availability of injunctive relief set out earlier, an arbitration clause (particularly in an international contract) will need to deal, at the very least, with the following.

- The place in which the arbitration proceedings will take place should be specified, as well as the language of the proceedings. In this context, it may be helpful to remember the international reputation which London has for resolution of disputes.
- The rules governing the arbitration proceedings should be specified.
- The parties should consider how any award of an arbitrator will be enforced. Whilst the New York Convention on the Recognition and Enforcement of Foreign Arbitral Awards 1958 may be of some assistance, it should be understood that difficulties may nevertheless arise if the party against whom the award has been made simply chooses to ignore it. In this scenario, arbitration proceedings may eventually lead to court proceedings by another route.

Jurisdiction of the court

Even if it is decided that disputes will be dealt with by the courts, rather than by any other means, it is necessary in international contracts to try to avoid lengthy arguments about which country's court will have jurisdiction over the contract. It will generally be in the interests of an HEI for an international franchise agreement to be subject to the jurisdiction of the UK courts, and (unless, in the circumstances, there are special factors which apply) for that jurisdiction to be exclusive. Whether or not this is achievable will depend upon the relative bargaining strengths of the parties, but any UK institution should be very wary about being drawn into a contract which is subject to the jurisdiction of the courts of the country in which the franchisee is located, or indeed the courts of any neutral country. If this is unavoidable, the implications of a foreign jurisdiction should be clearly understood, with advice taken from foreign lawyers if necessary. Also, there is a need to take care that the enforceability of any award made by a foreign court is properly considered. (See Collins, 1996 and Kappenol-Laforce, 1996.)

Choice of law

Whatever method of dispute resolution is chosen, it will also be necessary to specify the law which will apply to the contract. This need not necessarily be the same as the country whose courts will have jurisdiction. However, once again, a UK HEI will generally want the contract to be governed by English law, unless special factors apply. Whatever decision is made, it should be recorded in the contract. Failure to do so may lead the parties into very complex arguments concerning governing law.

Further legal considerations

In addition to those matters explored earlier, there are a number of other legal questions which may need to be considered, according to the circumstances of the franchise agreement. Some of these are listed briefly as follows, merely in order to identify where further thought may be necessary.
  Relevant areas would include:

- responsibility for health and safety;
- the effect of the Restrictive Trade Practices Act 1976 and international competition law, where the franchise agreement attempts to place restrictions upon either or both parties (for instance, in terms of exclusivity);
- the impact of taxation, particularly VAT in UK franchise agreements and the taxation regimes of other countries in international agreements;
- a careful consideration of what should properly constitute a *force majeure* event under a franchise agreement;
- provisions governing insurance, particularly in order to support any contractual indemnities.

Electronic delivery and distance-learning

In recent years, there have been rapid advances in multimedia and information highway technology. HEIs have been in the vanguard of the utilization of such technology in the UK. As these developments become more fully integrated within education, it is likely that there will be a vast increase in the opportunities for franchised delivery of education and for distance-learning. There are at least two important consequences of this for franchising within HE. First, written agreements need to be kept under review in order to ensure that they keep pace with changing methods of delivery. Second, as has been emphasized earlier, HEIs need to be sure that they are protecting the IP in teaching materials in an organized and efficient way, and that they are safeguarding their interests when they make those teaching materials available to other parties.

222 Nigel Sternberg and Michael Smith

Conclusions

The drafting of educational franchise agreements is not, it is submitted, an area for the uninitiated. At the same time, it should not be thought that the complexities outlined in this chapter make the drafting of such agreements inordinately difficult. Many issues can be resolved fairly rapidly, in order to achieve the level of protection for franchisors which good management, the requirements of quality control and commercial common sense make necessary.

Further reading

Abramson, M. *et al.* (1996) *Further and Higher Education Partnerships: The Future for Collaboration.* Buckingham: SRHE/Open University Press.

Adams, J. N. and Pritchard-Jones, K. V. (1997) *Franchising: Practice and Precedents in Business Format Franchising.* London: Butterworths.

Collins, L. (1996) *International Litigation.* Oxford: Oxford University Press.

Koppenol-Laforce, M. (1996) *International Contracts.* London: Sweet & Maxwell.

Mendelsohn, M. and Bynoe, R. (1995) *Franchising.* London: FT Law & Tax.

15

The Private Finance Initiative

Tim Costello (Eversheds)

Editors' introduction

Whatever the politics of the private finance initiative (PFI) as a supposed panacea for raising capital and whatever the economic and commercial realities of any particular PFI project, here we are concerned with the legal issues – with the contractual documentation drafted to structure the 'deal' and with the extent to which such documentation will try to address what are the duties of each party. Essentially, PFI attempts to procure an asset/ service for a higher education institution (HEI) at a lower cost than it alone could do so in a traditional way and while also somewhat shifting the risk of failure away from the HEI towards the provider. The provider will clearly be influenced by the predictability of the HEI's income-flows: the likely introduction of tuition fees paid by students and the possible negative impact on demand for HE places will probably create extra uncertainty and make the putting together of a PFI jigsaw even more difficult.

This chapter is also concerned with other more traditional ways of raising capital (e.g. the mortgage), and with the possibility of an HEI or group of HEIs raising capital in the money markets by launching a bond. For an account of one of the very few HE PFI projects, see McWilliam (1997) on student accommodation; for an accommodation PFI project of a somewhat different kind, see NAO (1997) on prisons!

Introduction

What is a PFI transaction?

PFI is a means by which private capital can be harnessed to deliver services required by the public sector. It is based on the concept that the public sector has duties to deliver services, but that it is immaterial whether it owns the assets through which those services are delivered. Although traditionally the public sector has owned these assets, there is no reason why this should be so. In the case of services which require a substantial level of capital investment, if the assets concerned are owned and financed by the private sector, the demands on the public sector borrowing requirement will be commensurately reduced.

Why does a PFI transaction take the form it does?

PFI may properly be regarded as a form of procurement – not of assets but of services. This is the fundamental concept, where the risk of ownership of the assets required for delivery of the service should remain with the provider.

Before current accounting conventions became applicable, leasing was a means by which finance for what was effectively the purchase of an asset could be kept off the balance sheet of the body acquiring the asset. It is curious that although a lessee becomes obliged to make payments of rent throughout the term of a lease, by accounting convention, the aggregate of the rents due does not have to be recognized as a liability at the outset. The effect was that, although very significant liabilities were incurred, none showed on the balance sheet nor did the asset. This was recognized as being misleading. Under the currently applicable accounting standard (FRS 5, The Accounting Standards Board Limited, 1994), financial statements must reflect substance and not form. Where the lessor recovers over the term of the lease rents which in aggregate amortize the whole cost to the lessor of purchasing and financing the asset, the asset and the finance to purchase it must be shown on the balance sheet of the procurer. By contrast, if by the end of the term of the lease the lessor will only have recovered part of the cost of acquiring the asset (and will, in order to realize a profit on the transaction, be looking to sell the asset or let it for a further hire period), neither the asset nor the finance need appear on the balance sheet of the lessee. It is a question of looking at which party bears the risk of the value of the asset at the end of the term of the lease.

In the purest form of PFI transaction, the procurer would never be the owner of the capital asset employed to deliver the services during or after the end of the contract. Normally, however, provided that there is a substantial transfer of the risks of ownership for a long period, neither the asset nor the finance required to pay for it need be recognized on the balance sheet of the procurer. In examining where the various risks relating to the acquisition lie, the standard seeks to determine the substance of the transaction. It is not simply a question of ascertaining whether sufficient risk has transferred to, or remained with, the provider. The issue is whether the risks of *ownership* of the assets required to provide the service lie with the provider or the procurer. Theoretically, this must mean that the residual value risk is paramount. Suppose, under a PFI transaction, an HEI starts with a vacant plot and at the end of the contract period has a hall of residence standing on it, having paid the provider for the use of the building throughout the contract period and not being obliged to make any further payment to the provider after the end of the period. It is hard to avoid concluding that the HEI has 'bought' the hall of residence. This is so, even if the provider has borne every conceivable risk in the meantime. In practice, all the risks which apply in a particular case and which party bears them are examined and, provided that the procurer is sheltered from the majority of the applicable risks, it is likely that the procurer will not be required to recognize the transaction in its accounts as the acquisition of an asset.

How is a PFI transaction achieved?

Since central government is able to borrow at the finest rates available, if the capital required for a project is to be provided from private sources, the cost of capital will inevitably be higher. Furthermore, the costs of setting up the transaction will be higher for the procurer, the successful bidder and those who are unsuccessful. These increased expenses will directly or indirectly increase the cost of the project. Accordingly, if PFI is to provide better value for money and given that the provider will be looking for a return on capital, the saving will need to be found in some other factor. For example, the provider may be able to deliver a given level of service by:

• making a smaller capital investment, or
• operating at lower running costs

than the conventional public sector solution. It might be able to use the assets at a time when they are not required to deliver services to the procurer. Buildings used for education are often not intensively used. A provider may be able to use them at times of the day or periods of the year when they are not required for their primary purpose. For this reason, it is important for the procurer to specify the services it requires and not the asset through which they will be delivered. This allows the provider maximum freedom in which to decide the nature and extent of its capital investment – reducing the cost to the procurer and maximizing the provider's return. A comparison can be made between the recurrent cost of conventional procurement and the charges which will be made for the services by the provider. In this way, one can determine whether PFI offers value for money.

Assets or services?

To some extent, the argument that the use of premises can be seen as the delivery of a service rather than the acquisition of an asset is specious. In the case of a pure service (e.g. a payroll computer bureau), the employer can use another bureau and the bureau can find another customer. Where there is use of a particular building, it is not the same. It is likely that the HEI will want to continue to use the building (even if dissatisfied with the service) and the provider may not readily find another user of the building. To the extent that it can be done without prejudicing the accounting treatment of the transaction, it is as well if the form of the transaction reflects this. The subject of the services might not be the use of a building, it might concern equipment (e.g. a computer network). In this case, although it may be impractical for the physical assets to be used elsewhere, the cost of the equipment is relatively small compared to the cost of delivering a computer service. Accordingly, it is possible to disregard the fact that part of the regular payments to the provider in fact pay for the hardware. The substance of the transaction will not be the sale of the equipment but the provision of services of which use of the equipment is only a part.

PFI in higher education

Since the 1988 reforms, all HEIs have been private bodies. One might ask why PFI had any relevance to them. The answer is partly for reasons of political expediency and partly because it is thought that the benefits which PFI can deliver to the public sector will also be applicable to a sector which is largely paid for by the taxpayer. HEIs are private, so their cost of funds is higher than that of the Government and the comparative cost of funds disadvantage of PFI is reduced.

Regulatory framework

HEIs are not currently required to consider using PFI as a means of procuring new projects. The Higher Education Funding Council for England (HEFCE) has said that in the future HEIs might need to show that they have explored opportunities for involvement of the private sector, but currently they do not need to (see HEFCE Circular 17/95). The financial memorandum between the HEFCE and an HEI may, however, encourage the HEI to consider PFI. Some of the newer HEIs inherited liabilities from the local education authorities of which they were once part. This means that borrowing to make capital investments is difficult, because they do not have strong balance sheets (even though HEFCE reimburses them for debt service costs on these loans). For such institutions, PFI can have a great benefit, provided that they have the income to support the recurring charges for the service provided.

Other factors

There is, nevertheless, political pressure on Government departments to demonstrate a flow of PFI transactions in the sector for which they are responsible. The Department for Education and Employment (DfEE) is no exception to this and the unit within it charged with this responsibility is active promoting PFI in higher education (HE) as elsewhere. The capital funds at the disposal of the HEFCE are now so paltry in relation to the size of the sector that new developments are likely to have to be funded from other sources. Some HEIs might be in the position of not having the capital available and not being willing or able to carry the debt required to fund development on their balance sheets. This will mean that for their own reasons they will be driven down the PFI route.

Parties

Conventional procurement

Figure 15.1 shows diagrammatically the various different parties who will be concerned in a building project. This might concern the construction of a new teaching facility on a site already owned by the HEI. The HEI will have direct contractual relationships with all the principal providers of finance, goods and services and will have the opportunity of structuring the transaction and choosing the various firms and companies involved as it wishes (within the confines of the public procurement rules and consistent with demonstrating value for money).

Figure 15.1   Parties in a building contract

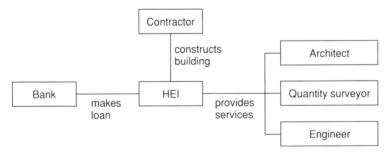

Procurement under PFI

If instead of obtaining a building, the HEI procures services, consisting of the making available of fully serviced teaching space, there will be one contractual relationship to which the HEI will be party together with the provider of the services.

The provider will have a multiplicity of relationships with the various entities contributing to the provision of the services. Figure 15.2 shows a

Figure 15.2   Parties in a PFI contract

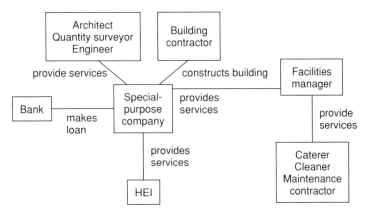

simple arrangement which illustrates this. Customarily, in bidding for the contract the provider will specify the names of the other firms and companies which will be providing goods or services, but the HEI will not have the opportunity of choosing them individually.

Special-purpose companies

In due course, no doubt, a kind of business will spring up specializing in delivering all aspects of PFI contracts. At present, however, in most cases the provider is a company specially established for the project, which typically is owned by the companies involved in the project. This raises the following two issues.

1. The special-purpose company is unlikely to be heavily capitalized. PFI contracts usually last for tens of years and the HEI must be concerned to ensure that the credit standing of the special-purpose company is sufficient. This means that in many cases a guarantee must be sought from its shareholders or a bank.
2. PFI has been embraced more or less enthusiastically by the building contractors. However, in the UK such companies normally need to devote their available resources to their core business. They can be expected not to be long-term holders of shares in a series of special-purpose companies set up for the various projects which they have built. In due course, there will be a need for the initial holders of the shares of the special-purpose companies to sell their shares. Indeed, the aggregation of these companies is likely to be the method by which specialist PFI providers emerge as a distinct business sector. Equally, the HEI may be concerned about the timing of any sales of shares and perhaps the identity of any future shareholders.

Anatomy of a PFI transaction

As with any procurement, the initial issues are value for money and affordability. It hardly needs saying that the concept of value for money requires competitive tendering. Even if this were not the case, it would be required by the public procurement rules.

Public procurement regime

As part of the completion of the single market, the European Council has adopted a series of measures regulating the procurement of goods, services and construction works not only by public sector bodies but by bodies which, while having a private character, exist for the purpose of meeting needs in the general interest with respect to education and are financed mainly from public sources. This definition includes almost all HEIs. The underlying purpose of the rules is to ensure that all enterprises within the European Economic Area (the 15 members of the European Union (EU), Iceland, Liechtenstein and Norway) have the opportunity of bidding for publicly financed projects in whatever country the project may be taking place. The public procurement rules may seem to be bureaucratic and mechanical regulations which are of comparatively little significance. However, they impose a procedure that underlies the whole procurement process. The regime only applies if the cost of procurement exceeds certain limits – ECU 5,000,000 for works and ECU 200,000 for services and supplies. The value in national currencies is fixed biennially by the European Commission and for 1997 is £3,950,456 for works and £158,018 for services and supplies. A substantial new facility for an HEI will be covered either by (works) Directive 93/37/EEC and the Public Works Contracts Regulations 1991 (SI 1991 No. 2680) or by (services) Directive 92/50/EEC and the Public Services Contracts Regulations 1993 (SI 1993 No. 3228). If the facility is to be obtained under PFI, it is a matter of debate which directive applies. With the exception of the differing threshold this issue is of no consequence. One of three award procedures must be followed:

1. the *open procedure* under which contract documents must be prepared and issued to all those who request them for the purpose of submitting a tender;
2. the *restricted procedure* under which interested suppliers apply to be included on a shortlist of those invited to bid on the basis of contract documents supplied only to them with the invitation;
3. the *negotiated procedure* under which selected applicants are invited to negotiate the terms of the proposed contract until the contract is let to the one of them with which the most satisfactory agreement can be reached.

The negotiated procedure can only be used in limited circumstances. One of these is where prior overall pricing is not possible. (See the Public Services Contracts Regulations 1993, Regulation 10(2)(*b*): 'exceptionally, where the nature of the services to be provided, or the risks attaching thereto, are such as not to permit prior overall pricing'.) There are two difficulties with this exception to the rule that the open or restricted procedures must be used rather than the negotiated procedure:

1. the provision commences with the word 'exceptionally', at least implying that the negotiated procedure may not be used in all cases where the nature of the services or assessment of risks makes overall pricing impossible;
2. the output specification giving details of the services required, produced at the beginning of the procurement process, will in all cases be very precise and the risks will not be obscure.

The reason why one seeks to use the negotiated procedure is in order to tailor the documentation to the actual proposals put forward by the provider, so as to permit the provider to be as free as possible in configuring the physical environment in which the services will be delivered. Post-tender negotiations are not permitted under the open and restricted procedures. Nevertheless, the Treasury, responsible for enforcing the public procurement regime, is convinced that the negotiated procedure can be used in PFI.

Mechanics

An HEI intending to use the negotiated procedure for a project would send a notice for publication in the *Official Journal of the European Communities*. The notice, in the form specified in the Public Services Contract Regulations 1993, Schedule 2, Part D, invites requests to be selected to negotiate. The notice must allow at least 37 days from the date of despatch of the notice for interested parties to submit their requests.

In the intervening period, the HEI and its advisers would be preparing:

- initial details of the project which would provide sufficient information for the applicants to make a preliminary proposal;
- a questionnaire which would form the basis of the HEI's decision on whom to invite to negotiate.

Having received these requests, the papers would be sent to all applicants by way of reply. Replies to the questionnaire would be examined and suitable respondents would be invited to make an oral presentation. After this, a final selection would be made and an invitation to negotiate sent to those chosen. At least three applicants must be invited to negotiate (or all the applicants if requests are received from fewer than three people).

The Public Services Contract Regulations 1993, Regulations 14–20 contain detailed provisions dealing with the selection of those to be invited to negotiate.

The invitation to negotiate would contain a detailed output specification of the project and indicative heads of terms, if not a draft of a proposed contract. Those to whom it was issued would be required to submit detailed proposals by a fixed date. Following receipt of these proposals and an oral presentation, the preferred supplier would be chosen. Detailed negotiations on the terms of the contract would then follow. The period from issue of the *Official Journal* notice to signature of the contract would be likely to be about 10 months.

Form of the transaction

The exact relationship of the procurer and the provider will naturally vary according to the nature of the services. Suppose the subject matter of the arrangement is a hall of residence which will be made available to students during term time but used for purposes unconnected with the HEI at other times of year. In this case, the transaction might well not give the HEI any interest in the building. It could essentially:

*   oblige the provider to make the accommodation available during term time to students nominated by the HEI;
*   oblige the HEI to nominate students to occupy 95 per cent of the available space or pay for the unused rooms.

It would doubtless deal with other matters (e.g. the risk of students failing to pay their lodging charges), but there would be no question of the building's being an asset of the HEI. (See McWilliam, 1997 and NAO, 1997.)

Another typical example might be a laboratory building which would be required for research and teaching purposes 24 hours a day throughout the year. The HEI would want to make sure that only its staff and students, contractors and other visitors authorized by the HEI had access. In this case, the HEI itself would be the occupier of the building with exclusive possession and however the agreement between the provider and the HEI is described it will take effect as a lease.

How the provider acquires the property in order to be able to make it available will normally depend on where the site is and what the parties want to happen at the end of the contract term. Where the site is already owned by the HEI and/or where the HEI wishes to be sure of retaining the property at the end of the contract period, it makes sense for the HEI to have an interest in the property superior to that of the provider (either the freehold or a superior lease) and to grant a lease to the provider. The provider then grants an underlease to the HEI so that it can occupy the building. For the transaction to be regarded as qualifying under PFI, it will be essential for the provider to bear all the risks of occupation. This means that the lease by which it holds the property will be a full repairing and insuring lease under which it has to deliver the property at the end of the term in first-class repair or the provider will have equivalent obligations under the operating agreement. By contrast, the underlease to the HEI would contain no such obligations since it would be paying a fully inclusive service charge which would not vary according to the actual costs of the provider.

Ancillary services

As mentioned earlier, PFI is concerned with services not assets. Accordingly, where the subject matter is occupation of a building, it will be much more credible as a PFI project if as many of the services required for use of the building are bundled together and delivered under the PFI contract. These services could include maintenance, energy supply, cleaning, telecommunications, catering, security, porterage and possibly even office services (e.g. photocopying and secretarial help).

This raises the following difficulties.

- Normally, contracts for these services would run for a much shorter period than the 25 or 35 years common for a PFI contract. The discipline in such relationships is exerted by the fact that the contractor knows that if standards fall the HEI will simply fail to renew the contract or terminate it on notice. This means that there is no need to satisfy any objective test before replacing the contractor. If the contract runs for even 10 years, when the service declines, the HEI will be obliged to prove that the contractor has not complied with the terms of the contract. This is not necessarily easy, even in simple cases such as frequent breakdowns of equipment. It is even more difficult if, for example, the food provided tastes bad or if cleaning is inadequate. This is the case however well the output specification is drawn.
- Neither party may want to agree a price for such a long period. Indexation may be an adequate adjustment tool for up to five years, but after that either the increase in the cost of delivery or the market price for such services will diverge from the index or both.
- The needs of the HEI are likely to change over the period of the contract.

The first problem can only be fully addressed by having the period of the ancillary service contract shorter than the main PFI contract term. The pricing issue can be solved by a benchmarking process. Effectively, this is done by comparing prices for equivalent services on the review date and adjusting the contract price to the cheapest. However the nature of services under a PFI contract for occupation of buildings is that they will be bespoke to that building. It will not be easy to ascertain comparable prices without asking other suppliers to tender. They are not likely to be prepared to do so unless they have a chance of being awarded the contract. So, again, it may be a question of having shorter-term contract periods for the services. Logically, this calls into question the wisdom of bundling everything up together at the outset.

Change can be addressed by a mechanism in the contract which allows either party to propose changes in the contract, obliges the provider to quote a variation in the price and permits the HEI to decide whether to proceed with the change. This should work well for increases in service, but may be less robust in the case of reductions where the provider quotes a reduction in the price which the HEI considers to be too small. The final difficulty can probably be overcome by reference to an independent expert for a decision.

Timetable

Table 15.1 gives the typical timetable for a project involving a new building.

Table 15.1   Timetable for a new building project

Date	Step accomplished
End of month 2	Complete initial appraisal of project and issue notice to the *Official Journal*
End of month 4	Complete evaluation of responses to the *Official Journal* notice, draw up short list of providers, issue invitation to negotiate
End of month 7	Evaluate detailed responses to the invitation to negotiate and identify the preferred provider
End of month 10	Conclude negotiations with preferred provider and sign contracts
Completion of construction and fitting out	Take up occupation and commence paying the periodical amount for the services supplied

Conclusions and practical considerations

There are a number of reasons why an HEI might want to procure a new project by PFI:

- the recurrent cost might be cheaper because of the skill of the provider in specifying the assets required to deliver the required service;
- the provider might have an alternative use for those assets when they would otherwise be idle and be prepared to reduce the charge to the HEI accordingly;

- it might be good politics to support the initiative which the Government is promoting;
- the HEI might need to avoid borrowing the money required to fund the capital costs of the project because its balance sheet would not be strong enough.

If either or both of the first two motives are applicable, the HEI need not be concerned whether the transaction actually qualifies under the PFI. If the third motive is dominant, it may be possible to come sufficiently close to a PFI transaction, to satisfy those who are concerned to promote the PFI without fully conforming to the strictest requirements. It is only in the last case of the fourth motive where strict compliance will be necessary, otherwise FRS 5 may require the facility concerned to be considered an asset of the HEI and the obligations under the contract to be recognized as a loan.

Unless PFI is likely to be a significantly cheaper option, an HEI will be wise to choose conventional procurement. The transaction costs are cheaper and the process will be quicker. Where PFI might offer benefits, it will be well to test the opportunities. Given the constraints imposed by the public procurement rules, it will usually be possible to test whether the market can produce a solution under PFI which is more cost effective than conventional procurement. If this turns out not to be the case, it will be possible to switch to conventional procurement at that stage. It is important that the original notice to the *Official Journal* allows for this. Otherwise the need to issue a fresh notice may cause cost and delay.

If the PFI route is started the key issues are:

- formulation of the output specification;
- establishing an investment appraisal;
- dealing with the legal requirements for properly authorizing the transaction, compliance with the public procurement rules and establishing the contractual documentation.

The HEI will require advice from surveyors (if the subject matter is the occupation of buildings), accountants and solicitors. There could be a significant cost saving if the professional advisers are used only as required rather than all of them attending every meeting of the project team. Legal advice will be required at every stage and solicitors can usefully be appointed as lead advisers.

Other private sources of finance

If PFI does not seem worth considering in detail or has been rejected, HEIs are usually able to obtain finance by way of loans from banks. Debt finance would also be available from the bond market. Leasing should also be considered for plant and machinery.

Regulatory framework

Under Circular 5/96 of the HEFCE, HEIs are required to obtain the consent of the HEFCE for borrowing, if the annualized servicing costs of borrowing exceed 4 per cent of total income as reported in the latest audited financial statements. Annualized servicing costs are the cost of capital repayments and interest spread evenly over the period of the borrowing. (The annualized servicing costs of debt inherited from local education authorities is excluded from the calculation.) For this purpose 'borrowing' includes finance leasing and other schemes where borrowing is the substance of the transaction.

Borrowing

As well as borrowing from banks – for which there is ample opportunity – HEIs can consider raising finance in the long-term bond market. One university has done this directly. The cost of this can be high as it involves giving a great deal of information about the activities, assets, liabilities and financial state of the HEI. Financiers have also suggested a cooperative approach to the market. This would involve a specially incorporated company issuing the bonds which would have the benefit of the guarantee of an insurance company. The funds raised would be on-lent to the participating institutions. Because of the credit enhancement provided by the guarantee, minimal information about the participating HEIs would be required. The advantage of using the bond market is that a rate of interest is fixed for a period up to 25 years. A complicating factor is that the investors like the whole amount of the face value of the bond to be repaid by one instalment on the due date of the bond. The HEI using the money raised, however, will need to provide for repayment out of its income throughout the period of the bond. There is bound to be a difference between the interest rate payable on the bond and the interest which can be earned on the amounts set aside to make repayment. Nevertheless, the bond market offers a form of finance which HEIs should probably use for part of their borrowing requirements.

Leasing

Because HEIs are charities, they do not usually have income which is taxable for corporation tax purposes. Accordingly, when they make an investment in plant and machinery for which a commercial entity would be able to obtain capital allowances, they cannot obtain the benefit because they have no tax liability in the first place. If they are able to lease the plant and machinery from a leasing company which can obtain the capital allowances and, as is normal, pass on part of the benefit to the lessee, the financing cost of obtaining the use of the plant and machinery will be less than if the money to purchase it had been borrowed by the HEI.

Conclusions

For the foreseeable future, the Government will not be providing significant funding for capital projects. HEIs will be forced to find the capital required from private sources. Since they are private bodies, their borrowings do not form part of the national debt and they are not required to use PFI rather than conventional procurement. The HEFCE does not oblige HEIs to consider PFI for their capital projects, whereas FE colleges are obliged by the FE Funding Council to evaluate the PFI option (see FE Funding Council Circular 95/25). Nevertheless, in some cases, PFI will be the preferred option. In some ways, HE has the best of all worlds: it is able to take advantage of the fact that PFI is being developed as an innovative way of providing services more economically in some cases than conventional procurement. On the other hand, it is not forced to use PFI or even to incur the expense of evaluating it in depth where it is unlikely to be more cost effective.

Further reading

Deacon, M. (1997) Capital funding and the private finance initiative: panacea or poison chalice?, *Perspectives: Policy and Practice in Higher Education*, 1(4), 133–8.

McWilliam, J. (1997) A commissioner's tale: Avery Hill Student Village, University of Greenwich, *Public Money and Management*, 17(3), 21–4.

Morrison, N. (1996) *Private Finance Initiative*. London: FT Law & Tax.

NAO (1997) *The PFI Contracts for Bridgend and Fazakerley Prisons*. London: HMSO.

Warner, D. A. and Kelly, G. (1994) *Managing Educational Property*. Buckingham: Open University Press.

16

The Legal Status of the Students' Union

Ian Leedham (Shakespeares)

Editors' introduction

What is the legal status of the students' union (SU)? Who is in charge of it – the community of students or the higher education institution (HEI) itself? If not the latter, what legal responsibilities does it have for the proper management of the SU, and what powers (if any) to ensure the proper management of the SU? Who owns the building itself and the land on which it stands? What happens if something goes wrong – if the SU becomes bankrupt or is sued for breach of contract and has to pay substantial damages, or if there is a death arising from neglect of health and safety matters? Who clears up the financial mess, who pays the financial penalty and who faces the criminal prosecution brought by the Health and Safety Executive? If things became difficult in this way, can the HEI, which earlier might have wanted to be in control of the SU, now try to distance itself from all responsibility, especially in terms of being a financially deeper pocket for the payment of those damages? Is the gap between the SU and the HEI sufficiently wide for no liability of the former ever to transfer to the latter? Can the gap be made wider?

This chapter deals with all these questions and more issues besides, including the relevant legislation under which SUs exist, their extensive trading activities and their governance. Clearly, there are links to Chapter 3 (governance), Chapter 4 (trusteeship), and Chapter 12 (trading companies).

In a case in 1996, four students were expelled from the SU for alleged financial and procedural impropriety by South Bank University and were refused leave by the Court of Appeal for judicial review (JR). They were reported in *The Higher* (26 July 1996) to be considering an appeal to the European Court. The case highlighted whether the university had the power to take over the running of the SU, to install a caretaker manager and to impose an interim constitution on the SU.

Definition

Prior to the Education Act (EA) 1994, the term 'students' union' was a generic one which did not require further definition. The EA 1994 made significant changes to the law regarding SUs and imposed certain onerous obligations on HEIs in relation to their SUs. These statutory obligations came into force on 1 April 1995 and their existence should be recognized and carefully observed by all HEIs.

The EA 1994, Section 20(1) defines an SU as being:

(*a*) an association of the generality of students at an establishment . . . whose principal purposes include promoting the general interests of its members as students; or

(*b*) a representative body (whether an association or not) whose principal purposes include representing the generality of students at an establishment . . . in academic, disciplinary or other matters relating to the government of the establishment.

This is a wide definition and its purpose is to encapsulate the spectrum of differing types of SUs that exist. In fact to emphasize this, the EA 1994, Section 20 goes further to highlight that the definition of an SU extends to include bodies or societies which represent undergraduates or postgraduates, committees, and halls of residence and colleges within a university (i.e. Oxford and Cambridge colleges). The 'association' referred to does not require a majority of students to be classed as 'a generality of students'. It is doubtful that the definition extends to include specific subject societies (e.g. Electrical Engineering Society), but it may cover a more general organization (for example, the Faculty of Engineering Society), depending upon the objects of the organization. The provisions of the EA 1994 do not apply to organizations whose principal purposes are the organization of social activities. This is because this type of organization is not promoting the general interests of its members or representing them in disciplinary matters (e.g. Friends of the University, sports clubs and social committees).

Any affiliated associations or bodies which are classed as an SU under the EA 1994 and who have a 'branch' at another establishment must comply with the provisions of the EA 1994, Section 20(4) at both establishments. However, this requirement does not extend to include nationwide or worldwide organizations such as the National Union of Students (NUS). Organizations such as the NUS are excluded from complying with the EA 1994. Another recognized exclusion is that part-time students may be excluded from union membership, if an HEI determines that part-time students are not eligible for union membership. Therefore, the EA 1994 may, if the HEI decides, only apply to SUs which represent the 'generality' of full-time students. It is important to remember that, for these obligations to apply, the organization must come within the definition of an SU, not just have that title. The basic premise being, an HEI which has an association which promotes the general interests of students or which represents students in relation to academic or disciplinary matters, would have to comply with the requirements under the EA 1994.

The requirements

The intention of the EA 1994 is to provide a framework to ensure that an SU operates in a fair and democratic manner within its constitution and accounts for its finances. However, the EA 1994 does not regulate all the activities of SUs. It is the responsibility of the governing body of HEIs to ensure that the specific provisions in the EA 1994, Section 22 are followed. An HEI is 'to take such steps as are reasonably practical to secure' compliance of the SU with all the more specific requirements under Section 22. These are as follows.

1. The SU should have a written constitution, which should be made freely available to all students.
2. The constitution should be approved by the governing body and be subject to review at least once every five years.
3. A student has the right not to be a member of the SU and a person who chooses not to be a member of the SU should not be unfairly disadvantaged in respect of the provision of services which members receive. This provision allows membership of the SU to be voluntary. Students have the opportunity to 'opt out' of the SU. The original bill intended students to 'opt in' to the SU, until the House of Lords reversed it. The aim is to allow greater choice and democracy in SUs. Students and prospective students must be notified at least once a year of their right to 'opt out' of the SU. To ensure that students are not unfairly disadvantaged in respect of the availability and provision of facilities and services, the governing body can make an agreement with the SU to continue to provide facilities for students who have 'opted out' or provide separate parallel facilities. The EA 1994 does not detail exactly what facilities and services should be provided for students who have 'opted out' and the Parliamentary Under Secretary of State stated that:

> it is not for the Government to say what services should be available; that is quite properly a matter for the Institution to decide. I emphasized that in initiating the measures, we are leaving matters to local decision wherever possible and not seeking to prescribe in concrete the exact procedures to be followed.
> (*Hansard*, Standing Committee, Col. 386, 21 June 1994)

It has been suggested that 'opted out' students should have equal services in relation to welfare, catering and sport. Obviously, voting rights in relation to the SU would not be open to non-members. Again, HEIs must ensure that at least once a year 'opted out' students are informed of the alternative services available to them.

4. Secret ballots should be held for elections to major SU offices (e.g. President and Vice-President). It is up to the HEI to determine which are the 'main offices' of the SU as no further guidance is given. However, Baroness Blatch said that she would 'expect the requirement to apply to the Union President and others with a significant role in running the Union' (*Hansard*, House of Lords, Vol. 553, Col. 167). So the main offices subject to a secret ballot would normally include the President, Vice-President, Secretary and Treasurer. The requirement of a secret ballot does not apply to the open university or any distance learning colleges (see the EA 1994, Section 22(9)).
5. The SU elections should be 'fairly and properly conducted'.
6. An SU office (e.g. President or Vice-President) should not be held for longer than two years.
7. The financial affairs of the SU should be properly conducted and scrutinized. Arrangements should be made for the approval of the SU's budget and the monitoring of expenditure by the governing body. According to the NUS finance survey (1995), the average turnover of an SU is £1,486,037, which represents an increase of 5 per cent on 1994. This turnover is larger than many businesses. How a governing body addresses the requirement for the SU's budget being approved and its spending monitored is again left to the HEI's discretion.
8. The financial reports of the SU should be published annually and copies made available to the governing body and all students. All the external organizations to which the SU is affiliated or to which it has made grants or donations should be published annually along with details of all fees and donations made to such external organizations. This is to prevent an SU making donations which are contrary to charity law. External relations and affiliations should be in pursuit of the objectives for which the SU was established and within its objects and powers. This requirement follows a line of legal actions brought by students with regard to the donation of funds to external, political or non-charitable organizations by their SU.
9. The allocation of resources to groups or clubs should be fair and there should be a detailed, written procedure available for examination by all students. This requirement is essentially a codification of what has already been common practice within most HEIs.
10. If the SU decides to affiliate to a new external organization, then a notice should be published detailing the cost of the affiliation or donation the SU will be making along with its application. This notice should be brought to the attention of the governing body and all students.
11. The annual reports should contain a list of the external organizations to which the SU has made donations in the period and the amount of those individual donations.
12. There should be a procedure for the review of affiliations to external organizations. Every year the current list of affiliations should be approved by the members. The EA 1994 does not provide specific details

as to how this review may be conducted, but this requirement would be best dealt with at an annual general meeting. A proportion of SU members (not less than 5 per cent) may requisition a ballot to question the continued affiliation to a particular organization. The decision on continued affiliation is conducted by secret ballot of all SU members.

13. A complaints procedure should be implemented to allow students who are dissatisfied with their dealings with the SU or who claim to be unfairly disadvantaged by reason of opting out of it to air their grievances. The written complaints procedure should be brought to the attention of the students by the governing body. The complaints procedure must provide for an independent person to investigate and report to the governing body. This independent person has not been defined within the EA 1994, but it was envisaged that he or she would be appointed by the governing body and not be connected with the HEI. The complaints procedure is intended to provide an independent and impartial review procedure. It is left to the governing body to decide whether to accept the independent person's report but it has to ensure that, where a complaint is upheld, there is an effective remedy available.

14. All complaints should be dealt with promptly and fairly. The HEI must provide an effective remedy, when a complaint is upheld following investigation.

15. The governing body of an HEI should prepare and issue a code of practice detailing how each of these requirements are secured and observed. This code of practice should be brought to the attention of all students at least once a year along with instructions as to the restrictions imposed on SUs by charity law and the rights of students to freedom of speech. This is, of course, in addition to the SU's written constitution and the complaints procedure.

The governing body of the HEI has discretion on how to implement these requirements – no specific assistance, model constitution or code of practice has been supplied by the Government. This increases the burden of the task and leaves sufficient scope for varying methods of implementation and infringement! The legal responsibility for ensuring compliance with the requirements listed is that of the governing body of the HEI, and failure to comply with them or misinterpretation of them could result in JR proceedings (see Chapter 9). The HEI must decide what are 'reasonably practicable' steps to implement, observe and monitor the provisions within the HEI.

Freedom of speech

Under the EA 1994, Section 224, HEIs must outline to students the provisions of the Education (No. 2) Act 1986, Section 43, regarding the freedom of speech in HEIs and issue them with a copy of any code of practice relating to it. Section 43 requires the HEI to 'take such steps as are reasonably practicable to ensure freedom of speech for students and employees of the HEI and for visiting speakers.' This duty includes the use of any HEI premises, so far as it is possible. The use of the premises cannot be denied on the grounds of the beliefs, views, policies or objectives of the individual or organization requesting the use of the venue. The HEI should issue, and keep up-to-date, a code of practice outlining the procedures to be followed by students or employees with regard to meetings or other activities involving speeches or debates. The conduct required of any students or employees organizing or arranging such meeting may also be outlined in the HEI's code of practice along with disciplinary measures to ensure compliance.

There is very little guidance on what is 'reasonably practicable' in relation to this obligation. However, the case of *R v University of Liverpool*, ex p *Caesar Gordon* has helped to clarify the position. The case concerned a proposed meeting of the University of Liverpool Conservative Association, to which members of the South African Embassy in London had been invited to give a speech. The university gave provisional permission for the meeting, subject to the cooperation of the police. After consultation with the local police, the meeting was cancelled because the university was not satisfied 'that adequate arrangements could be made to maintain good order'. It was feared that public violence would break out in neighbouring areas, which had a large black and Asian population. There was an internal appeal in accordance with the university's code of practice. On appeal, the university agreed to allow the meeting to be held under certain special conditions, but later cancelled the meeting again following further consultation with the police.

The Chairman of the University of Liverpool Conservative Association brought judicial review proceedings against the university on the grounds that the university's decision was *ultra vires* and in breach of the Education (No. 2) Act 1986, Section 43. The court held that 'good order' could only relate to 'good order' within the precincts of the university. The university in discharging its duty under Section 43(1) was not entitled to take into account threats of 'public disorder' outside the confines of the university by persons not within its control. The police's concerns of public disorder in the surrounding area was not a good reason for the university to refuse permission for the meeting to be held. It would be for the police, not the university, to consider whether a breach of the peace would occur and to forbid or cancel the meeting on the grounds of public interest.

An interesting point in this case was that the court decided that the university was acting reasonably by imposing conditions. The special conditions that the university imposed were that:

- attendance of the meeting would be confined to a limited number of staff and students;
- there would be no publicity of any kind for the meeting;
- entrance to the meeting would be granted only on production of a valid university identity card.

This case is useful in establishing that an HEI can concern itself with disruption on its premises but not in the surrounding areas, and that it is perfectly within an HEI's authority to impose special conditions (provided that these are reasonable). This case also demonstrates the effectiveness of having a good code of practice.

Status

SUs are usually unincorporated associations separate from the HEI, although some are now considering acquiring corporate status. The majority of the SUs are established either by charter, statute or equivalent articles of government of the HEI itself. The only real exceptions are Cambridge, Essex and York universities where there are SUs established by an 'ordinance'. The difference between an ordinance and a charter, statute or articles of government is that an ordinance may be terminated by the institution without the consent of the Privy Council. The various charters, statutes, articles of government and ordinances vary considerably in their definition and regulation of an HEI's SU.

Before proposing any major change to the status, organization or constitution of the SU it is advisable to examine the HEI's governing document for the provisions regarding the SU. It is also necessary to examine the 'objects' within the constitution of an SU as these differ in their detail and comprehensiveness from institution to institution. An SU should have clearly defined objects, which are in accordance with the university's own objects and, as far as possible, able to be construed as charitable. The objects should certainly not be broader than those of the HEI.

Unincorporated association

An unincorporated association (which most SUs are) was defined in *Conservative Central Office v Burrell* as:

> two or more persons bound together for one or more common purposes, not being business purposes, by mutual undertakings, each having mutual duties and obligations, in an organisation which has rules which identify with whom control of it and its funds rests and upon what terms and which can be joined or left at will.

An unincorporated association is governed by its own constitution, which acts essentially as a legally binding contract between its members. It must have identifiable rules and an identifiable membership (which should satisfy the provisions for a written constitution – see the EA 1994, Section (2)(*a*)). An unincorporated association has no separate legal existence itself, unlike a company, and is seen in law as a group of individuals who have duties and liabilities to one another. There are no statutes dealing directly with unincorporated associations and so the law applies to unincorporated associations in the same way as it does to individuals. Therefore, a member of an unincorporated association who enters into a contract on its behalf is personally liable on that contract, although the member may be entitled to be indemnified out of the association's funds under its rules.

The SU and charity law

HEIs are normally charitable institutions. They are classed as 'exempt charities' (for more details, see Chapter 4). Under the Charities Act 1993, Schedule 2, all institutions or colleges connected with an HEI or any institution which is 'administered by or on behalf of an institution' and 'is established for the general purpose of, or for any special purpose of or in connection with the . . . HEI' is also an exempt charity. Accordingly, as long as there is this congruence of administration and of purpose, the SU will have exempt status.

Advantage of charitable classification

The advantage of being an exempt or registered charity is that the rules relating to certainty of a trust and perpetuity are no longer applicable. However, the biggest benefits, of course, are in relation to tax advantages – exemption from capital gains tax, income tax, corporation tax (other than on trading income) – and business rates reduction. HEIs are also normally exempt from VAT on the supply of education and research. However, VAT is payable in relation to trading activities. The advantage of exempt status is that the SU does not have to comply with as many statutory requirements as a registered charity, making its administration easier. However, it is important to remember that the rules regarding trustees acting 'reasonably and prudently' in all matters, and the careful application of funds in accordance with the charity's objects and powers of investment, still apply.

Charitable status and donations

Basically, an SU exists to further the educational purposes of the HEI, to promote the general welfare of the students and to advance the interests of the HEI in the appropriate ways. Any non-charitable activities should be supplemental or incidental to the overall development of scientific, artistic, cultural, athletic, political, religious and social activities among students. Any expenditure or donation by an SU should be made only to further these objects. The subject of charitable status and donations by SUs has been raised in the courts on a number of occasions, where it was questioned whether funds were being correctly applied in donating money to charitable (but non-educational) organizations and political organizations.

In 1972, the University of Sussex SU intended to make donations to 'War on Want' and to a campaign protesting against the abolition of free school milk. The matter came before the courts and Mr Justice Brightman said:

> it is not open to the Unions . . . to authorise the use of the Union's funds for the purpose of promoting any object which may happen to interest the members of the Union regardless of whether such object is charitable and educational or not . . . If the members of the Union wish to express their views financially that money should come from their own personal funds and not from trust money. Admittedly, part of the educational business is research, discussion, debate and reaching a corporate conclusion on social and economic problems, but, in my view the provision of money to finance the adoption outside the University of that corporate conclusion does not form any part of the educational process.
>
> > (*Baldry v Feintuk*)

It was held that the payments to 'War on Want', despite being a charity, were not educational and that 'it is not open to one charity to subscribe to the funds of another charity unless the recipient charity is expressly or by implication a purpose or object of the donor charity'. As for the campaign against abolition of school milk, it was held that this was a non-charitable purpose and, therefore, 'charitable funds cannot be lawfully used for setting up such a fund'.

In 1985 another case came before the courts (*Attorney General v Ross*). The North London Polytechnic proposed making a substantial payment towards the striking miners and in aid of victims of the Ethiopian famine. The Attorney-General took the view that these payments were outside the scope of the SU's objects and *ultra vires*. The SU argued in this case that some of its objects were charitable, but others such as its affiliation with the NUS and other outside bodies demonstrated that its main purpose was not charitable. Therefore, the SU should not have charitable status and should be free to make any donations it wanted. Mr Justice Scott disagreed and, in holding that the SU did have charitable status, said:

> there is, in my view, no reason in principle why a Students' Union being a charity should not affiliate itself to the NUS, a non-charity and pay the subscriptions or fees. The NUS is the leading National Student Organisation. I do not, therefore, accept Counsel's argument that affiliation to the NUS and payment of affiliation fees is inconsistent with the Union having a charitable status.

Therefore, if the SU's constitution, as well as expressing charitable objects, allows certain non-charitable activities to be carried on, provided these non-charitable activities are regarded as being merely ancillary or supplementary to the SU's main objects, it is not fatal to charitable status (which, anyway, should be well worth preserving for tax reasons).

Another interesting case considering the more detached relationship the SU had with its HEI, is *London Hospital Medical College v Inland Revenue Commissioners and Others*, which concerned a medical college attached to a hospital. An SU had been formed with the objects of promoting, encouraging and coordinating 'social, cultural and athletic activities amongst the members so as to add to the general comfort and enjoyment of the students', but qualified hospital staff could also be members of the SU. The SU was reliant on the college for a proportion of its funding and regarded itself as under the control of the college. However, the Inspector of Taxes challenged the SU's charitable status on the grounds that its activities solely benefited its members. The court decided that the SU did exist solely to further educational purposes and it achieved this aim. The SU was heavily dependent on the college and the benefits given to members were for the purpose of encouraging and carrying out the main educational purpose of the college. Mr Justice Brightman took into account that if the college took away its support, the SU would close and that the main object of the SU was furthering the purposes of the college and not for private benefit. The SU was, therefore, charitable.

In the light of these cases, the provision in the EA 1994, Section 22, regarding the publication of external organizations to which the SU is affiliated or wishes to be affiliated or donate funds can now be appreciated. Furthermore, the requirement under the EA 1994 to bring to the attention of all students the restrictions imposed on the activities of the SU by charity law also becomes evident.

Risk and liability

The activities of SUs are frequently the subject of media attention. The SU undertakes a variety of events, entertainments and sports which can often lead to publicity and legal actions. Governing bodies of HEIs are obviously concerned about being held liable for the actions, omissions or debts of the SU. The question of whether an HEI could be held liable for the SU will depend on the nature of the claim that has been brought.

Health and safety aspects

Injury or damage caused by defects in buildings or health and safety prosecutions will usually remain the responsibility of the HEI as the owner of the building. Health and safety regulations are extensive and leave few grounds for a defence in relation to occupiers' liability.

An HEI could transfer ownership of the SU building to the SU to reduce its potential liability, but this then creates difficulties in that the SU may mortgage the property, sell it or lease or licence parts of it to third parties. Furthermore, if the students were to go into 'occupation', the university would have little or no powers to intervene. There is also no guarantee that the SU would keep the building in adequate repair or satisfactory condition. HEIs could consider the possibility of leasing or licensing the SU premises to the SU itself. A lease or licence may provide for repair and upkeep of the building and for its general safety and security, which again should reduce the potential liability of an HEI.

Employment and staff disputes

Within an unincorporated association, the person who is liable to an employee is the person who actually engaged or appointed the employee (e.g. the SU President or the SU Executive Committee). This obviously creates difficulties should a member of staff bring an action against the SU for wrongful or unfair dismissal or a Wages Act (1990) claim.

Contractual and tortious liability and the unincorporated association

Perhaps more of a concern for an HEI is the possibility of liability for the debts, breaches of contract and injuries or damage caused by negligence, which could result from the activities of the SU. In a contractual situation, an unincorporated association enters into a contract through individuals, who may remain personally liable for the debts or breach of contract resulting from that agreement. If authority to enter into a contract was given by a committee, then the committee members would be liable for breach of the contract. An ordinary member of the SU (i.e. a full-time student) or the HEI itself would not usually be liable for the debts or breach of contract by an SU, because he, she or it has not been given any implied authority to make that contract, nor contracted personally. Liability under a contract is for the full amount of the claim and not limited to the funds which the unincorporated association holds. However, liability may be limited by a specific provision in the contract to the funds of the association provided such a provision is considered reasonable under the Unfair Contract Terms Act 1977. In cases of negligence and other torts some or all of the members of the SU may be liable depending upon the extent to which they held overall control of the activities concerned.

As there is little existing case law, it is difficult to establish or predict a court's approach or conclusions. However, it is important for the SU to maintain adequate insurance for all types of public liability, which, in the case of an unincorporated association will need to be taken out by an officer or the committee of the SU, who then holds it on behalf of all the members of the SU. This insurance must be capable of indemnifying individual members.

Potential HEI liability

HEIs have always recognized that SUs are a potential risk in terms of liability and have tried to emphasize to parents, students and others that the HEI itself is not responsible for the SU and is not liable for its activities. Normally, an HEI will not be liable for breach of contract by an SU as it is not a party to the contract and, therefore, cannot be held liable on it. However, liability could arise if the HEI has given a guarantee in relation to the contract.

The issue of whether an HEI could be liable for the negligent activities of an SU is an interesting question. A plaintiff (e.g. a student) bringing a claim for negligence has to show that there was a duty of care owed by the defendant and that this duty of care has been breached (e.g. lack of safety equipment, slippery floors or inadequate facilities), which has caused damage to the plaintiff and which was foreseeable in the circumstances. This is a very simplistic view of the tort of negligence (it is not possible to discuss here all the possible circumstances in which a duty of care may arise: see *Winfield & Jolowicz on Tort*, 1994). In the absence of any substantive case law, it is difficult to predict quite how far a court would go in determining the extent to which an HEI owes a duty of care to members of an SU.

The HEI has a duty of care to ensure, for example, that the buildings in which students study and work are safe and that examination papers are marked fairly and correctly. The HEI is also vicariously liable for the negligent actions of its staff in the course of their employment. However, whether an HEI's duty of care extends to activities which are not part of a student's course (e.g. climbing or diving) is an interesting discussion point. The courts have held that social and sports activities are part of HEI objects and that this is the reason why SUs maintain exempt charitable status, so it is arguable that injuries may be foreseeable as a result of students engaging in social or sporting activities organized by an SU, or a particular section of it, and that the HEI has a duty of care to ensure such activities are conducted properly. On the other hand, the HEI is certainly not any longer *in loco parentis* and is not obliged to supervise student social activities (see Chapter 7).

Where an individual has been severely injured or killed as a result of negligence, the courts are often anxious to compensate the plaintiff for the damage they have suffered and the duty of care may be constructed all too easily for the HEI as a 'deep pocket', (and probably carrying insurance) in those cases where the SU itself is unable to meet the liability.

Reducing the risks

The incorporation of the SU is now seen as a way for the HEI to reduce its risks and liabilities associated with the everyday running of the SU.

Incorporation of the SU does not guarantee exemption from liability, but it may improve the chances of successfully avoiding liability should it arise.

However, before considering incorporation, it is worth remembering that faced with either 'bailing out' the SU financially and accepting responsibility or defending a potentially high profile court action and its media publicity, the HEI may be caught between the devil and the deep blue sea. However, at least it would solve the problem of a lack of case law in this area!

Incorporation

The use of trading companies by HEIs has become more common. These companies are used for structural, commercial and tax reasons (for more on trading, see Chapter 12). The publication of the bar turnover of universities (*The Times*, 23 July 1996) showed some SU bars with a turnover of up to £2 million, with a large proportion over £1 million. It may soon become essential, as opposed to advisable, for SU bars to be run through trading companies to avoid difficulties with their charitable status.

The following brief outline of some of the difficulties which may be experienced if full incorporation of the SU were envisaged, is accompanied by some possible solutions. Incorporating an SU is not a simple task and there are many issues to be considered. The success of incorporating an SU, its continued development and its efficient governance would depend on the objects and powers which are given by the memorandum and articles of association. An HEI should consider exactly how much influence or control it wants over an SU.

Format

An SU would probably be incorporated by means of a company limited by guarantee (see Chapter 12), which has independent status but which differs from a company limited by shares in that:

- it has no shares;
- each member of the company agrees to contribute to the assets of the company to a specified amount (e.g. 5p) should the company be wound up for any reason;
- the members of the company are the original subscribers and any other persons who agree to become members in accordance with its articles of association;
- it may operate without using the word 'Limited' after its name provided the company's objects are the promotion of commerce, art, science or education and that any profits are spent promoting these objects.

Memorandum and articles of association

A company limited by guarantee must have a memorandum and articles of association setting out the objects and powers of the company, the directors' powers and the members' rights and voting powers. These documents are the governing document of the SU and should satisfy the requirement for a written constitution – see the Companies Act 1985, Sections 288(*b*) and 574(2)). These documents have to be carefully drafted so that the administration procedures it lays down are workable and capable of compliance.

Running an incorporated SU

The SU (as a company) must comply with the various provisions of the legislation concerning companies. The obligations placed on a company by this are too numerous and extensive to discuss in detail here. However, briefly the company's day-to-day obligations are that it must:

- print the company name, registration number and registered office on all notepaper and invoices;
- keep statutory books with details of directors, members, debentures and charges and directors' interests;
- file an annual return with Companies House;
- file annual audited accounts with Companies House;
- register and keep Companies House notified of any changes of director;
- hold an annual general meeting;
- make any changes to the constitution of the company by holding an extraordinary general meeting and having the resolution approved by 75 per cent of the members present;
- comply with the provisions in the Companies Act with regard to the calling and holding of meetings.

The requirements are extensive – there are 80 circumstances in which documents are to be submitted to Companies House. The task of ensuring that an incorporated SU complies would not be a simple one. Failure to file returns or accounts will result in substantial fines or even criminal liability being imposed on directors and officers. It may be wise for the company secretary to be a permanent member of staff of the HEI itself in order to ensure compliance and provide continuity.

Directors and members

An important issue to consider is who will be the directors and members of a company. One approach would be to appoint the sabbatical officers as the directors of the company and all students (except those who have expressed a wish to 'opt out' of the SU) as members of the SU. The register of members could be maintained by keeping a list of all students attending at the HEI. If this list is kept or printed from a computer database the HEI and the SU should consider compliance with the 1984 Data Protection Act before any information is transferred.

If this approach is adopted, the HEI will lose all direct control over the governance and conduct of the SU, although it may retain some considerable indirect influence if it is the main provider of financial support. The students may enter into contracts, change the constitution, change the name, secure finance and alter the membership provisions, without the consent or approval of the HEI. This would be a dangerous situation, particularly considering the legal obligations of an HEI's governing body under the EA 1994 which they may be unable to monitor if the SU were completely self-governed.

HEIs may, therefore, wish to consider the following ways of maintaining some control over the company.

- Appoint members of the HEI staff as directors of the company. This carries some risk of personal liability for those directors, particularly if the company were to become insolvent, or, as a charitable trustee, if the directors acted imprudently or unlawfully in relation to the memorandum and articles of association. An HEI may consider it sensible to invest in directors and trustees liability insurance. It is also important to remember that appointing a director does not give the HEI control of the company and that control is ultimately given by membership voting rights.
- Give the HEI enhanced voting rights either in all situations or only in specified situations. Alternatively, the HEI could be given a right of veto in certain circumstances.

Incorporation and charitable status

On incorporation, an SU will become a separate legal entity from the HEI but should be able to maintain exempt charitable status by virtue of its association with the HEI – see the Charities Act 1993, Schedule 2(w). As we have seen earlier, in order to obtain exempt charitable status an SU must have congruence of administration and of purpose with the HEI. The congruence of administration should be satisfied by the requirement in the HEI's constitution, charter or articles for the establishment and funding of the SU and the requirement for the SU to account for its funds to the HEI. The congruence of purpose should be satisfied by the objects of the SU being educational, charitable and compatible with those of the HEI.

It is advisable to submit copies of the articles and memorandum of association in draft to the Charity Commissioners for their examination and comments to avoid difficulties later. There is also the issue of remunerating the sabbatical officers who would normally be directors of the SU. Remuneration of charitable trustees is normally only allowed in 'special circumstances' and, although this should be possible, clearance with the Charity Commissioners is again highly advisable.

Shadow directors

A shadow director is a person in accordance with whose directions or instructions the directors of a company are accustomed to act. However, a person is not deemed a shadow director by reason only that the directors act on advice given by him or her in a 'professional capacity'. Therefore, if the directors of an SU are 'accustomed to act' in accordance with the instructions of the HEI, the HEI is likely to be deemed to be a shadow director. All the directors or at least a governing majority of them must be accustomed to act on the directions of a shadow director. In order to establish 'accustomed to act', there must be examples of more than one act to establish a course of conduct. It is not essential for any element of compulsion to be proved in the relationship between the shadow director and the board of directors. The HEI may be regarded as a shadow director by reason of a director (e.g. the permanent full-time company secretary) being employed by it or by its enhanced, special or majority voting rights as a member of the company which results in the directors being accustomed to act in accordance with the HEI's instructions. If an HEI is deemed to be a shadow director, it will be liable in the same way as an ordinary director and may become liable for the actions of the company. This could be of particular concern should the company become insolvent. However, it could also be used as a method of 'lifting the corporate veil' in an instance involving tortious liability.

Incorporation and drink!

The SU will need to consider the nature of any licence to sell intoxicating liquor. If this is a club registration and so requiring a registration certificate under the Licensing Act 1964, Schedule VII, then the use of enhanced or reduced voting rights for members may not be permissible. This problem could be circumvented by making an application for a Justices Licence.

Conclusions

Of all the matters discussed in this chapter, incorporation is perhaps the most complex, interesting and important. Incorporation will not necessarily guarantee the HEI protection from tortious liability in particular, but it *might* help by thickening the veil between the SU and the HEI (depending on the exact balance of distance between, control of, and involvement within, the SU by the officers of the HEI). It might also at least ensure a clearer regime for the routine management of the SU by invoking the procedures of the legislation concerning companies – the key element here probably being the competence of the SU permanent secretary acting as the company secretary. So far, only one HEI is known to be seriously exploring incorporation, but it is likely to be a topic of increasing significance.

Further reading

Farrington, D. J. (1994) *The Law of Higher Education*. London: Butterworths.
Warburton, J. (1992) *Unincorporated Associations*. London: Sweet & Maxwell.

Part 6

The Higher Education Institution and its Property

17

Security: Surveillance, Trespass, 'Reasonable Force' and 'Clamping'

Catriona Webster (Shakespeares)

Editors' introduction

Some higher education institutions (HEIs) in the USA have their own police forces and some of those forces are armed! Oxford University has had its Proctors and the University Marshall, backed up by 'bulldogs' (porters in bowler hats) for many centuries (but not (yet) armed!). All HEIs have security problems and all have security cover (usually from directly employed porters and security officers, sometimes by way of a contract with a private security firm). This chapter explores the power these security forces have in law when trying to maintain good order on the campus. Just how much force can a porter reasonably use in removing a protestor from the animal house or in restraining a car thief? When does reasonable force become unreasonable and excessive force, leaving the porter (or, vicariously, his or her employer, the HEI) open to being charged with assault? What is the legal position as regards the clamping of cars? When does a non-member of the HEI cease to be a welcome member of the public, entitled by implicit invitation to enjoy certain campus facilities (e.g. to stroll around the lake, to browse in the bookshop or to buy a loaf in the Student Union shop) or by explicit invitation to join the sports centre, to watch a play in the theatre and to attend a public lecture, and become a trespasser whom the HEI can order off the campus?

Linking back to the disciplining of students in Chapter 7, this chapter also examines the options open to the HEI authorities in dealing with student protest in the form of the threatened occupation of HEI buildings or their actual occupation. What is the law concerning the reasonable use of force to prevent the building being occupied? Once occupied, what are the steps in the legal process to repossess it?

This chapter also explores the legal issues surrounding the use of surveillance cameras and what happens to the film 'footage'.

Introduction

Regardless of the size or locality of the HEI, some system of security will already exist. However, given the ever-increasing petty crime in educational establishments, there is an even greater demand for increased levels of security no matter where the property is situated. Although security must now be regarded as a necessity, there is the need to create a balance among:

- the necessity to protect the safety of students and staff at the HEI but in such a manner to enable them to move on and off campus freely at various times;
- the need to maintain the security of the HEI's property;
- the benefit in allowing members of the public access to campus facilities (such as bookshops, theatres and sports centres), which the HEI may encourage the public to use.

Achieving a balance may not be easy, particularly with pressures from various action groups attempting to promote civil liberties and the individual's right of freedom. However, the lack of proper security systems may result in claims of negligence against the HEI. Security systems in operation in HEIs at present range from flood lighting and surveillance cameras to guard dogs and security patrols. Further attempts have been made by many HEIs to protect the individual's security (for example, by issuing personal alarms to staff and students – male and female).

Occupiers' liability

Whether the HEI is an owner or merely an occupant of the property, it owes a duty of care to anyone who may come on to that property – see the Occupiers' Liability Acts 1957 and 1984. This duty relates to the state and condition of the property and imposes an obligation on the HEI to warn of hazards that may be present on the property. To consider whether the HEI is an occupier for the purposes of the duties imposed by law, the test to be applied is whether the HEI has some degree of control associated with its use of the property – see *Wheat v Lacon*. Where there is a sufficient degree of control, the HEI will be considered to be an occupier and obligations will, therefore, be imposed on it.

The duty imposed on HEIs for visitors and those entering the property lawfully differs from those who enter as trespassers – a higher level of care being required for the visitors and those entering the property lawfully. The duty imposed by law on the occupier in respect of lawful visitors is to take such care as is reasonable in the circumstances to ensure that the visitor will be reasonably safe in using the property for the purposes for which that visitor is invited. Therefore, one would expect property to be free from obstacles and hazards, particularly those areas being used by staff and students. Routes should be kept clear and the fabric of the building itself should be in a safe state so as to avoid injury to any visitors. The occupier must be prepared for children to exercise less care than adults, which means that greater effort will be required where children have access to the property (which will even be the case where a child trespasses onto the land). If an HEI offers crèche facilities or play groups for children, it must exercise extra care to ensure that the property is safe and specially designed for such purposes.

Liability to those who are not the HEI's visitors and who are on the land without authority (i.e. trespassers) arises only:

- if the HEI is aware of a danger or has reasonable grounds to believe that a danger exists;
- if the HEI knows or has reasonable grounds to believe that a person is in the vicinity of the danger or may come into that vicinity (whether or not it is lawful for that person to be in the vicinity);
- if the risk is one against which the occupier may reasonably be expected to offer some protection.

The HEI duty is to take such care as is reasonable in the circumstances to see that the person on the land does not suffer injury on the property resulting from the danger contemplated. This will apply to trespassers as well as authorized visitors. The HEI should be aware that old security methods (such as fixing glass in cement on top of walls) may create such a danger and, should injury result, is likely to be a breach of the duty owed by the HEI. Although the HEI does have a duty to the trespasser, this extends only to the person and not to the personal property of the trespasser. The HEI may, depending on the individual circumstances, discharge its duty by giving warning and notice of the danger in order to discourage any person from taking the risk. Such warnings should be especially clear for any property where children are likely to be enticed onto the property.

The HEI's duty of care is not limited only to the buildings. It extends to all parts of the property belonging to or used by the HEI. The public often have rights of access to cross HEIs' land by means of footpaths or roadways. These routes should be adequately maintained and, if any hazard does arise, an appropriate warning in a clear place should be given. The HEI must exercise a duty of care in these circumstances in order to avoid negligence claims which may arise if, for example, pathways are uneven and a pedestrian is injured when tripping.

Health and safety

Although occupiers' liability places some control on HEIs for the standard of their properties, HEIs are also subject to stringent health and safety legislation. The Health and Safety at Work Act 1974 places a duty on employers and those responsible for places of work to ensure that employees, visiting staff and other individuals are protected from risks arising out of work activities. This will include protection for students, members of the public and contractors. Specific duties regarding high-risk areas (such as radiation and genetics) have been introduced by various regulations following the 1974 Act, and the European Union (EU) has called for the implementation of further directives to ensure the health and safety of the workforce. These have been implemented in the Health and Safety Regulations 1992.

It is suggested by the Committee of University Chairs in their *Guide for Members of Governing Bodies of Universities and Colleges in England and Wales* (CUC, 1995) that HEIs and other organizations should make sure that:

- a health and safety statement in which management responsibility for health and safety issues is clearly designated;
- those with designated responsibility are aware of and have access to regulations, advice and training;
- the institution plans the implementation of its policy and sets health and safety standards which it expects to be achieved;
- the institution has structures and arrangements for implementing its safety policy (e.g. safety officers and appropriate committees);
- the institution monitors its activities to ensure that the agreed standards are being met.

A large range of requirements is set out in legislation governing such matters. This chapter is focused merely on security and, hence, does not discuss this aspect in detail. Suffice to say, health and safety, although concerned with hazards, also places great emphasis on the existence of reporting procedures and constant review by employers and occupiers. A good health and safety policy will aid in a defence against any negligence claim.

Controls on parking and wheel-clamping

Parking arrangements on private property can often be problematic and solutions for easing parking problems may cause controversy. (**Editors' note**: remember the jocular definition of a university: 'A collective of academics united only by a common grievance over car-parking'!) It is often necessary to implement constraints or restrictions on parking, thereby easing congestion and keeping emergency access ways clear. Pay-and-display machines, barrier systems, parking attendants, individual parking passes and wheel-clamping are a few methods which may be considered. Some methods of control will only prove effective where the number of access routes onto the property are limited. Unauthorized parking can amount to trespass on the property and wheel-clamping may be considered a solution. However, where wheel-clamping is operated on private land, various conditions must be satisfied – otherwise, the clamping may be deemed to be illegal. HEIs in Scotland should be aware that wheel-clamping is clearly illegal and it is taken to fall within the limits of extortion (depriving a motorist of his of her vehicle by detaining it against his or her will can amount to theft). The conditions necessary to ensure legality in England and Wales apply even where the person parking the car clearly enters the land as a trespasser. The following conditions need to be satisfied.

1. There must be a notice in an obvious place stating that wheel-clamping is in operation. If no notice is given, the motorist may not realize that he or she is trespassing on the land. If a motorist then parks his or her car on the land where notices are clearly placed, he or she accepts the risk that the car will be clamped. If the motorist did not realize there was a risk of clamping, he or she could claim trespass and conversion amounting to wrongful interference with goods under the Tort (Interference with Goods) Act 1977.
2. Once the motorist does park, he or she then accepts that a fee will need to be paid to release the car. Any release fee must be reasonable. If a sum is excessively high, it may be held to be unwarranted. The 1968 Theft Act, Section 21, provides that the unwarranted demand for revenues with a view to gain or with an intent to cause loss can amount to the offence of blackmail. The law does not establish what sum of money would be deemed reasonable for a release fee and the amount may vary according to the circumstances of the case. It would probably be looked on unfavourably by the court if the intention of the release fee was to make profit as opposed to deterring illegal parking.
3. The vehicle must be released without delay once the motorist offers to pay the fee. If the vehicle is not then released, there could be deemed an intention to permanently deprive the motorist of the vehicle. This could give rise to an accusation of theft.
4. There should be a means by which the motorist can communicate his or her offer of payment. The notice should state a telephone number or contact point, and it is necessary for someone always to be available to release the car (*Arthur v Anker*).

The practicalities of operating such a system may be difficult to meet, particularly if no one is available at certain hours to release the car. If a private firm is employed to take on the responsibility of clamping, then the individuals concerned should be easily identifiable (by means of a uniform or identification badge). It is *not* considered illegal for a motorist to remove a wheel-clamp provided he or she does not damage the clamp.

Security guards

Although private policing may be considered an expensive security arrangement, it does have its advantages – most noticeably by the fact that someone is physically available on site to deal with issues as and when they arise. Further, the mere presence of security guards may prevent incidents from arising. It must be remembered, however, that private security guards do not have the same powers as police, particularly in respect of arrest and detention. Common law (as opposed to statute) does vest certain powers of arrest in the ordinary citizen where:

- an arrestable offence is being committed or there are reasonable grounds to suspect such an offence is being committed;
- an arrestable offence has been committed and there are reasonable grounds to suspect the person is guilty;
- a breach of the peace is committed in the presence of the person making the arrest;
- the arrestor reasonably believes that such breach will be committed in the immediate future by the person arrested;
- a breach has been committed and there is reasonable belief that renewal of it is threatened – see *Albert v Lavin.*

Every citizen in whose presence a breach of the peace is being, or reasonably appears about to be, committed, has the right to take *reasonable* steps to make that person refrain from doing so – see the Criminal Law Act 1967. There is a duty for the arrestor to hand over the arrested person to the police as soon as is reasonably possible. If the person arrested claims that the arrest has been made falsely, then that person can claim damages for trespass to the person, including a claim of false imprisonment if the individual is detained. In the event that security guards are employed at the property, they are not permitted to use *un*reasonable violence or force on a trespasser even if that individual is engaging in a criminal activity – see *Revill v Newbury.*

As the use of security firms is becoming more widespread, it is important that the security staff do not invade the private rights of students and staff. Concerns may arise since the background of security staff is often unknown, particularly as to whether they have criminal records. It should be the case that any member of security staff can be easily identifiable by means of a uniform and/or badge, particularly where a private firm is contracted to do the task of security. The HEI must consider the risk that they will be held vicariously liable for the actions of any security guards they employ. It is, therefore, sensible for the HEI to consider insuring for such liability, or, if a security firm is instructed to provide such service, checking to see that it has insurance cover for wrongful or unlawful arrest, or for false imprisonment. Damages for trespass may be given even if there is no proof of damage. If the security personnel are employees of the HEI, then the HEI would be wise to check the records of prospective employees.

The reasonable use of force to defend the property or eject a trespasser is lawful. The trespasser must first be asked to depart before any attempts to physically eject him or her. Excessive force must not be used – for example, a security guard using a cosh or truncheon on an unarmed drunken student would be excessive, as would four guards being 'over-zealous' with just one trespasser. The force should be matching – that is, only if the guard is attacked or has reasonable cause to believe himself to be about to be attacked, should he or she resort to violence, using something to hand as a *defensive* weapon only if the assailant has an *offensive* weapon. If it is a matter of removing a trespasser, the guards should take care not to inadvertently cause injury by using certain risky arm-locks or neck-holds. Clearly, self-defence training provided by the HEI for its security force will help establish that it had not only discharged its duty of care as an employer to its employed security staff, but that it had also attempted to ensure that they were less likely to land the HEI in court by way of vicarious liability. Where any staff are employed on the premises for promoting security, the landowner should be aware that it is responsible not only for those employed (employer–employee relationship), but also for the actions of those so employed (vicarious liability).

Security of property

As well as the safety and security of the people using the HEI's buildings, the security of the buildings themselves must be considered. Floodlighting, for example, can help to improve safety and security on campus, but HEI managers should be aware that the erection of floodlights may require planning permission. As for the security of an individual's property and belongings, the HEI will not wish to accept responsibility for these. Disclaimers stating that the property is left at the owner's risk could go some way to avoiding responsibility, particularly with cars parked on campus. It might be worth considering putting notices disclaiming responsibility for loss on any tickets needed to park. Ideally, this notice should be brought to the attention of the individual prior to the purchase of any tickets. Responsibility for death or personal injury cannot, however, be contracted out of under the Unfair Contract Terms Act 1977. Furthermore, the implementation of the UTCCR 1994 means there is now an even greater requirement for clarity and reasonableness in notices and contracts directed at 'the consumer'.

Occupation of HEI property by students

Security of HEI property may be put into question by some form of sit-in or protest by the students, or even just by the threat of such action. Where this occurs, the HEI can commence proceedings in the High Court either for an injunction to restrain students from occupying or an order for possession once they have done so. The HEI need not identify every individual involved, as long as reasonable steps to identify individuals have been made. It will often be impracticable to obtain the names of everyone concerned. Usually the injunction or order names officers of the Students' Union (SU) as the representatives of the student community. Orders for possession under the Rules of the Supreme Court, Order 113, can now be made even when all occupying students cannot be identified – see *University of Warwick v De Graaf and Others*. Courts have made possession orders not only for those parts of the property adversely occupied, but also in situations where there has been a threat that the students might occupy other parts of the HEI's premises. So, the order may be extended by the court to cover the whole of the HEI – see *University of Essex v Djemal and Others*. There are also criminal repercussions if damage or injury to persons is caused as a result of the occupation. The SU, however, will often be made to pay for damage to the premises of the HEI from its grant or budget.

When areas of HEI property have been invaded as part of a demonstration, the fact that an individual is not motivated by the desire for personal gain will be taken into account in sentencing. In circumstances where criminal welfare campaigners entered and destroyed property in a university department and removed slides showing rodents being injected, it was decided that, whilst the law cannot be taken into the hands of campaigners even if they believed they were morally justified, such behaviour should result in a custodial sentence but that such a sentence should be suspended – see *R v Adams*.

It remains to be seen whether the Criminal Justice and Public Order Act 1994 may yet be used by the police in the context of a student occupation. This makes trespass a criminal offence under certain circumstances (e.g. 'raves', the Stonehenge summer solstice gathering and 'squatters' in private houses), giving, for once, some force to the old 'wooden lie' of 'Trespassers will be prosecuted'. The Criminal Justice and Public Order Act 1994, Section 69, creates the offence of 'aggravated trespass', whereby a person who intimidates others so as to deter them from following a lawful activity or who obstructs or disrupts that activity, may be liable for up to three months' imprisonment. This is really aimed at 'hunt saboteurs' and relates to an offence 'on land in the open air'. Hence, even if the police were willing to act under Section 69, they could do so only if the trespassers were 'occupying', say, a playing field or a car park, rather than the Animal House or Registry.

Freedom of speech

There is a duty on the HEI to take reasonable steps to ensure freedom of speech for its members, students, employees and visiting speakers – see the Education (No. 2) Act 1986, Section 43. The HEI is not, however, under any duty to take into consideration persons and places outside its control, but the premises of the SU will normally be deemed part of the HEI premises and under its control – see the Education (No. 2) Act 1986, Section 43(8), and *R v University of Liverpool, ex p Caesar Gordon*.

Closed-circuit television

Closed-circuit television (CCTV) is being used more widely for security purposes. It can also help promote a sense of security. Despite its benefits, the argument arises as to whether such use of CCTV interferes with an individual's privacy. There are no controls in law on the use of surveillance equipment, unless the equipment is used to such an extent that it causes a nuisance: the concept of privacy is relatively underdeveloped in English law. This type of complaint would only tend to arise where one person or a few people believed they were falling victim to surveillance, but the use of CCTV in HEI property is primarily for reasons of safety and security. The HEI should carefully consider who will assume responsibility for monitoring the screens and who should be permitted access to the film footage. The footage can often be very helpful in deterring crime and may also assist police in solving crime. The main benefit of security cameras is that they seem to reduce crimes related to theft of cars. It is unlikely that the student population, bearing in mind the benefits of CCTV, would, therefore, object to its presence if it is made clear to them that the recordings will be closely controlled and that cameras will not be placed in areas which might be considered private by the students (such as common rooms).

Further reading

Smith, J. C. and Hogan, B. (1996) *Criminal Law*. London: Butterworths.

18

Houses in Multiple Occupation and what is a 'House'?

Sharon Ranouf (Mills and Reeve)

Editors' introduction

Is a hall of residence a house in the terms of the relevant legislation governing fire safety, sanitation, overcrowding, etc., in houses in multiple occupation (HMOs)? Even if such a structure can be a house in law (whatever the man on the Clapham omnibus may see it as in common-sense and architectural terms), is it actually in multiple occupation? Is a higher education institution (HEI) hall of residence an HMO? Is an Oxford college quadrangle or a Cambridge college court a hall of residence or even a house? If the relevant legislation is applicable, what impact might it have in terms of the need to meet the standards set for HMOs? Are grants available for the costs of meeting those standards? What powers of enforcement are there?

Where an HEI operates a property leasing scheme, whereby it rents whole houses from landlords and in turn acts as a landlord in renting the house or a room within it to students, what are its responsibilities to these students under HMO legislation?

Introduction

With the ever-increasing demand for HEI places and particularly as a result of the changes which were required for certain HEIs to achieve their status as statutory universities, the requirement for accommodation in HEI towns has reached an all time high. The legislation governing HMOs was primarily introduced to deal with problems encountered by local authorities faced with irresponsible landlords (both in the student market and the other sectors of the private rental market) who failed to make adequate provision for the prevention of fire, but it is now being looked to as legislation which might counter the perceived social 'problems' which have arisen as a result of a growing student population. With local authorities being required by members of the public to look closely at both existing and new cases involving potential HMOs, the HEIs and their managers will no doubt find themselves increasingly involved in ensuring compliance with the legislation itself and with the particular requirements of each individual local authority. Typically, however, a good number of the houses occupied by students will not actually be classified in law as HMOs. Even if this is the case, the HEI managers are still likely to incur costs – in money and time – in establishing the position. They may also encounter difficulties when planning new developments within the local community or when considering further or new head tenancy leasing schemes.

This chapter provides an overview of the law and its sanctions and looks at the approach which has been taken by some local authorities with the aim of providing an understanding of the issues which arise. Taking the law itself as a starting point, it is necessary to consider how the law has been interpreted, how the interpretations will affect HEIs and what action may be required as a result.

What is an HMO?

The legal definition of an HMO can be found in the housing legislation and not, as one might expect, in planning law. An HMO is defined in the Housing Act 1985, Section 345(1), as 'a house which is occupied by persons who do not form a single household'. It is clear that the legislation will include much more than the traditional 'picture book' house. Decided cases have defined a 'house' as 'a place fitted and used and adapted for human habitation' (*Reed v Hastings Corporation*). Flats in multiple occupation are also HMOs – see the Housing Act 1985, Section 345(2). The definition is a wide one from which individual local authorities can derive differing interpretations of what does and what does not constitute an HMO.

HEIs will be primarily concerned with two types of student accommodation and whether or not that accommodation constitutes an HMO. These are

1. shared student houses;
2. halls of residence (and similar types of accommodation within the HEI itself, such as the Cambridge college courts or Oxford quadrangles).

Shared houses

The all-important factor in determining whether or not a shared house is also an HMO appears to turn on whether, as a matter of fact, the sharers live together as a single household. Does a shared house operate as a home? Ministerial guidance has been issued to local authorities on this point (and generally, in relation to what does and does not constitute an HMO). However, the final decision is particular to each case which is looked at by each local authority and turns on the individual facts of that case – see Department of the Environment (DoE) Circular 12/86.

The guidelines suggest a set of relevant questions to be looked at in each case, including:

- whether the student occupiers share cooking, washing and cleaning;
- whether they occupy on separate contracts;
- whether the individual rooms can be locked;
- the extent of the shared rooms and facilities;
- whether the landlord is entitled to fill a vacancy at the property should one arise.

In most cases, local authorities have found it helpful to identify categories of potential HMOs. Where lists have been drawn up, these include a category for the 'traditional' HMO (i.e. a house divided into bedsits with shared kitchen or bathroom facilities), a category for houses converted into flats with a shared access but no shared living or dining facilities and a category for a house shared by a number of individual people. It is this third category into which the typical shared student house will fall. What is very clear, however, is that individual local authorities take different approaches (notwithstanding the ministerial guidance) to determine whether or not a house shared by a number of individuals does or does not constitute an HMO.

In a report to the Development Control Sub-Committee (27 January 1995), the director of development of Newcastle-upon-Tyne City Council considered whether there should be a strict application of the requirement to occupy as a single household failing which the property would be classified as an HMO. The director concluded that making a distinction between occupation as a single family or occupation as a single household was difficult to establish both on a practical and a factual level. The director pointed out that changes can be easily effected beforehand to ensure that, on inspection, the house appears to be in single household occupation. Reference was made to a decision by one housing inspector on appeal who accepted that the use of a property by students was a communal one on the basis that there was joint decision-making and sharing of facilities and services, and notwithstanding the fact that the bedrooms were lockable or that desks, chairs and kettles were kept in each individual's room.

This approach can be contrasted with that of Hart District Council (from their guide *Standard for Houses in Multiple Occupation*, revised 22 August 1994) who made a clear statement that one of their categories of HMOs comprised:

> houses occupied on a shared basis where occupants may belong to a specific group or have a common background, e.g. students. Tenants normally have an individual room and share the kitchen and bathroom, together with a communal living area.

Most authorities seem to take the view that a household with a degree of shared use of facilities (such as kitchen and sanitary accommodation) will not fall within one of the categories as being an HMO and will, therefore, be outside the regulations. Arguably, it is these shared households which fall outside the ambit of the HMO regulations (and the provisions of planning law which regulate change of use) which can give rise to some of the greatest problems. This is discussed later in relation to planning control.

Halls of residence

Although, using a wide interpretation, halls of residence could be brought within the meaning of an HMO for the purposes of the Housing Act 1985, it is arguable that, in drawing up their categories, local authorities have impliedly excluded halls of residence. There can be no doubt that a hall of residence is 'a place fitted and used and adapted for human habitation'. However, given that the categories listed by the various local authorities expressly include hostels, hotels (where a reasonable proportion of the guests are occupying as their principal place of abode) and residential homes involving an element of care, then it is arguable that halls of residence are not intended to be caught.

In practice, the housing authorities may be unlikely to take steps to investigate the condition and status of a hall of residence unless a complaint is received. In all probability, if the HEI and its managers are maintaining the halls to a reasonable standard, then the issue is unlikely to arise. In practice, it is far more likely that students with complaints about HEI halls of residence will take the matter up direct with HEI accommodation officers or bring pressure to bear through the SU. If the local authority is thought of at all in such cases then it will most likely be as the very last resort.

Does planning law have any impact?

In planning law, there is no definition of what constitutes an HMO. A dwelling house is defined, however, and includes occupation by not more than six unrelated residents living together as a single household as well as occupation by a single person or by people living together as a family – see the Town and Country Planning (Use Classes) Order 1987, Class C3.

No planning permission is required to change the use of a property from use as a dwelling house in the occupation of an individual or in the occupation of a single family to use by six or fewer sharers. Thus, there is no opportunity at the planning stage for local authorities to 'catch' houses which may or may not become HMOs and to seek to regulate them. Certain changes to properties would require planning consent, including dividing a house into self-contained flats or bedsits or changing the use of a property to use it as a hostel or residential home. As most halls of residence are purpose built, planning consent will be required anyway for any new halls before the commencement of the development. Similarly, any new development of HMOs will require planning consent and planning authorities have separate factors which will be taken into account. For example, in Newcastle-upon-Tyne the Development Control Sub-Committee takes account of:

- the nature of the locality and the impact on the area of HMOs;
- the size and suitability of the premises;
- the privacy of prospective occupiers;
- the impact of any necessary fire escapes;
- availability of car-parking;
- provision for refuse storage.

However, in the majority of cases, there will be no recourse to planning law where, for example, disaffected local residents wish to complain about unkempt gardens, traffic congestion, car-parking problems or problems with refuse.

Effect of a student residence being an HMO

Having established that a certain property (either within the HEI's own portfolio or forming part of a property leasing scheme) is an HMO, it is necessary to consider what action might be needed as a result. The relevant housing authority has various means of control in the form of registration schemes, associated 'control provisions', the imposition of management regulations and control orders. Brief details of each of these controls are set out here, but for more comprehensive information the reader is referred to Arden and Partington (1994) and to Jordan (1996) for changes implemented after 1 January 1997.

Registration schemes

The purpose of the schemes is to allow the local housing authorities to gather and record information. Authorities should be approached on an individual basis to ascertain whether or not a registration scheme has been put in place and whether the scheme affects the area in which the particular property is situated and the type of HMO concerned. A local authority search should reveal this information when a property is purchased.

The law in relation to registration schemes is presently governed by the Housing Act 1996. The provisions of the 1996 Act do not apply until 1 January 1999 to registration schemes already in existence. In the meantime, if the local housing authority wishes to do so, the existing registration schemes can be revoked and new schemes implemented. If the HEI is renting a property to students which it believes may be an HMO or indeed if the HEI is operating a head tenancy leasing scheme involving such properties, the HEI will be under a duty to register the property if a registration scheme is in operation. It is, therefore, necessary to consider the existing registration schemes and to comment on any changes which might occur over 1997 and 1998 as a result of the Housing Act 1996. Under the existing law the local housing authority has power to require owners or occupiers or any other person with an interest in the property (which would include HEIs operating head tenancy leasing schemes) to provide information to enable the authority to establish the particulars which are to be registered. It is an offence punishable by a fine not to provide information if requested to do so or to make a deliberate misstatement – see the Housing Act 1985, Section 350.

Control provisions

The registration scheme usually incorporates control provisions. Typically, such provisions make it an offence to permit occupation of a property which is not registered or to allow occupation of the property by more people than the registration permits. The first offence is punishable by a fine of up to £1000 plus £100 for each day the offence continues, and the second by a fine of up to £2500 plus £250 for each day the offence continues. In addition, the control provisions usually allow the local housing authority to refuse to register an HMO if the house is unsuitable for use as an HMO and cannot be adequately altered. Alternatively, requirements could be imposed as a prerequisite to registration of the property as an HMO. Registration and control provisions under the Housing Act 1985 required DoE confirmation before implementation by local housing authorities. A model scheme was developed and individual schemes conforming to the model scheme would be readily approved whereas other schemes would need to be justified by reference to local conditions if they were to be implemented.

Following the Housing Act 1996, all registration and control schemes must follow a statutory model which is to be drawn up. In seeking to establish the model scheme, the Government plans to limit the types and sizes of property which will be covered. There will be consultation in respect of the model scheme before the provisions of the Act relating to it are brought into force. However, even before this consultation, the Government has indicated that HEIs (among other organizations) will *probably* be excluded from the requirement to register (*Hansard*, H of L, Vol. 572).

Under the Housing Act 1996, Section 65(1), landlords will have to apply for re-registration every five years. This allows the local housing authority an opportunity to re-assess the landlord and the relevant properties. There will also be a positive duty on landlords to register with increased fees being levied for registration in order to help fund the cost of the schemes (£60 per room has been mentioned).

A further completely new element of the legislation is the introduction of special control provisions. These are aimed at protecting the neighbourhood from particular types of tenant rather than protecting the tenants from adverse conditions in the HMO. Special control provisions will not be included within model schemes and local housing authorities will need to make out a strong case for specific approval. Again, the Government has already indicated that those bodies and organizations excluded from the model schemes will also enjoy exclusion from the special control provisions. It seems, therefore, that such special control provisions will not necessarily assist disgruntled local residents who are at odds with the student population and who are seeking to prohibit HMOs being set up in their neighbourhood.

Although the registration schemes and associated control schemes allow the local housing authorities an opportunity to deal with HMOs, there will be many more student properties which 'escape' registration and the requirements which can be imposed thereafter. Birmingham City Council has implemented an owner's charter, which allows responsible landlords an opportunity to apply voluntarily for chartered status in respect of their rented property. The charter sets out standards of repair, safety measures and amenities which should be provided, and sets out legal and other guidelines for landlords to follow in managing their properties. The benefit to landlords of working to achieve chartered status is that their properties will be more likely to be included on lists of approved accommodation which are held by the HEIs in the city and perhaps afford them the opportunity to be included by the HEIs as part of an HEI head tenancy leasing scheme.

Power to require works

The provisions contained in the Housing Act 1985 relating to houses unfit for occupation or in serious disrepair will apply equally to HMOs as to other properties. In addition, the Housing Act 1985, Section 352, gives the housing authority power to serve notice on the person having control of the house or managing it. This clearly includes HEIs operating head tenancy leasing schemes. The notice can require works to be carried out to ensure that there are:

- satisfactory facilities for the storage, preparation and cooking of food (to include adequate sinks with hot and cold water);
- adequate toilet, bath, shower and wash-basin facilities;
- adequate means of escape from fire and other fire precautions.

The notice will set out a reasonable period within which the work must be carried out. Failure to comply is a criminal offence punishable by fine and if works have not been carried out the local housing authority can undertake them and pass on the cost (both of the works and of any administrative and other expenses) to the owner or the manager.

The Housing Act 1996 imposes a duty on landlords to keep HMOs up to the standard of fitness required for the number of occupants. This no longer depends on service of a notice by the local housing authority. Breach is punishable by fine and landlords may also face civil action by their tenants. This is unique in relation to HMO provisions.

Power to stop overcrowding

The local authority has power to serve an overcrowding notice if the number of people occupying the premises or likely to be occupying the premises is thought to be excessive. Alternatively, a direction to reduce overcrowding could be issued with a limit being placed on the number of people who may be accommodated at the property. This could have an impact on some HEIs, particularly at the beginning of a new HEI year, when students arrive to enroll without accommodation and need to be temporarily housed in rooms shared with other students until alternative accommodation is available. Again, offences are punishable by fine.

Imposition of management regulations

There are a number of matters required by statute and certain matters which can be required by the local authority exercising its discretion, all of which seek to ensure that the property is kept in good repair and good order. The management regulations are enforced by service of a notice on the manager of the property requiring the works to be carried out within a reasonable time. The local authority has power to carry out the works in default and to recover the expenses from the manager, as is the case with repair notices.

Control notices

If all else fails, the local authority can take possession of the property (subject to the rights of the existing occupiers) by making a control order and by assuming responsibility for the management of that property. The local authority acts as manager and has very wide powers (including the power to collect the rents and to discharge the expenses of management from those rents). In addition, removal expenses and rehousing expenses for those who may need to move out in order to allow works to be carried out may be claimed, together with the cost of the works themselves. The owner or manager from whom the local authority has taken over control is generally entitled to receive one half of the rental value of the property, by way of compensation, for the duration of the control order.

Control provisions – summary

Clearly, any of the control provisions, if invoked, will have a considerable costs impact on the owner or manager of the property. The onus is, therefore, on the owners and managers to ensure that their properties are 'up to scratch' without the need for the local authority to rely on the control provisions. With ever-decreasing funds available to HEIs, the requirements in respect of HMOs are likely to leave a further damaging hole in the annual budget.

Availability of grants

Housing repair and improvement grants are in short supply. There is provision under the Housing Act 1985, Section 464, for an application to be made for repair and improvement grants. However, such grants are only available where the property is to be owner-occupied or let as a residence. Grants are not available where the property is to be let in separate parts not as a home.

In the case of *R v Parker* it was decided that a dwelling 'let as a residence' did not comprise an HMO. The decision prevents entrepreneurial landlords profiting further from repair and improvement grants by applying for and using them to increase their stock of houses available for letting. The decision will, however, do little to assist HEIs who may be struggling to provide sufficient suitable HMO accommodation for their students. It is worth noting, however, that such grants should be available for the typical student shared house which does not actually constitute an HMO.

Special grants are available for improvements to the sanitary facilities and fire precautions at the HMO, and the amounts available were originally set out in a DoE circular (12/86). In addition, discretionary grants may be given for repair and replacement work. It should be noted that the local housing authority has power to restrict the work which the grant will cover so as to ensure that the repairs and replacements do no more than to place the property in a reasonable standard of repair. The HEIs will need to approach their individual local housing authorities to determine whether or not the proposed repairs will attract a discretionary grant.

Conclusions

In looking at the housing available, whether it is already in the HEIs portfolio or being considered for purchase or for inclusion in a head tenancy leasing scheme, the distinction between houses which are HMOs and fall within the legislation and those which are not will clearly be of great importance.

The primary impact will be the cost of ensuring that, if the property is an HMO, all the necessary regulations are complied with. For those who have not already done so, HEI managers would be well advised to establish good working relationships with the officers at the local housing authorities in order to establish a spirit of cooperation in the management of all the HEIs' properties whether or not these are HMOs. Although the law in relation to housing has been radically overhauled with the passing of the Housing Act 1996, it is not inconceivable that further legislation could follow in the wake of public criticism about those areas of towns and cities which are being given over to student housing. In the shorter term, and in the face of complaints from local residents about noise, anti-social hours, poor standards of maintenance and increased crime (particularly during student holidays), the local housing and planning authorities will be increasingly looked to as the powers able to tighten up local plans and restrict future development of what would otherwise be properly regulated HMOs. In such cases it will undoubtedly be easier for the HEI to plan for the future if it is working with the cooperation of its local housing authority.

In summary, for the average HEI involved in three main types of student residential accommodation the position is as follows.

1. For *halls of residence*, there are likely to be no HMO implications unless students bring in the local authority by making complaints and the local authority finds the premises to be seriously defective.
2. For *houses owned and run directly by the HEI*, again they are probably not to be defined as HMOs, and, even if they are, there will probably be no requirement to register them under the new model registration and control schemes which will be established under the Housing Act 1996. However, an existing scheme may trap them until 31 December 1998, and, even under the new model schemes, an authority could seek a property out and label it an HMO if it really wanted to be persistent.
3. For *head tenancy schemes*, there is probably a duty to register, whether under existing schemes or under the proposed new model schemes, but at least the liability for meeting HMO standards will lie with the owner not the HEI.

That said, any HEI directly running (or involved via head tenancy schemes in) overcrowded and ill-maintained property with inadequate fire precautions, whether a hall of residence or house, is subject to stringent local authority controls should student complaints bring the property to the attention of the local authority and whether or not the property is deemed an HMO. But, if the property is an HMO, the HEI under the Housing Act 1996, is under a stringent duty to keep the property up to standard and should not simply be waiting around to be 'caught' by the local authority. Being found in control of defective residential premises is not only a criminal offence under the Housing Act 1996, for the HEI, but, in the event of injury to occupants, a likely source of expensive and time-consuming action in tort (fire precautions and means of escape, plus the potential for carbon monoxide poison from gas appliances, being the most risky areas for HEIs incurring liability in tort).

Further reading

Arden, A. and Partington, M. (1994) *Housing Law*. London: Sweet & Maxwell.
Blair, B. (1997) *Liability of Landlords*. London: Sweet & Maxwell.

19

The Implications for Higher Education Institutions of the Disability Discrimination Act 1995

Daff Richardson (Manches & Co.)

Editors' introduction

This is an example of the kind of increasingly complex and ever-encroaching legislation which tends to creep up on the unsuspecting manager of a higher education institution (HEI). Another is the over-enthusiastic interpretation and application of legislation on houses in multiple occupation (HMOs) by some local authorities (see Chapter 18), and a third is the regulations concerning the use of flammable materials in furniture. Before a luckless HEI knows where it is there is a technical breach of the law and a potential bill for civil damages, for minor works and improvements of one kind or another. In some cases, there can also be scope for criminal prosecution of the HEI (and even of individual officers within it). Sometimes the pressure for an increasingly stringent legislative regime is Brussels/EC-driven (see Chapter 21). The particular piece of legislation described in this chapter is not only new, complex and wide-ranging (hence, potentially expensive) in its applicability to HEIs, but also it involves matters of some moral force (if not also ones of great sensitivity in terms of 'political correctness'). The HEI manager needs to tread carefully.

The recently (July 1997) reported out-of-court settlement concerning an NHS employee dismissed after contracting chronic fatigue syndrome (CFS, sometimes called ME, and once known pejoratively, and most unfairly, as 'Yuppie Flu') underlines the general need for employers to be 'reasonable' about obtaining proper and competent medical opinion, about *sympathetically* exploring part-time or an alternative type of work, and now also about determining whether the particular employee might be covered by the Disability Discrimination Act 1995. For example, CFS could be an *impairment* which has a *substantial, long-term* and *adverse* impact on the employee's ability to carry out day-to-day activities, including work, and hence the individual employee has become 'disabled' for the purposes of the Act. Many employers would have a much more simplistic view of what constitutes a disability (NB a US Court recently ruled that persistent lateness in an employee's arrival at work was, in the special circumstances of that case, a disability under the 1990 Americans with Disabilities Act!). Reasonable employers should have nothing to fear; macho managers who fire first and only belatedly when under legal pressure bother to ask questions, will need to be rational.

From a US perspective Kaplin and Lee (1995a) comment on the 'Section 504' comprehensive legislation, dating back to the Rehabilitation Act 1973 and reinforced by the Americans with Disabilities Act 1990, outlawing any discrimination against disabled applicants, students and employees – much stronger provisions than in the UK legislation discussed here, especially since it does directly cover applicants and students. A recent survey in the USA estimates a $9 billion price-tag if all US HEIs were to comply with the 1990 legislation, and that, in 1993–94 alone, $300 million was spent on appropriate modifications.

A UK survey estimates that new lifts cost about £150,000 each, an automatic door about £6000 and a disabled lavatory conversion about £1000. The CVCP has called for £50 million; HEFCE has allocated £6 million to cover the three academic years 1996–7 to 1998–9.

Introduction

The key provisions of the Disability Discrimination Act (DDA) 1995 came into force during 1996 and 1997. The DDA 1995 gives disabled people a range of new rights and remedies aimed, particularly, at combatting discrimination in employment and by the providers of goods and services. This is a brief guide to the DDA 1995 as it affects HEIs.

HEIs should be aware of:

- the duties of employers;
- the duties of 'service providers';
- the provisions affecting education.

The DDA 1995 is a complex piece of legislation. Its provisions are frequently supplemented and qualified by regulations, many of which are, at the time of writing, still to be published. Commentators perceive the DDA 1995 as having a number of shortfalls and it is expected that there will be a good deal of litigation surrounding, for example, its practical interpretation.

Employment

HEIs are, of course, large-scale employers of academic, academic-related and non-academic staff. The employment provisions of the DDA 1995 apply to all employers who have 20 or more employees. This threshold can be reduced, but not increased, by regulations. HEIs may have subsidiary companies with fewer than 20 employees. As a matter of good practice, these subsidiary companies should comply with the DDA 1995. It will be important to establish who is a disabled person for the purposes of the DDA 1995. Under the DDA 1995, a person has a disability if they have a physical or mental impairment which has a substantial and long-term effect on the ability to carry out normal day-to-day activities. The DDA 1995, Schedule 1 and subordinate regulations add to this definition and, no doubt, it will continue to be refined. The Secretary of State has published detailed guidance (*Guidance on the matters to be taken into account in determining questions relating to the definition of disability*, HMSO, 1996).

The DDA 1995 outlaws discrimination against disabled people at every stage of the employment process, from the advertisement of a vacancy to dismissal. Discrimination is the treatment of a disabled person (or a person who has had, but no longer has, a disability) for a reason relating to their disability in a way which is less favourable than the employer treats or would treat a person who does not have the disability in question, and where such treatment cannot be 'justified'. Adverse treatment will be justified where the reason for the treatment is material to the circumstances of the particular case and is substantial. The DDA 1995 also obliges employers to take reasonable steps to prevent their 'arrangements' or the physical features of their premises putting disabled people at a substantial disadvantage, when compared to people who are not disabled.

Arrangements are:

- procedures for selection of employees;
- terms and conditions on which employment, promotion, transfer, training or any other benefit is offered.

If an employer fails to make a reasonable adjustment, it *may* escape liability if the failure can be justified.

The DDA 1995 gives a non-exhaustive list of examples of reasonable adjustments, which include making adjustments to the premises or training, altering working hours and providing a reader or interpreter. Again, the Secretary of State has published detailed guidance (*Code of Practice for the elimination of discrimination in the field of employment against disabled persons or persons who have had a disability*, HMSO, 1996). Practical steps which employers can take to combat potential discrimination problems before they become a reality include:

- having a detailed disability policy, complementing the institution's equal opportunities policy;
- the monitoring of candidates and existing staff (perhaps by using confidential questionnaires) to establish whether any of them have disabilities.

It is good practice, where an employer has a disabled candidate for a post, or has an existing employee who becomes disabled, for the employer to consult the candidate or employee to discuss ways in which problems faced at work by the disabled person can be alleviated. The Employment Service, charities concerned with disabled people and disability consultants may also be able to give assistance in helping the HEI determine what adjustments should reasonably be made. Grants and other financial assistance may be available. Where the employer's premises are leased, the employer should contact the lessor, if this is required under the lease, for the lessor to give consent to those alterations which the employer proposes to make in order to comply with the DDA 1995. The lessor is obliged not to unreasonably withhold its consent. It can, however, attach reasonable conditions to the consent. These provisions will affect HEIs which rent property in which their staff work, and HEIs which themselves are the landlords of commercial premises.

The DDA 1995 also outlaws victimization of any person, whether or not they are disabled, if they have complained that discrimination has taken place against a disabled person, or given evidence in the course of such a complaint. If an employee of an HEI commits an act of unlawful discrimination in the course of their employment, the HEI may be vicariously liable for that act. The HEI may, however, have a defence if it can prove that it took reasonably practicable steps to prevent the discrimination. A key element to such a defence would be having and using an appropriate disability policy. Complaints under the DDA 1995 will be dealt with by an industrial tribunal. There is no qualifying period of service which an employee must accrue before a complaint can be entertained. As with sex and race discrimination complaints, there are no limits on the amount of compensation which may be awarded, and an award can include damages for injury to feelings. An industrial tribunal can also make a declaration as to the rights of the employer and the employee, and can recommend that the employer takes action to alleviate the problem about which the complaint has been received.

Provision of services

The DDA 1995 makes it unlawful for providers of goods, services and facilities to the general public ('service providers') to discriminate against disabled people by:

• refusing to serve a disabled person;
• failing to comply with the duty to make reasonable adjustments;
• discrimination in the standard of service provided to the disabled person;
• the terms on which the service is provided.

A service provider is expected to:

• make reasonable changes to policies, practices or procedures that make it unreasonably difficult for disabled people to use the service;

- take reasonable steps to obtain aids that will help disabled people use the service;
- take reasonable steps to remove or alter any feature of their premises that makes it difficult or impossible for a disabled person to use the service or, where reasonable, to find an alternative way to provide that service.

The rules about leased premises apply to service providers as well as to employers.

Regulations will guide service providers as to what is 'reasonable' and will also prescribe a maximum outlay for adjustments. There is guidance on the obligations for service providers (*Code of Practice containing guidance on access to goods, facilities and services*, HMSO, 1996). The rules relating to provision of services do *not* apply to the provision of education, including education funded by the HEFCs. It should be noted, however, that the legislation does not define 'education'. The status of services to students which are ancillary to the provision of education (such as catering, accommodation and leisure facilities) is unclear, and HEIs would be prudent to assume that the DDA 1995 applies to such services. In any event, HEIs (or their trading subsidiaries) will be service providers for the purposes of the DDA 1995 if they provide:

- conferences;
- public dining facilities;
- out-of-term accommodation to non-students;
- public access to sports and leisure facilities;
- public access to entertainment (e.g. plays and concerts), which are held on the HEI's premises.
(**Note.** This is not an exhaustive list.)

Given that HEIs will need to comply with the DDA 1995 in respect of these 'public services', the possibility that 'ancillary services' may be caught by the DDA 1995 may not be overly significant.

Depending on the subject matter of the courses, provision of commercial summer schools or evening classes might not count as 'education' and might be the provision of services for the purposes of the DDA 1995.

HEIs should consider all areas of their activities where they provide non-educational services to the general public, including 'indirect' provision of such services (e.g. by letting conference facilities to commercial organizers). The HEIs should then explore whether there are any particular problems in relation to those services for disabled people who might wish to take advantage of them. They should consider whether any changes ought to be made to the arrangements for the provision of the services, including the physical features of buildings. They also need to ensure that any staff who will be dealing with members of the public understand that they must not discriminate against disabled people. A person who has a complaint against a service provider may claim damages, including damages for injury to feelings.

Education

In introducing the DDA 1995, the Government has tried to avoid any suggestion that it is trying to compromise academic freedom. The DDA 1995, therefore, attempts to keep the regulation of HEIs, in so far as they are providers of education (but not as employers or service providers) within the ambit of the funding councils. It obliges the funding councils to have regard to the requirements of disabled people in exercising their functions and to make the publication of a disability statement by each HEI one of the conditions for grant. The thrust of the DDA 1995 is, therefore, not to impose any direct duties on HEIs with regard to their selection of students, the courses they offer or the arrangements for the provision of those courses, but to encourage HEIs to have regard to the needs of disabled students. The phrase 'to have regard to' is not an uncommon one in legislation; it is also a woolly one. Moreover, whether or not an HEI is being 'reasonable' within the law in, for example, not making extensive and costly changes to certain parts of its premises in order to provide access to disabled employees and conference trade users (having paid due regard to the DDA 1995), there will be the question of what the funding council should reasonably expect of HEIs in relation to disabled students and of what political pressures there are within the HEI for action even if it is not strictly required by the law. Thus, the individual disabled student or disabled applicant may not have direct access to the courts in relation to a dispute with a given HEI, but he or she will be able to exert a degree of moral or political pressure and may raise the matter with the funding council. She or he might also encourage the HEI to fund improvements reasonably required by virtue of its being an employer and/or it using the premises to provide services to non-students.

Summary

Although the provision of education by an HEI is exempt from the DDA 1995, an HEI will have significant duties as an employer and a 'service provider'. HEIs need to implement detailed disability policies covering all aspects of their employment practices, and covering the interface of the HEI and its staff with the general public in providing services. The measures in the DDA 1995 which affect higher education came into effect in July 1996. The employment provisions are effective from December 1996, as are most of the provisions relating to service providers.

Further reading

Doyle, B. (1997) *Disability Discrimination: Putting the New Act into Practice.* Bristol: Jordans.

Gooding, C. (1996) *Disability Discrimination Act 1995.* London: Blackstone.

Thomas, B. (1997) *Disability Discrimination.* London: Sweet & Maxwell.

Part 7

Consequences

20

A Guide to Litigation

Jonathan Leslie (Travers Smith Braithwaite)

Editors' introduction

Standard texts on litigation will normally run to over 500 pages (O'Hare and Hill, 1996; Osborne, 1995a and 1995b). The excellent layperson's short guide – Travers Smith Braithwaite (1996) – is a hardback book of over 250 pages (available subject to stock levels, one copy per higher education institution (HEI), free on application to Travers Smith Braithwaite by the Registrar, Clerk to the Governors or similar, in an HEI). We recognize that the author of this chapter was being set a near impossible task in being asked to summarize litigation in only a few thousand words. Yet is has been achieved *and* made relevant to HEIs in terms of the particular potential problems of handling litigation within, and on behalf of, an HEI. Litigation and even arbitration is not territory for the DIY legal enthusiast within HEI management, unless the HEI does not mind losing a case and running the risk of having to pick up the legal costs of the opponent. The process of litigation – the tactics – are the same for any person or organization. Hence, one would not need to address here such an issue in great detail since the ground is covered in any standard text on litigation. However, for an HEI, during litigation, there can be confusion about who has authority to speak for it, and, especially in the chartered universities, there may well be a distinct lack of corporate unity and responsibility (reflecting the relatively weak management structure as compared with most organizations and even as compared with 'managerially minded' statutory HEIs).

Kaplin and Lee (1995a) devote several pages from the US perspective to exploring the degree to which a member of staff not directly authorized to do X or Y can be seen to act as an agent and bind the HEI on the basis that to a third party he or she has 'apparent authority' to act and that it was reasonable of the third party to rely on the words of the member of staff or agent (Markesinis and Munday, 1992). They also comment on the de-mands of litigation:

administrators should never trivialise the prospect of litigation. Involvement in a lawsuit is a serious and often complex business that can create internal campus friction, drain institutional resources, and affect an institution's public image . . . Particularly for administrators, sound understanding of the litigation process is predicate to both constructive litigation planning and constructive preventive planning.

(Kaplin and Lee, 1995a: 709)

This chapter also explores alternative dispute resolution, as an option besides full litigation in the courts. There are, of course, always the concepts of negotiation (Tribe, 1994) or even mediation (Noone, 1996), as attempts to avoid legal costs, but care must be taken that exploration of informal routes does not create hostages to fortune if and when matters escalate.

Introduction

Recent years have witnessed an escalation of contentious legal disputes. These have affected all areas of life, both commercial and private, as legislation and the judgements of the courts in the UK and the European Union (EU) have assertively extended Government controls and the involvement of the common law into new areas. This trend, coupled with what is perhaps a modern cultural tendency to take disputes to the law, has greatly increased the volume of contentious issues that proceed through the courts.

HEIs may be involved in contentious legal disputes as much as bodies in other walks of life. Except, perhaps, in the case of those chartered bodies that remain subject to the exclusive jurisdiction of the Visitor when that jurisdiction is properly exercised and is not excluded by statute, HEIs are subject to the jurisdiction of the courts both in relation to their internal operations and in respect of their relations with the outside world. They are also free to submit those disputes to arbitration or to assisted methods of resolution. Students and staff aside, HEIs are as likely to end up in dispute over a building contract as any other 'employer' of the services of the UK construction industry.

This chapter aims to:

- describe briefly the types of dispute in which HEIs may become involved;
- explain the practices and procedures most typically followed in the resolution of disputes if any internal methods of resolution fail;
- describe in outline the chief remedies available at law and how they can be enforced;
- give some examples of practical safeguards that may be followed to protect the interests of the parties should a dispute need to be resolved at law.

Types of dispute

Disputes affecting HEIs may be characterized (for present purposes, very broadly) as either internal or external disputes. Internal disputes are those that affect the relationships between members of the institution – among themselves or between individuals or groups and the HEI. External disputes are those that arise between the institution or members of the institution and the outside world. The former may be easier to contain than the latter, and may in many cases be dealt with by internal procedures and by reference to codes of practice. It will only be if those *ad hoc* methods fail that the more formal steps referred to later may have to be invoked. In some cases, the internal procedures may be subject to the exclusive jurisdiction of the Visitor. The courts generally decline to adjudicate on legal challenges to decisions of the Visitor provided that the jurisdiction has been properly exercised (see Chapter 8). Exceptionally, the jurisdiction of the Visitor to determine employment disputes has been removed by statute. In cases where the Visitor has no jurisdiction, the internal procedures of the institution will generally be subject to the jurisdiction of the courts or to arbitration. External disputes will always be subject to the jurisdiction of the courts or to arbitration.

Examples of internal disputes are those involving:

- employment;
- sexual harassment;
- internal discipline;
- the quality and nature of tuition;
- property rights (e.g. student accommodation);
- conflict between the HEI and the students' union (SU).

External disputes may typically involve the following areas of law:

- intellectual property (IP) (e.g. disputes concerning copyright, trade-marks and patents);
- the construction industry;
- real property (i.e. those concerning the ownership and use of land);
- the management of investments of the institution;
- commercial contracts.

Although each type of problem may be different, there are broad similarities of approach in relation to each of them and they are all generally subject to the same procedures for their resolution.

The resolution of disputes

If internal procedures have failed, there are three principal ways in which legal disputes may be resolved: litigation, arbitration and alternative dispute resolution (ADR). *Litigation* is the name given to the process of the compulsory determination of legal disputes through the courts. *Arbitration* is the voluntary determination of such disputes by a procedure agreed by the parties which creates a binding result without recourse to the courts. These two systems have dominated the procedural landscape for generations. Their efficiency has come under increasing scrutiny. As a result, recent movements have led to reforms of the system of arbitration and there are also impending reforms to the system of litigation. Outside the area of formal dispute resolution, one of the most popular responses to problems associated with litigation and arbitration has been ADR, which is the term used to describe the consensual process of mediation intended to by-pass contentious methods.

Historically, English civil procedure (certainly that applicable in litigation and, in certain cases, in arbitrations) has been distinguished from the procedures of many other systems by a number of important features. First, it is adversarial – it involves the court sitting impartially to determine disputes among a number of hostile participants each of whom has a case to assert or to defend. The court plays little part in the process of identifying the facts or legal issues to be tried. This is different from those civil law systems that adopt an inquisitorial role in which the courts dominate the procedure and place greater emphasis on ascertaining for themselves the relevant facts. Second, the participants to a large extent formulate the issues for the court to decide, dictate the pace of the case and the general way in which it is conducted, and decide on the evidence to be adduced. Despite some recent judicial exhortations to the contrary, the judge currently plays a less interventionist role than in some other countries and will not normally interfere of his or her own volition with the way in which the case is put in law, the way in which it is presented or with the lengthy pre-trial preparations. It is for the parties, not the courts, to ensure that all necessary evidence is made available. Further, there are often much more onerous obligations than exist in some other countries to disclose documents to an opponent, even though they may be damaging to the discloser's case. Finally, in England cases are ultimately decided in public in open court after oral argument and the examination of witnesses. Although recent innovations have placed rather greater emphasis on written submissions than before, this tradition of orality lies at the heart of the English process.

Litigation in England is conducted under procedural rules that are derived from a mixture of statute, common law and what is called the 'inherent jurisdiction of the court', which is the power of the court to regulate its own procedures, subject to statute and common law precedents. The rules are updated frequently to reflect changes in the substantive law. Substantive law is the term for the general system of law that creates rights and liabilities (e.g. the law of contracts, trusts and torts). Procedural law governs the system by which those rights and liabilities are adjudicated by the courts. It is equally important, as without it there is no means of giving effect to the substantive law. In addition to the rules themselves, it is possible to discern various principles and objectives underlying the English procedural process.

For example, the rules are designed to ensure that all parties may know before trial the nature and extent of the case against them. There must be no 'trial by ambush'. Proper notice must be given at all times of the points the parties will rely on and of all steps to be taken in the case. Where time does not permit this, stringent penalties apply to any abuse at the court's discretion. Subject to legal professional privilege, all relevant documentary evidence, however harmful, must be disclosed before trial, as must statements of factual and expert witnesses. Sham or shadowy claims or defences will not be allowed to proceed. The settlement of disputes is encouraged. Often with the adversarial system, these principles and rules are only invoked at the instance of the party aggrieved. The courts will not generally intervene of their own volition to see if an abuse has been practised behind the scenes, nor will they volunteer a remedy. It is for the parties and their lawyers to take steps to protect themselves. They may even, and frequently do, agree to waive procedural requirements if it is sensible to do so, and the court will not usually object.

The conduct of court cases in adversarial litigation is often likened to a game, in which tactics enable the participants to take advantage of the weaknesses of their opponent. Thus, a plaintiff's lawyers will usually try to use every rule to force the defendant to face trial as quickly as possible, whereas the defence team will strive to create tactical delays in the hope that the claim will lose impetus or the plaintiff will run out of money or interest. To a very large extent, the courts permit the parties to fight as they will and they seldom intervene to assist someone whose lawyers or resources put him or her at a disadvantage to a better organized and more powerful opponent. It is a system in which the parties must look after themselves and within the procedural rules 'no holds are barred'. Although the courts will not police the day-to-day conduct of the parties they will, when confronted with procedural defaults, impose penalties that, in extreme cases, can be severe enough to strike out a claim or a defence. The rules of litigation may be seen as the way in which the courts regulate the relatively liberal environment in which the parties run their actions. It is not, therefore, possible to play fast and loose with the rules and lawyers must exercise their judgement responsibly.

The litigation regime in England involves a fundamental distinction between the High Court and the County Court, each of which currently has separate rules and procedures, the most important of which are summarized as follows. There is usually a choice between starting an action in the High Court or in the County Court. Although the historical limitations on the powers of the County Court have now to a large extent been removed, in practice the more important cases (especially those involving a degree of specialist knowledge) are begun and tried in the High Court. This in turn is divided into the Queen's Bench, Chancery and Family Divisions – each of which caters for different types of case. At this level, there are some specialist courts such as the Commercial Court, which regularly tries actions involving insurance, shipping and commodities transactions; the Companies

Court, which deals with cases concerning the constitutions and liquidations of companies; and the Official Referee's Court, which deals mainly with construction industry matters. Above the High Court is the Court of Appeal. Higher still, is the judicial committee of the House of Lords, which (excluding the European courts) is the last appellate court of England, Wales, Scotland and Northern Ireland.

Litigation begins with the issue and service of a writ. Unless the matter is settled, it ends with a trial in open court involving oral argument, the analysis of documentary evidence and the examination of witnesses, after which judgement is given by the court. Cases are invariably presented by counsel (a barrister). All civil trials are heard by a judge, usually after hearing oral evidence. Subject to any appeals, that judgement can be enforced against the defendant personally or against his or her assets. Between the issue of the writ and the trial, there is a prolonged pre-trial period during which 'interlocutory' steps (i.e. steps before trial) are taken when the issues are identified and preparations for trial are made. This period can be frustrating because it may seem that nothing serious is happening, but in fact it is during this period that foundations of the case are being laid and tactical positions taken that will influence the outcome of the trial or, as is usually hoped, lead to a favourable settlement. It is, therefore, a crucial period of tactical development. This phase is characterized by a series of time limits, set by the rules of the court, for taking various preparatory steps (e.g. for service of the writ, acknowledging service, serving a defence, giving discovery of documents and exchanging witness statements and experts' reports). The lawyers instructed on the case must use their initiative to carry on with the preparations. These will involve meetings with their clients, contact with witnesses and correspondence with their opponents in which papers are exchanged and the preparations developed. However, if progress cannot be achieved – if the other side is intransigent or if the court is required to help on any points in issue – an application to court must be made. Preliminary matters are dealt with by senior judicial officers (known as 'masters' in the High Court and 'district judges' in the County Courts) on the basis of evidence given by affidavit, which is a written statement made on oath. In the specialist courts (e.g. the Commercial Court), the judges alone deal with preliminary matters. The average time that elapses between the issue of a writ and judgement is about two years. It may be more or less depending on the complexity of the issues, the amounts at stake and the urgency of the case. It is the trial which usually absorbs the extensive costs most frequently associated with litigation, although in cases involving significant volumes of documentation or a large number of witnesses, the stages of discovery and the preparation of witness statements can also involve significant expenditure.

Litigation procedures: step-by-step

The issue of proceedings

As stated earlier, in English litigation, there is a fundamental distinction between the High Court and the County Court. Under the current procedures, the two courts have different sets of rules which arise largely from the historical differences in their jurisdictions and the fact that the County Court jurisdiction has been geographical and determined by the amounts at issue. In recent times, the formal distinctions between the two courts have to a great extent been removed and now the jurisdictions are substantially co-extensive, although the courts have the power to transfer a case begun in the High Court to the County Court, and vice-versa. As a general rule of practice, the High Court deals with disputes involving in excess of £50,000 and the County Court deals with those involving less than that sum, unless the case is one of unusual complexity. There is, however, provision for the Central London County Court to determine disputes worth up to £200,000. Generally, the High Court offers greater freedom to the parties to control the procedure than they have in County Court actions. In the High Court, it is usually possible to make applications in person to the court's administrative departments and this gives much greater flexibility when, for example, obtaining a hearing date or entering judgement in default. In the County Court, much administrative business is done by post and there is often a slow response to correspondence or applications.

Although nowadays the jurisdiction of the High Court and the County Court is often co-extensive, there are certain cases that must be brought in the County Court. These mainly relate to personal injury claims where the sum in issue is less than £50,000. Conversely, some actions (for example judicial review and defamation cases) must be begun in the High Court. Even if it is likely that a case will eventually be judged in the County Court, it can be advantageous to bring proceedings in the High Court. For example, the administrative procedures of the High Court tend to be more efficient and High Court proceedings tend to be taken more seriously by defendants than do County Court proceedings. In many cases for simple debts, the action is begun in the High Court even though it would inevitably be tried in the County Court. This is because of the greater opportunities for obtaining a default judgement in the High Court.

High Court

Proceedings are usually begun in the High Court by the issue of a writ (or an originating summons). A writ is usually drafted by the plaintiff's solicitors or counsel and to be valid must be issued by the court. This involves the payment of a court fee and the writ being stamped and entered in the court's records. It is important to remember that it is the date of the issue of the writ that determines whether the claim has been brought in time for the purposes of any relevant statutory or contractual time limits. In most

cases, a writ is only valid for four months from the date of issue and must
be served within this period, although in limited circumstances its validity
may be extended by order of the court. The writ must either be 'generally
endorsed' with a brief description of the plaintiff's claim sufficient for the
defendant to know what is alleged or be endorsed with a detailed statement
of claim. If the writ does not contain a detailed statement of claim, the
plaintiff must serve one within 14 days of the defendant acknowledging
service of the writ.

County Court
Proceedings are commenced in most cases in the County Court by the issue
of a summons (or an originating application). As with a writ issued in the
High Court, the summons is usually drafted by the plaintiff's solicitors or
counsel and needs to be entered formally into the court's records to be
valid. The summons has to contain a reasonably detailed statement of the
plaintiff's claim. There are two main types of action in the County Court,
the default and the fixed-date action. The former is used in money claims
and the latter in cases involving, for example, a claim for possession of
property. A default action can be begun in any County Court, usually the
one which is nearest or most convenient to the plaintiff, but cases involving
claims for a liquidated sum (i.e. one fixed in advance within the contract)
are automatically transferred to the court in which the defendant resides,
if a defence is filed. Claims for unliquidated damages (i.e. where the court
will be deciding the amount) are not automatically transferred, but may be
on application by the defendant. Fixed-date summonses must be issued in
the County Court where the defendant resides or where the cause of action
arose.

Service of proceedings

Service of proceedings is the process by which the writ or summons is
formally delivered to the defendant. There are various important rules setting
out which methods of service are acceptable. For example, if service is
not effected through solicitors, an English company ought to be served by
delivering the writ or summons to its registered office and a writ may not
be served by fax. The date of service is generally the date on which the
relevant court documents are received by the defendant (or his or her
solicitors). Where, as is usually the case, a plaintiff cannot prove the exact
date of receipt, the court assumes that the writ was served on a particular
date that is calculated in accordance with set rules and hence it may be
useful to retain the envelope as well as the documents enclosed in it. In
the High Court, service is usually carried out by the plaintiff's solicitors –
the court itself will not effect service. In the County Court, service can be
carried out by the plaintiff's solicitors, but, unless the court is notified that
this is intended, service will be carried out automatically by the court.

Acknowledgement of service

In High Court proceedings, the defendant must enter an acknowledgement of service with the court within 14 days of the service of the writ. By doing so, the defendant will register acceptance of the jurisdiction of the court to hear the case and indicate whether he or she intends to defend the action. If the defendant fails to file an acknowledgement of service within the prescribed time, it can be done later. However, the defendant then runs the risk that the plaintiff may first enter judgement. Although such judgements may be set aside, this is only possible on application by the defendant. Such an order will not be made unless the court is satisfied either that the judgement was irregular, for example because the writ was not properly served; or that, if the judgement was regular, the defendant has shown on affidavit that there is a proper defence. The court will not set aside judgement unless there is some real point to be achieved and will not do so where, for example, the plaintiff could apply successfully for summary judgement. It is, therefore, vital that these time limits are observed. If the defendant does serve an acknowledgement of service within the time prescribed or before the plaintiff enters judgement, he or she must then serve a defence.

Defence

In the High Court, a detailed written defence must be served either within 28 days of the service of the writ, or within 14 days of service of the statement of claim (whichever is later). It is possible to extend this time limit by agreement. If agreement cannot be reached, an application to court for an extension can be made on one day's notice. It is usual for the initial time limit to be extended at least once by agreement. As is the case with failure to acknowledge service of proceedings, failure to serve a defence within the time specified enables the plaintiff to obtain from the court judgement in default of defence and similar provisions apply in relation to applications to set aside such judgements. If the defendant also has a claim against the plaintiff (called a 'counterclaim'), the defence should preferably be served together with a pleaded counterclaim. Such a pleading is, in effect, a claim in its own right and puts the plaintiff in the action under similar obligations in respect of the counterclaim as the defendant is under in respect of the claim.

In the County Court, whilst there is no separate requirement to acknowledge service of a summons, the defendant must serve a defence within 14 days. If, in a default action or certain fixed-date actions, he or she fails to do so, the plaintiff may enter judgement for a fixed sum, for damages to be assessed or for such other relief as may be appropriate. In fixed-date actions (including those relating to recovery of land or delivery of goods), there is no default procedure and the plaintiff must still prove the case before obtaining judgement. The problems associated with obtaining judgement in default in the County Court (which are exacerbated by administrative delays caused by the requirement to make such applications by post) represent one of the chief drawbacks to County Court litigation, and might explain why many actions that ought to be begun in the County Court (by reason of the amounts in issue) are started in the High Court. The time limit for service of the defence can be extended by agreement. In the absence of agreement, it is possible to apply to the court for an extension. However, the procedure for making such an application differs from one County Court to another. In some courts, procedural difficulties will make a court application an unattractive option.

Reply and defence to counterclaim

In the High Court, a plaintiff is entitled to serve a written reply to the defence. This will only be necessary where the defence raises factual matters not covered in the writ and statement of claim. However, if the defence includes a counterclaim, it is essential for the plaintiff to serve a defence to counterclaim. If not, the defendant may obtain judgement on the counterclaim by default, in the same way as may the plaintiff in the original action. The time limit for service of the reply and defence to counterclaim is 14 days from the service of the defence, although once again this time limit can be extended by agreement or court order. In the County Court, the rules do not require the service of a reply but it is permissable to serve one. It is, however, usual to serve a defence to counterclaim.

Further and better particulars

The statement of claim, defence and reply and defence to counterclaim (together with any further submissions) are called 'the pleadings'. Any party to proceedings may seek additional details of the other side's pleadings. These are known as 'further and better particulars'. Further and better particulars can be very useful for clarifying the other party's position where it is not clearly set out in the pleadings. If the other party does not provide the particulars voluntarily, an application can be made for a court order forcing it to provide them. The court will require a party to provide such particulars which it thinks are necessary to explain the nature of the case. However, it will wish to ensure that an application is not being used merely to exert pressure on the other party.

Amendments to the writ and pleadings

The rules of court generally allow a party to make at any stage (even during the trial) amendments to the writ or pleadings. Often, these will be agreed by the other parties but, if that is not possible, an application must be made to court for an order permitting the amendments. This is usually granted on terms that require the party amending to bear the costs of any consequential amendments made by his or her opponent.

Joinder of other parties

A party (usually the defendant) may join into the action other parties not originally sued. For example, a defendant may by counterclaim bring an action not only against the plaintiff, but also against a new party. A defendant may also bring third party or contribution proceedings against those whom he or she claims are equally or to some degree responsible for the plaintiff's losses. Such steps may be taken at any stage in the action, but the leave of the court is required unless they are taken within the time prescribed for the service of the defence.

Directions for trial

After the parties have served their pleadings, the next stage is for the court to give directions setting a timetable for the preparation of the case for trial. The exact directions required will vary depending on the nature of the case. They will tend to deal with such matters as discovery, witness statements and experts' reports. The judges in the High Court have developed a closer involvement in cases, especially by the encouragement of the system of 'pre-trial reviews' in the most complex cases. In the County Court, it is not usually necessary to make an application for directions because its rules often provide for specific directions to apply automatically. These require most of the preparations for trial to have been completed within 12–14 weeks of service of the defence. In some cases, there will be a pre-trial review, which is similar to a summons for directions.

Subsequent procedures

Of the various ensuing stages of pre-trial preparation, three stand out as especially important. The first stage is the discovery of documents. This is the compulsory process whereby each party is required to disclose to the other the existence of all documents that it has or had in its possession, custody or power that are relevant to the issues or that contain information that may – directly or indirectly – enable the other party to advance its own case or damage the case of the other, or may fairly lead it to an avenue of enquiry that may have either of these two consequences. This process can be critical to the outcome of litigation. It is important to remember that for this rule the definition of 'document' is extremely wide and catches computer databases, tape recordings and means of recording information other than documents. Note also that there are a number of important exceptions to the rule that all relevant material must be disclosed. Thus, communications between a party and lawyers for the purpose of taking legal advice and communications between a party and anyone else for the purpose of actual or prospective litigation, are privileged from production; whilst communications, even if prejudicial, that are entered into for the purpose of settling a dispute, may be protected from disclosure. This is known as the 'without prejudice' rule. The second stage is the preparation and exchange of witness statements. These reveal what oral evidence a party will produce at trial, and will show to the other the strengths and weaknesses of its case. The third stage is the exchange of experts' reports. These are important in many cases, especially those involving professional judgements such as occur in negligence cases, and can also determine the outcome of the trial. In addition, in the pre-trial period there are crucial opportunities available to the parties to take initiatives that may either dispose of the litigation entirely or, alternatively, protect their positions pending trial. These include the following.

Summary judgement

The courts will enable a plaintiff (or a defendant who has made a counterclaim) to obtain judgement without a full trial where it is possible to demonstrate on oath (by affidavit) that there is no arguable defence.

The striking out of bad claims and the penalizing of misconduct

The courts will also assist a party whose opponent refuses to follow the correct procedures and will allow a defendant who is unfairly subject to unmeritorious claims to apply to strike them out, rather than to have to defend up to trial. Penalties in costs and, in extreme cases, the striking out of the claim or defence, may also be applied where a party is guilty of delay or abuse of the processes of the courts.

Injunctions and pre-trial preservation of property

One of the remedies awarded by the courts is a final injunction, which restrains a defendant from starting or continuing a wrongful course of conduct. In many cases, however, a plaintiff will be prejudiced if he or she has to wait until trial for his or her remedy. In such cases, the courts will on certain terms and subject to various conditions grant interim injunctions restraining the conduct of the defendant or preserving disputed property or his or her assets, pending trial.

Security for costs and interim payments

Where a plaintiff may be unable to meet the costs of litigation, he or she may on application by the defendant be ordered to provide security for the defendant's costs, either in the form of cash or a bond or a bank guarantee. The court also has power in some cases to make an order that the defendant pay to the plaintiff before trial some part of the damages claimed.

Arbitration

Arbitration is an alternative method of dispute resolution that largely avoids recourse to the courts. The object of arbitration is to enable the parties to have their dispute resolved in a binding and enforceable way by a tribunal of their own choice and pursuant to procedures to which they have expressly agreed. It is a popular means of dispute resolution where privacy is important or in areas that habitually involve specialist commercial customs and practices (e.g. in shipping, commodity, insurance, commercial leases and partnership disputes).

Historically, arbitrations in England have tended to follow the practices and procedures of litigation, with complex pleadings and discovery culminating in an oral hearing involving counsel. Owing to a number of factors, including the need to pay the fees of the arbitrator (which could be considerable), the fact that the arbitrator had fewer powers than a judge to enforce rulings against recalcitrant parties and the comparative freedom of the parties to refer issues of procedure or substance to the courts over the head of the arbitrator, a system that was intended to be flexible, cost-effective and quick had become discredited as a less efficient and costlier surrogate of litigation. In response to this concern, the Arbitration Act 1996 was enacted. Arbitration is consensual – that is, except in certain limited cases when arbitration is imposed by statute, a party will only be able to instigate an arbitration if his or her opponent agrees. The agreement will either be entered into as part of a larger contract at the time of reaching an agreement on other matters, for example in a charterparty or a building contract, and before any dispute has actually arisen, or at the time when the dispute arises. The main features of modern arbitration under the new legislation are as follows.

The autonomy of the parties

Arbitration recognizes the freedom of the parties to have their dispute resolved outside the courts of law if that is their wish. This involves the freedom to apply whatever procedures they choose, subject to the duty of the arbitrator to adopt procedures that will avoid unnecessary delay and expense.

The supportive role of the courts

The courts are now given a less interventionist role in arbitration and are confined to supporting the process of arbitration, if the process has broken down in any particular case. Appeals to the court from the decision of the arbitrator will be confined to important points of law where the arbitrator has made a serious mistake.

Flexibility of procedure

Litigation involves a prescribed procedure. In arbitration, there is no set procedure and the parties may adopt whatever rules they consider to be appropriate. Sometimes, they may choose to adopt the rules of one of the recognized arbitral bodies. In other cases, they may, for example, agree to dispense with all formality and have the dispute adjudicated without an oral hearing, even on general principles of 'equity and fairness' rather than in accordance with the substantive law of the land.

Increased powers of the arbitrator

Under the new system, the arbitrator is given enhanced powers to compel compliance with interim orders and to make more far-reaching final orders such as injunctions and specific performance.

The advantages and disadvantages of arbitration

The advantages of arbitration can be summarized as follows.

- **Privacy** An arbitration takes place in private and not in open court. This makes it suitable for disputes that concern confidential commercial matters that the parties do not want to be aired in public.
- **Simplicity** In many cases (for example in disputes arising out of commodities markets) arbitration can be dealt with purely 'on paper' (i.e. a submission of essential contractual documents to an arbitrator who determines the dispute without hearing oral evidence). Other, more complex cases, can often be more protracted.
- **Expense** It is likely that an arbitration will be less costly and speedier than litigation.
- **Specialization** An arbitrator is an adjudicator chosen by the parties rather than imposed by the court and may be selected because of knowledge and experience of the commercial transactions and issues.
- **Enforceability** In some cases involving international disputes, it is easier to enforce abroad the award of an arbitrator than a judgement of the court, owing to the sophisticated system of international enforcement treaties that apply to most arbitrations.

A disadvantage of arbitration is that it is not possible to force parties other than those who have agreed to participate in the arbitration, and this makes the procedure inappropriate in cases where a respondent wishes to seek in the same proceedings redress from a stranger to the arbitration agreement. As a result of the changes brought about by the new legislation, it may be expected that arbitration will be restored to the position it once occupied as a genuine and popular alternative to litigation.

Alternative dispute resolution

ADR has only recently emerged and become recognized in England as a useful technique for resolving disputes outside traditional litigation or arbitration methods. It has, however, been widely used in one form or another in other countries, particularly in the USA, and it is fast gaining ground in England as lawyers and their clients have embraced it as a means of achieving a cost-effective solution that promotes the clients' real objectives. ADR bears no real comparison to litigation or arbitration – its function is not to *impose* the resolution of a dispute on the parties, rather to help them to agree a resolution between themselves.

The overriding purpose of ADR is to help parties who have been unable to settle their dispute by traditional negotiation to find an amicable solution without the need for (further) intervention by the courts. It may be seen as an alternative to litigation or arbitration in the sense that it may precede the commencement of proceedings. Alternatively, it may be seen as complementary to those processes by assisting the resolution of disputes once they have developed into legal action. These purposes are achieved by a variety of somewhat different but flexible means, the most typical of which is a structured meeting or series of meetings between the parties and a neutral mediator or adviser whose job it is to:

- help each party conduct a realistic assessment of his or her opponent's case;
- facilitate common-sense dialogue;
- assist in solving problems or breaking deadlocks;
- encourage a settlement that is agreed as opposed to a resolution that is ultimately imposed by the court or arbitrator.

ADR is a wholly consensual process. ADR is generally conducted on a 'without prejudice' and confidential basis. In England, almost all ADR procedures can loosely be described as either 'mediation' or as 'mini-trials'. Mediation is by far the most common form of ADR in use in England. Mini-trials are more formalized settlement conferences involving the abbreviated presentation of evidence by representatives of the parties to a panel usually consisting of one neutral member and one senior executive of each disputant who, ideally, has no detailed knowledge of the dispute. Mini-trials can be more appropriate than mediation in large commercial cases involving particularly difficult questions of fact or law.

ADR provides the following benefits that are usually not available with other methods of resolving disputes: cheaper, quicker, more flexible and more private. Apart from the inevitable fact that the process is not mandatory, there are few disadvantages to ADR. It is sometimes said that ADR involves an unfortunate show of 'weakness' and denotes lack of resolve to fight and the need to show one's hand. This may be true, up to a point; but if settlement can be achieved nevertheless, no harm has been done. If settlement cannot be achieved, images can be restored soon enough. Further, as has been shown, litigation itself is conducted on the basis of full disclosure, so whatever is revealed in ADR processes will usually have to be disclosed in court proceedings in any event.

Remedies

The following are the main awards that a court (or arbitrator) may make.

Damages

Damages are the pecuniary compensation paid by a defendant to a plaintiff to compensate, in so far as money can, for the wrong which the defendant has committed. The object of an award of damages is to give the plaintiff compensation for a loss or injury he or she has suffered. It is the principal and most frequently sought remedy.

Specific performance

In some cases, damages will not be adequate to compensate the plaintiff. When the subject matter of a contract has special value or unique features which make damages an inadequate remedy, the court may order a defendant to perform the contract rather than pay damages for its breach.

Rectification

The court may order that a contract that does not properly record the agreement between the parties should be rectified to reflect the true agreement.

Injunction

In certain circumstances, damages will not be adequate to compensate the plaintiff because he or she needs to restrain the defendant from starting or continuing a wrongful course of conduct or to force him or her to do certain things in the plaintiff's interest, and not just to be compensated for continuing losses. The court may, in certain circumstances and on conditions, grant an injunction to restrain the defendant from acting wrongfully or require him or her to do things in the plaintiff's interests. In many cases, a claim to injunction is coupled with a claim to damages.

Declarations

In some cases, the plaintiff seeks to have rights determined by the court by a declaration. This may be coupled with a claim to damages or other forms of relief. This is appropriate in cases, for example, in which rights over land or in respect of contracts or the interpretation of legal documents that will affect rights in the future are involved.

Restitution and tracing orders

Where it is alleged that the defendant has acquired property of the plaintiff, for example, unlawfully or for no consideration and in circumstances where he or she has been unjustly enriched, the plaintiff is entitled to reclaim the property or an equivalent sum from the defendant. Such claims are often linked to a separate claim for a tracing order in which property of the plaintiff which has fallen into the hands of the defendant can be traced and recovered.

Possession of land

In an action under a lease or in respect of real property the court can order that the land, or the right to possession of it, be returned to the plaintiff.

Action for an account

In certain cases, the court will order the defendant to provide to the plaintiff an account of profit arising from use or misuse of the plaintiff's property and to give to the plaintiff the money so accounted for. This frequently arises in cases involving breach of copyright or trade-mark where it is proved that a defendant is accountable to the plaintiff for earnings from the infringement.

Judicial review

In addition to those awards referred to earlier, the court may also quash unlawful decisions of public bodies (which may include HEIs – see Chapter 9), restrain them from acting unlawfully or order them to take certain steps (by a process known as 'judicial review').

Enforcement of orders

It is outside the scope of this chapter to describe in detail the ways in which orders of the court or arbitrators may be enforced. The principal means available include:

• insolvency proceedings;
• attachment of assets and bank accounts;
• seizure of goods.

Safeguards for the HEI

Litigation and arbitration in England are, by nature, hostile and involve contested evidence. Cases are frequently won or lost as much because of the weight and type of evidence that is adduced as because of the underlying strengths and weaknesses of the cases in law. It frequently happens that cases are lost before a dispute develops by making unguarded statements or writing ill-advised letters or documents, or even simply by a failure to realize that a dispute is likely to become serious and needs to be dealt with professionally. Disputes involving HEIs could possibly give rise to serious problems of this nature because of a relatively informal and unstructured student–tutor relationship, and a generally individualistic approach within organizations which are, in management terms, relatively unhierarchical (especially in some chartered HEIs). The following account sets out in summary some of the safeguards that can be taken at an early stage in litigation to prevent such mistakes from being made. The safeguards may also help with internal procedures of dispute resolution and disciplinary hearings.

Identifying the dispute

It often happens that a dispute becomes litigious without it having previously been considered to be genuine or serious – too relaxed an initial approach may cause difficulties later. The ability to recognize when a dispute may become litigious, apart from enabling the problem to be controlled, can give an immediate advantage. For example, an admission may be obtained on a point that might later be contested or the imprudent disclosure of documents may be provoked. Equally, notes of conversations can be made and records kept that may help later if someone's word is doubted. Realizing that a problem may develop into a legal dispute will also alert those involved as to the potential damages and generate a more cautious and disciplined approach. It is only when the dispute has been identified that the basic precautions outlined as follows can be taken in order to ensure that nothing is done before lawyers are instructed which may make their job more difficult or prejudice the prospects of success in ensuing litigation.

Time limits

One of the most important threshold issues in any contested action is the time within which the claim must be brought. Great care should be taken over such issues as sometimes it is not clear that a dispute has arisen and the other party may not voice tacit concerns, hoping the time limits for claiming will pass unnoticed. Limitation periods, which are mainly governed by contract or statute, usually start to run, in contract cases, from the date when the contract is breached or, in the case of most other wrongful acts, from the date when loss or damage is suffered. In most cases, the relevant period is six years from the applicable starting date, but it may be longer or shorter depending on the circumstances and the precise nature of the claim. It is especially important to note that there are cases where untypically short limits are imposed (such as in contracts of employment or where a contract requires litigation or arbitration to be started within a shorter than usual time from the accrual of a cause of action or the arising of a dispute).

If the remedy sought is the recovery of a debt or damages, the only timing issue will be the statutory or contractual date beyond which no claim is to be brought. If, however, the aim is to obtain certain remedies such as an injunction or specific performance of a contract, proceedings should be brought as soon as possible after the existence of the claim has become known. This is because if the court finds that the plaintiff has unduly delayed the issue of proceedings and that the opponent has been prejudiced as a result, the remedies may be refused solely on the basis of delay.

Delegate effectively

Where there are a number of points of contact between the parties, consideration should be given to who ought to handle the case and to who ought to conduct any negotiations. This may be particularly relevant for HEIs where disputes may arise, for example, between students and staff. In such cases, it should be made clear at the outset whether a member of staff who becomes involved in a dispute has authority to act on behalf of the institution and is equipped to make statements and representations on its behalf. A student, who will inevitably be regarded as being in a subordinate position, may claim to be entitled to rely on what is said by a member of the academic staff even where that person has no actual authority. It is generally wise to delegate the handling of a dispute to one person who (subject to reporting to whomever is appropriate) is in charge of the matter and can coordinate the efforts of everyone involved. This will help to avoid confusion, inconsistency and mistake. It is a matter of judgement whether the individual most closely associated with a dispute or who has the closest relationships with the opponent's personnel should be responsible for negotiating a settlement. Those who are the most obvious individuals to negotiate a settlement may often be the best choices, but they may be so closely connected to the problem and the people involved that it will be difficult for them to negotiate effectively, or for continuing relationships or existing contacts to continue undamaged. Appointing an independent person may, therefore, be the most appropriate response. It may also be prudent to suggest that someone who might be regarded as being in a subordinate position should be independently advised or represented by another person. It would also be prudent to ensure that discussions take place in the presence of an independent witness.

When to involve lawyers

If the dispute is limited to fact or if the chosen negotiator is experienced, the instruction of lawyers may be delayed. However, it may be considered expedient to instruct lawyers at once if legal issues are involved or if the opponent has instructed lawyers. This is particularly true in those areas of law where complex legal issues are involved and where time limits are short.

Admissions and the 'without prejudice' rule

Where a dispute arises, it should be ensured that during negotiations no admissions are made which the opponent might later exploit. Admissions on a point of law or fact may be admissible in later proceedings and could be damaging.

To overcome this problem and to encourage parties to settle disputes, a general rule has been developed whereby it is not possible to use in evidence admissions made at meetings or in letters the purpose of which is to try to achieve a settlement of a dispute. It is important that all such meetings and communications are expressed to be 'without prejudice', lest the dispute not be settled. It should be noted that the mere use of the words 'without prejudice' at meetings or in correspondence will not automatically prevent admissions from being deployed in court. The rule only applies to a communication the genuine purpose of which is to advance the settlement of a dispute. If in doubt, it is probably sensible to stipulate that all such negotiations are without prejudice, but beware of using the term loosely in any circumstances that may appear to have a legal effect. Meetings or communications that are intended to be part of a formal record should be 'open' (i.e. without prejudice).

Documents and discovery

Litigation in England is increasingly document-oriented and cases can be won or lost by documents that evidence material facts. It is, therefore, sensible to be cautious about what is put in writing at this (or indeed, at any) stage of the process. An essential safeguard is to avoid the creation of documents that may be damaging and that may need to be shown to an opponent if proceedings are commenced at a later stage. Particular care should be taken of manuscript notes made on documents, whether originals or copies. If a manuscript is added to a letter or document, this would have to be disclosed and may materially damage the case when so disclosed and prejudice a possible settlement. Equally, documents should not be destroyed or lost if they are likely to be required for litigation. It is, nevertheless, sensible to make a careful contemporaneous record of what is said and done in the course of a dispute or its attempted resolution so that any misleading evidence given later may be challenged.

The future of dispute resolution in England

The system of arbitration in England has already been reformed by the Arbitration Act 1996 and it will be interesting to watch how the process of arbitration will respond. Equally, ADR is well established and it has already frequently stipulated in commercial contracts as a preliminary means of settling disputes. The procedures of litigation are also undergoing rejuvenation, initially by a more experimental approach taken by some of the judges in their day-to-day conduct of cases, but more importantly in the form of the review undertaken by Lord Woolf under the auspices of the Lord Chancellor's Department. The Final Report of the Woolf Committee was published as recently as July 1996 and it would be unwise to try to predict in what respects its recommendations will be adopted or when new systems will be introduced. It is, nevertheless, clear that a major reform of the system may be expected to come about in the relatively near future and that, consequently, the description given in this chapter will need to be updated.

It is likely that the following features will characterize the new procedures:

- The dichotomy between the High Court and County Court procedures and those differences that exist between the various divisions of the High Court will be removed and replaced by a uniform procedure for all courts and all types of case.
- The procedures will concentrate on the need for speed and economy and, to that end, will draw a distinction between 'fast track' and 'multi-track' cases.
- There will be an emphasis on reducing the number of pre-trial court applications and pre-trial activity generally.
- The judges will play a much more pro-active role in the conduct of cases so that litigation should to a greater extent be taken out of the hands of the parties and their lawyers.
- The process of discovery of documents that has for a long time been regarded with concern as a tool of oppression and delay will be curtailed and kept within more sensible boundaries.
- The length of trials will be cut down and the cross-examination of witnesses and the involvement of expert witnesses will be restricted.

Further reading

McFarlane, J. (1996) *Rethinking Disputes: The Mediation Alternative*. London: Cavendish.
Noone, C. (1996) *Mediation*. London: Cavendish.
O'Hare, J. and Hill, R. N. (1996) *Civil Litigation*. London: FT Law and Tax.
Osborne, C. (1995a) *Civil Litigation*. London: Blackstone.
Osborne, C. (1995b) *Commercial Litigation*. London: Blackstone.
Salzedo, S. and Lord, R. (1996) *Arbitration*. London: Cavendish.

Travers Smith Braithwaite, (1996) *The Travers Smith Braithwaite Guide to Litigation.*
   London: Travers Smith Braithwaite.
Tribe, D. (1994) *Negotiation.* London: Cavendish.
York, S. (1996) *Practical Alternative Dispute Resolution.* London: FT Law and Tax.

21

The Impact of European Law

Euan Temple, Joss Saunders and
Philip Turpin (Linnells)

Editors' introduction

The aim of this chapter is to review the impact so far of European law on English law in relation to higher education institutions (HEIs) and to contemplate what *might* happen as European law evolves. Some of the relevant ground has been covered in earlier chapters and this chapter will, therefore, simply refer back to that coverage where appropriate. Other areas, not mentioned elsewhere, are covered in detail in this chapter – notably:

- the definition of European Union (EU) nationals and their entitlement to local education authority (LEA) awards as students at UK HEIs;
- the residence rights of EU nationals (and their families) as students in UK HEIs;
- the recognition of qualifications within the EU.

The chapter ends by predicting that the development of European law 'will continue to have a profound effect' on English law and hence our HEIs. The 1996 ruling of the European Court on the 48-hour working week may prove significant if AUT and NATFHE surveys of the long working hours of HEI academics and administrators are to be believed. Similarly, the experimentation with two-year degree courses needs to be considered in the context of the EU arrangements for the mutual recognition of degrees and qualifications which envisage post-secondary courses of *at least* three years in duration (it has to be remembered that the English and Welsh three-year single honours degree is not only unusually specialized by international comparison, but also unusually short, even compared to the four-year norm in Scotland).

Introduction

According to Lord Denning in *Bulmer v Bollinger*: 'When we come to matters with a European element, the Treaty is like an incoming tide. It flows into the estuaries and up the rivers. It cannot be held back.'

The European Treaty of Rome 1957 contained no express reference to education. The first major revision of the Treaty, by the Single European Act 1986, introduced new provisions on social policy and on research, but still contained no express reference to education. Only in 1992, in the Treaty of European Union at Maastricht 1992, was education included as one of the policies of the EU, in order to help it meet its newly amended and extended objectives. Article 3(p) provides that the activities of the EC shall include a 'contribution to education and training of quality'. New Articles 126–7 on vocational training were introduced. 'Vocational training' is, in Euro-speak, defined widely. For most purposes, it includes what would usually be called academic study in the UK. So the considerable body of European law relating to vocational training is relevant to all HEIs. Even before Maastricht, HEIs were affected by the growing body of European law in their capacity as employers, providers of services, purchasers, managers of property, and in many other aspects of their activities both in the public sector and in their business dealings. Education has become a key area of EU activity.

HEIs are affected by rules governing both public and private institutions. The rules are found partly in legislation and partly in case law, particularly the decisions of the European Court of Justice (ECJ) in Luxembourg. The rules affect public procurement, employment law, intellectual property licensing, data protection, financial services, Research and Development agreements and other joint ventures, health and safety at work, the re-cognition of degrees in Europe, environmental issues, the movement, employment and residence of academics and students, and the burgeoning programmes for research grants and international educational links.

Which countries are covered? In the first place, European law applies to the members of the EU. European law is not to be confused with the rules of the Council of Europe, although that too has an impact on HEIs through the rules on free speech in the Convention on Human Rights, which is a measure of the Council of Europe, not of the EU. However, much European law also involves other countries. Norway and Iceland are partners of the EU through the European economic area (EEA) agreement, which came into effect on 1 January 1994. As is seen at airports, special immigration rules apply. Less visible, but equally important, are the EEA rules on public procurement and employment.

The EU also has association agreements with a number of countries and such agreements can give rise to rights enforceable by nationals of those countries in the UK and other EU members. Thus, for example, some EU rules on free movement can be relied on by Turkish nationals. There are also association agreements in place with many of the countries of Central and Eastern Europe. Although such agreements do not give rise to the same generous treatment of nationals, they do contain important rights and obligations.

In this chapter, three categories of people are referred to:

1. EU nationals;
2. EEA nationals (including EU nationals and nationals of Norway and Iceland);
3. nationals of other states who have enforceable rights under certain EU treaties. As this category is subject to change, the up-to-date position should always be checked.

The main laws

Articles, regulations and directives

The foundations of European law are contained in the European Treaty of Rome 1957, the Single European Act 1986 and the Treaty of European Union (Maastricht) of 1992 (which came into force on 1 November 1993).

Articles
References to articles usually means the clauses of the European Treaty of Rome 1957 or clauses of regulations or directives. Practical expression of the principles laid down in the articles of the European Treaty of Rome 1957 is largely contained in regulations or directives (issued by the European Council) and in decisions of the European Commission in Brussels and judgements of the ECJ in Luxembourg.

The most important articles for HEIs are:

- Article 7 (which prohibits discrimination on the grounds of nationality);
- Articles 30–6 (which require free movement of goods);
- Article 48 (which requires free movement of persons);
- Article 52 (which requires freedom of establishment);
- Article 59 (which requires free movement of services);
- Article 85 (which bans certain anti-competitive practices);
- Articles 126–7 (on vocational training, which is defined widely).

Regulations
These are binding and directly applicable in all members of the EU. Assuming they are sufficiently clear and unconditional, the regulations themselves create direct legal rights and obligations for individuals and companies, which are specifically effective from the date of issue and do not need prior Parliamentary approval. Such regulations have 'direct effect' and override any conflicting provisions in English law. They are enforceable in the English courts and tribunals.

Directives

These are binding on the members of the EU as regards the result to be achieved (usually expressed in great detail), but leave it to each country to implement the directive by bringing into force national legislation (usually by statutory instrument) within the time scale allowed, which is often two years from the date the directive is made. Since a directive is addressed to the Governments of the EU members, it does not create directly effective rights which can be enforced against private persons or companies, but it can be enforced against the country if the date set for implementation passes without it being implemented by that country. As a result of the ECJ's case law, directives may have legal effect even if they have not been implemented by the deadline date or if they have been implemented incorrectly. In some cases, the Governments of EU members can be sued by individuals or organizations who have suffered as a result of non-implementation or faulty implementation.

Decisions, recommendations and opinions

Commission decisions are binding on the organizations to whom they are addressed, and recommendations and opinions are not legally binding but may have some legal effect.

European Community or European Union?

Since most of the law affecting businesses is based on the provisions of the European Treaty of Rome 1957 it is correct to continue to refer in that connection to European Community law. Law arising from the provisions of the Maastricht Treaty, relating to education, common foreign and security policy and cooperation in justice and home affairs, is properly called EU law. However, both are referred to in this chapter as forming part of European law.

Public procurement

'Public procurement' for European law purposes is the sum total of the individual buying decisions of the thousands of public bodies within the European Community. For this purpose 'public bodies' specifically include Government departments, local authorities, fire authorities and police authorities (these bodies are called 'contracting authorities').

Do the public procurement regulations apply to HEIs?

There have been doubts expressed as to whether the regulations apply to HEIs. It is necessary to refer to Directive 93/37 the relevant part of which is given as follows.

'contracting authorities' shall be the State, regional or local authorities, bodies governed by public law, associations formed by one or several of such authorities or bodies governed by public law. The phrase 'a body governed by public law' means any body:

- established for the specific purpose of meeting needs in the general interest, not having an industrial or commercial character, and
- having legal personality, and
- financed, for the most part, by the State, or regional or local authorities, or other bodies governed by public law, or subject to management supervision by those bodies, or having an administrative, managerial or supervisory board, more than half of whose members are appointed by the State, regional or local authorities or by other bodies governed by public law.

In *Commission v Spain ('Madrid University')*, the European Commission instituted proceedings in response to the award by the University of Madrid of a works contract without advertising it in the *Official Journal* (OJ). The Spanish Government argued that it was exempt because of conditions of 'extreme urgency'. This was the need to complete the work before the start of the next academic year. The ECJ rejected this argument, finding that the exemption should be interpreted strictly and applied only where there was 'extreme urgency brought about by events unforeseen by the contracting authority'. Student numbers had been increasing steadily over a period of years and the influx due at the start of the next academic year, was neither unforeseeable nor would it cause any greater overcrowding than in previous years. In addition, the ECJ considered that, had the accelerated time limits provided for in the directive been applied, there would have been sufficient time (around six weeks) to advertise the contract and organize a proper selection procedure, whilst still achieving completion of the work before the start of the academic year. The opinion of Advocate-General Lenz in that case stated that a 'State University, even if independent from an organisational point of view, is as a rule a State Institution'. He added that 'No doubts have been raised in the course of the action, either as to the status of the University as a legal person governed by public law, or as to the applicability of the Directive.' The court found that Spain had not complied with the public procurement rules.

A view on this topic expressed by HM Treasury to the Committee of Vice-Chancellors and Principals (CVCP) on 22 July 1996 was that:

we agree that the critical test of whether universities are covered by the Directives, and hence our Regulations, is whether they are publicly funded, which in our view means funded as to more than 50 per cent; we have no difficulty whatsoever in notifying the Commission to that effect so that Annex 1 to the Works Directive can be amended; we consider 'public funding' to include both student grants, channelled via local authorities, and research funding (as opposed to payment under research contracts).

Annex 1 to Directive 93/37 includes as one of the categories to which public procurement rules apply 'Universities and Polytechnics, maintained Schools and Colleges, Research Councils'. So the University of Buckingham and some Oxbridge colleges *might* escape as being less than 50 per cent public funded, even allowing for the LEA and Research Council/British Academy payment of college fees. On these bases, it is fairly clear that most (if not all) HEIs are 'contracting authorities' subject to the regulations. Updating regulations are likely to cover the few institutions that *might* be outside the net.

A frequently quoted estimate (COM (94) 55: 78) is that the public sector in the European Community generates about 14 per cent of its GDP. Although not all of this vast amount is amenable to public procurement procedures, the European Commission estimates that a total of between 240 and 340 billion ECU of public sector annual purchasing power can be opened to competition. This is a formidable amount of purchasing power. As most of it in the past was purchased domestically, it has shut out potential cross-border providers. Although the European Treaty of Rome 1957 does not set any specific requirement in the field of public procurement, a number of its basic articles are fundamental to the arguments about opening up competition. To avoid cluttering up the tendering process, the public procurement regulations apply primarily to contracts over a certain threshold, quoted in ECU. For this purpose only, an exchange rate is fixed every two years, so that money market fluctuations do not bring contracting authorities arbitrarily in and out of the net.

The £ currency conversions for the thresholds until 31 December 1997 are set out in Table 21.1. The aim of the legislation is not to create uniformity, rather to harmonize all national public procurement rules. It introduces a minimum body of common rules for contracts above a defined threshold. The new rules set down a detailed code of strict procedures when contracting authorities start to consider buying in goods, works or services. These procedures drive right through, until after the contract is awarded. There are many types of action which can deliberately or unwittingly contribute to the infringement of the rules, including the artificial fragmentation of effectively one big contract into several small ones so that individual contracts fall below the threshold, the failure to provide full information to potential tenderers and the use of discriminatory terms in contracts (e.g. the specification of products of a specific make).

Table 21.1 Currency conversions for the thresholds of contracts (to 31 December 1997)

Public works contracts	5m ECU	£3,950,456
Public services contracts	200,000 ECU	£158,018
Public supply contracts (goods)	200,000 ECU	£158,018
Public supply contracts (information technology)	100,000 ECU	£79,009

A complaint could be made to the national courts by disgruntled would-be tenderers in respect of 'unlawful decisions' taken by contracting authorities. Failure to comply with the procedures could lead to a claim for damages or prevent the tendering process from continuing. After a contract has been awarded, the High Court cannot cancel the contract. However, it may award damages. Particular problem areas are:

- which set of regulations apply (supplies, works or services);
- thresholds – there may be a need to aggregate two or more connected contracts for threshold purposes, but aggregation of works contracts does not apply if the total value is less than 1 million ECU (£790,091). Likewise for services contracts, where the threshold is 80,000 ECU (£63,207) and the total estimated value of all the contracts worth less than this sum does not exceed 20 per cent of the total estimated value of all the contracts relating to the work (or services);
- filing the correct notices in the OJ at the right time and in the right form;
- use of the correct contract award procedure (there are several) and complying with specific time limits;
- potential provider appraisal – rejection of the potential provider for unpermitted reasons;
- tender appraisal – rejection of the tender for unpermitted reasons (the usual criterion will be either the 'lowest price' or 'economically the most advantageous' at the choice of the contracting authority);
- technical specifications being used which may be technically accurate, but which are phrased in a way contrary to the new rules.

If a contracting authority makes a mistake in any of the required procedures, it can lay itself open to a great deal of trouble, including claims for damages by aggrieved potential tenderers.

Table 21.2 The contract award notices filed by HEIs in January–March 1996

Germany 29	Spain 13
France 17	Sweden 5
Italy 15	Netherlands 3
UK 15	Ireland 1

Concerning HEI contracts, during January–March 1996 there were 98 contract award notices filed by HEIs in the OJ summarized in Table 21.2. Of these, 97 contracts were awarded by the HEI to firms in the home country – the single exception being a Swedish contract which was awarded to a French firm. If these figures reveal anything, it is only what might perhaps be expected. An evolutionary system has been put in place and it has hardly yet begun to break down years of national protectionism. Furthermore, a key fact which the statistics conceal, is that a number of commercial tenderers to HEIs have established subsidiaries in other members of the EU or find their way into these markets by way of joint venture partners, or by taking on smaller parts of large contracts. These would not appear on this unscientific survey as 'non-home country' winners of contracts.

Filing procedures

Public notices for advertising contracts (maximum 650 words) need to be placed in the OJ. The address is: The Official Journal, Office for Official Publications of the European Communities, 2 Rue Mercier, L-2985 Luxembourg. Tel: (from UK) 00–352–49.92.81 Fax: (from UK) 00–352–49.57.19 There is no fee payable for the insertion and it is sufficient to file it in English. The European Commission arranges for translation into the various languages as appropriate, free of charge. The notice may be faxed through, but must be followed up by hard-copy letter. The OJ is obliged to publish notices within 12 days of the date of despatch of the notice and to endeavour to publish notices within five days of the date of despatch if requested to do so under the accelerated procedure, if sent by telex, fax or e-mail.

Public Works Contracts (Directive 93/37) SI 1991/2680, amended by SI 1992/3279 and SI 1995/201

This directive applies to public contracts for construction or civil engineering works of 5 million ECU sterling equivalent (£3,950,456) or more. It also includes 'design and build' contracts. Tenders must be advertised in the OJ and strict time limits for the publication and provision for bid documents must be specified and observed. Contracts may be awarded by open or restricted procedures or negotiated procedures in certain limited circumstances. Even projects below the 5 million ECU threshold must avoid matters such as a specification which indirectly discriminates. By way of example, an HEI wishes to embark on a substantial building project, which is likely to cost about £4 million. The architects have suggested that buildings should be roofed in Welsh slate, as in keeping with the other roofs in the neighbourhood, but the HEI is aghast to hear that the plans should be offered to prospective tenderers with a more neutral description of the roof material. It is concerned that the extended advertising procedures that it must embark on will delay and interrupt the project itself, and that its failure to comply may lead to a withholding of funds from the Government. It is aware that there is slate on the market that is fairly similar in appearance to Welsh slate, but it would prefer to stipulate the real thing if possible.

The HEI is not allowed to put in technical specifications which refer to goods of a specific make or source, or to a particular process, and which have the effect of favouring or eliminating particular goods or contractors. This includes references to patents, trade-marks, etc. However, only if the goods cannot otherwise be described by sufficiently precise and intelligible technical specifications, is it possible to use the references basically banned, provided the references are accompanied by the words 'or equivalent', if that is justified because of the subject matter of the contract. There is, however, no clarification as to what an acceptable justification might be. Where 'or equivalent' is used, the HEI ought to make it clear that it is prepared to take into account any evidence the tenderer wishes to adduce that the goods are equivalent to the named type.

Public Supply Contracts (Directive 93/36) SI 1995/201

This directive applies to contracts for the purchase, renting, leasing or hire purchase of goods by contracting authorities of 200,000 ECU sterling equivalent (£158,018) or more. If an HEI has a recurrent need for meat supplies, for example, and enters into a series of supply contracts at different times, then it should project the next 12 months' expenditure on goods of that type, to ascertain whether the threshold of 200,000 ECU is exceeded. If it is, then the prescribed tendering procedure must be followed. There is an additional and separate ruling concerning contracts for the supply of information technology (IT) and telecommunications. The threshold here is 100,000 ECU (£79,009) and reference must be made to particular standards in the field for open systems (i.e. 'systems interoperability') unless very limited exceptions apply. So if an HEI wished to purchase IT equipment costing £79,009 or more, it would need to use the relevant standards in the contract, whether or not the 200,000 ECU threshold is reached. If it is reached, then the public procurement rules apply in addition.

   Contracts in relation to public supplies must, as a rule, be put out to competitive tender. In other words, tendering is by an open procedure. Recourse to restricted (with pre-selection) or negotiated (with pre-selection and negotiated terms) procedures must be justified by a written statement. The UK regulations require a contracting authority which has used the negotiated procedure to submit a report to the Treasury. Finally, obligations are imposed on contracting authorities to publish, not later than 48 days after the award of a contract, basic information on the contracts which have been awarded.

Public Services Contracts (Directive 92/50) SI 1993/3228 amended by SI 1995/210

This directive applies to priority services (part A services in the UK regulations) and includes maintenance and repair services, financial services, IT and related services, insurance, data-processing, accounting, market research, advertising and architecture and tenders for these contracts must be advertised in the OJ. The threshold is 200,000 ECU or more. Services such as contracts for legal services and for educational and vocational services (classified as residual services – part B services in the UK regulations) should be awarded in accordance with the rules as to technical specification. Open advertising under the public procurement rules for Part B services need not take place, though there may be other regulations which encourage this. If an HEI wishes to appoint external maintenance contractors to maintain all its buildings and the fee level comes above the threshold, the contract must be put out to tender in the OJ (if it has to be advertised in the first place). Employment of in-house staff will avoid the regime, if the contract does not need to be advertised.

Government Procurement Agreement (GPA) 1994

In parallel with the conclusion of the Uruguay Round, on 15 April 1994, a new GPA was signed in Marrakesh. This came into force on 1 January 1996. The World Trade Organization (WTO), the new institutional basis of GATT (General Agreement on Tariffs and Trade), will encompass not only the general agreement itself, but also all agreements and arrangements concluded under its auspices such as the GPA 1994. The WTO GPA 1994 applies to the 15 members of the EU and Switzerland, Norway, the USA, Canada, Japan, Korea, Hong Kong and Israel. It is open to other Governments to negotiate their accession.

Fees and awards

Educational establishments and award-giving bodies have for many years distinguished in the level of fees charged and the eligibility for awards, between those students who have a specified connection with the UK and those who do not. Students with the UK connection have often been referred to as 'home students' and those lacking the connection have been referred to as 'overseas students'. We will see that 'home students' can include foreign nationals, from within the EU and elsewhere, provided they have a 'relevant connection'.

'Home' fees and fees awards

Educational establishments (other than Oxbridge colleges) are *prima facie* entitled to charge higher fees to students who do not have a relevant connection with the UK. LEAs, research councils and other specified award-giving institutions are entitled to adopt criteria for eligibility based on the specified connection with the UK (and, in the case of awards by the research councils, the required connection may be with Great Britain). The rules are found in the Education (Fees and Awards) Regulations SI 1994/3042 amended by SI 1995/1241 and SI 1996/1640, and in the Education (Mandatory Awards) Regulations SI 1995/3321 amended by SI 1996/2088.

The 'relevant connection' is that the student must have been:

- ordinarily resident in the UK throughout the three years preceding 1 September, 1 January or 1 April closest to the beginning of the first term of the student's course;
- not resident wholly or mainly for the purpose of receiving full-time education.

Such a provision on its own would offend against Article 7 of the European Treaty of Rome 1957. Consequently, there are a number of 'excepted students' who are eligible for the lower 'home' fees, discretionary fees awards and fees-only mandatory awards. Eligibility as an 'excepted student' is that the student must be:

- a national of an EU member (or the son or daughter of such a national) who has been ordinarily resident within the EEA for the same three-year period and was not resident therein for any part of that period wholly or mainly for the purpose of receiving full-time education;
- a person not ordinarily resident in the UK or an EC national (or son or daughter of such a national) who was not ordinarily resident in the EEA only because he or she was temporarily employed outside the UK (or in the case of an EC national employed outside the EEA) or the student's spouse or parent was temporarily employed outside the UK or the EEA;
- a person who is in the UK as an EEA migrant worker who has throughout the three-year period been ordinarily resident within the EEA and was not resident there wholly or mainly for the purpose of receiving full-time education;
- an EEA national migrant worker who is not ordinarily resident for the three-year period only because he or she, his or her spouse or parent was temporarily employed elsewhere.

The test of 'ordinary residence' in the UK means that the citizenship of the student is irrelevant. A British citizen who was resident for two years in, say, the USA and then returned to the UK to study could be treated as liable to pay overseas fees, whereas a French citizen working in Germany for a couple of years and then coming to the UK to study would be treated as eligible for home fees. Ordinary residence has not been defined in statute or regulation, but has been considered by the courts and interpreted to mean the place where a person is living for settled purposes as part of the regular order of his or her life. Ordinary residence must not be simply equated with physical presence, because it is possible to retain ordinary residence throughout the period of a temporary absence from a place. Indeed, it is possible to be ordinarily resident in two places at the same time.

Maintenance awards

Maintenance awards still fall outside direct EU competence, being a matter of 'educational and social policy'. The requirement of three years' ordinary residence in the UK, not being wholly or mainly for the purpose of education, is a condition for the receipt of a mandatory award from an LEA. It can also be a condition attached to a discretionary award. Article 7 of the European Treaty of Rome 1957 has not so far extended to this area of educational and social policy, although it is difficult to predict future decisions of the ECJ. As matters stand, therefore, three years' ordinary residence within the EEA will not suffice. A European national residing in the UK for three years, not wholly or mainly for the purpose of education, will of course satisfy the requirement of the relevant connection with the UK.

An EEA national who is a migrant worker in the UK, together with his or her family, will be eligible for a mandatory award if the migrant worker:

- has been ordinarily resident within the EEA for the previous three years, not wholly or mainly for the purposes of education;
- has been in employment since last entering the UK (but not simply in order to qualify for a grant);
- intends to study a vocational course related to the previous employment or intends to transfer to a new employment sector in the case of involuntary unemployment;
- meets with all the other requirements of the mandatory award regulations.

Free movement of academics and students

Articles 48 and 52 of the European Treaty of Rome 1957 are relevant to the rights of entry and residence in the UK of academics and students who are EEA nationals and the families of EEA nationals whatever their nationality. The rights of free movement and residence possessed by students, academics and their families, are found in the European Treaty of Rome's (1957) directives and regulations, which provide for free movement for:

- workers;
- the self-employed;
- providers and recipients of services;
- students;
- members of the families of any of these.

Employees and potential employees have the right to enter the UK and remain in order to seek and take up employment. EEA students have the right to enter the UK and remain in order to pursue their studies. Employees and students can be accompanied or joined by their families. Their position in England and Wales is governed by the Immigration (European Economic Area) Order 1994. This order is designed to reflect the rights of free movement of workers, students and others found in the directives and regulations.

The Immigration (European Economic Area) Order 1994 provides that an EEA national shall be admitted to the UK on production of either a valid national identity card or passport issued by an EEA country. The order also provides for the admission of non-EEA members of the family. Except in the case of students, family members are defined in the order as the EEA national's spouse, a descendant of the EEA national or the spouse who is under 21 years or is their dependant, a dependent relative in the ascending line of the EEA national or the spouse. Regulation 1612/68 does, however, go further and, with Directive 68/360, requires EEA member countries to facilitate the admission of any member of the family not falling within the definition just given, if dependent on the EEA national or living under the same roof in the country from which they have come. A more distant family member such as this would, therefore, have to invoke the regulation and ignore the imperfect Immigration (European Economic Area) Order 1994. The 1994 Immigration (European Economic Area) Order provides that only the spouse and dependent children of a student are his or her family members. It mirrors, therefore, the more limited family rights contained in Directive 93/96. The non-EEA family members seeking to enter the UK to reside with the EEA national must first obtain an 'EEA family permit', which is a type of visa issued (free of charge) by the British Embassies and High Commissions Overseas. The 1994 Immigration (European Economic Area) Order further provides that the EEA national having been admitted, he or she shall be entitled to reside in the UK for as long as he or she remains a 'qualified person', that is:

- a worker;
- a self-employed person;
- a provider or a recipient of services;
- a student enrolled at a recognized educational establishment in the UK for the principal purpose of following vocational training.

A qualified person is entitled to be issued a residence permit by the Home Office Immigration Department as proof of his or her right of residence in the UK. A family member of the qualified person is also entitled to be issued with a residence permit.

In most cases, an EEA national working (or pursuing studies) in the UK will not have cause to approach the immigration department for the issue of a residence permit. He or she will arrive, present his or her passport or identity card, reside in the UK and later embark on completion of the work or studies. The student will have no cause to demonstrate that he or she is a qualified person by virtue of one or more of the definitions in the 1994 Immigration (European Economic Area) Order. However, where the EEA worker or student seeks to be joined or accompanied by a non-EEA family member, it becomes necessary to acquire a residence permit proving his or her right of residence in order to then obtain a family permit for family members coming to the UK or a residence permit for family members already here.

It is possible for a student to be a qualified person under any of the headings already identified. If the student is working as well as studying, he or she can potentially qualify as a worker – it matters not that the employment might be part-time or that the pay might be at a level which attracts family credit, so long as the employment is 'effective and genuine'. Similarly, the student might qualify as a self-employed person, pursuing a self-employed activity concurrently with the individual's studies. Fee-paying students at a private establishment will qualify as persons receiving services. If the student cannot fall within the definition of a worker, self-employed person or provider or recipient of services, then, to obtain a residence permit as a qualified person, he or she will need to be studying full-time on a vocational course, be covered by comprehensive sickness insurance and declare an ability for self-support without recourse to public funds. With these requirements, the 1994 Immigration (European Economic Area) Order reflects Directive 93/96 governing the position of students.

In conclusion, it can be stated that there is an effective regime in place for the free movement of European students and employees. In practice, the only problems that are likely to arise concern members of the family of the student or employee, who are not themselves EEA nationals.

The HEI as employer

By reason of Article 48 of the European Treaty of Rome 1957, an HEI is not entitled to refuse a position to a foreign academic, secretary or cook, on grounds only of nationality provided they are EC nationals. There is an exception for employees in the public service, but the ECJ has rightly not allowed HEIs to rely on that provision to avoid the rules where no issue of public security arises. The ECJ found that the University of Venice could be sued for discriminating against non-Italian nationals – see *Allue and Coonan v University of Venice*. The same principle would apply in the UK if there was discrimination against an EC national, or other national entitled to protection under certain EC Treaties. HEIs should keep a careful eye on their recruitment procedures. In *Scholz v University of Cagliari*, Ms Scholz argued that she had been unfairly treated under the University of Cagliari's recruitment procedure. The procedure gave credit for previous employment in the public service, but only if the public service was in Italy. The ECJ held that the restriction was invalid.

The issue of what amounts to discrimination on grounds of nationality can be difficult to resolve. For example, the ECJ found that a requirement that teachers in Ireland pass a test in the Irish language was justified, even though they would not need to use the language in their jobs – see *Groener v Minister of Education and City of Dublin Vocational Education Committee*. HEIs need to be aware of the pitfalls in their dealings with potential foreign recruits and actual employees just as they need to be aware of sex and disability discrimination legislation, much of which also originates in European law.

Mutual recognition of degrees and qualifications

The recognition of degrees between EU members is of importance to HEIs, students, potential students, employers and professional bodies. When must an HEI recognize a degree from an overseas HEI? Will its own degrees be recognized abroad? Will students be able to obtain work on the basis of their UK qualification? Will potential foreign students be dissuaded from studying in the UK if the UK diploma is not recognized abroad? What rules are there as to the length or content of courses which will determine whether or not they are recognized? Will professional bodies recognize qualifications obtained in other countries? Such questions are important for all HEIs, but those institutions offering vocational and professional courses are particularly affected. Articles 7, 48 and 52 provide the legal basis for the recognition of degrees. Degrees obtained by nationals of EU members in any EU member country must be recognized throughout the EU if they were obtained following a post-secondary course of at least three years duration. Degrees obtained in an EU member country by non-EU nationals do not need to be recognized in the same way.

In the 1960s and 1970s a series of directives provided for recognition of diplomas in relation to specific subjects, in particular the medical and allied professions (i.e. doctors, nurses, dentists, veterinary surgeons, midwives and pharmacists). Those directives required the coordination of training criteria so that a professional diploma was only recognized if certain subjects were included in the training. Some of these directives are still in force. For example, the European Commission in 1996 challenged French legislation which permitted psychiatric nurses to obtain a general care nursing qualification based on their psychiatric nursing qualification, without complying with the minimum standards in Directive 77/453. There was no general system by which degrees could be recognized, so instead of regulating diplomas profession by profession, Directive 89/48 provided for a general system. The directive uses the word 'diploma' rather than the word 'degree'. This directive was entitled 'For a general system for recognition of higher educational diplomas awarded on the completion of professional education and training of at least three years duration'. It also provides rules for the right to use academic titles. Directive 92/51 supplemented Directive 89/48 for diplomas of shorter duration.

What degrees must be recognized?

The definition of a diploma in Directive 89/48, Article 1(a) is:

> any diploma, certificate or other evidence of formal qualifications or any set of such diplomas, certificates or other evidence:
>
> - which has been awarded by a competent authority in a Member State, designated in accordance with its own laws, regulations or administrative provisions; and

- which shows that the holder has successfully completed a post-secondary course of at least three years duration, or of an equivalent duration part-time, at a University or establishment of higher education or another establishment of similar level and, where appropriate, that he has successfully completed the professional training required in addition to the post-secondary course; and
- which shows that the holder has the professional qualifications required for the taking up or pursuit of a regulated profession in that Member State.

There are special provisions where part of the education and training was received outside the EU. It is significant that the directive does not include any rules for minimum content requirements and there is no prerequisite of curriculum coordination.

The main points to be borne in mind are that the degrees are for three-year courses, that they are awarded by the institution on the basis of its own rules (not on the basis of any internationally coordinated procedure) and that they apply only to regulated professions. The last requirement is a significant limitation on the usefulness of the directive.

Vocational and professional courses

Both directives also govern professional training and professional qualifications. Directive 89/48 presupposes a higher education course of at least three years. Directive 92/51 governs other post-secondary education and training courses, other equivalent education and training, and some secondary courses (sometimes complemented by professional training and experience).

Additional requirements for some professions: aptitude tests and adaptation periods

Some regulated professions lobbied hard and were able to provide additional requirements. Lawyers' professional bodies, perhaps unsurprisingly, were the main group that insisted on additional requirements, and were widely criticized as a result. In some member countries of the EU this was no doubt for protectionist reasons, although additional requirements were agreed on the basis that although medicine or engineering require the same knowledge and skills throughout the EU, a professional lawyer requires a knowledge of the law of a particular country.

A German national, Mr Kraus, was awarded an LLM from Edinburgh University. He tried to use the LLM in his legal training in Germany. However, German law provided that he needed to obtain approval beforehand. This was expensive and time-consuming. The ECJ decided in *Kraus v Land Baden-Württemberg* that such rules, where they created an obstacle to the free movement of workers, could only be justified if they tried to further an objective in the public interest and were compatible with the European Treaty of Rome 1957. If such restrictions are permitted, they may go no further than what is necessary and they must be proportional.

Directive 89/48 achieved a compromise by requiring an aptitude test or adaptation period for certain professions. For example, in the UK, lawyers who have completed a diploma and relevant professional training in another EU member country can take the Qualified Lawyers Transfer Test. Many EU lawyers have taken advantage of this and have a dual qualification as an English solicitor.

Right to use academic titles

It is important for HEIs, graduates and employers that degrees be authentic and that their merit be known. Directive 89/48, Article 7, makes provision for use of academic titles. The addition of the name of an institution to the degree title is optional. So it can be hard to discover a degree's origin, and even more difficult to evaluate its merit, a problem exacerbated by the international nature of the directive. In some EU member countries recognition of degrees is a matter for Government; in others it is for the HEIs themselves. Directive 89/48, Article 7, sets out formal rules as follows.

- Nationals of other member countries who fulfil the necessary conditions for a regulated profession are entitled to use the professional title of the host member country.
- Such nationals are allowed to use their lawful academic title, and the abbreviation for it in the language of the host country, but the host member country may require the title to be followed by the name and location of the awarding institution.
- Where the profession is regulated by an association, nationals can only use the professional title on proof of membership, and if membership is subject to qualification requirements, then a foreign diploma may be recognised as fulfilling a requirement for a diploma, if it fulfils the criteria in the Directive.

Restrictions on the application of Directive 89/48

A significant restriction on the rights granted by directives is that they only apply to nationals of EU member countries. Thus, a US citizen who has graduated in the UK is not awarded the same rights of recognition as would be a UK or other EU citizen.

A number of institutions are listed in the directive as being regulated professional bodies. They include the principal institutions for accountants and engineers. The list is non-exhaustive. In *Aranitis v Land Berlin*, the ECJ said that a Greek geologist wishing to practise in Germany could not rely on the directive, because in Germany geologists practise on the basis of their degree only and so the profession was not regulated. However, the other aspects of European law (e.g. the rules on freedom of establishment) would still apply (see 'Recognition outside the terms of Directive 89/48').

The directive is also limited to diplomas awarded in EU member countries. A strange situation arose in the case of *Tawil-Albertini v Ministre des Affaires Sociales.* Mr Tawil-Albertini was a French national who obtained a doctorate in dental surgery in Beirut in 1968. His doctorate was recognized in Belgium in 1979 and he was subsequently authorized to practise dentistry in the UK and Ireland, where the authorities recognized his Lebanese qualifications. He next applied to practise in France and was refused. He sued the French Ministry and the case went to the ECJ. The court held that although Directive 78/686 required EU member countries to recognize diplomas awarded in other EU member countries, it did not require them to recognize diplomas from third countries, even where the diploma had already been recognized in a number of other EU member countries. This meant that the French national was entitled to practise in Belgium, the UK and Ireland, but not in France.

Recognition outside the terms of Directive 89/48

Quite apart from the Directive, Article 52 of the European Treaty can be used to obtain the right to use professional titles. In a recent case, the ECJ was faced with the issue of whether a German lawyer in Italy could use the title Avvocato in Milan. He was not a member of the Italian bar. The court ruled that restrictions on the use of the title must not be discriminatory and there have to be strong public interest reasons before a restriction would be allowed. The Italian Government had to take into account the lawyer's qualifications and experience – *Gebhard v Consiglio dell'ordine degli Avvocati e Proccuratore.* MEPs from the European Parliament's Committee on Legal Affairs are still discussing a directive on Lawyers Rights of Establishment.

In *Vlassopoulou v Ministerium Für Justiz Baden-Württemberg* the German Ministry refused to recognize a Greek law diploma as equivalent to a German law diploma. The Court was not able to rely on the directive as it had not been brought into effect at the relevant time, but it did require Germany to implement a system for recognition of qualifications which would enable the authorities to determine whether a graduate with a foreign diploma had the required knowledge to practise as a lawyer in Germany.

Recent developments

'Supplement' to be attached to degree certificate

Early in 1995, the European Commission raised the issue of the recognition of qualifications for academic and professional purposes in a communication. It identified four areas of action: information, creation of networks, consensual adaptation and quality appraisal. As a result, it is now draft-ing a model for a European 'Supplement', or form, which could set out details of the content of the course taken and the level of the qualification obtained. The form would be attached to the diploma, so that HEIs in other EU member countries could evaluate it and decide whether it should be recognized.

Disputes about recognition of qualifications
A second European Commission proposal was for a system of mediation for disputes about recognition. An idea for a mediation institute was rejected by EU member countries. Now mediation is being considered in the con-text of existing frameworks (e.g. HEI networks).

New directive
On 8 February 1996, the European Commission proposed a new directive (COM (96) 22 final) for a mechanism for the recognition of certain pro-fessional qualifications not covered by the existing directives. Under the new proposal, individuals can apply for the recognition of qualifications if they do not have the necessary professional experience to qualify under other directives. The relevant professions are listed in Annex A to the directive.

Simplified legislation
The European Commission is planning a simplification of the legislation concerning the recognition of diplomas under its initiative on simplified legislation for the internal market ('SLIM').

Anti-competitive practices

The European Treaty, Article 85, is concerned with the activities of under-takings (including HEIs) which in some way actually or potentially distort trade between EU member countries. The basic rule is that any commercial contract, arrangement or concerted practice which may affect trade be-tween EU member countries and which has as its object or effect an adverse impact on free competition, is void and unenforceable. 'Arrangement' has a very wide interpretation. It need not be formalized and can even relate to an understanding between undertakings not to compete in each other's territory.

The following examples have been found to be in breach of the Euro-pean Treaty, Article 85:

- if one party to a technology transfer agreement is required (without an objectively justified reason) to keep out of the selling market;
- if one party to a Research and Development agreement is restricted in its freedom to carry out Research and Development independently, or in

cooperation with third parties, in a field unconnected with that to which the programme relates or, after its completion, in the field to which the programme relates or in a connected field.

The increasing level of total fines for breaches of the competition rules in recent years points to the European Commission's greater stringency both in enforcing the articles and in punishing breaches: 1982, £18 million; 1988, £62 million; 1994, £373 million.

The scope of the European Treaty, Article 85 is devastatingly wide. The possibility of a large fine is real. The precise wording of contracts needs careful checking, but just as important are their objects and practical effects. Otherwise, possibly many years later, unforeseeable 'effects' may make what started out as a valid contract void and unenforceable. What are the consequences if an agreement, arrangement or concerted practice is in breach of the European Treaty, Article 85?

• Risk of very heavy fines on the undertaking from the European Commission for all parties involved in the anti-competitive behaviour.
• The parties may have to renegotiate the agreement, in which case care is needed because market conditions may have changed.
• The infringing undertaking may be liable for damages to third parties who suffer as a result of the unlawful conduct.
• Independent third parties may complain to the European Commission, as may a party to the agreement. This can result in fines as just described.

Anti-competitive practices which are permitted are as follows.

• If the European Commission gives clearance. Achieving this can be time consuming and very expensive. If granted, clearance may also be subject to conditions.
• If the contract is 'of minor importance' (i.e. if the market share is small enough to have no significant effect on competition and the combined group worldwide turnover of both parties is within relatively small limits). **Note:** Use of the exemption may be unreliable in the longer term (for instance, if another group takes over the holding company of one of the parties and the group turnover limits are thus exceeded, the exemption fails and the risk of liability for Article 85 penalties revives).
• If there is a 'block exemption' regulation available. These are exemptions, from the penalties of Article 85, in the overall interest of an efficient free market, for complete types (or blocks) of contract. However, there are two conditions:

  – the contract's wording must comply strictly with the block exemption;
  – the contract's intention and effect must comply strictly with the block exemption.

The technology transfer block exemption and the Research and Development block exemption are the principal block exemptions used by HEIs.

Technology transfer licensing agreements (Regulation 240/96)

Agreements between two parties are permitted for exclusive licensing (with a view to manufacture) of a patent for a period which may not exceed the patent's remaining life and which may include a ban on 'active' selling outside the territory and a ban on 'passive' selling for a period not exceeding five years. Pure know-how licensing and mixed patent and know-how licensing agreements are permitted. 'Know-how' is non-patented technical information which is secret, substantial and in any appropriate form. This exemption replaces (with a more liberal and commercial bias) the former patent licensing block exemption and the know-how block exemption.

Research and development agreements (Regulation 418/85)

These are permitted on certain terms where the contract is for pure Research and Development or where the Research and Development is for joint manufacturing or joint licensing (i.e. not for joint sale, which would have to comply with the main terms of Article 85 or be subject to a separate exemption).

Caution

The substance of a contract is more important than what it is called. For example, many contracts are called 'franchises' but they are really distribution agreements or something else. Each contract must be checked against the correct regulation, because precise details of each regulation are different.

It is essential to have some mechanism for periodic review of compliance with European law on commercial contracts. Market conditions can change and what started out as a valid contract may later be void and unenforceable, with consequent risk of fines.

Recommendation

Wherever European law collides with English law, European law prevails. Any agreement or practice which contravenes European law may prove void and unenforceable and can attract swingeing fines, even though it may comply with English domestic law. This can be the case even where the agreement or practice is between two English entities. HEIs must be able to rely on a secure contractual framework. The complexities involved between European and English law means that specialist help is essential to avoid unforeseen problems. Preventative help can be available from many law firms in the form of a compliance review service (i.e. a legal health check for the academic body).

Compliance review

The core of a compliance review for an HEI usually relates to competition law aspects on technology transfer, intellectual property (IP) licensing, Research and Development agreements and public procurement contracts, as these are the areas which most frequently give rise to difficulty. Every such agreement needs to be reviewed on a regular basis and, if necessary, redrawn to ensure it complies with European law regulations as they emerge and change. There is also a particular need to keep updated on aspects of employment law (which seems to be coming out of Brussels in increasing volume) and immigration rules applying to visiting academics and students. Compliance reviews can be extended or limited, to include whatever areas are required.

Future developments

Some commentators are of the opinion that 80 per cent of current domestic law in the UK has derived from Brussels. It may be regulations (which are immediately binding on all EU member countries with identical provisions) or directives (which can give a limited latitude in precisely how they are implemented into domestic law by Parliament). It is not possible to ignore the European dimension in running an HEI. At the time of writing, the EU member countries are moving towards the Inter-Governmental Conference to determine the future shape and development of the EU. In truth, the end of 1992 was only the end of the beginning for development of the single market. Further discussions continue to take place (the Maastricht Treaty 1993, the LEEA Agreement 1993, the WTO Government Procurement Agreement 1994 and the IGC 1996) on the introduction of new members (Austria, Finland and Sweden), on how far and how fast moves should be towards extra members and towards economic and monetary union, and on the relationship of the EU as a trading bloc with the rest of the world, in particular with the states of Central Europe. European Commission President Jacques Santer said in November 1996: 'Job security should mean ensuring the employability of workers, rather than the guarantee of keeping one's current job.' Commissioner Edith Cresson said, 'the free movement of ideas goes hand-in-hand with human mobility. In this respect, Europe is not in a very good position, compared with the US and Japan.'

One development is certain. The move towards harmonization of standards and mutual recognition in relation to employment law, health and safety and environmental issues, and the elimination of discriminatory barriers is likely to speed up rather than diminish. All this will continue to have a profound effect on all UK HEIs.

Further reading

Arrowsmith, S. (1996) *The Law of Public and Utilities Procurement.* London: Sweet & Maxwell.

Bovis, C. (1997) *Public Procurement Law in the EC.* London: Addison-Wesley Longman.

Clarke, P. F. and Temple, E. M. F. (1994) *Spicer's European Union Policy Briefing: Public Procurement Policy.* London: Longman.

Geddes, A. (1996) *Public Procurement: Practical Guide.* London: Sweet & Maxwell.

Lindrup, G. (1996) *Butterworths Public Procurement and Compulsory Competitive Tendering Handbook.* London: Butterworths.

Temple, E. M. F. and Bright, C. E. (1994) *Public Procurement Contracts: A Guide.* London: Croner.

Weatherill, S. and Beaumont, P. (1995) *EC Law.* London: Penguin.

Wyatt, D. and Dashwood, A. (1993) *European Law.* London: Sweet & Maxwell.

Case List

Albert v Lavin [1981] 3 All ER 878
Allerdale, The Times, 20 May 1996
Allue and Coonan v University of Venice (Case C-33/88)
Aranitis v Land Berlin (Case C-164/94)
Arthur v Anker, The Times, 1 December 1995
Associated Provincial Picture Houses Ltd v Wednesbury Corporation [1948] 1 KB 223
Attorney-General v De Winston [1906] 2 Ch 106
Attorney-General v Ross [1985] 3 All ER 345
Aztech Systems PTE Ltd v Creative Technology Ltd [1996] FSR 54
Baldry v Feintuk [1972] 2 All ER 85
Banks v CBS Songs Ltd and Others [1996] unreported, 26 July 1996
Bishopsgate Investment Management Limited (in liquidation) v Maxwell (No. 2) [1994] 1 All ER 261
Botzen v Rotterdamsche Droogdok Maatschappij BV (1986) 2 CLMR 50
Bulmer v Bollinger [1974] Ch 401
Chapple v Cooper [1844] 13 M & W 253
Claridge's Patent Asphalte Company Limited [1921] 1 Ch 543
Commission v Spain ('Madrid University') (Case 24/91)
Conservative Central Office v Burrell [1987] 2 All ER 2
Corporation of Mercer University v Smith [Ga 1988] 371 SE 2d 858
Customs and Excise Commissioners v Hedon Alpha Limited [1969] 2 Ch 365
Czarnikow v Roth, Schmidt and Company [1922] 2 KB 478
D'Mello v Loughborough College of Technology, The Times, 16 June 1970
Edmunds v Brown and Tillard [1688] 1 Lev 237
Framlington Group PLC and Another v Anderson and Others (transcript) 7 February 1995
Gebhard v Consiglio dell'ordine degli Avvocati e Proccuratore (Case C-55/94)
Glynn v Keele University [1971] 1 WLR 487
Green v St Peter's College, Oxford, The Times, 10 February 1896
Groener v Minister of Education and City of Dublin Vocational Education Committee (Case-379/87)

Harries v Church of England Commissioners [1992] 1 WLR 1241

Hegel v Langsam [1971] 29 Ohio Misc 147, 237 NE 2d 351, 55 Ohio 2d 476

Herring v Templeman and Others [1973] 2 All ER 581

Income Tax Special Purposes Commissioners v Pemsel [1891] AC 531

Jackson v Horizon Holidays [1975] 3 All ER 92

Joobeen v University of Stirling (1996) Ed LM 3(4)2

Kraus v Land Baden-Württemberg (Case C-19/92)

Liverpool and District Hospital for Diseases of the Heart v Attorney-General [1981] Ch 193

London Hospital Medical College v Inland Revenue Commissioners and Others [1976] 2 All ER 113

Moran v University College, Salford (No. 2), [1994] ELR 187, CA

National Trustees Company of Australia v General Finance Company of Australia [1905] AC 373

Naylor v Cornish [1684] 1 Vern 311n (1)

Noah v Shuba [1993] FSR 14

Norwich City Council v Harvey [1989] 1 All ER 1180, CA

Patel v University of Bradford Senate [1978] 1 WLR 1488; [1979] 1 WLR 1066, CA; [1979] 2 All ER 582

Pickering v Gunning [1628] Palm 528

R v Adams [1985] 7 CR App R (S) 97, CA

R v Aston University, ex p Roffey [1969] 2 QB 538

R v Camden London Borough Council, ex p H. (a Minor), The Times, 15 August 1996; [1996] Ed LM 3 (10)

R v Civil Service Appeal Board, ex p Cunningham [1991] 4 All ER 310

R v Coventry University, ex p Ali [1997] unreported, 11 February 1997

R v Derbyshire County Council, ex p Noble [1990] ICR 808

R v de Montfort University, ex p Cottrell [1996] unreported, 15 October 1996

R v East Berkshire Health Authority, ex p Walsh [1985] QB 152

R v Fernhill Manor School, ex p A [1994] ELR 67

R v Gough [1993] 2 All ER 724

R v Haberdashers' Aske's Hatcham College Trust, ex p T, The Times, 19 October 1994

R v Higher Education Authority Funding Council, ex p Institute of Dental Surgery [1992] 1 All ER 651

R v HM The Queen in Council, ex p Vijayatunga [1989] 3 WLR 13

R v Horsham DC, ex p Wenman [1995] 1 WLR 680

R v Ireland, The Times, 22 May 1996

R v Jockey Club, ex p Aga Khan [1993] 1 WLR 909

R v Lancashire County Council, ex p Maycock [1994] ELR 479

R v London Borough of Camden and Governors of Hampstead School, ex p H [1996] ELR 360

R v London Borough of Newham, ex p X [1995] ELR 305

R v London Oratory School, ex p Regis, The Times, 17 February 1988

R v Lord President of Privy Council, ex p Page [1992] 3 WLR 1112

R v Manchester Metropolitan University, ex p Nolan [1994] ELR 380

R v Panel on Take-overs and Mergers, ex p *Datafin* [1987] 3 WLR 1112
R v Parker, The Times, 11 March 1994
R v Rochdale MBC, ex p *Schemet* [1994] ELR 89
R v Secretary of State for Education, ex p *Prior* [1994] ELR 231
R v Secretary of State for Education, ex p *S* [1995] ELR 71
R v Secretary of State for Transport, ex p *Factortame Ltd* [1966] 1 All ER 301
R v Secretary of State for Wales, ex p *Rozhan* [1994] LGR 667
R v Sheffield Hallam University, ex p *Rowlett* [1995] Ed LM 2(4) 11
R v Staffordshire County Council, ex p *Ashworth, The Times*, 18 October 1996
R v University College London, ex p *Riniker* [1995] ELR 213; [1995] Ed LM 2(6) 1
R v University of Cambridge, ex p *Evans* [1997] unreported, CO/1031/97, 22 August 1997
R v University of Humberside, ex p *Cousens* [1995] Ed LM 2(6) 11
R v University of Liverpool, ex p *Caesar Gordon* [1990] 3 WLR 667; [1990] 3 All ER 821
R v Warwickshire County Council, ex p *Collymore* [1995] ELR 217
Rajah v Royal College of Surgeons of Ireland [1994] 1 LRM 233
Re D'Jan of London Limited [1993] BCLC 328
Re Duomatic Limited [1969] 2 Ch 365
Re Home Treat Limited [1991] BCLC 705
Re Hydrodam (Corby) Ltd (in Liquidation) [1994] BCC 161
Re Kirbys Coaches Limited [1991] BCLC 414
Re Leeds and Hanley Theatres of Varieties [1902] 2 Ch 809
Re Pinion [1965] Ch 85
Re Shaw's Will Trusts [1952] 1 All ER 49
Re Welfab Engineers Limited [1990] BCLC 833
Reed v Hastings Corporation [1964] 62 LGR 588
Reilly v University of Glasgow [1996] ELR 394
Religious Technology Center v Netcombe Online Communications Services, 21 November 1995, ND Cal
Revill v Newbury, The Times, 3 November 1995
Rosemary Simmonds v United Dominions Trust and Partners [1986] 1 WLR 1440
Sammy v Birkbeck College, The Times, 3 November 1964
Scholz v University of Cagliari (Case C-419/92)
Smolden v Whitworth and another, The Times, 23 April 1996, and 18 December 1996 (Court of Appeal)
Spijkers v Gebroeders Benedik Abattoir CV (1986) 2 CMLR 296
Spring v Guardian Assurance [1994] 3 All ER 129
Stern v Lucy Webb Hayes National Training School for Deaconnesses and Missionaries [DDC 1974] 381 F Supp 1003
Target Holdings Limited v Redferns (A Firm) and Another [1942] 2 All ER 320
Tawil-Albertini v Ministre des Affaires Sociales (Case C-154/93)
Thirunayagam v London Guildhall University [1997] 14 March, unreported (CA), but see *Education Law Monitor* 4(8) August 1997
Thomas v University of Bradford [1987] 1 All ER 834

Tweddle v Atkinson [1861] 1 B + S 393
University of Essex v Djemal and Others [1980] 2 All ER 742
University of Warwick v de Graaf and Others [1975] 1 WLR 1126; 3 All ER 284
Vlassopoulou v Ministerium Für Justiz Baden-Württemberg (Case C-340/89)
Walker v Northumberland County Council [1995] ELR 231
Waltham Forest, The Times, 20 May 1996
Waterlow Directories Ltd v Reed Information Services Ltd [1992] FSR 409
Wheat v Lacon & Co. Ltd [1996] 1 All ER 582
X (Minors) v Bedfordshire County Council [1995] 2 AC 633
Young v Naval, Military and Civil Service Co-operative Society of South Africa [1905] 1 KB 687
Zemco Limited v Jerrom-Pugh [1993] BCC 275

Bibliography

Abramson, M. *et al.* (1996) *Further and Higher Education Partnerships: the Future for Collaboration.* Buckingham: SRHE/Open University Press.

Adams, J. N. and Pritchard-Jones, K. V. (1997) *Franchising: Practice and Precedents in Business Format Franchising.* London: Butterworths.

Arden, A. and Partington, M. (1994) *Housing Law.* London: Sweet & Maxwell.

Arrowsmith, S. (1996) *The Law of Public and Utilities Procurement.* London: Sweet & Maxwell.

Association for Colleges (AfC) (1995) *Model Code of Ethics.* London: Association for Colleges.

Bainbridge, D. (1996) *Intellectual Property.* London: Pitman.

Bargh, C., Scott, P. and Smith, D. (1996) *Governing Universities: Changing the Culture?* Buckingham: SRHE/Open University Press.

Belbin, R. M. (1989) *Management Teams.* London: Heinemann.

Blair, B. (1997) *Liability of Landlords.* London: Sweet & Maxwell.

Bovis, C. (1997) *Public Procurement Law in the EC.* London: Addison-Wesley Longman.

Boyle, A. (1986) *Gore-Brown on Companies.* Bristol: Jordans.

Brooke, M. Z. and Skilbeck, P. M. (1994) *Licensing.* London: Gower.

Burton, M. and Patfield, F. (1994) *The Conduct of Meetings.* Bristol: Jordans.

Cabinet Office (1996) *Spending Public Money: Governance and Audit Issues.* London: HMSO

Cadbury (1994) *The Cadbury Report.* London: HMSO.

Cairns, E. (1996) *Charities: Law and Practice.* London: Sweet & Maxwell.

Cane, P. (1996) *Introduction to Administrative Law.* Oxford: Oxford University Press.

Carroll, A. J. (1994) The abuse of academic disciplinary power, *New Law Journal,* 144(729).

Carter Ruck, P. (1991) *On Libel and Slander* London: Butterworths.

CEF (1995) *Model Code of Conduct.* London: College Employer's Forum.

Charlesworth, T. and Morse, G. (1995) *Company Law.* London: Sweet & Maxwell.

Charity Commission (1993) *Decisions of the Charity Commissioners,* No. 6, Royal Holloway and Bedford New College. London: HMSO.

Chartered Institute of Patent Agents (1995) *CIPA Guide to the Patents Acts.* London: Sweet & Maxwell.

Chartered Institute of Patent Agents (1996) *European Patents Handbook.* London: Longman.
Chartered Institute of Patent Agents and Institute of Trade Mark Agents (1996) *The Trade Mark Handbook.* London: FT Law & Tax.
Cheffins, B. R. (1996) *Company Law.* Oxford: Oxford University Press.
Claricoat, J. and Phillips, H. (1995) *Charity Law A to Z: Key Questions Answered.* Bristol: Jordans.
Clarke, P. F. and Temple, E. M. F. (1994) *Spicer's European Union Policy Briefing: Public Procurement Policy.* London: Longman.
Clarke-Williams, H. (1997) *Defamation Law: A Practical Guide.* London: Butterworths.
Clayton, R. and Tomlinson, H. (1993) *Judicial Review: A Practical Guide.* London: FT Law and Tax.
Cobban, A. (1988) *The Medieval English Universities.* London: Longman.
Collins, L. (1996) *International Litigation.* Oxford: Oxford University Press.
Cornish, W. R. (1996) *Intellectual Property.* London: Sweet & Maxwell.
Cracknell, D. (ed.) (1996) *Charities: The Law and Pratice.* London: FT Law and Tax.
Cripps, Y. (1994) *The Legal Implications of Disclosure in the Public Interest.* London: Sweet & Maxwell.
CUC (1995) *Guide for Members of Governing Bodies.* Bristol: HEFCE (Chairs of University Councils).
CUC (1997) *Advice on Whistleblowing.* Bristol: CUC.
CVCP (Committee of Vice-Chancellors and Principals) (1994). *Notes of the Zellick Report. Guidance on Student Disciplinary Procedures.* London: CVCP.
CVCP (1995) *Recruitment and Support of International Students in UK Higher Education.* London: CVCP.
CVCP (1996) *Sport in Higher Education.* London: CVCP.
CVCP (1997) *Independent Review of Student Appeals and Staff Disputes: Interim Report of the CVCP Nolan Group.* London: CVCP (N/97/11).
Dale, H. P. and Gwinnell, M. (1995/6) Time for change: charity investment and modern portfolio theory, *The Charity Law & Practice Review,* 3(2), 65–96.
Davies, Sir Michael (1994) *The Davies Report: The 'Great Battle' in Swansea.* Bristol: Thoemmes Press.
Deacon, M. (1997) Capital funding and the private finance initiative: panacea or poison chalice?, *Perspectives: Policy and Practice in Higher Education,* 1(4), 133–8.
Dearing, R. (1997) *Higher Education in the Learning Society: Report of the National Committee of Inquiry into Higher Education.* London: HMSO.
Dearlove, J. (1995a) Collegiality, managerialism and leadership in English universities, *Journal of Tertiary Education and Management,* 1(2), 161–9.
Dearlove, J. (1995b) *Governance, Leadership, and Change in Universities.* Paris: UNESCO (IIEP).
DfEE (1993) *The Charter for Higher Education.* London: HMSO.
de Smith, S. *et al.* (1995) *Judicial Review of Administrative Action.* London: Sweet & Maxwell.
Doyle, B. (1997) *Disability Discrimination: Putting the New Act into Practice.* Bristol: Jordans.
Drysdale, B. and Silverleaf, T. (1994) *Passing Off.* London: Butterworths.
Duke, A. (1996) *Importing Oxbridge: English Residential Colleges and American Universities.* New Haven: Yale University Press.
Evans, G. R. (1996) *Raising Concerns and Handling the Consequences in Further and Higher Education: a Handbook.* London: Council for Academic Freedom and Academic Standards.

Evans, G. R. (forthcoming) *Accountability in Higher Education.* Buckingham: SRHE/ Open University Press.

Farrington, D. J. (1994) *The Law of Higher Education.* London: Butterworths.

Farrington, D. J. (1997) *Handling Student Complaints,* UCoSDA Briefing Paper 48. Sheffield: UCoSDA.

Farrington, D. J. and Mattison, F. (1990) *Universities and the Law.* Reading: Conference of University Administrators.

FEFC (1994a) *Report of Inquiry into Derby Tertiary College Wilmorton.* London: FEFC.

FEFC (1994b) *Report of Inquiry into St Phillip's Roman Catholic Sixth Form College.* London: FEFC.

Fine, R. (1997) *Being Stalked.* London: Chatto & Windus.

Flint, M. J. (1997) *User's Guide to Copyright.* London: Butterworths.

Fordham, M. (1995) *Judicial Review Handbook.* London: John Wiley.

Franks Report (1966) *University of Oxford: Report of Commission of Inquiry.* Oxford: Oxford University Press.

Fraser, A. and Neville, S. (1993) *Teambuilding.* London: The Industrial Society.

Furmston, M. P. (1992) *Universities and Disclaimers of Liability.* London: CVCP N/92/ 112 (29/5/92).

Galligan, D. J. (1996) *Due Process and Fair Procedures.* Oxford: Oxford University Press.

Geddes, A. (1996) *Public Procurement: Practical Guide.* London: Sweet & Maxwell.

Goode, R. (1995) *Commercial Law.* London: Penguin.

Gooding, C. (1996) *Disability Discrimination Act 1995.* London: Blackstone.

Gordon, R. (1996) *Judicial Review: Law and Procedure.* London: Sweet & Maxwell.

Gordon, R. and Barlow, C. (1996) *Judicial Review Deskbook.* London: John Wiley.

Gray, H. (1997) Higher education institutions as corporations, *Perspectives: Policy and Practice in Higher Education,* 1(3), 78–80.

Greenbury Report, The (1995) *Directors' Remuneration.* London: HMSO.

Griffiths, J. A. G. (1977 and subsequent editions) *The Politics of the Judiciary.* London: Fontana.

Gringas, C. and Nathanson, N. (1997) *Nabarro Nathanson: The Law of the Internet.* London: Butterworths.

Hall, J. (1990) Confidentiality on the Campus, *Education and the Law,* 2(1), 117.

Hall, J. (1994) College governors–understanding the checks and balances, *Education and the Law,* 6(4), 187.

Harbottle, M. (1995) *Investing Charity Funds.* Bristol: Jordans.

Harris, B. (1995) *Disciplinary and Regulatory Proceedings.* Chichester: Barry Rose.

Harrison, J. (1992) *Managing Charitable Investments.* London: ICSA Publishing.

Harrison, J. (1994) *Charity Investment Matters.* London: Lazard Investors Limited.

HEFCE (1996) *HEIs Related Companies: Recommended Practice Guidelines.* Bristol: HEFCE.

HEQ (1991) Mergers in Higher Education, *Higher Education Quarterly,* 45(2), entire issue.

HEQC (1995) *Code of Practice for Overseas Collaborative Provision in Higher Education.* London: HEQC.

Holloway, J. (1994) The rights of individuals who receive a defective education, *Education and the Law,* 6(2), 207–19.

Holyoak, J. and Torremans, P. (1995) *Intellectual Property Law.* London: Butterworths.

Hyams, O. (1994) The potential liabilities of governors of higher education institutions, *Education and the Law,* 6(4), 191–205.

Inglis T. and Heath, S. (1997) *Using Trade Marks in Business: Commercial Guide to Trade Marks Law.* London: John Wiley.

Jarratt Report, The (1985) *Report of the Steering Committee for Efficiency Studies in Universities*. London: CVCP.

Jordan (1996) *The Housing Act, 1996: A Practical Guide*. Bristol: Jordans.

Joynson, M. and Wood, J. (1987) *The Committee Business*. Reading: CUA.

Kaplin, W. A. (1979) *The Law of Higher Education*, 1st edn. New York: Jossey-Bass.

Kaplin, W. A. (1985) *The Law of Higher Education*, 2nd edn. New York: Jossey-Bass.

Kaplin, W. A. and Lee, B. A. (1995a) *The Law of Higher Education*. New York: Jossey-Bass.

Kaplin, W. A. and Lee, B. A. (1995b) *Cases, Problems and Materials: An Instructional Supplement to the Law of Higher Education*. New York: Jossey-Bass.

Koppenol-Laforce, M. (1996) *International Contracts*. London: Sweet & Maxwell.

Laddie, H., Prescott, P., and Vittoria, M. (1995) *The Modern Law of Copyright and Designs*. London: Butterworths.

Lai, J. P., Martin, S. and Cranidge, C. (1996) *Company Secretary's Handbook*. London: Tolley Publishing.

Lever, J. (QC) (1995) *Independent Inquiry Report*. Portsmouth: University of Portsmouth.

Lewis, C. B. (1983) The Legal Nature of a University and the Student–University Relationship, *Ottawa Law Review*, XV.

Lewis, C. B. (1985) Procedural Fairness and University Students: England and Canada Compared, *The Dalhousie Law Journal*, 9(313).

Lindrup, G. (1996) *Butterworths Public Procurement and Compulsory Competitive Tendering Handbook*. London: Butterworths.

Manning, J. (1995) *Judicial Review Proceedings: A Practitioner's Guide*. London: The Legal Action Group.

Markesinis, B. S. and Deakin, S. F. (1994) *Tort Law*. Oxford: Oxford University Press.

Markesinis, B. S. and Munday, R. J. C. (1992) *An Outline of the Law of Agency*. London: Butterworths.

Marshall, E. A., Morris, R. and Crabb, B. S. L. (eds) (1995) *Charlesworth and Morse: Company Law*. London: Sweet & Maxwell.

McFarlane, J. (1996) *Rethinking Disputes: The Mediation Alternative*. London: Cavendish.

McGregor, H. (1997) *McGregor on Damages*. London: Sweet & Maxwell.

McWilliam, J. (1997) A commissioner's tale: Avery Hill Student Village, University of Greenwich, *Public Money and Management*, 17(3), 21–4.

Mendelsohn, M. and Bynoe, R. (1995) *Franchising*. London: FT Law & Tax.

Miceli, M. P. and Near, J. P. (1992) *Blowing the Whistle*. New York: Lexington.

Michaels, A. (1996) *Practical Guide to Trade Mark Law*. London: Sweet & Maxwell.

Moore, M. (1979) *The Law and Procedure of Meetings*. London: Pitman.

Morrison, N. (1996) *Private Finance Initiative*. London: FT Law & Tax.

NACUA (National Association of College and University Attorneys) (1989) *Student Legal Issues*. Washington: National Association of College and University Attorneys.

NACUA (1994) *The Formbook*. Washington: National Association of College and University Attorneys.

NAO (1995) *Severance Payments to Senior Staff in the Publicly Funded Education Sector*. London: HMSO.

NAO (1997) *The PFI Contracts for the Bridgend and Fazakerley Prisons*. London: HMSO.

Nolan, Lord (1995) *First Report of the Committee on Standards in Public Life*. London: HMSO.

Nolan, Lord (1996) *Second Report of the Committee on Standards in Public Life*. London: HMSO.

Nolan, Lord (1997) *Third Report of the Committee on Standards in Public Life*. London: HMSO.

Noone, C. (1996) *Mediation*. London: Cavendish.

Oakley, A. J. (1996) *Trends in Contemporary Trust Law*. Oxford: Oxford University Press.

O'Hare, J. and Hill, R. N. (1996) *Civil Litigation*. London: FT Law & Tax.

Osborne, C. (1995a) *Civil Litigation*. London: Blackstone.

Osborne, C. (1995b) *Commercial Litigation*. London: Blackstone.

Oxford (1995) *Commission of Inquiry: Framework Document*. Oxford: University of Oxford.

Oxford (1996) *Governance*. Oxford: University of Oxford.

Palfreyman, D. (1995–6) Oxbridge fellows as charity trustees, *The Charity Law and Practice Review*, 3(3), 187–202.

Palfreyman, D. (1996/97) The Oxford Colleges and their College Contributions Scheme, *The Charity Law and Practice Review*, 4(1), 51–65.

Palfreyman, D. (1997) Gift horses – with strings attached! *Perspectives: Policy and Practice in Higher Education*, 1(4), 133–8.

Palfreyman, D., Thomas, H. and Warner, D. A. (forthcoming) *Managing Mergers*. Leeds: Heist Publications.

Parlour, J. W. and Burwood, L. R. V. (1995) Students' Rights, *Education and the Law*, 7(2), 63–78.

Pettit, P. H. (1993) *Equity and the Law of Trusts*. London: Butterworths.

Phillips, H. and Claricoat, J. (1995) The sale of chattels held on charitable trusts, *Christie's Bulletin*, Summer 1995, 1–9.

Picarda, H. (1995) *The Law and Practice Relating to Charities*. London: Butterworths.

Powell-Smith, V. (1967) *Blackwells Law of Meetings*. London: Butterworths.

Public Law Project (1994) *Is it Lawful? A Guide to Judicial Review*. London: Sweet & Maxwell.

Public Law Project (1995) *Applicant's Guide to Judicial Review*. London: Sweet & Maxwell.

Quint, F. (1994) *Running a Charity*. Bristol: Jordans.

Richens, N. J. and Fletcher, M. J. G. (1996) *Charity Land and Premises*. Bristol: Jordans.

Ryder, A. (1996) Reform and higher education in the enterprise era, *Higher Education Quarterly*, 50(1), 54–70.

Salzedo, S. and Lord, R. (1996) *Arbitration*. London: Cavendish.

Scott-Bayfield, J. (1996) *Defamation: Law and Practice*. London: FT Law & Tax.

Shackleton on the Law and Practice of Meetings, 9th edn (1997) London: Sweet & Maxwell.

Sharman, D. (1993) *The Perfect Meeting*. London: Century Business.

Shattock, M. L. (1994) *The UGC and the Management of British Universities*. Buckingham: SRHE/Open University Press.

Shaw, R. and Smith, D. (1979) *The Law of Meetings: Their Conduct and Procedure*. London: Macdonald & Evans.

Sheridan, L. (1993/4) Cy-près Application of three Holloway pictures, *The Charitable Law and Practice Review*, 2(3), 181–4.

Shilling, A. and Sharp, T. (1997) *Corporate Governance*. London: Butterworths.

Smith, J. C. and Hogan, B. (1996) *Criminal Law*. London: Butterworths.

Sparrow, A. P. (1996) *The Role of the Company Director*. London: Technical Communications (Publishing) Ltd.

Sparrow, A. (1997) *The Responsibilities of Company Directors*, FT Management Briefings series. London: Pitman.

Stratford, A. (1988) *The Committee Book*. London: Foulsham.

Supperstone, M. and Goudie, J. (1992) *Judicial Review*. London: Butterworths.

Temple, E. M. F. and Bright, C. E. (1994) *Public Procurement Contracts: A Guide*. London: Croner.

Thomas, B. (1997) *Disability Discrimination*. London: Sweet & Maxwell.

Thomas, P. (ed.) (1975) *Universities and the Law*. Manitoba: Legal Research Institute, University of Manitoba.

Tolley's Company Law Handbook, 3rd edn (1997) London: Tolley.

Travers Smith Braithwaite (1996) *The Travers Smith Braithwaite Guide to Litigation* London: Travers Smith Braithwaite.

Treitel, G. H. (1996) *The Law of Contract*. London: Sweet & Maxwell.

Tribe, D. (1994) *Negotiation*. London: Cavendish.

Tudor on Charities, 8th edn (1995) London: Sweet & Maxwell.

Underhill, T. and Hayton, D. J. (1995) *Law of Trusts and Trustees*. London: Butterworths.

Wade, H. W. R. and Forsyth, C. F. (1994) *Administrative Law*. Oxford: Oxford University Press.

Warburton, J. (1992) *Unincorporated Associations*. London: Sweet & Maxwell.

Warner, D. A. and Crosthwaite, E. (1995) *Human Resource Management in Higher and Further Education*. Buckingham: SRHE/Open University Press.

Warner, D. A. and Kelly, G. (1994) *Managing Educational Property*. Buckingham: Open University Press.

Warner, D. A. and Palfreyman, D. (1996) *Higher Education Management: The Key Elements*. Buckingham: SRHE/Open University Press.

Warren, R. C. (1994) The collegiate ideal and the organisations of the new universities, *Reflections on Higher Education*, 6(6), 34–55.

Warren, R. C. (1997) Corporate temperance in higher education, *Perspectives: Policy and Practice in Higher Education*, 1(3), 82–7.

Weatherill, S. and Beaumont, P. (1995) *EC Law*. London: Penguin.

Whincup, M. H. (1993) The exercise of university disciplinary powers, *Education and the Law*, 5(1), 19–31.

Whittaker, S. (1995) *Privity of Contract and the Law of Tort: the French Experience*. Oxford: Oxford University Press.

Williams, J. (1910) *The Law of the Universities*. London: Butterworths.

Winfield & Jolowicz on Tort, 14th edn (1994) London: Sweet & Maxwell.

World Bank, The (1994) *Higher Education: The Lessons of Experience*. Washington DC: World Bank.

Wyatt, D. and Dashwood, A. (1993) *European Law*. London: Sweet & Maxwell.

York, S. (1996) *Practical Alternative Dispute Resolution*. London: FT Law & Tax.

Zellick, G. (1994) *Final Report of the Task Force on Student Disciplinary Procedures*. London: CVCP.

Note

See 'A Bibliographical Essay on the Visitor' for a list of further material on the Visitor.

A Bibliographical Essay on the Visitor

David Palfreyman

For corporations being composed of individuals, subject to human frailties, are liable, as well as private persons, to deviate from the end of their institutions. And for that reason the law has provided proper persons to visit, inquire into, and correct all irregularities that arise in such corporations, either sole or aggregate, and whether ecclesiastical, civil or eleemosynary.

(Sir William Blackstone, *Commentaries on the Laws of England*, Vol. I: 480, 1787, 10th edition)

Introduction

This bibliographical essay reviews the literature (textbooks, monographs, articles as listed in Appendix A) on the role of the Visitor under English law with respect to the chartered ('old', pre-1992) universities and colleges. It will be appreciated that the statutory ('new', ex-polytechnic universities) do not have the institution of the Visitor, being subject to judicial review (JR) as the creatures of statute. Thus, Carroll (1994) divides HEIs into the post-1992 statutory universities subject to JR, the traditional chartered universities and Oxbridge colleges with their Visitors, and the ancient chartered Oxford and Cambridge which, he argues, as civil rather than eleemosynary corporations have no Visitor and hence the student–university relationship is simply a matter of contract law for arbitration in the courts as for any other contract (and as for the statutory universities). See Samuels (1973) on the student–HEI contract, along with Farrington (1994) and Chapters 6 and 7, and also Chapter 8.

The analysis of the literature has been divided into several sections:

- the history and evolution of the Visitor;
- the strengths and weaknesses of the Visitor as an institution;
- the jurisdiction of the Visitor;
- the Visitor's powers of enforcement and ability to award damages;
- the procedures for visitation;
- the scope for JR relevant to the Visitor.

A further section compares the role of the Visitor in Australia, Canada, England, New Zealand and Nigeria. Key cases relevant to the interpretation(s) set out in the texts and articles are listed in Appendix B, which includes brief notes on especially significant cases.

Reference is also made to the recent enquiry undertaken by Lord Nolan (1996) into the governance of UK HEIs, including how they deal with student and staff complaints and problems. There is some, inevitably speculative, consideration given to the future of the Visitor – a medieval relic, a ghost clanking its chains, an anachronism awaiting abolition, or a sound model for retention within the chartered HEIs and possibly even extension into the statutory HEIs?

Thus, Samuels (1973) describes the Visitor as being 'redolent of monarchist paternalism in an isolated, unworldly community of scholars' and Farrington (1994) concedes that the concept of visitation has 'a distinctly medieval, ecclesiastical ring'. Farrington and Mattison (1990) compare the Visitorial Court to the other remaining vestiges of domestic tribunals left over from the Middle Ages – the Court Martial in relation to military law, the Consistory Court for Church of England ecclesiastical law and the Court of Chivalry dealing with claims to coats of arms. Farrington, however, still sees the Visitor as a legal entity having 'much to commend it' and as 'perhaps a model to which the rest of the system should give close attention'. Similarly, Isaac in Chapter 8, having reviewed the strengths and weaknesses of the Visitor as a fair, speedy and inexpensive mechanism for dealing with disputes, concludes that it:

> is a valuable one which should not be abandoned . . . [and which] generally works well. Rather than being abolished the Visitorial system should be developed and extended to all HEIs. On closer scrutiny surprisingly few of its features are anachronistic. The majority of criticisms lie in practical considerations where new procedures and experienced personnel could straightforwardly minimize current problems. The debate has already recently moved on because of the recommendations of Lord Nolan.

The Visitor debate post-Nolan is the subject of a later section in this essay.

As noted earlier, the Visitor is to be found in the chartered universities and in the Oxford and Cambridge colleges, but *probably* (see 'The history and evolution of the Visitor') not in the two 'ancient universities' of Oxford and Cambridge – these are civil corporations, not eleemosynary corporations, albeit created by Royal Charter. (The new universities created from the former polytechnics by statute under the Further and Higher Education Act 1992, also do not have a Visitor.) Picarda (1995: 522) notes that 'The distinction in nature between the two ancient universities and the modern [chartered] universities is to be ascribed to history rather than logic'! Picarda (1995: 519) also provides two definitions of the Visitor. First, from the *Shorter Oxford English Dictionary* (3rd edition), 'one who visits officially for the purpose of inspection or supervision, in order to prevent or remove abuses or irregularities' and, second, from Mitcheson (1887), 'persons having a private or domestic judicial authority over eleemosynary, lay and ecclesiastical corporations for the correction of the life and conduct of the members and the adjudication of disputes between them'.

The history and evolution of the Visitor

Shelford (1836), Mitcheson (1887) and Williams (1910) provide historical accounts of the origin and evolution of the Visitor, all of which are echoed in the modern texts of Pettit (1993), Picarda (1995) and *Tudor on Charities* (1995). Mitcheson notes that:

> though the visitation of eleemosynary lay corporations is part of the common law of England, yet both the name and duties of the Office are derived from the canon law on which the principles of ecclesiastical visitation are based.
>
> (Mitcheson, 1887: 3)

Apart from the question of the petitioner's *locus standi* (see 'The jurisdiction of the Visitor'), Mitcheson's 1887 account holds good in all respects of jurisdiction, practice and procedure. He also provides a little gem in quoting the Bishop of Winchester's 1611 letter to James I, in which the author, as Visitor to St John's College, Oxford, explains his duties, noting that his visits are at his own expense ('I must visit at mine own no small charge') and beseeching his Majesty to ignore grumblings from St John's about his carrying out of those duties ('a few factious fellows to cover their diverse abuses, should by causeless complaints or clamorous noise' Mitcheson, 1887: 39–40)!

Shelford ('at the expense of much labour . . . by a careful perusal of the reported cases', Preface) provides an early version (1043 pp) of *Tudor on Charities* or of Picarda's equally monumental work. In the section on visitation (Shelford, 1836: 322–98), he notes that the Sovereign is the Visitor of *all* civil corporations, via the King's/Queen's Bench, and hence, on that basis, Oxford and Cambridge, the ancient universities, *do* have a Visitor despite the assertion in some textbooks that, since they are not eleemosynary, they do not (unlike their constituent colleges). He says:

> this is what is understood to be the meaning of lawyers, when they say that these civil corporations are liable to no visitation – that is, the law, having by immemorial usage appointed them to be visited and inspected by the King, their Founder, in his Majesty's Court of King's Bench, according to the rules of the common law, they ought not to be visited elsewhere, or by any other authority.
>
> (Shelford, 1836: 324)

Later, Shelford (1836: 333) notes that 'It was adjudged that the King had an undoubted right to visit the two universities of Oxford and Cambridge'. Early editions of *Tudor on Charities* cite the Supreme Court of Judicature (Consolidation) Act 1925, Section 56(2)(*a*) which, in turn refers back to the Supreme Court of Judicature Act 1873, Section 34, in terms of the King's/Queen's Bench having a range of miscellaneous duties (including, presumably, that of visitation to Oxford and Cambridge). The latest edition of *Tudor on Charities* (1995) continues with this interpretation. See, however, Picarda (1995: 521–2), Pettit (1993: 278), Farrington (1994: 1.14 and 2.35) and Carroll (1994) for another view. In fact, Picarda (1995: 521) notes that 'Civil corporations are subject to the jurisdiction of the Queen's Bench Division: the Crown's prerogative to visit such corporations is exercised by the judges, administering the common law of England.' A footnote then refers to Shelford and states '*Quaere* whether the court acts in the capacity of Visitor.' Later (1995: 522), however, Picarda comments 'The Universities of Oxford and Cambridge being civil corporations do not have a Visitor: they are subject to the control of the courts'. In fact, the different interpretations are not that far apart and all this is very largely a matter of semantics: when is a Visitor not a visitor?!

Shelford praises the Visitor model:

The domestic forum of the Visitor is peculiarly adapted for determining all disputes which arise between the members of learned societies . . . If the learning, morals, or proprietary qualifications of students were determinable at common law, and subject to the same review as legal actions, great confusion and uncertainty would follow.

(Shelford, 1836: 330–1)

Thus, the Visitor watches over the endowment, the foundation, on behalf of the Founder:

for it is fit the members that are endowed, and that have the charity bestowed upon them, should not be left to themselves (for divisions and contests will arise amongst them about the dividend of the charity), but pursue the intent and design of him that bestowed it upon them . . . where they who are to enjoy the benefit of the charity are incorporated there, to prevent all perverting of the charity, or to compare differences that may happen among them, there is by law a visitational power.

(Shelford, 1836: 332)

Williams follows Mitcheson and Shelford in his account of the Visitor (1910: 29–46), and includes a very detailed 'Appendix of Cases' (1910: 120–51), many of which are Visitor cases. Williams also discusses whether Oxford and Cambridge are visited by the Crown (the most recent example, he says, being in the reign of James II): 'As the law stands at present, a civil corporation has the Crown for a Visitor, the visitation being exercised by the King's Bench Division, not by the Lord Chancellor, as in eleemosynary corporations' (1910: 31). However, 'There is a doubt whether Oxford and Cambridge have visitors . . . The matter must be considered doubtful' (1910: 32). It is unclear why by 1910 what in 1836 had apparently been certain should have become doubtful, but it may be linked to the dispute detailed shortly. As for the colleges, Williams notes that 'The right of visitation is in law an incorporeal heriditament' (1910: 35).

The 1852 Report of the Oxford University Commission notes that:

The University of Oxford is a corporate body . . . Its privileges have been granted or renewed in many Royal Charters . . . Whether there be power in any hands ordinarily to superintend this great Institution, and to reform it, when reform becomes necessary, and what is the extent of that power, if it exists, has often been a subject of dispute. Such a power has, however, been generally supposed to reside in the Sovereign, as Visitor. It has often been exercised by the Crown, and has often been recognised by the University . . . the right of visitation . . . has never been formally denied by the University . . . Even if the fullest authority ever claimed by the Sovereign were demonstrated to be constitutional, the long interruption of its use might render it difficult to discover the proper mode of exercising it.

(Report of the Oxford University Commissioners, 1852: 3–4)

The material in the Report's appendices includes an opinion from the Attorney-General in 1836 that there is indeed a Visitor 'and that the power of visiting that University is in the Crown' (1852: D54). But the 1851 'Opinion of the Legal Advisors of the Heads of Houses and Proctors' is that the Crown possesses no such visitational authority:

The visitatorial right, properly so called, is annexed to eleemosynary foundations alone . . . The University, however, is not an eleemosynary foundation, but
a civil corporation, and, as such is subject to the control of the Court of Queen's
Bench, which, upon complaint, acts with regard to it by mandamus, or otherwise, as it acts respecting other civil corporations. This species of control has
sometimes, though inaccurately, been called Visitatorial . . . but where there is a
Visitor a mandamus will not be granted as to any matters within his jurisdiction.
(Report of the Oxford University Commissioners, 1852: D54)

A 'Postscript to the Evidence of the Rev. J Wilkinson' (245–9) discusses 'the
visitatorial power of the Crown over the University' and notes that the University
had on various occasions acknowledged the right of visitation. It concludes:

the assumption by the Crown; if not of the title of Visitor, at least of the right
to visit is beyond dispute. Indeed, it does not appear that the Royal right of
visiting the Universities was ever questioned; on the contrary, it was gloried in
as a University privilege, and urged in bar of jurisdiction by other parties.

Dr Bentley's Case, R v Cambridge University is cited: 'Dr Bentley's counsel admitted
"that if the University had returned that the King was their visitor, as they might
have done, it would have put an end to the dispute here" . . . I am contending that
the University has this incident [visitation] of an eleemosynary corporation.' Counsel's view is presumably based on the acknowledged exclusivity of jurisdiction of the
Visitor.
   More recently in a case (and, so far, the only modern one of a student versus the
University of Oxford – as opposed to a student versus his or her Oxford college
within the jurisdiction of the college Visitor) the university did *not* invoke the jurisdiction of a Visitor. See *R v Oxford University*, ex p *Bolchover*, where Bolchover claimed
(unsuccessfully) that the proctors had acted unfairly.
   The present official stance of the University of Oxford is that it does *not* have a
Visitor, although, for the purposes of attempting to demonstrate that, post-Nolan,
it has an independent arbitrator of disputes, it currently argues that the proctors,
a medieval office carried over the centuries into modern times, are truly independent of the 'management'/executive by definition and behaviour, while the high
steward is of Visitor-like gravitas: between these two officers, student and other
disputes will, says the university, be dealt with impartially and fairly. If, however, the
complainant remained aggrieved, there is certainly no exclusion of the courts as
would be the case with a real Visitor, and hence the only practical issue is whether
such a case goes direct to the Queen's Bench as the appropriate court or starts off
in the County Court as would most similar disputes. Or, unless in fact the Queen's
Bench is not functioning *qua* Court but *qua* Visitor. Hence, presumably, a judge
would be despatched to Oxford or Cambridge to act as Visitor (speedy, informal,
less expensive?), with the result that the decision would be final (absolute jurisdiction?) and subject only to limited (?) JR by the courts. If the latter, and given that
the Visitor system is generally a sound mechanism (see 'The strengths and weaknesses of the Visitor model'), there seems little purpose in Oxford denying that
it might have such a convenient Visitor. Similarly, Cambridge at present believes
itself not to have a Visitor and the 1997 case of *R v University of Cambridge*, ex p
Evans notes in the judgement of Mr Justice Sedley that 'Cambridge University has
no Visitor'. Hence the High Court in that case considered whether leave should
be granted to Dr Evans to seek judicial review of the fairness of the University's

promotions procedures: the judicial review route would, of course, be barred by the exclusive jurisdiction of the Visitor, had Cambridge been deemed to have one.

The better interpretation, however, is that Oxford and Cambridge do technically have a Visitor in the form of the Queen's Bench Division, but that any dispute would be dealt with by *and physically in* that court (a one-man 'court' would not helpfully be coming to Oxford!), and hence that invoking the concept of the Visitor in relation to what would in effect be JR of the university's procedures would make no difference to the speed/cost dimension. In disputes short of JR, the aggrieved student could and probably would proceed by way of the usual court hierarchy for a claim in contract or tort: there would not, in fact, be exclusive jurisdiction for the Queen's Bench Division as would, in the case of an Oxbridge college with a real Visitor, preclude a contract (and perhaps a tort) claim in relation to any alleged failure to provide the appropriate educational 'experience'.

The strengths and weaknesses of the Visitor model

If our friendly Visitor did not already exist, would we invent him or her? Ricquier (1978) puts it well:

> Does the Visitor matter? The question has to be asked. Recent cases upholding his jurisdiction have been greeted with wailing and the gnashing of teeth, and slow emergence of this antediluvian functionary into the twentieth century cannot be expected to be greeted without misgivings. There are, however, strong arguments for its retention, and indeed encouragement.
>
> (Ricquier, 1978: 211)

Smith (1986) believes the Visitor to 'have a useful and important role to play in our universities . . . he is invariably a person of the highest standing and authority . . . disputes can then be determined swiftly, cheaply, and with the minimum of formality' (Smith, 1986: 666). *Tudor on Charities* (1995) notes that 'in recent years it has been commended as providing a practical and expeditious means of resolving disputes' (1995: 369), and argues that the House of Lords in recent cases has been 'concerned to retain the visitor's jurisdiction as a speedy, cheap and final answer to internal disputes' (1995: 387). The praise of Shelford (1836) has already been noted.

Peiris (1987) notes that 'The rationale of the visitational jurisdiction is essentially pragmatic' and he quotes Megarry, Vice-Chancellor, in *Patel v University of Bradford Senate*:

> In place of the formality, publicity and expense of proceedings in court with pleadings, affidavits and all the apparatus of litigation, there is an appropriate domestic tribunal which can determine the matter informally, privately, cheaply and speedily, and can give a decision which, apart from any impropriety or excess of jurisdiction, is final and will not be disturbed by the courts.
>
> (Peiris, 1987: 1499)

Howells (1989), however, queries whether the Visitor route is private and any less formal. Samuels (1973) considers the Visitor 'redolent of monarchial paternalism for an isolated unworldly community of Scholars . . . inappropriate for a large place of work'. He endorses the idea of an HE advisory board which might 'exercise appellate disciplinary functions, in order to bring consistency into the university world'. This has echoes of calls, post-Nolan, for an HE Ombudsman (see 'The Visitor post-Nolan').

Finally, the Report of the Oxford University Commissioners noted that 'For the settlement of internal disputes nothing can be better than the decisions of a wise Visitor. The decisions of Visitors have in point of fact been usually just and speedy' (Report of the Oxford University Commissioners, 1852: 183).

The jurisdiction of the Visitor

Although in recent decades there has been some debate and confusion about the extent of the jurisdiction, there is now clarity on the boundaries, which have been confirmed along the traditional lines (with one key exception regarding academic staff contracts of employment). Thus, Farrington and Mattison noted that 'there seems to be no dispute about the exclusivity of the Visitor's unique jurisdiction' (1990: 79). They cited authority back to 1747: Wright J. in *R v Bishop of Chester*, 'Visitors have an absolute power; the only absolute one I know in England'. They also cited Lord Hardwicke LC in *Attorney-General v Talbot*, 'The powers are absolute and final, and cannot be taken away by the courts of law in this kingdom . . . the most convenient jurisdiction; for though perhaps it may be sometimes absurd, yet it is less expensive than a suit in law or equity'. Farrington sees the Visitorial jurisdiction as 'a true "Alsatia in England"' (1994: 42). Pettit declares that the 'power of the Visitor is absolute and exclusive' (1993: 279).

Bridge (1970), writing in the context of the 'present unrest in the universities', saw the powers and duties of the Visitor as having been settled as early as 1692 in *Philips v Bury*: 'his determinations are final and examinable in no other Court whatsoever', Sir John Holt, CJ. The Visitor should not, argued Bridge, be dismissed as being just a figurehead, having only a nominal role ('not merely a social and ceremonial adornment of the university'). Again, Lord Hardwicke is quoted from *Attorney-General v Talbot*: 'the general powers of a Visitor are well known; no court of law or equity can anticipate their judgement, or take away their jurisdiction, but their determinations are final and conclusive'.

Smith (1981) traces cases from even earlier than *Philips v Bury*, such as *Daniel Appleford's Case* where Appleford sought *mandamus* to restore him to his fellowship against the warden and fellows of New College, Oxford, only to be told by Hale CJ. that 'We ought not to grant a *mandamus* where there is a visitor'). Smith's trail carries him through the 18th century (*R v Bishop of Chester; Attorney-General v Talbot; St John's College v Todington*) and the 19th century (*Thomson v University of London*) to the 20th century (*R v Dunsheath*, ex p *Meredith; Thorne v University of London*) before culminating in *Patel v University of Bradford Senate* where Megarry VC said, 'it seems to be clear that the visitor has a sole and exclusive jurisdiction, and that the courts have no jurisdiction over matters within the visitor's jurisdiction'. Smith sums up the Visitor as 'a private judge'. Smith (1986) takes the story on, noting a revival of interest in the concept of the Visitor ('A Ghost from the Past'), and citing especially *Hines v Birkbeck College* concerning the overlap of membership of the foundation with the contract of employment. Does the latter 'bring the cognisance of any dispute involving such internal rules within the jurisdiction of the common law courts?'. Smith argues it will not, on an analogy with the application of ecclesiastical law solely by the ecclesiastical courts:

the general courts of law will not attempt to enter the jurisdiction of another which they recognise as possessing a competent authority over its own special laws and subject matter in order to enforce rights and duties derived from the law appropriate to that jurisdiction, even though they may appear at first sight to have a *prima facie* right to do so by virtue of some other relationship such as contract.

(Smith, 1986: 107)

On the other hand, Smith recognizes that the generality of employees are not within the jurisdiction of the Visitor. He says: 'The relationship is entirely contractual . . . Such persons may be said not to have any "status" within the foundation itself derived from its statutes, etc., however much they appear superficially to be part of the university community' (1986: 569). Smith's four-part running article in the *New Law Journal* was cited by the House of Lords in *Thomas v University of Bradford*.

Ricquier (1978) examining *Patel v University of Bradford Senate*, defines the jurisdiction as including anybody with *locus standi* to the internal rules of the foundation on which the Visitor arbitrates, and not just, as had been thought, corporators or actual members of the foundation. Here he agrees with Christie (1974) who had been prompted by *Herring v Templeman and others*, and differs from Bridge (1970):

It has been noted elsewhere [Christie] that the determining factor [in deciding whether a matter is within the Visitor's jurisdiction] should be not so much the status of the complainant as the subject-matter of the complaint . . . the cases that go against it [this interpretation] can be discredited as being dependent on anachronistic distinctions between scholars and commoners at Oxbridge.

(Ricquier, 1978: 653)

Ricquier, however, does query whether the Visitor covers disputes about admission to the university, as do Smith (1986: 568) and Picarda (1995: 529) who also accept that the jurisdiction applies to all 'of the foundation' and not just corporators. *Tudor on Charities* (1995) cites *Oakes v Sidney Sussex College, Cambridge* where the Court 'declined to follow the previous view that the Visitor of an Oxford or Cambridge college has jurisdiction to determine a dispute with a scholar (i.e. a member of the college) but not an ordinary student' (Ricquier's point as noted earlier).

Ricquier (1979) in a lengthy review of the history, role and jurisdiction of the Visitor cites a Canadian case in support of the exclusive jurisdiction line, *Vanek v Governor of the University of Alberta*, a case, however, which prompted the Alberta legislation to abolish the office of Visitor altogether! He regards Sir Richard Kindersley's statement in *Thomson v University of London*, as 'the obvious starting-point for a discussion of visitational power' ('Whatever relates to the internal arrangements and dealings with regard to the government and management of the house, of the domus of the institution, is properly within the jurisdiction of the Visitor'). *Thomson v University of London* concerned the exclusive jurisdiction of the Visitor in relation to examinations and was affirmed in *Thorne v University of London*: 'the High Court does not sit as a court of appeal from university examiners' (Diplock LJ.). *Langlois v Rector and Members of Laval University* is also cited as a Canadian case confirming this proposition. Ricquier went on to identify the 'areas of doubt' as regards jurisdiction – overlap with the general law of the land, including trust law, where the courts can intervene since the issue is no longer solely local law, and the problems of admissions ('essentially one of discretion').

The Visitor's jurisdiction most recently (1987) and definitively came up for consideration by the House of Lords in *Thomas v University of Bradford*, here concerning not student discipline or progress as in *Patel v University of Bradford Senate* but an academic's contract of employment. Lord Griffiths, dismissing a contrary Commonwealth case, *Norrie v Senate of the University of Auckland*, declared that 'the exclusivity of the jurisdiction of the Visitor is in English law beyond doubt and established by an unbroken line of authorities spanning the last three centuries'. Thus, in reviewing *Thomas v University of Bradford*, Hadfield (1987) concludes, 'The Visitor is clearly here to stay'. Lewis (1987) was not so sure, noting that 'having apparently reestablished the orthodox position, the House then significantly altered the traditional understanding of the visitorial jurisdiction' by confirming that an aggrieved academic employee (a member of the foundation) *can* utilise the Employment Protection (Consolidation) Act 1978. In fact, this ambiguity was little more than briefly academic in that the Education Reform Act (ERA) 1988 promptly removed tenure, the issue at large in *Thomas v University of Bradford*, for all academic staff appointed (or even promoted) after 20 November 1987, and, via the notorious model statutes imposed by the University Commissions set up under the ERA 1988, introduced non-Visitor mechanisms for dealing with disputes regarding the contracts of employment of academics (see Zellick, 1989; Pettit, 1991). Pettit (1991) reviews *Pearce v University of Aston in Birmingham* as a case concerning an academic in dispute over his contract of employment.

Peiris (1987) and Howells (1989) also consider *Thomas v University of Bradford*, the latter contemplating 'the protection currently available to aggrieved university academics' in the context of the 1980s universities no longer being ivory towers as they become 'more management orientated'. Hence, Howells comments, 'The appropriateness of the Visitor to resolve these disputes must be doubted'. Pitt (1990) considers the ERA 1988 'attack on tenure' and the work of the University Commissions, now virtually complete as even the Oxbridge colleges have had their messy statutes forcibly revised to incorporate the draft model statute regarding redundancy. He notes that the Visitor may still have a role as part of the university appeal mechanism prior to a dispute reaching the Courts.

Tudor on Charities (1995) quotes from *R v Committee of the Lords of the Judicial Committee of the Privy Council acting for the Visitor of the University of London*, ex p *Vijayatunga*: 'the Visitor enjoys untrammelled jurisdiction to investigate and correct wrongs done in the administration of the internal laws of the foundation to which he is appointed; a general power to right wrongs and redress grievances'.

The Visitor's powers of enforcement and ability to award damages

Farrington states that, although the Visitor 'apparently has wide powers to grant relief . . . he or she has no power to order compensation in the nature of damages' (1994: 51). Lord Hailsham LC, in *Casson v University of Aston in Birmingham*, is quoted:

> the only substantive prayer for relief in this case is a monetary claim for compensation in the nature of damages. After considerable research I have been unable to find any precedent in the long history of visitatorial powers in which a visitor has made such an order and in my view he has no such power.

Farrington notes that this view was accepted by Kelly LJ. in *Re Wislang's Application* and by Sir Michael Davies (1994) in the University College of Swansea case in 1993.

In contrast, however, Pettit declares, 'Contrary to the view expressed by Lord Hailsham LC, the House of Lords has now said that there is no reason why the Visitor should not award damages in an appropriate case' (1993: 281). He cites *Thomas v University of Bradford*, which is the subject of two articles (Hadfield, 1987 and Lewis, 1987), both of which note that it 'overruled the statement in *Casson* that the Visitor possessed no power to award damages' (Hadfield's words). *Tudor on Charities* (1995) agrees with Pettit.

Farrington, therefore, seems to be wrong, but at least he is in good company with Lord Hailsham! In fact, Smith (1986: 667), following Hailsham, recognizes an 'inability to award damages'.

Peiris (1987), however, comments that 'In this state of the authorities it would certainly be rash to take for granted that the Visitor could be presumed upon to order the payment of damages for breach of contract', not least because he or she 'would in all probability take into account the general interest and welfare of the institution . . . This erodes disconcertingly the plaintiff's legitimate interests which are protected by the common law action for contractual damages'.

The procedures for visitation

Tudor on Charities (1995) agrees with Picarda (1995) on most aspects of the procedures for visitation:

- the Visitor is not obliged to proceed by way of common law rules;
- he or she is invoked by way of petitioning for an appeal;
- the visitation is a judicial act and, hence, all relevant parties must be heard but not necessarily personally by the Visitor (in that assessors can be appointed to advise, commissaries can be sent to whom the hearing of evidence can be delegated, e.g. the Crown will delegate via the Lord Chancellor to a High Court Judge or even a QC) and perhaps only in writing – a point Wade and Forsyth (1994: 537) also make.

In short, the Visitor has wide discretion over procedures, and, indeed, 'formalities should be kept to a minimum' (Picarda, 1995: 532).

de Smith (1974) discusses the applicability of the rules of natural justice to Visitor procedures in the light of *R v University of Aston Senate*, ex p *Roffey*, an interesting and controversial case: the Visitor must offer the student facing disciplinary charges the chance to offer a defence, to plead mitigating circumstances, but there needs to be no pretence that formal procedures are required as if in a court of law. Wade (1969) was critical of the legal reasoning displayed in *R v University of Aston Senate*, ex p *Roffey*: 'It was only a question of time before the high tide of litigation over natural justice reached the universities'; 'the whole legal paraphernalia' has been imported into academic life; the board of university examiners has mistakenly been viewed as a judicially reviewable statutory tribunal or Government agency.

Otherwise, the only detail on the practice and procedure for Visitor appeals is the article by Picarda (1992–3). The founder has delegated to the Visitor, so can the Visitor further delegate? Broadly, no, but he or she can appoint an assessor to assist on matters of law or send a commissary. The sovereign, instead of acting via the Lord Chancellor, may appoint a commissioner. The hearing of evidence may be delegated to an examiner (but better not to if the material is 'hotly in dispute, because the Visitor is then deprived of the opportunity of assessing the credibility of witnesses in the box'). The Visitor can visit of his or her own accord (a 'general visitation'), but this practice has died out in modern times. Otherwise, the Visitor will be activated by an appeal, launched by petition from anybody with the necessary *locus standi* (i.e. 'the petitioner's interest in having a matter determined by reference to the internal laws of the foundation in question': the petitioner could be the university itself, but this is much less likely than it being an aggrieved student or academic). Thus, we have a petitioner and a respondent, and a formal petition, but thereafter the formalities are entirely within the control of the Visitor as to whether proceedings mimic court practice (e.g. pleadings, discovery, interrogations, further and better particulars). Usually, 'subject to the need to conform with the principles of natural justice', the proceedings will be simple – a hearing, but one which does not necessarily involve oral evidence or, indeed, much by way of evidence (e.g. if it is about the interpretation of a statute). Evidence may or may not be on oath, 'as the visitor may direct'. Costs and damages may be ordered. Costs were indeed awarded in *Thomas v University of Bradford* (No. 2).

Mitcheson notes that the Visitor should proceed 'summarily, simply, and plainly, without the noise and formalities of a court' (1887: 5), and that 'visitors have in England generally adopted as closely as possible the procedure of the ecclesiastical courts; for if they are to give the parties interested a fair hearing, they can hardly adopt a more simple procedure' (1887: 14). Shelford also discusses powers and procedures: 'A visitor is not bound to proceed according to the rules of the common law' (1836: 361); his powers are 'absolute and final' (1836: 361); he may deprive the members of a foundation of their position if they refuse to take full part in a visitation (1836: 369); 'the acts of a visitor, whether right or wrong, cannot be examined in courts of law, where he has acted within the scope of his jurisdiction' (1836: 376); 'He may administer an oath or require an answer upon oath' (1836: 379). Williams echoes much of Mitcheson and Shelford, noting that the Visitor 'cannot, apart from statute, compel the attendance of witnesses' (1910: 44), and that 'No precise mode of procedure is necessary, as long as substantial justice is done.' (1910: 44).

JR of the Visitor

Although there has been uncertainty even until the 1980s concerning the extent to which the Visitor is subject to JR, the position is now clear. Wade and Forsyth (1994) state that the Visitor is subject to JR for any breach in the application of the rules of natural justice in relation to procedures, and for any lack of jurisdiction and authority, but not for any error of fact or of law (here the Visitor has an 'ancient immunity'). The full range of JR remedies applies – *mandamus, certiorari* and prohibition.

Similarly, Pettit (1993) and Picarda (1995) confirm Wade and Forsyth – the jurisdiction of the Visitor is exclusive, but there is limited control by the courts by way of JR in the form of prohibition if the Visitor exceeds his or her jurisdiction, *mandamus* if there is a failure to act, and (only more recently established within case law) *certiorari* in certain circumstances (*not* for errors of fact or law). Picarda makes the point that, in practice, matters are likely to be clarified by way of declaration rather than the issue of an order and also comments that a Visitor could have

damages awarded against him or her for exceeding his or her jurisdiction. Since
there is no JR for error of fact, there is effectively no appeal against the decision of
the Visitor. Picarda comments here that, as a result, the Visitor is unable to relieve
against his or her own sentence!? In relation to error of law, Pettit (1993: 281)
explains the logic in the ordinary courts not being able to review the Visitor's
interpretation and application of the internal laws of the foundation or institution
– the courts are not here concerned with English law but with the *forum domesticum*,
the local law of the university or college, and so they have no relevant expertise.
('The visitor is not applying the general law of the land but a peculiar, domestic law
of which he is the sole arbiter and of which the courts have no cognisance.')

Wade (1993), however, queries whether such an exemption from JR in respect of
error of law, as bestowed (or confirmed) by the House of Lords in *R v Lord President
of the Privy Council*, ex p *Page*, is sustainable. It has to be noted that the Lords
reversed the judgements of lower courts, and only by a majority of three (Lords
Browne-Wilkinson, Keith, Griffiths) to two (Lords Slynn and Mustill). The majority
'emphasised the considered judicial policy over 300 years in refusing to review
visitors' decisions on their merits . . . *certiorari* would never issue for mere error'.
Wade asks whether that line of argument, dating back to *Philips v Bury*, may be 'a
shibboleth', ready to be discarded as, like all else in the last 40 years (he says), it
will eventually fall to the incoming tide of JR. Otherwise, the Visitor is, indeed, with
this 'ancient immunity', in a unique position in the 1990s.

Smith (1993–4) also reviews *R v Lord President of the Privy Council*, ex p *Page*, noting
that the House of Lords had been unable to find 'anything inherently wrong with
powers vested in an inferior court from which there could be no appeal', given that
'the rules which are under consideration are not the general laws of the realm, but
the private rules of the founder, and the High Court is neither competent in such
laws, nor is it directly concerned whether or not such laws are observed or enforced'.
Smith is clearly more optimistic than Wade as to how much longer the Visitor can
enjoy the privilege of being subject to only limited review by the ordinary courts.
Certainly, as early as 1973, Fridman argued that universities:

- are *de facto* public bodies, not private and independent corporations;
- 'are totally, or almost completely financed by the public purse';
- provide 'a public service';
- are, as a result, 'amenable to the controls of administrative law'.

As explored in the following section, the balance of independence/regulation
and of reference to the Visitor/ordinary courts is rather different in Canada (Fridman
was Dean of Law, University of Alberta), Australia and New Zealand.

By way of comparison, see Baker (1992) on the scope for JR of the Visitors to the
Inns of Court, who are themselves judges. Can the court effectively review itself if
the Visitors are *de facto* judges, or are they 'mere' Visitors? The case explored by
Baker is *R v Visitor to the Inns of Court*, ex p *Calder*.

A comparison of the Visitor in Australia, Canada, England, New Zealand and Nigeria

US common law has no equivalent of the Visitor and in Scotland it once existed
(Farrington, 1994: 51: 'in principle the Visitorial jurisdiction in Scotland exists even
though it is in desuetude'). Matthews (1980) provides a review of what he calls

'Dominion cases', noting that 'Dominion Courts while acknowledging the force of the English authorities, have shown what appears to be a reluctance to apply them' (notably in Ex p *McFadyen*, an Australian case).

Willis (1979) explores *Patel v University of Bradford Senate* and 'examines its applicability to Australian universities', noting that 'the visitor's is a largely untried and unknown jurisdiction: one unwelcome, in the main, in the courts wherein it has been raised'. He considers three University of Sydney cases, including Ex p *McFadyen*, and quotes Halse Rogers J. in that case:

> I think . . . that probably nobody until *Ex parte King* [1944] . . . ever thought that there was any possibility of intervention by the visitor . . . it was never contemplated by the Legislature or by anybody from the time the Act was passed . . . that it did anything more than give the Governor an official connection with the University (*ie* the Visitor as a ceremonial feature). The conclusion is that *Patel* provides the basis for the revival of the exercise of visitatorial powers, but with what consequences it is impossible to predict.
>
> (Willis, 1979: 294)

Sadler (1980) contemplates similar territory, noting that, typically, in Australia various university acts provide for the governor to be the Visitor, and considering in particular *Murdoch University v Bloom* (unreported, 16 April 1980). This was a case concerning the contractual relationship between an academic and the university. The court decided that the matter was not *domus* and, hence, not within the jurisdiction of the Visitor, but there was a strong dissenting opinion. This dispute reflected the uncertainty in English courts surrounding *Hines v Birkbeck College* until *Thomas v University of Bradford*.

Sadler (1981) returns to the issue of visitatorial jurisdiction in Australia considering a range of cases dating back to 1871 and concluding that in Australia the Visitors 'consider that their jurisdiction is not appellate but is more akin to that of a court exercising supervisory jurisdiction. This view of the visitatorial role is both unsatisfactory and unprecedented'. Sadler prescribes as 'the only realistic avenue for reform' the 'detailed statutory delimitation of visitatorial jurisdiction together with the guidance of statutory criteria which visitors must take into account in exercising their jurisdiction' (the Visitor as ombudsman under statute, not as a venerable creature of common law). The Visitor, on balance, is worth preserving, says Sadler, as 'an objective independent appellate body' *providing* there is appropriate 'statutory elucidation of the visitor's jurisdiction, powers and procedures'.

Price and Whalley (1996) also argue for the retention of the Visitor, but only if revamped, noting recent calls for abolition in Western Australia and actual abolition in New South Wales, whereas Victoria has provided for the Visitor's jurisdiction to be concurrent with, not exclusive of, that of the courts – see the Administrative Law (University Visitor) Act 1985. Shaw (1986) is cited. They see the defects but argue for reform and renewal:

> there are real and practical ambiguities and uncertainties concerning the nature and extent of the appellate aspect of the visitorial jurisdiction . . . [hence the need] to clarify and redefine the scope of this jurisdiction in the light of such problems and contemporary needs [especially modern Administrative Law and the call for bureaucratic accountability] to enable it once again to serve the purpose for which it was originally intended.
>
> (Price and Whalley, 1996: 48)

Earlier in the 1996 article they memorably described the Visitor as 'one of the earliest forms of alternative dispute resolution'! Other Australian cases include *Re University of Melbourne, ex p De Dimone, Re Macquarie University*, ex p *Ong* and *Bayley-Jones v University of Newcastle*, in addition to those already cited.

Lewis (1985) compares England and Canada in the context of disciplinary and academic procedures for students and, with regard to the role of the Visitor, notes that in both countries the courts have been reluctant to become involved in 'purely academic assessments', leaving the Visitor to be the sole arbiter of the soundness of that procedure by which the academic decision was reached (but not actually reviewing the decision itself). With reference to student discipline rather than academic progress, the position is similar: 'There seems a reluctance to interfere in university matters which is reflected in the marked lack of clarity and precision in the judgements.' Lewis notes that 'Some of the legislation establishing particular Canadian universities have, *perhaps unwittingly*, endowed them with a university Visitor' (emphasis added). He hopes 'that the Visitor meets the same fate in other Canadian provinces that he met in Alberta where the legislature moved swiftly to abolish him on his reentry into the legal world' – (post *Vanek v Governor of University of Alberta*).

Brookfield (1985) reviews the role of the Visitor in New Zealand universities in the context of *Bell v University of Auckland*, the latter having 'authoritatively defined the place of the Visitor in New Zealand law, giving to that officer a jurisdiction less exclusive of the courts than that enjoyed in England, but ascribing in some respects wider visitatorial power than was thought at least by some to exist' (p. 384). As in Australia, the Governor-General was the Visitor, at least in 1860s legislation, but fairly quickly the role devolved on to the Minister of Education after a Royal Commission Report in 1879, before reverting to the Governor-General in the case of the 1960s universities. The New Zealand Visitor, however, post *Norrie v Senate of the University of Auckland*, is subject to full review by the Courts, whatever the position in England, on the basis that New Zealand universities are publicly-funded – the Visitor's jurisdiction does not so much exclude the courts as in England. On the plus side, for Visitor aficionados, 'the court has if anything expanded the Visitor's role as a judge of issues of substantive fairness'. Brookfield notes that in *Rigg v University of Waikato* the Visitor exercised the quasi-judicial scope awarded in *Norrie v Senate of the University of Auckland* 'with impressive skill'.

Caldwell (1982: 309), also writing from a New Zealand perspective, queries 'unquestioning deference to such an archaic institution . . . [as being] inappropriate in a period of creativity in Administrative Law and in a time when the courts are in the process of unshackling old limitations on their right to review'. This not least because 'the modern New Zealand University . . . is radically different from the Oxbridge Colleges in which visitatorial jurisdiction took root'. So, 'it should therefore be subject to public scrutiny in the courts', leaving the Visitor as 'a quasi-ombudsman' in the context of the modern university 'as simply another statutory body'.

Peiris sums up the comparative position thus:

> The lines of development of English and Commonwealth law suggest varying nuances and differences of emphasis largely attributable to historical and contractual factors . . . English Judges, in comparison with their colleagues in Australia and New Zealand, have conceded to the visitor ample powers.
>
> (Peiris, 1987: 377)

One reason for the difference of approach, Peiris argues, is that in Commonwealth jurisdictions 'visitors are often politicians or local worthies' and are, therefore, seen by the Courts as likely to be less independent-minded than the Lord Chancellor (or his commissary) acting on behalf of the Queen who is Visitor to most English/Welsh HEIs. Moreover, as Peiris notes, at least in New Zealand, universities are 'almost invariably the creature of statute', and, as a result, are, in fact, closer to the UK statutory HEIs which, of course, do not have the Visitor model – they are fully subject to judicial review. See Carroll (1994) as regards *R v Manchester Metropolitan University*, ex p *Nolan* (unreported, 15 July 1993). Howells (1989) considers the New Zealand situation post *Norrie v Senate of the University of Auckland* as having advantages over English law, where 'the weight of precedent' has prevented a similar rationalization of the Visitor – courts' overlap and conflict of jurisdiction.

Price and Whalley (1996) refer to 'vice-regal concerns', the fear of unreasonable intervention by the Governor-General in a university's affairs, and, similarly (but rather more understandably), Ikhariale (1991) discusses the problem of such intervention in Nigerian universities in the 1980s.

The Visitor post-Nolan Report (1996)

What can be said of the likely future of the Visitor within English chartered HEIs in the context of:

- the non-existence of the concept not only in all countries except England and certain key commonwealth common law nations, but also in its non-existence even in Scotland and under US common law;
- the Visitor having been summarily executed in the province of Alberta, as described earlier, and in Victoria;
- the ambivalence of the Australian, and to a lesser degree the New Zealand, courts towards the Visitor's jurisdiction, and the calls by law academics (Caldwell, 1982; Lewis, 1985; Sadler, 1981) in those countries for the reform if not the termination of the Visitor;
- the absence of the Visitor in at least half of the UK HEIs – the statutory HEIs – and all those in Scotland;
- the two inquiries by Lord Nolan (1995 and 1996);
- an HE system within an increasingly litigious and consumerist society, where students will be making an ever-greater financial sacrifice for their education, will be ever-more conscious of value for money, will more commonly be older, part-time and vocational-orientated?

Nolan refers to the Visitor and notes 'the advantage that in defined circumstances the Visitor's jurisdiction may exclude recourse to the courts' (1996: 107). The Nolan Report goes on, however, to state that: 'The visitorial system of hearing appeals is not by any means perfect. The process of appointing a Visitor's representative to investigate may be lengthy, visitorial law is complex, and the courts show an increasing disposition to intervene' (1996: 108). On balance, the Visitor is 'an outside judgement', 'an independent perspective' (1996: 108), and should be replicated in some way in the statutory universities ('a gap which needs to be filled' – 1996: 109). This leads to Recommendation 9 ('Students in higher education institutions should be able to appeal to an independent body, and this right should be reflected in Higher Education Charters') and Recommendation 10 ('The higher education funding councils, institutions, and representative bodies should consult on a system of independent review of disputes'). This system, suggests paragraphs 110–12, might take the form of:

> a statutory panel of senior persons experienced but no longer involved in further or higher education administration, from which a conciliator or arbitrator might be drawn when required . . . [It] would supplement the Visitorial system and provide an alternative for institutions without a Visitor.
>
> (Nolan, 1996: 109)

All this is, of course, reminiscent of Samuels (1973) calling for the creation of an HE advisory board. So, the Visitor seems to pass the Nolan test for public and quasi-public bodies to be seen 'to let an independent person or body review their activities if necessary' (1996: 102).

The CVCP (1997) has seen some advantage in trying to find a mechanism to meet Nolan criteria ('. . . to adopt a new procedure that is comparable to the visitorial jurisdiction, or a substitute for it . . . It may be possible to go a long way towards replicating the role of the Visitor, which does have the advantage of providing a relatively swift and cheap remedy . . .'), *but* it must not be one 'which would still leave them [HEIs] amenable to the jurisdiction of the courts'; it must be one 'that is effectively an alternative to the courts'. Hence the possibility is raised of the student–HEI contract including a term referring to *binding* arbitration under the Arbitration Act 1996, with the arbitrator being drawn from a 'Panel of Independent Persons' (such a panel might include 'independent persons who have experience in higher education, dispute resolution or related matters'). There is, however, some doubt as to whether the Unfair Terms in Consumer Contracts Regulations 1994 might make such an arbitration clause unenforceable, especially since the NUS has already expressed concern over any such proposal to terminate students' rights to bring court actions. Moreover, Legal Aid is not at present available for arbitration: would the HEI meet the student's legal bills, and, if so, would its cheque be open-ended? In the commercial sector arbitration has not proved to be significantly less costly than conventional litigation, and a reformed court system may yet make litigation a speedier process than at present, hence it is not obvious that arbitration is a panacea. It may be that only new legislation could achieve the CVCP objectives of both meeting Nolan and restricting the role of the courts in the creation of a Visitor-like system for the statutory HEIs, a direction, after all, in which Nolan seems to point.

So, post Nolan Report (1996) the Visitor seems to have a secure future, and perhaps even an expansionist one, subject to some elements of procedure (notably the process of actually commencing a Visitor action where somebody has to be found to act on behalf of the Queen/Lord Chancellor) being revamped. Summary execution by the legislation à la the demise of the Visitor in the province of Alberta, Canada, and the State of Victoria seems unlikely, as does a narrowing of jurisdiction in relation to interference and supervision by the Courts as in New Zealand. The recent 30 years of the 300 year or so history of the Visitor since *Philips v Bury* have seen the courts give recognition in key cases to its exclusive jurisdiction and powers: *Thorne v University of London; Patel v University of Bradford Senate; Hines v Birkbeck College; Thomas v University of Bradford; Oakes v Sidney Sussex College, Cambridge; Pearce v University of Aston in Birmingham; R v Committee of Lords of the Judicial Committee of the Privy Council acting for the Visitor of the University of London,* ex p *Vijayatunga; R v Lord President of the Privy Council,* ex p *Page.* The Visitor may yet survive well into a fourth century.

On the other hand, in the event that legislation was required to establish some form of compulsory independent appeal system for the statutory universities (and possibly Oxford and Cambridge), not least to ensure that such a system then really did preclude the courts being involved (which could not be guaranteed under a voluntary arrangement) other than in the context of Wednesbury-style JR for unreasonableness, it is possible that the apparently anachronistic chartered university Visitor could be replaced by also calling upon such a panel to provide for the chartered universities a recently retired HEI administrator or manager (to sit in conjunction perhaps with a senior solicitor or barrister) as a last resort appeal tribunal, all internal procedures having been exhausted.

Appendix A

Baker, J. H. (1992) *Judicial Review of the Judges as Visitors to the Inns of Court* Pub L 411.

Bridge, J. W. (1970) *Keeping Peace in the Universities – The Role of the Visitor* 86 LQR 531.

Brookfield, F. M. (1985) *The Visitor in the New Zealand Universities* 11 NZ ULR 382.

Caldwell, J. L. (1982) *Judicial Review of Universities: The Visitor and the Visited* 1 Cant. L. Rev. 307.

Carroll, A. J. (1994) *The Abuse of Academic Disciplinary Power* 144 NLJ 729.

Christie, D. (1974) *A Problem of Jurisdiction and Natural Justice* 37 MLR 324.

CVCP (1997) *Interim Report of the CVCP Nolan Group.* London: CVCP (N/97/11).

Davies, Sir Michael (1994) *The Davies Report: The 'Great Battle' in Swansea.* Bristol: Thoemmes Press.

de Smith, S. A. (1974) *Aston's Villa – Replay for Visitors?* 33 CLJ 23.

Farrington, D. J. (1994) *The Law of Higher Education.* London: Butterworths.

Farrington, D. and Mattison, F. (1990) *Universities and the Law.* Reading: CUA.

Fridman, G. H. L. (1973) *Judicial Intervention into Universities' Affairs* 21 Chitty's LJ 181.

Hadfield, B. (1987) *The Visitor Stays – Thomas v University of Bradford* Pub LJ 320.

Howells, G. G. (1989) *Employment Disputes within Universities* 8 CJQ 152.

Ikhariale, M. A. (1991) 'The institution of the Visitor in English and overseas universities: problems of its use in Nigeria', *International and Comparative Law Quarterly* 699.

Lewis, C. B. (1985) *Procedural Fairness and University Students: England and Canada Compared* 9 Dal LJ 313.

Lewis, C. J. (1987) *Universities, Visitors and the Courts* 46 CLJ 384.

Matthews, T. G. (1980) *The Office of the University Visitor* 11 University Qld LJ 152.

Mitcheson, R. E. (1887) *Opinion on the English Law and Practice of Visitation of Charities.* Archive item in the Bodleian Law Library.

Nolan, Lord (1995) *First Report of the Committee on Standards in Public Life.* London: HMSO.

Nolan, Lord (1996) *Second Report of the Committee on Standards in Public Life.* London: HMSO.

Peiris, G. L. (1987) *Visitorial Jurisdiction: The Changing Outlook on an Exclusive Regime* 16 AALR 376.

Pettit, P. H. (1991) *Academic Tenure and the Education Reform Act 1988* 54 MLR 137.

Pettit, P. H. (1993) *Equity and the Law of Trusts.* London: Butterworths.

Picarda, H. (1992–3) *Practice and Procedure on Visitorial Appeals* 1 CL & PR 63.

Picarda, H. (1995) *The Law and Practice Relating to Charities.* London: Butterworths.

Pitt, G. (1990) *Academic Freedom and Education Reform: The Tenure Provisions of the Education Reform Act 1988* 19 ILF 33.

Price, D. M. and Whalley, P. W. F. (1996) 'The university Visitor and university governance', *Journal of Higher Education Policy and Management,* 18(1), 45–57.

Report of the Oxford University Commissioners (1852).

Ricquier, W. T. M. (1978) *The University Visitor* 4 Dal LJ 647.

Ricquier, W. T. M. (1979) *Failed Students and Access to Justice* Pub L 209.

Sadler, R. T. (1980) *The University Visitor in Australia: Murdoch University v Bloom* 7 Mon LR 59.

Sadler, R. T. (1981) *The University Visitor: Visitorial Precedent and Procedure in Australia* 7 U Tas LR2.

Samuels, A. (1973) 'The student and the Law', *Journal of the Society of Public Teachers of Law,* 12, 252.

Shaw (1986) 'Disputes within universities: the Visitor or the Courts?', *The Australian Universities Review* 29(1).

Shelford, L. (1836) *Law of Mortmain.* London: Longman.

Smith, P. M. (1981) *The Exclusive Jurisdiction of the University Visitor* 97 LQR 610.

Smith, P. M. (1986) *Visitation of the Universities: A Ghost from the Past* 136 NLJ 484, 519, 567, 665.

Smith, P. M. (1993/94) *The Jurisdiction of the University Visitor: How Exclusive is Exclusive?* 2 CL & PR 103.

Tudor on Charities (1995). London: Sweet & Maxwell.

Wade, H. W. R. (1969) *Judicial Control of Universities* 85 LQR 468.

Wade, Sir William (1993) *Visitors and Error of Law* 109 LQR 155.

Wade, H. W. R. and Forsyth, C. F. (1994) *Administrative Law.* Oxford: Oxford University Press.

Williams, J. (1910) *The Law of the Universities.* London: Butterworths.

Willis, P. (1979) *Patel v University of Bradford Senate* 12 MULR 291.

Zellick, G. (1989) *British Universities and the Education Reform Act 1988* Pub L 513.

Appendix B: key cases

Attorney-General v Talbot [1747] 3 Atk

Bayley-Jones v University of Newcastle [1990] 22 NSWLR 425

Bell v University of Auckland [1969] NZLR 1029

Casson v University of Aston in Birmingham [1983] 1 All ER 88

Daniel Appelford's Case [1672] 1 Mod 82

Dr Bentley's Case, R v Cambridge University [1723] 1 Stra 557

Ex p *Buller* [1855] 1 Jur (NS) 709

Ex p *McFadyen* [1945] 45 SR (NSW) 200

Ex p *King, R v University of Sydney* [1994] 44 SR (NSW) 19, FC

Herring v Templeman and Others [1973] 1 All ER 581; 3 All ER 569, CA

Hines v Birkbeck College [1985] 3 All ER 156

Hines v Birkbeck College (No. 2) [1991] 4 All ER 450

Langlois v Rector and Members of Laval University [1974] 47 DLR (3d) 674

Murdoch University v Bloom [1980] unreported, No. 2294 (16/4/1980) of 1979, WASCFC

Norrie v Senate of the University of Auckland [1984] 1 NZLR 129

Oakes v Sidney Sussex College, Cambridge [1988] 1 WLR 431
Patel v University of Bradford Senate [1978] 1 WLR 1488; [1979] 1 WLR 1066, CA; [1979] 2 All ER 582
Pearce v University of Aston in Birmingham [1991] 2 All ER 461, 469
Philips v Bury [1692] 1 Ld Raym 5; 2 TR 347; Skin 447; 4 Mod 106
R v Bishop of Chester [1747] 1 WM BV 22
R v Committee of the Lords of the Judicial Committee of the Privy Council Acting for the Visitor of the University of London, ex p Vijayatunga [1988] 1 QB 322; [1989] 2 All ER 843
R v Dunsheath, ex p Meredith [1951] 1 KB 127
R v Her Majesty the Queen in Council, ex p Vijayatunga [1989] 3 WLR 13
R v Lord President of the Privy Council, ex p Page [1992] 3 WLR 1112; [1991] 4 All ER 747
R v Manchester Metropolitan University, ex p Nolan [1993] unreported, co/2856/92, 15 July 1993
R v Oxford University, ex p Bolchover, The Times, 7 October 1970
R v University of Aston Senate, ex p Roffey [1969] 2 QB 538
R v University of Cambridge, ex p Evans [1997] unreported, CO/101/97, 22 August
R v University of London, ex p Vijayatunga [1987] 3 All ER 204
R v Visitor to the Inns of Court, ex p Calder [1993] 2 All ER 876; *The Times,* 20 March 1992
Re Macquarie University, ex p Ong [1989] 17 NSWLR 112
Re University of Melbourne, ex p De Dimone [1981] VR 378
Re Wislang's Application [1984] CLY 2462, NI 63
Rigg v University of Waikato [1984] 1 NZLR 149
St John's College v Todington [1757] 1 Burr 158
Thomas v University of Bradford [1987] 1 All ER 834
Thomas v University of Bradford (No. 2) [1992] 1 All ER 964
Thomson v University of London [1864] 33 LJ CH 625
Thorne v University of London [1966] 2 QB 237; [1966] 2 All ER 338, CA
Vanek v Governor of University of Alberta [1975] 3 WWR 167; [1975] 5 WWR 429

Notes

Hines v Birbeck College concerned, and confirmed, the exclusivity of the jurisdiction of the Visitor in relation to employment disputes between an academic and the university (approved in *Thomas v University of Bradford*). Hoffman J. noted that the subject of the exclusivity of the Visitor 'is a subject rich in authority', and referred to *Patel v University of Bradford Senate, Casson v University of Aston in Birmingham* and *Re Wislang's Application* as well as *Thomson v University of London* and *Thorne v University of London.*

Hines v Birkbeck College (*No. 2*) concerned the overlap between the Visitor and the court in relation to the ERA 1988, Section 206, and the court applied *Pearce v University of Aston in Birmingham.*

In *Oakes v Sidney Sussex College, Cambridge* it was established that the Visitor's jurisdiction in relation to students depended not on the student's membership of the college (as a corporator, rather than simply *in statu pupilari*), but on whether he or she sought to enforce rights under the domestic or internal law of the college (i.e., all students and academics are covered). Thus, the *dictum* of Megarry Vice-

Chancellor in *Patel v University of Bradford Senate* was not followed. He had held that the Visitor's jurisdiction applied only to those 'of the foundation' (e.g. warden, fellows and scholars (not commoners) in an Oxbridge college context). *Thomas v University of Bradford*, however, was followed.

In *R v Lord President of the Privy Council*, ex p *Page* the House of Lords, applying *Philips v Bury* and *Thomas v University of Bradford*, reaffirmed that the decision of a Visitor was not amenable to challenge by JR on the grounds of error in fact or in law, but only in cases where the Visitor has acted outside his or her jurisdiction, has abused his or her powers or has acted in breach of other rules of natural justice. Lord Griffiths in his judgement clarified that an abuse of the Visitor's powers did *not* include the Visitor having made an error in the interpretation of the domestic law of the university:

> *certiorari* should not lie to reverse the decision of a visitor on a question of law. The value of the visitatorial jurisdiction is that it is swift, cheap and final. These benefits will be largely dissipated if the Visitor's decision can be challenged by way of judicial review . . . to admit *certiorari* to challenge the Visitor's decision on the grounds of error of law will in practice prove to be the introduction of an appeal by another name . . . If it is thought that the exclusive jurisdiction of the Visitor has outlived its usefulness, which I beg to doubt, then I think it should be swept away by Parliament and not undermined by judicial review.

Lord Browne-Wilkinson quoted from *Philips v Bury* as 'the locus classicus of the law of Visitor . . . repeatedly applied for the last 300 years' and also cited the judgements in *R v Bishop of Chester*: 'Visitors have absolute power; the only absolute one I known of in England' (Wright, J.) and 'This Court cannot control visitors' (Dennison, J.). In Ex p *Buller* he noted that Lord Benyon, CJ had commented that 'a member of a college puts himself voluntarily under a peculiar system of Law, and asserts to being bound by it, and cannot thereafter complain that such a system is not in accordance with that adopted by the common law'. Thus, despite the recent growth of JR, it is not a concept generally applicable to the Visitor since the Visitor is not dealing with the common law, but with 'a peculiar, domestic law of which he is the sole arbiter and of which the courts have no cognisance'. Hence, if that means 'the position of the visitor is anomalous, indeed unique', then so be it, especially since 'it provides a valuable machinery for reducing internal disputes which should not be lost'. Lords Mustill and Slynn, however, dissented from Lords Griffiths, Browne-Wilkinson and Keith, with Lord Slynn emphasizing that 'there has been a considerable development in the scope of judicial review in the second half of this century' – citing Wade (1993) – which should take in the Visitor as it has other areas of legal and quasi-legal activity.

In *Patel v University of Bradford Senate* the Court of Appeal upheld the exclusivity of the Visitor's jurisdiction in relation to a students' complaint over the decision of a Board of Examiners to fail him. The Court applied *Thorne v University of London*, another complaint about examination failure (i.e. in a chartered university possessing a Visitor disputes about the fairness of examination decisions are solely for the Visitor and there can be no appeal from the Visitor's decision). See also *R v Committee of the Lords of the Judicial Committee of the Privy Council Acting for the Visitor of the University of London*, ex p *Vijayatunga*.

In *Pearce v University of Aston in Birmingham*, the exclusivity of the Visitor as confirmed in *Thomas v University of Bradford*, was taken as read. The dispute was about the 'relevant date' in the ERA 1988, Section 206(2), after which the Visitor's jurisdiction was excluded in relation to any employment issue between a university and its academic staff.

The House of Lords in *Thomas v University of Bradford* confirmed the jurisdiction of the Visitor as being exclusive 'beyond doubt' and found that the Visitor can award damages. Lord Bridge of Harwich, Lord Brandon of Oakbrook and Lord Mackay of Clashfern each concurred with the speeches of Lord Ackner and Lord Griffiths, in which the latter reviewed 'an unbroken line of authority spanning the last three centuries' and considered the articles by Bridge (1970) and Smith (1981, 1986). The authoritative cases cited ran from *Philips v Bury*, via *Attorney-General v Talbot, St John's College v Todington, Thomson v University of London, Herring v Templeman and Others, Patel v University of Bradford Senate, Re Wislang's Application*, to *Hines v Birkbeck College*. Lord Griffiths noted that *Norrie v Senate of the University of Auckland*, left the Visitor in New Zealand universities 'subordinate to the courts', but advised his colleagues that 'this is not the way in which our law has developed and in my view it is not open to your Lordships to . . . adopt the New Zealand solution'.

In *R v Committee of the Lords of the Judicial Committee of the Privy Council Acting for the Visitor of the University of London, ex p Vijayatunga* the Court of Appeal upheld the exclusivity of the Visitor's jurisdiction in considering matters of academic judgement (here the selection of examiners for a PhD thesis). The Court noted *Thomas v University of Bradford*, concluding that the appointment of examiners was 'wholly a matter of academic judgement in which this court should not interfere'.

A note on the Universities and Colleges Education Law Network

The Universities and Colleges Education Law Network (UCELNET) is designed to facilitate the exchange of information on legal issues affecting higher education institutions. Membership is open to all relevant institutions for a modest annual subscription. Benefits include an annual national conference, regional sessions and a biannual Reporter. Enquiries to the UCELNET office, c/o Dennis Farrington, Deputy Secretary, University of Stirling, FK9 4LA. Tel: 01786 467020 Fax: 01786 466699.

Contact Addresses for Contributors

Cole and Cole (Chapters 4, Emma Chamberlain; and 8, David Isaac)

Cole and Cole
Buxton Court
3 West Way
Oxford OX2 0SZ

Tel: 01865 791122
Fax: 01865 721367
DX 96200 Oxford West

Eversheds (Chapters 3, John Hall and Oliver Hyams; 12, John Boardman; 14, Nigel Sternberg and Michael Smith; and 15, Tim Costello)

Eversheds
Senator House
85 Queen Victoria Street
London EC4V 4JL

Tel: 0171 919 4500
Fax: 0171 919 4919
DX 83 LON/CH'RY LN WC2

Linnells (Chapter 21, Euan Temple, Joss Saunders and Philip Turpin)

Linnells
Greyfriars Court
Paradise Square
Oxford OX1 1BB

Tel: 01865 248607
Fax: 01865 728445
DX 82261 Oxford 2

Manches & Co. (Chapters 11, Stephen Dooley; and 19, Daff Richardson)

Manches & Co. (incorporating Morrell, Peel and Gamlen)
3 Worcester Street
Oxford OX1 2PZ

Tel: 01865 722106
Fax: 01865 201012

NB: Stephen Dooley moved in 1997 to
Sidley and Austin's
Information Industries Group
Royal Exchange
London EC3

Tel: 0171 360 3600
e-mail: sdooley@sidley.am
Fax: 0171 626 7937

Martineau Johnson (Chapters 2, Nicola Hart; 6, Simon Arrowsmith and Nicola Hart; 7, Simon Arrowsmith; 9, Paul Pharoah; and 13, Simon Arrowsmith)

Martineau Johnson
St Philip's House
St Philip's Place
Birmingham B3 2PP

Tel: 0121 200 3300
e-mail: education@martjohn.com
Fax: 0121 625 3330

Mills and Reeve (Chapters 10, Alasdair Poore; and 18, Sharon Ranouf) is a member of The Norton Rose M5 Group of independent legal practices.

Mills and Reeve
Francis House
112 Hills Road
Cambridge CB2 1PH

Tel: 01223 364422
Fax: 01223 355848
DX 122891 Cambridge 4

Shakespeares (Chapters 16, Ian Leedham; and 17, Catriona Webster) is a member of QLG, a national grouping of law firms

Shakespeares
10 Bennetts Hill
Birmingham B2 5RS

Tel: 0121 632 4199
Fax: 0121 643 2257
DX 13015 Birmingham 1

Travers Smith Braithwaite (Chapter 20, Jonathan Leslie)

Travers Smith Braithwaite
10 Snow Hill
London EC1A 2AL

Tel: 0171 248 9133
Fax: 0171 236 3728
DX79 LONDON

Index

The Society for Research into Higher Education

The Society for Research into Higher Education exists to stimulate and coordinate research into all aspects of higher education. It aims to improve the quality of higher education through the encouragement of debate and publication on issues of policy, on the organization and management of higher education institutions, and on the curriculum and teaching methods.

The Society's income is derived from subscriptions, sales of its books and journals, conference fees and grants. It receives no subsidies, and is wholly independent. Its individual members include teachers, researchers, managers and students. Its corporate members are institutions of higher education, research institutes, professional, industrial and governmental bodies. Members are not only from the UK, but from elsewhere in Europe, from America, Canada and Australasia, and it regards its international work as among its most important activities.

Under the imprint *SRHE & Open University Press*, the Society is a specialist publisher of research, having over 70 titles in print. The Editorial Board of the Society's Imprint seeks authoritative research or study in the above fields. It offers competitive royalties, a highly recognizable format in both hardback and paperback and the worldwide reputation of the Open University Press.

The Society also publishes *Studies in Higher Education* (three times a year), which is mainly concerned with academic issues, *Higher Education Quarterly* (formerly *Universities Quarterly*), mainly concerned with policy issues, *Research into Higher Education Abstracts* (three times a year), and *SRHE News* (four times a year).

The society holds a major annual conference in December, jointly with an institution of higher education. In 1995 the topic was 'The Changing University' at Heriot-Watt University in Edinburgh. In 1996 it was 'Working in Higher Education' at University of Wales, Cardiff and in 1997, 'Beyond the First Degree' at the University of Warwick. The 1998 conference will be on the topic of globalization at the University of Lancaster.

The Society's committees, study groups and networks are run by the members. The networks at present include:

Access	Mentoring
Curriculum development	Postgraduate issues
Disability	Quality
Eastern European	Quantitative studies
Funding	Student Development
Legal education	Vocational Qualifications

Benefits to members
Individual

Individual members receive

- *SRHE News*, the Society's publications list, conference details and other material included in mailings.
- Greatly reduced rates for *Studies in Higher Education* and *Higher Education Quarterly*.
- A 35 per cent discount on all SRHE & Open University Press publications.
- Free copies of the Precedings – commissioned papers on the theme of the Annual Conference.
- Free copies of *Research into Higher Education Abstracts*.
- Reduced rates for the annual conference.
- Extensive contacts and scope for facilitating initiatives.
- Free copies of the *Register of Members' Research Interests*.
- Membership of the Society's networks.

Corporate

Corporate members receive:

- Benefits of individual members, plus.
- Free copies of *Studies in Higher Education*.
- Unlimited copies of the Society's publications at reduced rates.
- Reduced rates for the annual conference.
- The right to submit applications for the Society's research grants.
- The right to use the Society's facility for supplying statistical HESA data for purposes of research.

 *Membership details*: SRHE, 3 Devonshire Street, London W1N 2BA, UK. Tel: 0171 637 2766. Fax: 0171 637 2781. email:srhe@mailbox.ulcc.ac.uk
World Wide Web:http://www.srhe.ac.uk./srhe/
Catalogue: SRHE & Open University Press, Celtic Court, 22 Ballmoor, Buckingham MK18 1XW. Tel: 01280 823388. Fax: 01280 823233. email:enquiries@openup.co.uk